WOMEN

Making America

WOMEN
Making America

Heidi Hemming
Julie Hemming Savage

Clotho Press

Text copyright © 2009 by Heidi Hemming and Julie Hemming Savage

Clotho Press
Silver Spring, MD 20906

First edition: March 2009

10 9 8 7 6 5 4 3 2 1

Library of Congress Control Number: 2008908741

Hard cover:
ISBN-13: 978-0-9821271-1-7

Paperback:
ISBN-13: 978-0-9821271-0-0

Printed and bound in China by Kings Time Printing Press

Designed by Elizabeth Woll

Front cover art, clockwise from top-left: Native American mother, Library of Congress LC-USZ62-115744; Anthony pin courtesy of Jo Freeman; Flappers, Scurlock Studio Records, Archives Center, National Museum of American History, Smithsonian Institution; Anonymous woman, Library of Congress LC-USZC4-10208; Chicago Women's Graphic Collection, Library of Congress LC-USZC4-7235; 14 February, 1999, Kristine Lilly (#13) of Team USA, Aubrey Washington/Allsport/ Getty Images; *The Readers*, Library of Congress LC-DIG-ppmsca-13707; The Granger Collection, New York
Back cover art: Working girls, Library of Congress LC-USZ62-86967; Midwife, Library of Congress LC-USZ62-121893; "Bathing Girl Parade," LC-USZC4-8150

Includes bibliographical references and index.

Visit www.womenmakingamerica.com

To the next generation:

Colin and Copeland Smith

Jeremiah, Lucy, and Eleanor Savage

Graham, Benjamin, and Truman Austin

Orpha and Daisy Foster Jewell

Contents

Acknowledgments

We realize that we never could have written *Women Making America* without the collective, painstaking work of scores of historians who have gone before us, searching for women's stories in often unlikely places. Their efforts have inspired and motivated us. If we can do nothing else to satisfy our debt, we hope to bring their ideas to new audiences.

We have identified with the women in this book as our work has progressed through the chaos of children, spouses, relatives and friends, sports teams, PTA, and piano lessons. This book has been an act of collective will, a group project requiring the insight, love, and patience of more people than we can name. Our parents, Alice and Val Hemming, insisted that we move forward with this daunting project, contributed substantial resources, and cheered us every step of the way. Thank-you to them, our siblings—Jill Hemming and Colin Austin, Patrick Hemming and Margaret Olsen—and our children for stepping in and out of our way as circumstances demanded. And thank-you to Karl, whose devotion, perceptiveness, support, and good humor have been unwavering.

We owe a great debt to the many individuals who graciously read and commented on chapters—Wendy Brown, Claudia Bushman, Penny Colman, Bob Cooney, Leigh Geis, Stephanie Gilmore, Jill Hemming, Patrick Hemming, Val and Alice Hemming, Emily Hickman, Peggy Jackson, Dena Leibman, Molly MacGregor, Robyn Muncy, Margaret Olsen, Natalie Prado, Karl Savage, Merikay Smith, Audrey Southard, Kimberlee Staking, Valerie Tripp, Judith Wellman, Sally Roesch Wagner, Linda Wharton, and many others. Vickie McCauley Lowe shared her personal Title IX archives, and students at West Junior High in Lawrence, Kansas, provided the original inspiration for the project. Lisa Jacobs helped us probe the adolescent mind by conducting focus groups with her teenage babysitters. Students at Rockville High School in Rockville, Maryland, also provided an audience on which to try our ideas.

This journey has brought us into contact with wonderful and kind people who have willingly shared their knowledge and expertise with us. We appreciate the help and friendship of Penny

Colman, who has mentored us through treacherous waters. Thank-you to the Library of Congress archivists, particularly Jeff Bridgers in Prints and Photographs, and Sheridan Harvey, Janice Ruth, and Barbara Orbach Natanson, who care deeply about women's history. Michael Summers is our Web hero.

We simply could not have done this without Cathy Jewell, our editor, advisor, and friend who has loved the book as we do. She led us to Elizabeth and Tom Woll of Cross River Publishing Consultants. Working with Elizabeth has been a complete pleasure, and her layout has brought our dreams of a beautiful book to fruition.

To our many friends and well-wishers we say thanks, and enjoy the ride!

Women Making America

"Everything that explains the world has in fact explained a world in which men are at the center of the human enterprise and women are at the margin 'helping' them. Such a world does not exist—never has. ***Men and women have built society and have built the world. Women have been central to it.***"

—**Gerda Lerner**, historian

omen Making America emerges from the realization that we could not find a single book wherein young as well as seasoned readers could gain a comprehensive view of women's multiple roles and many contributions to America's past. In the last thirty years there has been an explosion of scholarly work devoted to the history of women in America. Unfortunately, much of this has failed to reach audiences outside of academic circles.

Even more regrettably, in America's classrooms, women continue to be relegated to special-feature-box status in textbooks and curriculum. Students are regularly sent a not-so-subtle message that women aren't really a part of history. In this book we have distilled recent historical scholarship to make it accessible to a wide audience.

Women's rights advocate **Elizabeth Cady Stanton**'s radical words, spoken in 1851, remain keenly relevant today. She cried out for the "great work" of educating girls (and we would add, boys) to instill

"I think about [my great aunt], and about my own mother, about women whose pictures you see in other historic photographs, and the women whose lives and life's work have gone unrecognized—even in their own homes at times—and I feel that I'm here on the backs of so many women's shoulders, so many who have come before. We all are. *If we want our girls to benefit from the courage and wisdom of the women before them, we have to share the stories.*"

—**Shireen Dodson**, from *The Mother-Daughter Book Club*

A six-generation photograph taken in 1893 in Selma, Alabama. The oldest grandmother was probably born into slavery, while the baby may have lived to witness the civil rights movement.

in them the courage and freedom "to be, to grow, to feel, to think, to act. . . . We have had women enough befooled under the one system," she declared, "Pray, let us try another." *Women Making America* seeks to do just that.

ORGANIZATION AND FEATURES

Every historian has to choose where to begin her story. We have decided to commence this history in the years leading up to the formation of the United States of America. Embarking in 1770, we fully recognize that we are neglecting the rich early history of North America. Our decision was a practical one; we either needed to limit the book's timeline or reduce its details. Since we wanted a book brimming with anecdotes, images, stories, and voices from America's female kaleidoscope, we opted for the former.

The female experience in America has been far from universal. From the country's earliest days, beliefs about racial and cultural difference have profoundly influenced interactions between people. Geography, race, and class have always affected women's lives. Their lives have also shared some common threads. We have chosen to focus on health, paid work, home, education, beauty, amusements, and the arts in the lives of women through the centuries. In exploring these themes, readers can better trace the shifting perceptions of and expectations for women and girls from colonial times to the present.

HEALTH

Women's bodies have long inspired wonder and
suspicion, as well as misunderstanding. Until late in
the twentieth century, childbearing and child rearing
dominated most of a woman's adult life, regardless
of her race or class. Her understanding of her own
anatomy and health were incomplete and shaped by the
prevailing medical ideas of the time. This section sheds
light on how various generations viewed women's bodies
and their illnesses. It also traces the roles that women
often assumed as family and neighborhood health care
providers.

A 1938 Works Project Administration
(WPA) poster promoting proper health
care for pregnant women.

PAID WORK

When people today want to know if a woman is in the workforce or staying home with her children
they ask, "Does she work?" Women have always worked. The real question is, "Does she get paid

for her labor?" This section
follows the evolution of
women's work for pay, from
domestic servants to factory
workers, from teachers to
electricians and politicians.
We chronicle the uneven
path of women into wage
work and professional
advancement.

Corrections officer **Mary Herron** in
Winnebago County, Illinois (1993).

AT HOME

Today's ideal of home as a cozy emotional refuge is relatively new in the historical picture. Expectations about love, marriage, home, and homemaking have evolved over time. "At Home" surveys everything from courtship to life after marriage. It covers issues such as child rearing, material consumption, domesticity, and home decorating.

The "ideal woman" as portrayed on a 1915 magazine cover.

EDUCATION

The word *education* carries a different meaning for us than it did for many generations of Americans. Today, education tends to be formal, prolonged, and mandatory. Our current system attempts to educate children of all races, both girls and boys, rich and poor. That has not always been the case. In the past, fears abounded about the consequences of educating women. "Education" chronicles the struggles and triumphs of women and girls pursuing knowledge.

No longer "separate but equal," students integrate Anacostia High School in Washington, DC, in 1957.

For Preserving & Dressing The **HAIR.**

BEAUTY

What is beautiful? It depends. Today's love goddess may not seem so attractive to future generations. But that hasn't stopped women and girls from dedicating plenty of time and resources to achieving just the right look. Fashion has long been a marker of larger trends in society. What did it mean when teens in the 1960s grew their hair long, or when girls in the 1920s cut theirs? "Beauty" follows trends such as fashion, changing ideas about beauty, and the emergence of the cosmetics industry.

An 1860 ad for Hovey's Cocoa Glycerine.

AMUSEMENTS

For women, much more than men, the line between recreation and work has been very thin. With little time to call their own, America's women have found ways to transform necessary tasks into social occasions. However, even for those with time and money, fun has often been dictated by ideas about what was appropriate for females and males. "Amusements" spotlights women escaping to the movies, shopping, attending traveling shows, bowling, watching TV, and even dancing the "funky butt."

These girls play with their dolls and miniature tepees on the Northern Cheyenne Indian Reservation in 1909. **Julie E. Tuell** took this photograph after she moved to the Montana reservation as a young bride.

ARTS IN THE SPOTLIGHT

This section focuses on writers, artists, musicians, poets, playwrights, and others who broke through major barriers to make their voices heard. It is anybody's guess how many more women might have pursued the arts had they enjoyed the same resources and encouragement as men. In spite of obstacles, many women managed to create while at the same time juggling more traditional responsibilities as mothers, wives, and daughters. Others steered clear of these responsibilities and took less traditional paths.

Vinnie Ream, pictured here in 1865, helped to support her family by working as a sculptor. She created this bust of President Abraham Lincoln while he worked.

What One Woman Did

Some women have responded to the challenges of their respective time periods in creative and visionary ways. Consequently, most chapters feature one or more sections entitled "What One Woman Did." We hope these vignettes will help readers think about current problems and see themselves as makers of history.

GENERAL CONTENT

Many of the challenges and issues facing women were unique to the age in which they lived. Consequently, each chapter includes sections that are specific to that era. Discussions of historic events such as wars, immigration, migration, suffrage, the Great Depression, the civil rights and women's movements, and other topics fill out relevant chapters.

This 1863 image of *The Soldier's Memorial* was sold by Currier & Ives to commemorate the losses of the Civil War.

SIDEBARS

These provide a wealth of quotes, biographical information, facts, and stories. Examples of the types of sidebars follow.

Did you know?

In 1980, a group of women in California discovered that only 3 percent of material in school textbooks was devoted to women. Determined to change this, they formed the National Women's History Project. By 1987, they had succeeded in convincing Congress to set aside March as Women's History Month.

Have you ever heard of . . . Mary Beard?

An ardent women's rights activist and social reformer at the turn of the twentieth century, Beard became the first historian to truly envision women as an active force in the larger historical picture. Referring to a standard history book of her time, she wrote in 1915, *"A visitor from Mars reading it would imagine there had been not women in this part of the universe from the landing of the Pilgrims to the present day for scarcely a mention of women can be found in all the hundreds of pages."* Beard's lifelong, untiring efforts to increase women's historic visibility through numerous books and articles were met primarily with hostility or indifference.

"[Women's history] does not simply add women to the picture we already have of the past, like painting additional figures into the spaces of an already completed canvas. It requires repainting the earlier pictures, because some of what was previously on the canvas was inaccurate and more of it was misleading."

—**Linda Gordon**, historian

"*In order to keep their true selves and grow into healthy adults, [girls] need . . . to feel that they are a part of something larger than their own lives and that they are emotionally connected to the whole.*"

—**Mary Pipher**, *Reviving Ophelia*

In this book, you will encounter women of all ages, ethnicities, religious backgrounds, and classes making decisions about how to live their lives. It is sometimes easy to forget that, like us, people in the past had to make choices without knowing the outcomes. We invite you to join us in learning about the women who made America and hope that you will find your own ways to build a better future.

CHAPTER 1

A Revolutionary Generation

1770–1800

On April 26, 1777, with the Revolutionary war brewing, sixteen-year-old **Sybil Luddington** galloped off into the cold and rainy night to alert her neighbors of an impending British attack. The enemy had just burned nearby Danbury, Connecticut, where supplies for the region were kept. They were now prepared to occupy the surrounding countryside. Traveling forty miles over muddy tracks and through dense forests, Luddington rounded up 400 militiamen by daybreak. Though outnumbered, they drove the British from the area.

If Luddington's actions seemed heroic, the fact that she was female made them doubly so. Like other girls in this time period, she had not been prepared for public action, but for women's work in the home. She knew how to garden, raise livestock, keep house, care for children, and produce items that could be traded. She may have also helped with the family business, a gristmill. However, few women believed they should or could engage in "masculine" activities. Men and women took on one another's responsibilities only in the hardest of circumstances.

The colonies in which Luddington lived had been

An 1850 illustration of Sybil Luddington's heroic ride.

home to European colonists for more than 200 years. While most people lived on farms, cities like Boston, New York, Philadelphia, and Charleston had become bustling market centers with an emerging underclass of poor people. Slavery, which had come to the colonies in 1619, had become increasingly regulated and inescapable. With available lands along the eastern seaboard dwindling, young people migrated to the frontiers where life was difficult and conflict with native peoples unavoidable. Though many colonists loved Great Britain, they also craved more influence over how they were governed.

As tensions led to outright war, women struggled to feed, clothe, and protect their families in challenging settings. Like Sybil Luddington, many would also be called upon to step outside their usual range of activities. Extraordinary times called for extraordinary measures. Their contributions during a long and bloody war would alter American notions about women and instill a new sense of self-confidence.

AT HOME

"NOW I HAVE TURNED HOUSEKEEPER"

MARRIAGE AND FAMILY From birth, a girl in eighteenth-century America was taught to fill a well-defined role in society. Unlike today, she would not face choices about what to be when she grew up. With few exceptions, she could be quite certain her life would center on her family and home. Regardless of her talents, wealth, education, or intelligence, her primary roles would be those of daughter, wife, and mother. She would learn domestic skills by working alongside her mother, where she would also learn to defer to her father.

Upon marriage, she would turn her loyalty to her new husband. One of the founding fathers, Benjamin Rush, advised a young bride, *"From the day you marry you must have no will of your own. . . . if he is like others of his sex, [he] will often require unreasonable sacrifices of your will to his."*

The single most important decision a girl would ever make was whom to marry. Since a woman gave up most legal rights when she married, her future hinged on attracting the attentions of a young man who was honorable, kind, and financially promising.

Betty Haskel married Jonathan Bennet and bore nine children. Their names are recorded in this watercolor family record from Poland, Maine. What sorts of records will your family pass down to future generations?

With almost no possible escape from a bad marriage, a woman's choice of a spouse determined her future happiness or misery. Desertion, rather than divorce, was the most common way to end an unhappy union.

"The happiest marriages I have known have been those where the subordination I have recommended has been most complete."

—BENJAMIN RUSH

When a woman married, she ceased to exist legally. She became a "**femme covert**," which meant that her identity would be "covered" by her husband's and that he would represent her interests (as he saw them) to the world. As head of the household, he owned all property and made all financial decisions. A married woman could not sell or purchase land, make a will, sue or be sued, or even sign contracts. Her children, her earnings, and even her body did not legally belong to her.

If the woman was black, her choices were even more limited. Unless she was one of a small percentage of free blacks, she was a slave, and regardless of her talents and intelligence, would remain one. Her roles as a daughter, wife, and mother would always take second place to her bondage. As one Massachusetts slave named **Juliet** found, though she had married "an extreme fond Husband" and had borne a baby girl, she could readily be torn from both. Most masters weren't concerned with their slaves' feelings.

Though the law did not recognize slave marriages, within the slave community they were considered binding. While slave owners occasionally forced slaves together for the purpose of having children, most agreed that allowing slaves to choose spouses would encourage more babies, which would result in more slaves for the owners.

Among whites, some ideas about marriage had begun to change by the time of the Revolution. Increasingly, it was up to daughters to decide whom they would marry. With a decline in parental input, notions of love, romance, and personal happiness became as important as more practical concerns like economic security. **Mary Stevenson** declared that

"an union without affection is the most deplorable situation a woman can be in."

When youth wanted to avoid parental control, some either eloped or got pregnant in order to bring about the marriage. In many late-eighteenth-century New England towns, nearly one-third of all young women were pregnant at the time of their marriages—up from less than 10 percent in the 1600s.

WORK Affection did not mean that partners were equal or did the same jobs, Most couples viewed their relationship as an economic necessity as well as a partnership. Once a woman married, the hard work of maintaining her home began. As the vast majority of Americans barely eked out a living on small farms, there was plenty to be done. Shortly after her marriage, southerner **Mary Withers** mourned more carefree days: *"Now I have turned housekeeper for to my sorrow I know there is no romance in going from the smokehouse to the store room and from there to the cellar half a dozen times a day."* Whether she lived on the frontiers of Ohio or Tennessee, on a Southern plantation, or in the more settled portions of New England, a woman's domestic chores were endless and exhausting.

Take for example, one annual task: the December hog slaughtering. Once the several-hundred-pound pig was killed, it had to be dipped in hot water to remove the skin. The bristles were then removed to make brushes. The fat had to be rendered to make candles and soap, and the intestines cleaned out to make sausage. Next, in order to preserve the meat for the long winter ahead, it had to be salted—as one woman recalled, "until all the skin was nearly off my hands." Not a single portion of the hog was wasted.

Anna Bowen Mitchell, who had moved from Rhode Island to South Carolina, wrote,

"The detail of one day…would be the detail of the last six months of my life."

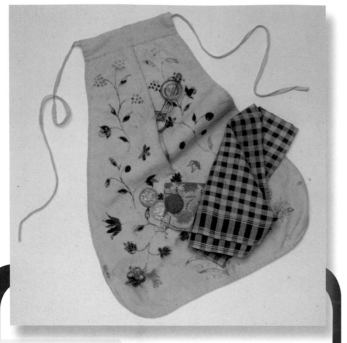

As you might imagine, cooking was quite a bit different than it is now. In **Eliza Pinckney's recipe for "Calves Head,"** the cook was instructed to do the following: "Boil the head till the Tongue will Peal, then cut half the Head into small pieces . . . make little Cakes of the Brains and dip them in and fry them, then pour the stew'd meat in the dish with the other half of the head, and lay the fried Oysters, Brains, and Tongue, with little bits of crispt bacon, and force meat Balls, on the Top and all about the meat garnish with horseradish and barberries and serve it hott."

Those details would likely include making and stoking fires, cooking, baking, preserving food, washing, ironing, milking cows, managing children, churning butter, carding, spinning, weaving, sewing, knitting, mending and altering clothing, cultivating a kitchen garden, and raising geese, chickens, and sheep.

Add seasonal jobs such as making soap and dipping candles, and it's easy to understand why cleanliness was rarely a priority. Farm homes and taverns had a reputation for being untidy and downright grimy. Flies, lice, and bed bugs, soot from the fireplace, as well as mud and manure from outside challenged even the most dutiful housekeeper.

For most, life was carried out in small, shared spaces or outdoors. Privacy was reserved for only the wealthiest of Americans. Neighbors wove in and out of each other's homes. Most people owned few belongings and packed as many as twelve or more family members, slaves, and servants into one- or two-room houses to sleep at night. Beds were pushed to the side during the day to make way for other activities. Luxury items such as napkins, tablecloths, plates, and bowls were rare.

If this work seemed unrelenting for white women, for slave women it was even more demanding. They had to complete a similar round of duties around the demands of heavy labor in the fields. Working from sun to sun and cradle to grave in urban homes and businesses, small farms, and enormous moneymaking plantations, they were forced to maintain their families late at night and on Sundays. Their housing was poor and their resources few.

CHILDREN AND HOMES By 1800, women bore an average of over seven children, though much larger families were not uncommon. This meant that while women were gardening, sewing, cooking, and hauling, they were often pregnant or nursing. And while space might have been tight, those who managed to have many children live to adulthood counted themselves lucky. Rural daughters spent much of their time spinning, helping their mothers, and exchanging work with their neighbors. Over a fifteen-year period, one Maine family recorded

Have you ever heard of... Amelia Simmons?

She wrote the first American cookbook, *American Cookery or the Art of Dressing Viands, Fish, Poultry and Vegetables, and the Best Modes of Making Pastes, Puffs, Pies, Tarts, Puddings, Custards and Preserves, and All Kinds of Cakes, from the Imperial Plumb to Plain Cake, adapted to This Country and All Grades of Life.* Published in 1796, it included uniquely American ingredients such as corn, pumpkin, and cranberries. Most housewives, however, cooked from memory or from handwritten recipes.

having 35 various young women living and working in their home. Unmarried girls made critical contributions to the survival of their families. A woman who had no daughters was in quite a predicament, having no one but paid help, if she could afford it.

Knowing the perils of marriage, it may seem surprising that a girl would choose to marry at all. The truth is that the alternative was not very appealing. A single woman, or "spinster," rarely gained independence, but rather relied upon her family for her upkeep. With few exceptions, she would work for others, without ever keeping her own house, or caring for her own children. **Rebecca Dickinson**, a single seamstress, complained in 1787 that "others and all the world was in Possession of Children and friends and a hous and homes while I was so od[d] as to sit here alone."

IN TOWN A woman living in town might escape some drudgery by purchasing many items and not

This image of an "old maid" is quite unflattering. Women who did not marry had little control over their lives.

Of her children, **Fanny Bland Tucker**, a Virginia plantation mistress, wrote to her absent husband, "The children are very well but intolerably noisy and troublesome—it is a hard day's work to attend to them & the drudgery of the house—their interruptions at this moment are so frequent I scarcely know what to write."

Once spinning and weaving was complete, some materials were dyed. This process ranged from simple to highly complex. Browns were often produced by boiling hulls of butternuts or black walnuts. That was easy. To dye things blue, on the other hand, was a long and stinky process. Smelly indigo was simmered in a pot of urine, and left for about two weeks. When yeast was added and the mixture turned brown, it was ready for dying. It was a good thing that indigo did not fade with multiple washings, because material had to be scrubbed multiple times to remove the stench.

keeping her own poultry. A trip to the market was not much like going to the grocery store today, however. When a woman bought a chicken, she brought it home alive and had to kill and pluck it before it made its way to the table. She, like her counterparts in the country, saved the feathers for beds, pillows, and quills. Town life offered some relief from hard labor, but with higher standards of cleanliness, townswomen spent more time cleaning their houses.

Middle-class and upper-class young women benefited most from the reduced demands of life in town. Compared to country girls, their existence was leisurely. These young women often had the time to read, learn to dance, and spend time with friends. Many held sewing groups where they took turns sewing and reading aloud to each other. Their work was less important for the family's survival and was intended instead to prepare them for their future lives as mistresses of their own houses.

ON THE FRONTIER Life was toughest for women on the frontier where many did not survive the primitive conditions. A man traveling through South Carolina noted that "in many places they have nought but a Gourd to drink out off Not a Plate Knive or Spoon, A Glass, Cup or anything." A New England traveler described one-room "wretched cabins" made with "tree trunks still covered with bark," where the chinks were "filled in with clay to stop the wind and rain," and the roof was made with large pieces of bark.

On the frontier, a woman often lacked the benefits of neighbors and family. She was also least likely to have any paid help. If she didn't reap enough from her garden, or store away enough supplies for winter, her family would face hunger and possible starvation. One woman who had moved with her husband to outlying Ohio in 1789 recalled that when she thought of her home in New England, she would "sob and cry as loud as a child" while milking her cows.

It is not surprising then, that most Indian women were not tempted to adopt white ways. Members of the Iroquois or Haudenosaunee League of Six Nations in the Northeast held women in high esteem. White men meeting with them to make

Captivity narratives helped to instill white settlers with fear and hatred of Native Americans. This fictitious 1815 account told the story of Mary Smith watching the "monsters of barbarity" kill her family.

treaties were completely baffled by spokesmen who negotiated wearing ceremonial skirts and carrying corn pounders. Whites assumed that these clothes revealed weakness. What they did not understand was that the spokesmen had been given the honor of transmitting the word of clan mothers, and that their outfits were signs of power. They had been made honorary women.

Haudenosaunee men built the longhouses, but women owned them. Men cleared the fields, but women grew and controlled the corn, squash, sunflowers, and beans. Family lines were traced through mothers. Clan mothers, or Gantowisas,

were judges, spiritual leaders, and counselors responsible for naming male leaders, distributing food, and sending off warriors to fight. Being part of a clan was a huge safety network. Clan members could arrive at the village from anywhere and know that women of the same clan would feed them. Both wives and husbands were free to end unhappy marriages. Rape was rare and severely punished.

Mary Jemison, taken captive at fifteen by the Shawnee, was one of numerous white captives who chose to stay with their Indian host families. Adopted by the Seneca in New York, she came to love her family "as I should have loved my own." Jemison later told a biographer, "No people can live more happy than the Indians did in times of peace." Though they dressed skins for clothing, Seneca women were free from the spinning, weaving, and sewing that consumed the hours of white women. Cooking was simple and required few utensils. Jemison concluded that even though

"Indian women have all the fuel and bread to procure, and the cooking to perform, their task is probably not harder than that of white women . . . and their cares certainly are not half as numerous, nor as great."

Did you know?

The word *squaw*, which has commonly been used to describe Indian women, is in fact a derogatory term taken from the Haudenosaunee word to describe female reproductive parts.

BEAUTY

"HOW AGREEABLE THEY WILL APPEAR"

It is a myth that wealthy Southern women merely sat around fanning themselves and looking lovely. In reality, their lives were consumed with the details of managing a household and estate. With husbands away on business or engaging in politics, women often ran plantations alone. One planter wrote to his wife in 1790, "I presume you have planted all the crop. I have only to add that I wish you good luck and good speed." In 1789 **Diana Dunbar** responded to her husband, *"I would willingly follow your advice and not go in the sun if I could avoid it, but there is many things to do about a place that you men don't think of."* In spite of the demands on their time, women worried about how they looked.

In 1777, the *London Magazine* warned new husbands that once wives took off their clothing, "you'll find you have lost half your wife." Though huge hoop skirts had largely disappeared by 1778, the new fashions relied on large hip pads with a full skirt in back supported by a "false rump" pad in back. Women weren't the only ones padding themselves. In a time when it was important for men to have good-looking calves, some took to padding those, as well.

One young man wrote in his diary of the importance of eyebrows to a woman's beauty. He described fourteen-year-old **Miss Hale** as *"a slim and silent girl and **a good set of eyebrows, which are esteemed in Virginia to be essential to beauty***." These eyebrows could be obtained by the seemingly modern techniques of trimming, plucking, and coloring with lead.

TOWERING HAIRDOS AND GIGANTIC DRESSES

France and England set the pace for colonial fashion. In France, especially, styles became increasingly extreme. Dresses reached tremendous proportions and hairdos grew to such towering heights that some fashionable women were forced to kneel in their carriages to protect their gargantuan hair. One woman observed that French women's "wooly white hair and fiery red faces make them look more like skinned sheep than human beings."

While Americans never reached the same extremes, many submitted to modified fashion tortures. In preparation for a ball or party, a woman's hair was worked over a wire frame, curled, and extended by fake hair and other materials. This was then plastered, powdered, and decorated with a display of plumes, bows, or beads. This hairdo was expected to last for many days, making sleeping difficult. Women suffered from itchy, aching heads and bug infestations.

One woman may have regretted her stylishness when a story about her hair showed up in the Boston *Gazette* in 1771. The paper reported that when she had been accidentally thrown from her carriage, her headdress was torn off to reveal an embarrassing mess of yarn, hay, and flax.

By the 1780s, women sported reduced, but still large "hedgehog" hairdos. In addition, fashions included a wide variety of hats, hoods, and bonnets made from gauze, silk, beaver skin, straw, and other materials. Hoods on cloaks had to be specially made to protect and not flatten elaborate hairdos. During this time it was difficult for even the most wealthy to keep up with fads. From 1784–86, Paris magazines noted seventeen shifts in hat fashions.

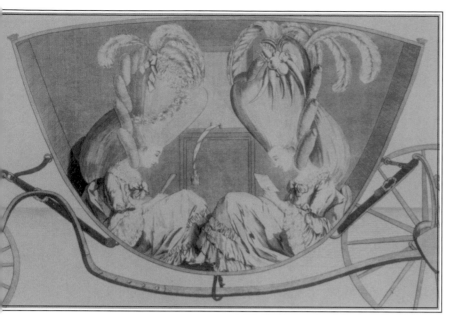

A 1776 British cartoon mocking the size of fashionable women's hairdos.

THE COMING OF A REVOLUTION

"TROUBLESOME TIMES A COMING"

The coming of the Revolutionary War would jarringly interrupt lives that had previously revolved around the seasons and cycles of work. During the 1760s, Britain had tried to recoup its financial losses from the French and Indian War by directly taxing the colonies. As colonists resisted, some of the most private and basic female responsibilities became public and political. In 1769, twenty-two-year-old **Charity Clarke** sent one of many strongly worded letters to her cousin in England. "If you English won't give us the liberty we ask," she warned. *"I will try to gather a number of ladies armed with spinning wheels . . . who shall all learn to weave and keep sheep, and will retire beyond the reach of arbitrary power, cloathed with the work of our own hands."* The image of helmeted women warriors toting looms might have made her cousin smile, but the British would soon discover that, in the colonies, patriotic women were no laughing matter.

REVOLUTIONARY HOMESPUN

Though politics were for males only, female colonists found that they, too, had a direct stake in the simmering conflict. Patriots hoped that by refusing to buy English goods they could force Britain to change its policies. This couldn't be achieved, however, without cooperation of the women. Suddenly, the choice of what to purchase became a public statement.

For years, wealthy Americans had enjoyed fine, imported European cloth rather than the homespun still produced and worn by poor country folk. So, when patriot women chose to wear unfashionable homespun dresses to fancy balls and church services, they were taking a political stand. What's more, they were agreeing to card wool, spin thread, and weave cloth or pay someone else to do it. Wearing homespun clothing thus became a visible display of patriotism.

Women were roundly praised for their sacrifice by some, and mocked by others. One New England paper reported, "in a large circle of very agreeable ladies in this Town, it was unanimously agreed to lay aside the Use of Ribbons, &c., &c., &c., How agreeable they will appear in their native beauty, stript of these Ornaments from the prevailing Motive of Love to their Country." Newspapers also applauded groups of New England girls who gathered to spin all day in public "spinning bees."

If women's patriotism didn't spur them to wear homespun, the prices of material might.

The switch to homespun actually improved the lives of some Southern slaves who were put to work carding, spinning, and weaving in converted tobacco barns. For the next forty years, many female slaves escaped harsher fieldwork by becoming expert spinners and weavers.

Sarah Franklin Bache complained to her famous father that she had paid an enormous amount for a "common calamanco petticoat without quilting." Unlike earlier times, she reported, "I buy nothing but what I really want, and wore out my silk ones before I got this." Only months later, she reported that "a pair of gloves cost seven dollars. One yard of common gauze twenty-four dollars." That would be $500 in today's currency.

THE WAR OF WORDS Men were unsure how to react as women began, cautiously, to share opinions about current events. In South Carolina, **Eliza Wilkinson** observed with a touch of humor that she and her female friends became armchair politicians. *"All trifling discourse of fashions, and such low little chat was thrown by, and we commenced perfect statesmen. Indeed, I don't know but if we had taken little pains, we should have been qualified for Prime ministers."*

BOYCOTTING TEA When the First Continental Congress met in Philadelphia in September 1774, it pled with colonists to stop drinking imported tea, "that baneful weed." The corresponding request to give up cockfighting, card playing, and horseracing was probably a relief to women. They were excluded from these activities anyway. Drinking tea was a different story. It was more than recreation; it was a way of life. Colonists universally adored tea.

Giving up tea was a great sacrifice. New Englander **Dorothy Dudley** wrote, "Its absence from our tables is cuttingly felt by many." Nonetheless, Virginia ladies filled the newspapers with letters encouraging one another to "banish India tea from your tables, and in its stead, substitute some of those aromatic herbs with which our fruitful soil abounds." One group of North Carolina ladies "burnt their tea in a solemn procession." Such public protests by women made some people uncomfortable.

When fifty-one women in Edenton, North Carolina, signed a petition in October 1774 declaring solidarity with the nonimportation resolutions, British officials ridiculed them. Newspapers carried this cartoon depicting very ugly and masculine women signing the document.

Living in the mountains of New Jersey, nineteen-year-old **Jemima Condict** couldn't see what all the fuss was about. *"It seems we have troublesome times a coming,"* she told her journal in October 1774, *"for there is great disturbance abroad in the earth and they say that tea caused it. So then if they will quarrel about such a thing as that, what must we expect but war."*

"Surely, my sisters, we cannot be tame spectators."

—A SOUTH CAROLINA PLANTER'S WIFE

SEEING IT COMING Attending a patriotic sermon in February 1775, one man noted that the men were "animated," but the women "were affected in quite a different manner; floods of tears rolled down their cheeks, from sad reflection of their nearest and dearest friends and relations entering into a dreadful civil war." The wives of politically active men were, perhaps, the first to understand not only the possibilities, but the sacrifices of war. Realizing that her husband was helping to forge a brand new government, **Abigail Adams** ventured what has become a famous suggestion. Writing to him privately, she requested that lawmakers

"Remember the Ladies, and be more generous and favorable to them than your ancestors. . . . Do not put such unlimited power in the hands of the Husbands. Remember all Men would be tyrants if they could."

Clearly Adams wanted the new government to pay attention to the needs of its women as well as its men.

Mary Bartlett of New Hampshire was accustomed to having her husband away on business. He often left her in charge of their busy household while he participated in local politics. However, in 1774, individuals loyal to the crown burned the Bartlett home to the ground. Mary Bartlett was forty-two years old and expecting her twelfth child when Josiah rode off to meet with the Second Continental Congress in 1776. On July 4th, he signed the Declaration of Independence, openly marking himself as a traitor to the crown. Mary Bartlett's pleas would be echoed by many other women in the years to come, *"Pray do come home before cold weather. As you know my circumstances will be difficult in the winter—if I am alive."* No one could guess how chaotic and bloody the next eight years would be.

Have you ever heard of . . . Mercy Otis Warren?

Warren's biting satire, published in Boston newspapers starting in 1772, fanned the flames of patriotic sentiment. Readers knew exactly who was being lampooned: British public officials. What they did not know was that the author was the busy mother of five boys between the ages of six and fifteen. Fortunate in that her father, brother, and husband recognized and respected her lively intellect, Warren was better educated than most women of her era. In addition to her plays and poems, she carried on extensive correspondence with many of the great thinkers of the time. Statesmen asked for her advice. She could never forget, however, that she was only participating in the male arena of political ideas because men allowed her to be there. Later, she was one of the first people to write a history of the Revolution.

THE REVOLUTIONARY WAR

CHOOSING SIDES

Though women had virtually no voice in politics, the ensuing war would forever change their lives. Depending on their circumstances, women viewed the start of the Revolution through very different eyes.

- On April 19, 1775, British soldiers destroyed the weapons depot and ransacked houses in Concord, Massachusetts, afterwards continuing on to Lexington. They burst into the bedroom where **Hannah Adams** lay with her newborn baby. One soldier "immediately opened my curtains with the bayonet fixed, pointing the same to my breast." She begged him not to kill her, to which he agreed if she went outside. *"I immediately arose,"* she told Congress, *"threw a blanket over me, went out, and crawled into a corn house near the door, with my infant. . . . They immediately set the house on fire, in which I had left five children and no other person."* Fortunately Adams was able to rescue her children and put out the fire.

- In May 1775, an Abenakis Indian woman "expressed much concern about the times," to a Maine settler. She said "their men could not hunt, eat, nor sleep; keep calling together every night" to counsel with each other. Native Americans wanted to view the conflict as one between white brothers, one in which they could remain neutral. However, long experience with European settlers suggested otherwise. The woman concluded, *"I think the world is coming to an end."*

- In July 1775, a fifteen-year-old slave girl ran away from her Virginia master. During the seven months in his possession, she had already attempted escape twelve times. After the first three, her master had whipped her severely. Even so, when the governor promised freedom to slaves escaping

In this 1776 British cartoon, the battle of Bunker Hill is playing out quite literally with a sea battle, infantry, and artillery in a woman's large hairdo. It's not so far from the truth, as women found the war right at their front doors.

to British lines, she took her chances yet again, running to the governor's mansion. Imagine her distress when, pursued by the slave patrol, she found the British forces had retreated. No one was home. The slave girl was returned to her master, who gave her eighty lashes, "well laid on" as he said, and then held "cold embers" to her back.

- Expecting her second child in December 1776, **Sarah Sherwood** saw her husband flogged publicly in their New Hampshire square after he declared himself loyal to the king. Convinced that he had been selling information to the British, townspeople rampaged through their house, destroying and stealing belongings. Now Justus Sherwood was on the run, openly aiding the British governor. To complicate matters for Sherwood, her husband's secret visit home to collect intelligence had resulted in another pregnancy. How would she explain this to

"What a scene has opened upon us. . . . If we look back we are amazed at what is past, if we look forward we must shudder at the view. Our only comfort lies in the justice of our cause."

—Abigail Adams to Mercy Warren, May 1775

everyone who believed her husband was far away? In October 1777, seven months pregnant, carrying a one-year-old and pulling a three-year-old by the hand, she and a slave boy set out for Canada.

In spite of the friction over taxes, many colonists deeply loved Britain. Many had family or friends in England, followed English fashions, and sent their children to Britain to be educated. Even after hostilities at Lexington and Concord, Congress sent a petition to King George, pleading that war be avoided. When the fighting began in earnest, no one knew how it would end. It seemed at the time that the largest, best-equipped army in the world was bound to win. However, this was a conflict in which nearly everyone would be forced to take sides, if they hadn't already.

In the example above, the concerns of the Abenakis woman were perhaps better founded than she knew. For Native Americans, the Revolutionary War would be nothing short of cataclysmic. Whether they supported the Americans, the British, or tried to remain neutral, the end results were the same: lost lives, homes, and self-rule. Their eventual displacement would send ripples across the continent.

In 1775 almost 500,000 slaves lived and labored in the colonies. During the chaos of war, individuals like the adolescent girl above weighed uncertain, and possibly deadly, options. Should they stay put and hope for the best? Should they run away to a city or swamp? Or should they offer their services to an army? For many slave women, the choice was shadowed by concern for their children. Yet with the talk of liberty all around them, they too hoped for freedom—their own. This might be the chance of a lifetime.

Not all colonists agreed with the course that America was taking. People who remained loyal to the king were called *loyalists* or *Tories*. A woman married to a Tory was guilty by association. Whatever her personal beliefs, people assumed them to be the same as her husband. The war dissolved the networks of friendship and love that would normally have provided loyalist women with security and aid. Some were mobbed, beaten, and even killed by people who had been their friends and neighbors.

Remaining neutral was also next to impossible, though many Quakers tried to do so. Opposed to violence, widow **Margaret Morris** and her four children stayed in their New Jersey town in spite of the fighting. As townspeople hunted out loyalists,

An 1863 depiction of the "First Blow for Liberty" of the battle of Lexington.

As a man left for war, he did not drop by the army warehouse to pick up a uniform. None existed. His wife or his mother knitted his stockings, hats, and gloves, wove his blankets, and stitched his jackets, shirts, and breeches. She also packed food, home remedies, and homemade candles and soap. Then she sent him on his way with the very real possibility that she might never see him again.

and as soldiers of both armies looted neighbors' homes, Morris risked the wrath of both sides by nursing anyone who needed her help. Complicating matters, her young son frequently tried to slip away to see soldiers and get in on some action.

Much blood had already been shed during the eighteenth century as European nations fought for control of the American continent, primarily in frontier combats with colonists backed by the powerful British military. Now this same military was arrayed against colonists in their own homes, towns, seaports, and farms. The Revolution fighting began mostly in New England, shifted to the middle states, and finally, expanded into the South. Though men would be the primary combatants, this war would have lasting repercussions for everyone.

Farm woman **Mary Draper** made bullets for her husband and young son. Instead of eating from wooden plates, or "trenchers" like many families, the Drapers used pewter passed down to Mary by her mother. It was probably a sad day when she took her beloved pewter platters and dishes from the shelf to melt them into buckshot.

STAYING BEHIND

Stirred by patriotic fervor, some women may have agreed with the New Jersey grandmother who requested of her sons, *"Let me beg you . . . that if you fall, it may be like men; and that your wounds may not be in your back parts."* In North Carolina, young women "entered into a resolution not to permit the addresses of any person . . . unless he has served in the American armies to prove by his valor, that he is deserving of their love." Others probably agreed with the wife who said of her soldier husband, "I was troubled to think that he should love to be going so much in the war and leave me with helpless children in very poor circumstances."

When a soldier enlisted, the entire family sacrificed. Maintaining a household required the efforts of husband, wife, and older children, not to mention a servant or slave or two. The loss of one or more contributing family members could quickly plunge a family into financial crisis. If the soldier died, the family's poverty was often permanent.

HIS AND HER TASKS Many women were left to fend for themselves. Without the basic goods imported from England, women had to

In June 1782, it had been five years since **Abigail Adams** had seen her husband and young son, who were in Europe. She patted herself on the back: "I will take praise to myself," she wrote. "I feel that it is my due, for having sacrificed so large a portion of my peace and happiness to promote the welfare of my country."

neck and tossed him into the cart." Once they had the keys, the women hauled out the coffee, put it in trunks, and drove away. *"A large concourse of men stood amazed silent spectators."* It has been estimated that women instigated at least third of the known food riots that erupted during the Revolution. While "unfeminine," these behaviors were still considered justified because women had to feed their children.

Women also took on new and unfamiliar tasks—those of their husbands and sons. While familiar with the workings of their farms, they had no more cut down trees or purchased land than their men had spun thread or made butter. Now, women strove to keep fields planted and harvested, orchards tended, and business affairs in order. They also learned how to manage a dwindling labor force and negotiate sales.

Leaders of the emerging government spent months if not years away while their wives managed their estates and raised their children. Their infrequent, short visits home often resulted in pregnancy. **Deborah Franklin** assumed responsibility for the national post office as well as the family finances while Benjamin was in Paris. Lonely, overburdened wives consoled themselves that their sacrifices served a greater cause.

As months turned into eight long years, many wives grew confident in their new skills. Some ceased to ask, or even take advice from their absent husbands, and came to think homes and farms as "ours" instead of "his." **Lucy Knox**, the wife of one of Washington's most trusted generals, felt that the experience had changed her. She wrote to her husband in 1777, *"I hope you will not consider yourself as commander in chief of your own house— but be convinced . . . that there is such a thing as equal command."*

"SURROUNDED BY AN ARMY"

In March 1776, British forces and their Hessian (German) allies occupied Boston. In June they moved on to New York City. The following year they were in Philadelphia. Lodging soldiers in her home was a challenge that every woman hoped to avoid, but both armies expected civilians to provide

get creative. Some experimented with hickory ashes and a little salt to preserve meat. In the absence of leather for shoes, others sewed rags around their feet. If a woman wanted cloth, she had to weave it herself. When her needles broke or got lost, she made do with thorns. She could replace English tea using local plants and herbs, but her children still had to eat. A foot soldier's wages, when he was paid at all, were pitifully low.

With the price of most staples beyond reach, the poorest families were pushed to drastic measures. Abigail Adams described a scene in July 1778 where at least a hundred women confronted a merchant accused of charging too much for goods. When he refused to give them the keys to his warehouse, "one of them seized him by the

housing and food to their troops. Many women found themselves with enemy soldiers snoring in the next room. With children to care for, and inflation making paper money nearly worthless, they were still obliged to feed and wash clothes for these uninvited strangers. When a British major moved in with **Elizabeth Drinker** and her children, he brought "3 horses, 3 cows, 2 sheep, and 2 turkeys, with several fowls…3 servants and one negro… [and] 3 Hessians who take their turns to wait on him as messengers." This entourage was loud and took over most of the house.

Mothers worried for their young daughters. Rape was common, if the boasts of one British officer housed on Staten Island are to be believed. He chuckled in August 1776, "The fair nymphs of this isle are in wonderful tribulation" because of unrestrained soldiers. "A girl cannot step into the bushes to pluck a rose without running the . . . risk

of being ravished." When soldiers were brought to trial for their misdeeds, he found it "entertaining." Sexual assaults often went unreported.

Everywhere soldiers went, epidemics followed. With diseases such as smallpox daily carrying off friends, relatives, and neighbors, Jemima Condict called January 1777 *"A sickly time and a very dying time, the people fleeing before their enemies."* To Abigail Adams's great grief, her mother, who had come to help care for the family during a dysentery epidemic, herself succumbed.

Wives of officers were not spared; they just housed higher profile guests. Although they were enemies, rules of etiquette governed the way elite commanders and their families treated one another outside of battle. After the Americans won the battle of Saratoga in 1777, General Schulyer's wife, **Catherine Schulyer**, was asked to house the same British officers who had just burned her country

What Catherine Schulyer probably didn't mention to the British while serving up their meals was that before the battle she had ridden to Saratoga and torched her ripe wheat fields so that the enemy could not harvest them.

estate to the ground. She gave them her best rooms and treated them like guests.

For young women, the arrival of friendly troops could seem a romantic opportunity. Fifteen-year-old **Sally Wister**, bored in the country and missing Philadelphia, was a little frightened but mostly filled with anticipation when she thought that soldiers might pass through. In October 1777, she heard the "greatest drumming, fifing, and rattling of waggons" and ran to watch what turned out to be American soldiers marching to a nearby town. When soldiers called at the house later in the day, Wister made sure she was looking her best. That night she wrote to a friend,

"I feel in good spirits, though surrounded by an army: the house is full of officers, yard alive with soldiers—very peaceable sort of men, tho'. They eat like other folks, talk like them, and behave themselves with elegance; so I will not be afraid of them. . . . I am going to my chamber to dream, I suppose of bayonets and swords, sashes, guns, and epaulets."

During their stay, Wister captured the attentions of a young "bashful" major. More than one marriage resulted from such encounters. The elite of both armies carried on a lively social life when not engaged in fighting.

Loyalists in large cities held lavish parties. New York's fashionable and quick-witted **Rebecca Franks** did not have her mind on war, but on bonnets and bows. In her letters, she shared the frivolous details of parties and balls, and the ins and outs of handkerchief pinning and brooch wearing. To her sister in Philadelphia, she wrote, "I shall send you a pattern of the newest bonnet; there is no crown, but gauze is raised on wire and punched in a sugar loaf at the top. The lighter the trimming the more fashionable." Reading her letters, you would never guess that a war was being waged not far from where she wrote.

"THE MULTITUDE OF WOMEN": CAMP FOLLOWERS

Not all women stayed home. **Sarah Osborn**, a young servant from New York, dodged bullets in more than one battle to feed hungry soldiers. While she was carrying food to soldiers at Yorktown, George Washington stopped her and asked if she "was not afraid of the cannonballs." She replied that *"It would not do for the men to fight and starve too."* Cooking and washing clothes for her soldier husband and his comrades, she became one of thousands of women who tended to the most basic needs of soldiers so they could keep fighting.

In this day of modern warfare, it is hard to imagine a war where families intentionally tag along. Yet, in many ways, the Revolution was a family affair. In addition to combat, soldiers were expected to care for their own needs and pay their own expenses. One bystander observed that American soldiers, "not being used to doing things of this sort, choose rather to let their linen, etc., rot upon their backs than to be at the trouble of cleaning 'em themselves."

Common prisoners of war were not given the same red-carpet treatment as officers. After Saratoga, 5,000 British and Hessian soldiers with their wives and children were marched 200 miles to Boston in the fall chill. In a letter to Mercy Warren, **Hannah Winthrop** described the "sordid set of creatures" who trudged through her town. There were 2,000 women, ragged and barefoot, carrying heavy bags full of pots, pans, and furniture, not to mention babies and children "peeping out." She was also shocked by the stench of their unwashed bodies.

Revolutionary War armies included great numbers of camp-following women and children. Why do you think they are rarely shown in war imagery?

Army camps were rife with bugs and disease. A soldier was more likely to die of sanitation-related diseases such as typhoid fever than from wounds received in battle. Smallpox brought down whole regiments. One critic reasoned, *"When at home, their female relations put them upon washing their hands and faces, and keeping themselves neat and clean; but absent from such montiors. . . . They have grown filthy, and poisoned their constitution by nastiness."*

In other words, soldiers needed women. Yet, female services came with strings attached. Most had children. An estimated 5,000 women and 12,000 children followed the British Army by the end of the war. When General Clinton's army evacuated Philadelphia in 1778, the procession was twelve miles long. Though poorer and more mobile, the American army also had thousands of women and children in its ranks. Wives able to get an official position as a "woman of the regiment" counted themselves lucky because in addition to wages, they also received half rations for themselves and quarter rations for their children. Both armies set quotas for the number of women they would officially hire, but many more women followed unofficially.

Though subject to military rules and discipline, women in camp often did whatever it took to survive, including looting the countryside

The story of one camp follower named **Mary McCauley** became quite famous. McCauley wintered over in Valley Forge, and at the battle of Monmouth, helped to fire the cannons, for which she was later awarded an army pension. She is remembered as "Molly Pitcher." In truth, there were many "Molly Pitchers" who helped the troops.

and robbing the dead. They were also accused of prostitution, disobeying orders, illegally trafficking alcohol, enticing men to desert, and spying. Camp followers blatantly defied General Washington's orders to skirt the city of Philadelphia while his soldiers marched through.

By all accounts, female camp followers were a tough bunch. Poor and displaced, they could not lay claim to treatment as respectable "ladies." One American soldier wrote, "A caravan of wild beasts could bear no comparison." Living outside in all kinds of weather, emptying the bedpans of dying men, marching hundreds of miles, scrubbing crusty clothes, cooking for hundreds, and toting water to cool down firing guns was no picnic—especially with children tagging along. Yet, those who followed the army were usually women who felt as if they had no other choice—daughters of poor families, widows, and runaway servants who faced destitution and starvation because of the war. And, in fact, though they received low wages, and even less respect, the army could not have carried on without them.

"WHAT PREPARATION COULD I MAKE?": TO STAY OR TO GO

As uniformed men appeared in their fields, blockaded their roads, and hammered at their doors, women had to make quick and vital decisions. Should they stay home and try to protect their property, or take to the "roads filled with frightened women and children, some in carts with their tattered furniture, others on foot fleeing into the woods"? It was often impossible to tell friend from foe until the last second. As redcoats pillaged her house and ripped the buckles from her shoes, **Eliza Wilkinson** was defiant. However, she recalled that *"when they were gone, and I had time to consider, I trembled so with terror that I could not support myself. I went into the room, threw myself on the bed, and gave way to a violent burst of grief."* For a long time after she slept in her clothes.

Did you know?

Though they did not share the same miserable conditions as poorer women, the wives of commanding officers also joined their husbands in camp, especially during the winter when fighting slowed. The portly and sharp-tongued **Lucy Knox**, Southern belle **Catherine Greene**, and practical **Martha Washington** must have made an unusual trio at winter quarters, where they worked to distract both officers and foot soldiers from their uncomfortable circumstances. Washington named her pet tomcat after her husband's dashing young aide, Alex Hamilton, who had all the ladies swooning.

Often rumors were the only source of information about troop movements. Hunkered down in their homes, women watched the roads and listened for news. Soldiers from both armies stripped farms of anything they could eat or wear. They tore down barns and fences for firewood. They also carried off slaves, separating slave families and leaving women without help to replant crops. Some families were plundered repeatedly. Having watched enemy soldiers carry all the bedding from her house, **Jane McJunkin** literally wrestled a man for her last quilt. When the soldier slipped and fell, she put her

The multitude of women . . . especially those who are pregnant, or have children, are a clog upon every movement."

—GEORGE WASHINGTON ON CAMP FOLLOWERS

In February 1776, sixteen-year-old **Mary Slocumb** dreamed that her soldier husband was dead. She hurriedly saddled her mare and rode more than thirty miles to where she could hear a battle raging. Hurrying past wounded men, she saw her husband's bloody cloak exactly as it had lain in her dream. Surprisingly, the man in the cloak turned out to be a wounded neighbor. "Why Mary," exclaimed her astonished husband when he found her binding wounds. "What are you doing there? Hugging Frank Cogdell, the greatest reprobate in the army?" Though relieved that her husband was alive, Slocumb was too embarrassed to tell him why she had come.

foot on his chest and wrenched the blanket from his hands. His commanding officer let her keep it, though his unit took everything else.

Refugees usually sought shelter with relatives, squeezing into small houses and adding extra burdens to those already barely surviving. Hosting seven extra people by 1775, **Sally Cobb Paine** wrote, "I have my house full and hands too." Often women and children who had moved to avoid the fighting found the war had followed them.

SLAVES Slave women faced a particularly difficult decision. If caught running away, they might be maimed, executed, or sold to hard labor in the West Indies. Staying may have seemed the safest option. However, both armies treated captured slaves as the spoils of war. More than one slave wife watched helplessly as family members were dragged away by marauding soldiers. Wartime shortages made life harsh even for those far from the battlefield. Many women who remained with their masters were given more work than ever, while receiving less food and clothing. Others, sensing the dwindling power of their owners, refused to work at all. South Carolina plantation owner **Eliza Pinckney** complained that her slaves thought they were "quite their own masters."

Voicing the common fear that slaves would side with the British against their owners, George Washington's steward rightly observed, "there is not a man of them, but would leave us, if they believed they could make their escape." Among those who ran away from the Washington plantation were "**Lucy**, a woman about twenty years old. **Esther**, a woman about eighteen years old," and "**Deborah**, a woman about sixteen years old." During colonial times, most runaways were male. However, when slave women found war on their doorsteps, many took their children and fled to British encampments. What was at first a small stream of fugitives became a raging river.

Thousands of escaped slaves offered their services to the redcoats, though only about a thousand fought as soldiers. The British initially welcomed escapees, not out of kindness, but because they needed people to do support jobs. Fugitive women foraged for food and firewood, tended horses, cooked meals, washed clothes, and nursed the dying. When General Charles Cornwallis's army marched from North Carolina to Virginia in 1781, between four and five thousand escaped slaves trailed behind.

"Neither sleep to my eyes, nor slumber to my eyelids, this night, but judge you, what preparation could I make . . . six children hanging around me, the little girls crying out, 'Mamma, will they kill us!'"

—**Mary Gould Almy** to her soldier husband

For most, however, escape was the beginning of more misery. **Judith Jackson** washed and ironed for Lord Dunmore's army. Though she successfully fended off the attempts of her former master to reenslave her, she later petitioned for help after another man "took all my clothes . . . took my money from me and stole my child from me and sent it to Virginia." If she successfully fended off slave catchers and robbers, a woman might still succumb to smallpox or starvation. Crowded together in camps with inadequate clothing and food, thousands died from infectious diseases. When times got hard for the British, they cut back on rations for black camp followers, or abandoned them altogether. If deserted by fleeing armies, fugitives faced punishment from vengeful masters.

LOYALISTS As thousands of loyalist men and their older sons fled to England or Canada, many wives and young children stayed behind, mistakenly believing that they would be spared what one woman called "disrespectful indignities." Petitions submitted by women after the war described how "rebels" carried off their animals, smashed their furniture, and burned their homes. Not only did crowds take **Elizabeth Wilstee**'s food storage and rip open her feather beds, they pulled logs loose so that her roof would cave in.

These scenes were especially common in the South, where one in five people was loyal to the crown, and the conflict became an all-out civil war. Considering loyalists to be traitors, state assemblies seized their homes, lands, and even their clothes, tools, and dishes—often selling them to

Imagine the terror of having soldiers come through your house to take away the food and blankets you need to survive.

raise revenue for the war. Some state governments officially banished anyone who would not pledge allegiance to the cause.

Grace Growdon Galloway remained in Philadelphia when her husband and daughter fled to New York and then London. After the British evacuated Philadelphia, representatives of the Continental government showed up to confiscate her home and belongings. She endured the same shortages as her neighbors, but without the benefit of friends. Lonely and sad, she asked her journal, "Shall I once more belong to somebody, for I am like a pelican in the desert." It galled her that people avoided her company. She wrote in 1779, *"For the whole town are a mean pack and as such I despise them."* She died before she could see her husband or daughter again.

"THE NESTS ARE DESTROYED": NATIVE AMERICANS

When the war began, both sides courted Indian allies. Until then, the Six Nations of the Haudenosaunee (Iroquois) had maintained their power in the Northeast by presenting a strong, united front. Now, in councils that included both women and men, they debated what to do. Their British trading partners had tried to protect their

This is a nineteenth-century illustration of a Mohawk village as it might have appeared in 1780.

lands from settlers. What had the Americans done for them? Not much. The choice split the Six Nations. The Senecas, Cayugas, and Mohawks sided with the British, and the Tuskaroras and some Oneidas and Onondagas with the Americans.

Mohawk **Molly Brant** knew where her allegiance lay. As the widow of Indian Commissioner Sir William Johnson, she strongly urged her people to remain loyal to "their father the King." Raised a Christian and educated in mission schools, she moved skillfully between cultures. "Her features are fine and beautiful . . . her complexion clear and olive-tinted," noted an Englishwoman who met Brant. "She possessed . . . a native pride and consciousness of power." The daughter of an influential Sachem (or chief) and an honored clan mother, she employed this power to keep the Six Nations allied with the British. Her son-in-law wrote: *"one word from her goes farther with them than a thousand from any white man."*

Brant sent her sixteen-year-old son to fight, but remained home with her other seven children, providing ammunition, food, shelter, and information to loyalists. Her timely tip led to the battle of Oriskany, where British and Indian allies ambushed American militia. Many Mohawks and Senecas died. More sobering still, the opposing side included their own brothers, the Oneidas. The conflict between whites was now an Indian civil war as well. Patriots drove Molly Brant and her children from their home.

The frontiers of New York, Ohio, Pennsylvania, Kentucky, and Tennessee became brutal killing grounds. Families left behind on the frontier became easy targets. Soldiers and warriors rejected their common humanity by killing and mutilating one another's wives, mothers, and children. Blacksnake, a Seneca warrior, recalled when loyalists and Indians slaughtered white settlers at Cherry Valley in 1778: "I just than took my tomehawk and strok one and to another. . . Dont minde anything about criing woman and children."

The next fall, 4,500 American soldiers marched through Iroquois country and destroyed forty villages. Other militias carried out similar attacks elsewhere. The only eyewitness account by an Indian woman is that of Mary Jemison, the captive mentioned earlier. She later recalled that when American soldiers came,

"A part of our corn they burnt, and threw the remainder in the river. They burnt our houses, killed what few cattle and horses they could find, destroyed our fruit trees, and left nothing but the bare soil and timber."

Cold and without shelter, "I took two of my little ones on my back, bade the other three follow." Jemison and her children survived the record bitter winter in a cabin with two generous escaped slaves. However, thousands froze and starved to death. Those who had fled before the American troops huddled around British forts, where smallpox raged.

Suspicious of all Indians, Americans frequently failed to distinguish friend from foe, raiding the towns of their allies and sending more groups over to the British side. The cycle of violence perpetuated itself throughout the war. Militia massacred unarmed, praying Delawares. Shawnees terrorized random settlements. American soldiers burned Cherokee farms. Wyandots besieged white towns.

Many Indian women were accustomed to seasonal migration, but this was different. Having lost everything and unable to return home, they could not grow food for the following year. With their agricultural base destroyed, clans could not rebound. Reducing Indian women and children to starvation and rags only spurred their husbands and fathers to fight harder. As one American officer observed, "The nests are destroyed but the birds are still on the wing."

FIGHTING THEIR OWN WAR

Though few toted guns, many women nonetheless fought their own war, from spying and sabotaging the enemy to driving marauders from their own homes. In some ways, females made perfect spies and messengers because they were not expected to do such things. With soldiers staying in their homes, women frequently overheard and passed on information that might be useful to military commanders.

Long after the war, **Dicey Langston**'s family recalled her bravery. Fifteen at the outset of the war, the South Carolina girl frequently eluded or faced down threatening loyalist neighbors, even wading a swollen river in the dead of night to warn her brother. On one occasion, she saved her aging father from Tory soldiers. On another, she tipped off a peaceable loyalist neighbor of an attack, but then had to turn around and warn the Patriots who planned to attack him that he had sent out friends to ambush them. People tended to overlook "unusual" behavior such as Langston's if they thought it was motivated by womanly affection.

Loyalist women also took great risks. After **Lorenda Holmes** helped smuggle loyalist refugees

When the British prepared a sneak attack on Washington's troops in 1777, **Lydia Darragh** is said to have overheard their plans and crossed British lines to warn the patriots. This 1845 illustration of that event is a bit romanticized, as Darragh was a nearly fifty-year-old mother of five at the time.

to a British camp outside New York, an American officer burned her foot with hot coals to teach her a lesson. This was actually her second warning. After she carried letters through the lines in 1776, city officials shamed her by displaying her naked in front of an open window. Because the prevailing wisdom was that women by themselves were not political actors, continental governments were unsure of how to deal with women who passed information to the enemy, hid soldiers, and smuggled supplies for them. These women could seriously undermine the cause.

What One Woman Did

Though born in England, **Esther de Berdt Reed**'s sympathies lay with the patriots. Busy with three young children, she wrote to her brother in March 1775, "You may judge...how interesting politics are, when they employ so much of my thoughts and attention, now I am surrounded by family concerns." Soon thereafter, her husband Joseph was made secretary to General Washington. *"I think the cause in which he is engaged, so just, so glorious, and I hope so victorious,"* she exulted, *"that private interest and pleasure may and ought to be given up without a murmur."*

These were not idle words. With her husband away, Reed moved her elderly mother and children six times to escape the fighting. In the midst of this, her two-year-old daughter died of smallpox. In 1780 she gave birth to her fifth child, George Washington Reed. Hearing of tattered and hungry American soldiers, Reed worried about her husband's troops. If demoralized men deserted the army, what would become of the cause for which everyone had given so much? While recovering from childbirth, Esther Reed had an idea.

Surely women could dress more simply and donate money to the troops. Though formal organizations were considered masculine, Reed needed an official avenue for collecting money. The resulting Ladies Association of Philadelphia was the first interstate women's organization. Elected president, Reed divided up the city and sent women out in pairs to knock on doors—a truly novel and somewhat shocking plan. In three days they collected more than $300,000 in paper money.

Reed wrote to women in other states who soon followed suit. The association wanted to give a small sum to each soldier to spend as he wished. George Washington was grateful, but had his own ideas. Convinced that soldiers would waste the money on liquor, he insisted that the donations be used to purchase cloth and make shirts.

Reed bowed to his wishes. She wrote to her husband, "I shall now endeavor to get the shirts made as soon as possible." She died before she could. Only thirty-three years old and nursing four-month-old George, Esther Reed succumbed to dysentery in September 1780. The people of Philadelphia mourned. Others, particularly Sarah Bache (Benjamin Franklin's daughter), were left to finish Reed's project. Individual women sewed 2,200 shirts, embroidering their names on the finished shirts so the soldiers would know who had made them. Washington thanked the ladies: "The Army ought not to regret its sacrifices or its sufferings when they meet with so flattering a reward."

In Georgia, a British courier and his soldier escort were waylaid by two young men who forced him to hand over the important papers he was carrying. At the nearby house where the soldiers stopped for the night, farmwife **Rachel Martin** did not tell them that the two "bandits" were her daughters-in-law, **Elizabeth** and **Grace**. The women quickly forwarded the message on to American General Greene, and then spent the evening chatting with the unsuspecting soldiers whom they had just robbed.

THE WAR ENDS

Early in the war, **Elizabeth Field**, the wife of a Virginia minister, had written, *"I hope after we have been well jolted, jumbled & shak'd together we may by some lucky hit be thrown into our old Places and stations, that the world will settle into its usual course, & things move in the same order and regularity as formerly."* When the war officially ended with the Peace Treaty of Paris on September 3, 1783, many probably hoped to return to the "usual course." However, this was not possible. The Revolution had changed America.

- When the British surrendered, they ceded all Indian lands south of Canada to the Americans. The Indian nations who had been their allies were "thunderstruck." How could these white men hand over what was not theirs to give? The British had been a buffer against expansion. Now it appeared that American "liberty" would simply be an excuse to take what colonists had wanted

all along: Indian lands. What many people don't know is that at the same time, those writing the U.S. Constitution were borrowing Haudenosaunee ideas about democratic governance. In the years after the Revolution, many Native American groups continued to resist, but it was a losing battle. Indian women lost more than land as imposition of white ways upset the balance of male and female relations within clans.

- While an estimated 80,000 to 100,000 slaves ran away during the war, only a small fraction of these managed to stay alive and free. In fall 1783, the British and their Tory allies evacuated the colonies. Aboard their ships were a small but unknown number of free black women bound for England, and 914 bound for Canada. Of these many would eventually seek their fortunes in the African colony of Sierra Leone.

- Between 75,000 and 100,000 loyalists left America by the end of the war. Many loyalist wives, bitter and penniless, eventually joined their husbands in exile, where they struggled to make new lives for themselves. Though they had sided with the king, they felt unwelcome and homesick in England. Emigrants to Canada found a rough frontier society. **Mary Fisher** later recalled her miserable first winter in a tent:

> "How we lived through that first winter I hardly know. There were mothers, that had been reared in a pleasant country enjoying all the comforts of life. . . . They clasped their infants to their bosoms and tried by the warmth of their own bodies to protect them from the bitter cold."

Although the English and American governments awarded compensation to some loyalists for their losses, they could never replace the lives shattered, and the friends forfeited for having chosen the losing side.

- For white patriot women, the Revolution represented both losses and gains. Many mourned lost loved ones and lost property. Some were thrust into irreversible poverty. At the same time, elite women realized with alarm that divisions between classes had become less fixed. Having weathered the storm, however, many women also possessed a new confidence in themselves and their abilities. They knew that their sacrifices and contributions had been important. While new ideas about female citizenship would result in better access to education for some and an emerging respect for motherhood, they would not ensure legal or political rights.

Revolutionary ideals, coupled with female contributions to the war, caused the fledgling country to look upon women with new eyes. Many people began to believe that to succeed, the new country needed citizens who were educated enough to act for the common good. And who would produce these educated citizens? Mothers. Unable to participate in politics directly, mothers could nonetheless raise noble, wise sons who would be the next generation of virtuous citizens. In the new United States of America, women were to rear what one young woman called "future heroes and statesmen." Their daughters, in turn, would be prepared to mother their own little patriots.

EDUCATION
"AN AGREEABLE COMPANION TO A SENSIBLE MAN"

Throughout the eighteenth century, a girl's most important education consisted of learning to spin, sew, weave, and keep house. Or, as one educated man put it, "Girls knew enough if they could make a shirt and pudding." Upper-class girls were polished for society in finishing schools where they learned to sing, dance, embroider, paint, and speak French. These "ornamental skills" were put to use in making the best marriage possible. Not one existing school taught girls the same academic subjects as those taught to boys. Why would females need to know of the world when their lives centered on the home?

Judith Sargent Murray, who wrote under a male pen name so people would take her seriously, was among those who challenged these notions. Seized by an "unaccountable itch for scribbling," Murray crafted a number of passionate and well-reasoned essays insisting that women had minds equal to men. At a time when women were still thought to be naturally irrational, she pointed out that women merely suffered from dismal educational opportunities. She lamented that in families, *"the sister must be wholly domesticated, while the brother is led by the hand through all the flowery paths of science. . . . The one is taught to aspire; . . . the other early confined and limited."*

Murray and others insisted that if mothers were going to teach their children and create able citizens, they needed to be educated themselves. An increasing number of children attended primary school, and literacy rates increased each year. Massachusetts mandated free elementary education for all children in 1789. For the first time, a critical mass of prominent men also argued that women needed improved education.

FEMALE ACADEMIES A few of these men, led by Benjamin Rush, established the Philadelphia Young Ladies' Academy in 1787. Here the daughters of well-to-do Philadelphians were taught a broad range of academic subjects. Students eventually came from as far away as the West Indies. Rush proclaimed that this education would prepare a young woman "to be an agreeable companion to a sensible man," and teach her the skills necessary for household management and

This 1778 British cartoon reveals woman's double bind. She is mocked for becoming what her society has asked to her become. The same society that scorns her has offered her few other opportunities.

Americans had only recently embraced the belief that children were born innocent, and needed to be taught and nurtured in the ways of goodness. This was a radical departure from the previous notion that children were sinful by nature and needed to be whipped into submission. This shift in thinking led parents to view their children's education differently.

Some parents foresaw dreary prospects for unschooled daughters. Thomas Jefferson wrote in the 1780s that he wanted his daughter Martha educated because "The chance that in marriage she will draw a blockhead I calculate at about fourteen to one. . . . The education of her family will probably rest on her own ideas and directions without assistance." His prediction turned out to be true, as Martha married poorly and raised twelve children almost single-handedly.

This is an 1873 reprint of Susanna Haswell Rowson's novel *Charlotte Temple,* a best-selling moral tale in which Charlotte dies after bearing a child out of wedlock.

In 1792, a book entitled *Vindication of the Rights of Woman* caused quite a stir. **Mary Wollstonecraft,** the book's British author, boldly declared that women should not be excluded from participating in a democratic society. She believed differences between men and women mainly to be the result of women's inadequate education and opportunities. Many Americans read and debated her ideas. After Charleston matron **Alice Izard** read the book aloud to her husband, she huffed to her daughter, "I have just finished. . . as much of it as I could read, for I was often obliged to stop, and pass over and frequently to cough and stammer it. **He is as much disgusted with the book as I am, and calls the author a vulgar, impudent hussy."**

shaping the values of her sons. Professor Samuel Magaw encouraged "habits of obedience, and a placid, graceful attention" to womanly duties. These characteristics would prepare young women "to please, charm and entertain, at home among their families and friends." Noticeably lacking was any reference to education preparing a girl for a future where she might support herself.

Eliza Southgate, born in Maine in 1783, benefited from the increasing number of female academies that were established during her lifetime. Born into a family with money, she took advantage of the new opportunities and attended author **Susanna Haswell Rowson**'s Young Ladies' Academy in Boston. A delightful series of letters she wrote to her cousin,

Moses Porter, reveals that the subject of women's education was still controversial. She asked him, "Do you suppose the mind of woman the only work of God that was 'made in vain'?" When Southgate's cousin chastised her for her ideas, she returned hotly, *"On what subjects shall I write you? I shall either fatigue and disgust you with female trifles, or shock you by stepping beyond the limits you have prescribed."* Educated women had to walk a thin line and remain carefully submissive to the men in their lives.

In one letter, Porter worried that educated women might seek a higher place in society. On the contrary, Southgate argued. She believed that educating women would help them to see the necessity of their lower place in society. Though most early educational reformers agreed with Southgate and believed that education would merely help women in the home, they were wrong about its long-term impact. As women became more educated, they would gradually pursue broader rights and opportunities.

Most women, however, were so busy running households that there was time for little else. Abigail Adams lamented that her younger sister's genius was "stifled through want of leisure." **Elizabeth Smith Shaw** echoed that claim in a 1781 letter: *"[I]f Ideas present themselves to my Mind, it is too much like the good seed sown among Thorns, they are soon erased, & swallowed up by the Cares of the World, the wants, & noise of my Family and Children."*

PAID WORK

"CHANGING WORKS" AND KEEPING TAVERNS

BARTERING Unlike today, in the 1700s, many of a woman's daily household tasks earned essential money and goods for her family. Where housework left off and paid work picked up was often unclear. On July 12, 1775, **Nabby Foot** wrote, *"I went to Mr. Otis's and spooled some of Mrs. Wrights yarn and come home about noon and got my piece to work and Eliza Wells was here and I helped Israel pole hay a little."* In this one simple journal entry, Foot reveals the fluid nature of work in the late eighteenth century. Her journal shows a world of "changing works" and sharing tools. Outside housework, there was a whole other round of labor that she bartered, traded, or exchanged with neighbors. Her contributions were significant not only to her own family, but to those around her.

The expectation that wives would contribute to the family economy is well illustrated in one man's complaints that his betrothed had tricked him into thinking she was a hard worker. According to his account, *"her friends had collected all the yarn in the neighborhood and hung it up around her room and made me think it was her own spinning."* Now he was

Bartering was so common that during the difficult war years, the Maryland *Journal,* under the direction of **Mary Katherine Goddard,** accepted all sorts of payments, including, "Beef, Pork, or any Kind of Animal Food, Butter, Hog's Lard, Tallow, Bees-Wax, Flour, Wheat, Rye, Indian Corn . . . tann'd Sheepskins, brown Linen . . . and Cotton Rags."

Producing flax for clothing was a constant, ongoing, process. First, women planted and tended the plants. At harvest, they pulled the stocks up by roots, placed them in neat piles, and then knocked off seeds. Next the plants were retted (wetted to break down the outer shell), pounded, and beaten until the husk and tow (short fibers) fell. Following this, they were hetcheled (carded until smooth). At this point, the flax was ready for spinning, weaving, and sewing. **Mary Stirling** *bypassed the early production by getting paid in flax for a nursing stint. She worked the flax, spun and wove it, and sold the finished product.*

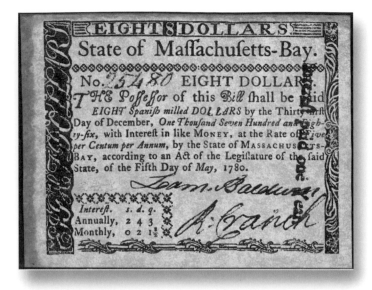

left with a lazy wife who did little to increase the family's prospects.

Because of women's *femme covert* status and the amount of bartering and trading going on, most married women's paid labor is hidden from the historical record. Transactions often went unrecorded. One Rhode Island blacksmith noted in his journal, "Rose Dyer to coum and help Rake & pull Flax." In this instance, Dyer was paid in pork that would help feed her family. Producing extra goods also provided a way to purchase items that couldn't be produced on the farm. Flax seed, eggs, butter, cheese, and the like could be traded for pots and pans, books, molasses, or imported cloth.

WAGE WORK We will never know how **Betty Foot** felt when she wrote in her diary for the ninth straight day, "Carded tow." We can guess, however, from the fact that she was also preparing to become a teacher. Could it be that she was tired of carding, spinning, and weaving every day? Outside of family production, there were other ways that girls and women could work to help support themselves and their families.

In Philadelphia in 1775, one quarter of adult women worked as servants. These included elderly widows, indentured servants, free and enslaved blacks, Indians, and young girls. One frustrated mistress referred to the latter group as "young Giddy Headed Girls." Because of a shortage of workers, these girls easily moved from one position to another, distressing their employers. Most servants received only room and board and meager wages.

Another 15 percent of women in Philadelphia worked in retail trades or managed property; 8 percent kept boarders. Others made gloves, washed clothes, taught school, or worked as midwives or seamstresses. It is believed that 20 percent of American taverns and 30 percent of shops were kept by females. Boston also has records of women working as saddlers, ironmongers, brew masters, soap makers, and bakers. Cut off from better-paying jobs, black women and the very poor often resorted to taking in other people's laundry, working as servants, and peddling supplies on the street.

Unless the woman was single or widowed, however, her work does not show up in the public record. Even if she were running a shop, all transactions were completed in her husband's name. It is, therefore, difficult to know the extent of women's involvement in their husbands' businesses. During Benjamin Franklin's long absences, Deborah Franklin not only kept her household running, she ran the printing shop and post office as well. She was far from alone. We have some indication that women were very involved in their husbands' businesses based on the large number of women who continued running them after their husbands' deaths. Those working as shoemakers or hatters probably learned the trade by working alongside their husbands. These women were the lucky ones, because for many others, widowhood almost guaranteed poverty.

A woman could be thrust into the ranks of the poor in multiple ways. She could be born poor. Her husband could die or desert her. Since her fortunes were completely linked with his, if he failed or his luck ran out, so did hers. The death of children also left elderly women without support. While work as a seamstress, midwife, or shopkeeper could pay well, most work did not pay enough to sustain life. Thus, women made up a majority of the ranks of the poor. With inadequate systems in place to care for them, many lived in grim circumstances.

What One Woman Did

"An Extensive and Benevolent Plan of Usefulness"

On September 26, 1771, **Elizabeth Murray Campbell Smith** chose to marry for a third time. From her first marriage, she had gained an understanding of the defenselessness of widowhood. From her second marriage, she had inherited a vast amount of wealth. She entered this last marriage at the age of forty-five with her eyes wide open.

Unwilling to give up her hard-won financial and legal independence, she had her third husband, Ralph Inman, sign a six-page prenuptial agreement that gave her continued control of her considerable estate. She wrote to her

brother that *"By contract [he] has put in my power to Will away every thing as if I was not married."* This turned out to be a wise move, since the marriage was a difficult one.

Before Elizabeth Murray (Inman) died in 1785, she did what few women of her time had power to do: she wrote her own will. She left few assets to her husband, and gave the rest to her own family and friends. A large share of her estate went to four of her nieces: Dolly, Betsy, Polly and Anne "for [their] own personal Use & Disposal."

For Murray, this final statement was in line with her life's work. For years, she spent considerable energy assisting the women around her to become self-sufficient. At one point she described her

A 1769 portrait of Elizabeth Murray Campbell Smith by John Singleton Copley.

efforts in behalf of her nieces as "an extensive and benevolent plan of usefulness." Her plans involved helping women to set up shops. She knew the business well, because at the age of 22, she had begun selling imported goods in Boston. Without friends or family nearby, she managed to run a successful business. This experience gave her a "spirit of independence" that informed the rest of her life.

Anne and **Elizabeth Cuming** were among those who benefited from her mentoring. According to them, they were "two young unexperienced Girls," when their mother died. Having lived a sheltered life, they were unprepared to provide for themselves. Elizabeth Murray helped them set up an import business that was successful until the coming of war. The sisters chose to leave Boston with other loyalists and the British troops in 1776. They removed to Halifax, Nova Scotia, where they set up a new shop.

One of Murray's protégés didn't enjoy the experience of keeping shop quite so well. Murray's niece Anne felt mortified by the loss of status involved in working for money. With her aunt's support, Anne came to America at the age of sixteen to work. She had been educated to be a genteel young woman. Consequently, she felt that this was "a plan of life for which from Nature and education I was totally unfit." Rather than gaining a sense of independence, Anne suffered from "humiliation" and a "state of degradation." Anne's sister Polly felt quite differently. Like many others aided by Murray, she was empowered by the experience. Having returned to England to be with her family, Polly assured her aunt, ***"The spirit of independence that you cherish'd in me is not yet extinct."***

Did you know?

Though Eli Whitney has been credited with inventing the cotton gin (a machine that removed seeds from cotton lint), it is believed that he got his ideas from Catherine Greene, widow of Revolutionary War General Nathanael Greene. In addition to suggesting that Whitney use wire rather than wood for the gin teeth (the most important part of the invention), she also financed his project. Whitney was a terrible businessman and as word got out, people simply copied the invention. He went broke and Greene received no credit, but their machine changed the course of American history.

SLAVERY IN THE NEW COUNTRY: UNPAID LABOR

Though the Revolution had been waged in the name of liberty, American lawmakers were reluctant to abolish slavery. At the end of the war, thousands of black women, men, and children were no freer than the day the war started. The 1790 census counted 750,000 blacks in America, 90 percent of whom were enslaved. In 1780 a slave woman named **Mumbet** heard the Declaration of Independence read in the public square of Sheffield, Massachusetts. This was not her first encounter with such ideas. Before the Revolution she had quietly served refreshments while a prominent group of men met to discuss British tyranny. She later recalled that she "kept still and minded things" as they drafted a statement that would soon be echoed in the Declaration of Independence—proclaiming all men created equal. Perhaps none but Mumbet noted the irony of a freedom declaration made by men who were themselves owners of people. Over the following years, as her husband died in the war and she endured the wrath of an unkind mistress, Mumbet thought about what she had heard.

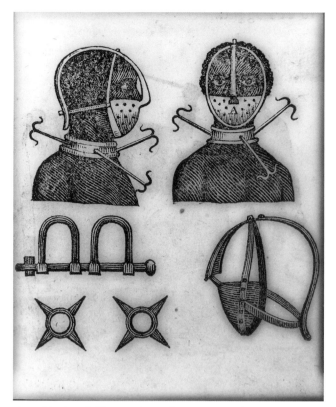

An 1807 book illustration of an iron mask, collar, shackles, and spurs used to restrict slaves.

The day after the reading in the square, she and another slave stepped into the law office of Theodore Sedgwick, one of her master's friends. She asked him if all were born equal, did that not mean her as well. Sedgwick agreed to represent her case. Surprisingly, the ensuing lawsuit was found in favor of the two slaves. Mumbet, now a free woman, chose to be called Elizabeth Freeman. This and a number of similar cases tried the same year resulted in the abolition of slavery in Massachusetts in 1782. Other Northern states also grudgingly enacted gradual emancipation, freeing their slaves over a generation.

At the same time, Southerners reopened the international slave trade. When members of Congress ratified the Constitution in 1787, they allowed slaves to be imported until 1808. Shackled

"Any time, any time while I was a slave, if one minute's freedom had been offered to me, and I had been told I must die at the end of that minute, I would have taken it—just to stand one minute on God's earth a free woman—I would."

—Elizabeth Freeman

The Old Plantation, a watercolor painted in the late 1700s.

Africans arrived in cargo ships by the thousands, reintroducing African cultures into the existing slave communities. Some Northerners quickly sold their slaves south rather than emancipate them. Between 1782 and 1810, 90,000 slaves were imported into South Carolina alone. In the South, slavery had become the way of life, even for nonslaveholders. The invention of the cotton gin in 1793 made growing cotton wildly profitable. Sugar cane and rice also fetched high prices. More than ever, the success of the Southern economy seemed to hinge upon forced labor.

ARTS IN THE SPOTLIGHT

THE SLAVE MUSE

When **Susanna** and John **Wheatley**, a devoutly religious couple, ventured to the docks of Boston in 1761 to purchase a slave, they did not see the action as contradicting their beliefs. Almost everyone of consequence in Boston society owned at least one slave. The sight of manacled people on the dock, however, must have moved the Wheatleys to pity because they bought a shivering little girl "of a slender frame and evidently suffering from a change of climate." The child, assumed to be about seven years old because she was losing her baby teeth, had just survived the terrifying voyage across the Atlantic Ocean from an African slaving port. Crowded into the dark and damp holds of slave ships, captives lay chained in their own excrement. It has been estimated that as many as one half perished before reaching America's shores.

Whatever the child's African name, the couple called her Phillis after the ship that brought her. The family was so taken with her charm and intelligence that they did not put her to work like other slaves. Not only did she quickly learn to speak English, but the Wheatley's twin daughters taught her to read and write. **Phillis Wheatley** was soon poring over philosophical, religious, and classical literature. By the time she was eleven, Wheatley was studying Latin and writing poetry. Modeling her work after her favorite poet, Alexander Pope, the adolescent girl dazzled Boston circles. In a time when many women were not literate, a poetry-writing slave, and a girl at that, raised eyebrows.

Though the family treated her well, Wheatley was always conscious of her status as a slave. She ate at a table nearby, but not with them. Only one poem, however, addressed her own state:

> I, young in life, by seeming cruel fate
> Was snatch'd from Afric's fancied happy seat:
> What pangs excruciating must molest,
> What sorrows labor in my parent's breast?

In 1773 Wheatley's mistress saw to it that a book of her poetry, *Poems on Various Subjects, Religious and Moral,* was published in England. She sailed to London, a much different voyage from that of her childhood, and was wined and dined by English nobility. London newspapers described her as "extraordinary."

"The people of Boston boast themselves chiefly on their principles of liberty. One such act as the purchase of her freedom, would, in our opinion, have done more honor than hanging a thousand trees with ribbons and emblems."
—London *Monthly Review,* 1774

This engraving of Phillis Wheatley was printed in her 1773 book, *Poems on Various Subjects, Religious and Moral.*

When Susanna Wheatley died the following year, her family set the writer free. This young woman who penned sublime poetry had few marketable skills with which to provide for herself. She joined the throngs of free blacks barely scraping by in a wartime economy. A successful poem about George Washington and an invitation to visit him in Cambridge kept poverty at bay for a time, but without her mistress to open doors, Wheatley had little hope of making a living as a poet. Like other free black women, she only had access to the most menial jobs.

Her 1778 marriage to a handsome tradesman John Peters may have been happy, but it did not provide much material comfort. Their first two children died in infancy. On a cold December day in 1784, the promising poet and her third child also died. None of her original manuscripts survived; it is not known what John Peters did with them.

As an elderly woman, Crow Indian **Pretty-Shield** recalled that she was no more than a child herself when she went into labor. Her mother took her to a lodge that had been built for the birth. "A fire was burning," Pretty-Shield recalled, "and my mother had made my bed, a soft buffalo robe folded with the hair side out. This bed was not to lie down on. Crow women do not lie down when their babies are born, or even afterward, excepting to sleep when night comes....Two stakes had been driven into the ground for me to take hold of, and robes had been rolled up and piled against them, so that when I knelt on the bed-robe and took hold of the two stakes, my elbows would rest upon the pile of rolled robes."

In a time when few people understood how to care for their teeth, a midwife might also act as a dentist. German immigrant and midwife **Liwwät Böke** noted in her diary, *"I have extracted many teeth with string and pliers. St. John [her village] is almost toothless."*

HEALTH

BATHING AND BIRTHING

BATHING In 1798, **Elizabeth Drinker**'s husband Henry came home with a newfangled contraption—a shower box. In a time when few people even owned washstands, this was quite something. It took Elizabeth Drinker, a sixty-five-year-old Quaker renowned for her "uncommon personal beauty," a full year to muster the courage to bathe. In 1799 she confided in her journal, *"I bore it better than I expected, not having been wett all over att once, for 28 years past."* Today, Drinker would be considered dirty and possibly crazy. But in 1798, she was far from alone in her lack of cleanliness. In fact, she and her husband were on the cutting edge of a new bathing fashion that was emerging in Europe.

It took a while for bathing as we know it to fully catch on in America. In the Drinker household, family members reused each other's bath water and never even considered using soap (soap was used only for washing clothes and didn't come into use for bathing until the mid-1800s). Bathing came into vogue in some wealthy households in the 1790s. By 1850, washing became important for the middle classes. Still, in 1851, when someone proposed that the White House could use a bathroom, it was ruled out as costly and unnecessary. It would take more than a century before most Americans considered weekly bathing a necessity.

CHILDBEARING One of the most defining features of a woman's life was that of pregnancy and childbirth. Watching anxiously as her daughter Sally give birth in 1799, Elizabeth Drinker mused on her own experience: *"This day is 38 years since I was in agonies bringing her into this world of troubles; she told me with tears that this was her birthday."* There was, however, a considerable difference between the two women's birthing experiences. Drinker's deliveries would have been traditional affairs, attended by female friends and a midwife. Her daughter, on the other hand, was on the forefront of another emerging trend. Instead of calling a midwife, she employed the services of a doctor. This was quite a shift from traditional ways.

For Drinker's generation, and those before her, childbirth, or being "brought to bed," was a communal female occasion. Mothers, sisters, cousins, and friends gathered to help and encourage the laboring woman. One midwife noted that after a birth, "There were 22 in number slept under that roof the night." A woman's friends were, according to one manual, "welcome companions" who helped the laboring woman to "bear her pains to more advantage. Their cheerful conversation supports her spirits and inspires her to confidence."

Someone also went for the midwife, a local woman experienced in delivering babies. Though a midwife had her own house to manage, she was always on call. She hurried to the home (often across streams and through fields and forests), made the laboring woman as comfortable as possible, and coached her through the delivery.

"This is the 600th Birth at which I have attended Since I came to this Eastern Clime," announced **Martha Ballard** to her journal on December 15, 1796. Midwives such as Ballard played multiple roles. Not only did they deliver babies, they acted as healers, nurses, pharmacists, morticians, herbalists, and confidants. On a single day in 1787, Ballard recorded that she "Put Mrs Claton to Bed with a son at 3 PM. Came to Mr Kenadays to see his wife who has a swelling under her arm. Polly is mending. I returnd as far as Mr Pollards by water. Calld from there to Winthrop to Jeremy Richards wife in Travil." Three days later, she laid Mrs. Claton to rest, "Her infant Laid in her arms." She was the first of Martha Ballard's patients to die as a result of childbirth.

Cures for various ailments sometimes included remedies that we might find quite strange. Ballard was glad to report that **Lidia Savage** felt relieved after she "Gave her some urin & honey & some Liquoris & put a plaster to her stomach." To relieve the shingles, she "bled a Catt & applid the Blood." Most cures, however, relied heavily on her expert knowledge of herbs. Slave midwife **Maria Jackson** believed that making a laboring mother angry would help her deliver faster. "My job was to cotch the babies, and see dat everything was alright fore I left the place, and I'se had 'er go back every day fer seven days to see dat dey was doin' alright. . . . You'se had to go, rain or shine, sleet or snow."

Because death was ever present, references to it appeared frequently in fine and popular art. Here, death is personified and carries on a chilling conversation with a lady.

These traditions changed as wealthy, urban women began to call in physicians rather than midwives to deliver their babies. Initially, physicians were only called in at times of crisis; they soon began to attend normal births. They criticized the old female customs. One physician wrote in 1769 of the "ridiculous custom" of gathering women for births: "These, instead of being useful serve only to crowd the house, and obstruct the necessary attendants. Besides they hurt the patient with their noise: and often, by their untimely and impertinent advice, do much mischief." Over the course of the next century, both attending midwives and other women would be gradually pushed out of the birthing process.

AMUSEMENTS

"VISITING"

AMONG THE COMMON FOLK A few days after her seventeenth birthday, New Englander **Ruth Henshaw** wrote in her journal, "Spun and sang songs." She and her friend Sally often worked together to relieve the dullness of their labors. Nearly five years later, Henshaw was still spinning. She complained about her day's work, *"I spun. I should think I might have spun up all the Swinging tow in America by this time."* When you consider the unrelenting monotony of jobs repeated over and over again for years on end, it's easy to see why people preferred to mix work and pleasure. Women gathered to husk corn, make quilts, attend births, and celebrate weddings.

Occasionally, people found time to just have fun. The upper classes looked down on the lower classes for their crude jigs, reels, and country dances. "These dances are without method or regularity," described one horrified observer. "A gentleman and lady stand up, and dance about the room, one of them retiring and the other pursuing, then perhaps meeting, in an irregular fantastical manner. . . . In this they discover great want of taste and elegance and seldom appear with the grace and ease which those movements are so calculated to display."

He might have also discovered the primitive eating habits of the common folk. One man described the fairly prevalent custom of "setting the large six-quart dish in the center of the table, while half a dozen or more children stood around it, each with a spoon, partaking of this homely but healthful repast of samp and milk." One European visitor complained about having to wipe his mouth on the tablecloth "which in consequence suffers in appearance." Even the upper classes in America often ate from the tips of their knives.

AMONG THE ELITE Wealthier women had more options that didn't involve work, such as card parties, concerts, banquets, dances, and picnics. Some even took vacations. But the most common form of diversion for women was "visiting." During visits with friends and neighbors, women could catch up with the latest news and gossip.

This form of visiting did not entail working together. One young married woman, **Ann Head**, found it difficult to complete her mending with the amount of visiting required of her. She complained to her journal in 1786 about the "great heap of work that decreases very slowly through gossiping about, which is unavoidable without giving my kind friends

Even with the somewhat reduced hairdos of the 1780s, fashion accidents could still occur. In one instance, a "fashionable belle" came to visit President Washington wearing a headdress of unusually high "ostrich plumes, waving high overhead." Regrettably, the drawing room ceiling "was rather low, and **Miss McEvers'** *plumes were ignited by the flames of the chandelier." One of Washington's aides "sprang to the rescue of the young lady and extinguished the fire by smothering it with his hand."*

offense." She said that by the time she finished one round of visits, it was time to "begin again." It was a challenge to find the right balance between work and leisure. Within a culture that valued work and industry, many believed that too much "frolicking" could become corrupting.

Wives of newly elected government officials tried to determine how to socialize without seeming too much like the British royalty they had just rebelled against. In October 1789, Martha Washington wrote to her niece, *"I think I am more like a state prisoner than anything else. There are certain bounds set for me which I must not depart from, and as I can not do as I like, I am obstinate and stay at home a great deal."* Whether or not they welcomed the part, officials' wives were thrust into public roles where they were required to hold highly formal social events and receive callers on a regular basis. Martha Washington, Abigail Adams, Lucy Knox, Sally Jay, and others established a sort of formal visiting in the capital city by hosting receptions and formal dinners on specific nights of the week. Anyone was welcome to call as long as they were dressed appropriately.

These events were an important part of life in the new republic and represented a sacrifice for the women who hosted them. When the capital was moved from New York to Philadelphia, Abigail Adams felt "low spirited and heartless." *"I am going amongst another new set of company, to form new acquaintances, to make and receive a hundred ceremonious visits, not one of ten from which I shall derive any pleasure or satisfaction."*

FEMALE CITIZENS

Amid all this working and playing, living and dying, there was one place where things were a bit different: New Jersey. A reverend passing through New Jersey in 1802 noted, "Stopping for dinner at an inn . . . I saw at the bar where I went to pay, a list of voters of the town stuck up. My eye ran

This couple is **sparking**, or courting. One somewhat surprising pastime of courting couples was the New England tradition of "bundling." In cold houses were privacy was rare, couples were allowed to become better acquainted by sleeping together for the night. They stayed fully clothed and were sometimes separated by a board.

On April 23, 1775, Betty Foot wrote in her journal, "Ellen & David lay abed till Sun about 3 hours high when they got up and he went home I suppose." The couple's wedding plans were announced in church on June 11, and they were wed on the 22nd.

When an illustrator sat down nearly one hundred years later to create this image of colonial women voting in New Jersey, the women of his century were still denied the vote.

over it, and I read to my astonishment the names of several women. *'What!' I said, 'do women vote here?' 'Certainly,' was the answer, 'when they have real estate.'"* We might assume that **Susan Boudinot Bradford**, daughter of a state politician, was one of these, as she congratulated the women of New Jersey for "being on a footing with the gentlemen." She also expressed surprise that the decision to grant women the vote "has been done by the gentlemen themselves."

Unlike any of its neighboring states, the New Jersey constitution of 1776 allowed all property owners to vote. Anyone with property could cast a ballot. Only single women voted because married women could not own property, but between widows and unmarried girls, there were apparently plenty of eligible ladies. Not only did they vote, they also actively participated in newspaper debates over important issues. Politicians paid attention, and both parties competed heatedly for women's votes.

When Thomas Jefferson won the 1800 election, the men in Bloomfield toasted female voters, saying, "May their patriotic conduct in the late elections add an irresistible zest to their charms."

However, others insisted that women, "timid...and unskilled in politics," simply cast the same vote as their men. One critic wrote, "Let them...consider that female reserve and delicacy are incompatible with the duties of a free elector, that a female politician is often subject of ridicule." In 1807 lawmakers rewrote the law to exclude women, blacks, and noncitizens. Loss of the women's vote in New Jersey appears to have been as much a fatality of bickering politicians as a commitment to keep females out of politics. The result, however, was the same. Like their sisters in other states, New Jersey women would no longer have a voice in elections or laws. Women of the new century would be convinced that their power lay in quietly influencing the world around them.

In 1787 a Cherokee woman wrote to Benjamin Franklin, "I am in hopes that if you rightly consider that woman is the mother of all, and the woman does not pull children out of trees or stumps nor out of old logs, but out of their bodies . . . they ought to mind what a woman says."

Circles of Influence
1800–1840

Migrating west with her family, **Mary Ellen Todd** was excited when her father taught her how to drive the wagon. She was even more delighted when she mastered the finer points of cracking the leather whip. A few days later her "heart bounded" as she overheard her father say to her mother, "Do you know Mary Ellen is beginning to crack the whip?" Her mother's response was not, however, what she might have hoped, "I'm afraid it isn't a very lady-like thing for a girl to do." Todd later recalled, *"After this, while I felt a secret joy in being able to have the power that sets things going, there was also a sense of shame over this new accomplishment."*

The turn of the nineteenth century was a time that presented women with tensions between ideal and reality. On the one hand, womanhood was being redefined, narrowing a woman's circle of influence to home and children. Cherokee Indian women were taught to spin and weave on the assumption that doing so might transform them

Georgianna Buckham and Her Mother, 1839.

into the white ideal. On the other hand, more girls attended school, young women tried wage work, and women started charity, missionary, and social reform associations. Exempt from the consideration given to other women, a new generation of slave mothers toiled in the fields and tried to shield their children from sale and exploitation. Finally, a handful of little girls growing up during this time, confronted with these inconsistencies, emerged as America's first champions of true equality for women.

EDUCATION

"THE HIGHEST MENTAL CULTIVATION OF WHICH SHE IS CAPABLE"

Twenty years after the Revolution more girls went to school than ever before. Even so, their education continued to be seriously inferior to that of their brothers. Although most New Englanders laid claim to at least some public education by 1800, schools were not necessarily free, and many girls attended only in the summer when the boys were working. Private academies tended to be little more than "finishing schools" that taught girls to serve tea, dance, paint a little, and chat in French. Critics such as writer **Jane Swisshelm** dismissed this curriculum as creating students who sat around *"reading novels, lisping about fashions and gentility, thumping some poor tired piano until it groans again, and putting airs on to catch husbands."* But what was the alternative?

People debated about the mental capacities of females, but most could agree that the ultimate goal was to make better mothers and wives. Even individuals who believed that women were as smart as men insisted, "It is no more the business of women to lead our armies, to vote at the ballot box . . . than it is for a man to darn her stockings, nurse children, or superintend a kitchen. . . . Educate her not only to be a graceful and accomplished being, but a help-mate and a wife."

THE FEMALE SEMINARIES Young **Emma Hart Willard** believed that even future homemakers should understand the mysteries of science, philosophy, mathematics, and Latin. The

A ceremony at a young ladies' seminary in 1810.

sixteenth of seventeen children, Willard recalled, *"My father, happily for his children . . . used to teach us of evenings, and read aloud to us; and this way I became interested in books and a voracious reader."* In 1821 she opened a new kind of school, the Troy Female Seminary in New York. Her curriculum was "First, moral and religious; second, literary; third, domestic; and fourth, ornamental." Within a few years, the seminary had more than three hundred students who learned everything from trigonometry, Greek, and astronomy to art and

Future women's rights activist Lucy Stone received some of her education at Mount Holyoke. You might not guess her radical leanings or her steely determination from the sweet look on her face.

"We are taught . . . that we must seek to obtain the graces and accomplishments which will make us better pleasing to men. My soul loathes such meanness with perfect loathing! If there were no being in the world for her to influence, I would, for the sake of her own deathless nature, insist that **for herself alone, woman should receive the highest mental cultivation of which she is capable**."

—**Lucy Stone**, women's rights activist

homemaking. In addition to producing upper- and middle-class virtuous wives and mothers, however, Willard turned out graduates who were prepared to teach in the ever-increasing number of common schools.

Mary Mason Lyon acted on an even broader vision. Breaking social rules about female assertiveness, this self-made educator traveled through dozens of towns raising money to endow a college that would teach traditionally masculine subjects to a broader range of young women. More than one stagecoach rider got an earful of ideas while riding with Lyon over bumpy roads. Hers would not be a school for wealthy girls alone; those who lacked money could attend if they

Black women had a particularly difficult time getting an education. Following slave rebellions in the early nineteenth century, states passed laws that forbade slaves to read. Few Northern schools were open to black students. Free blacks and Quakers set up schools for black students in cities such as New York and Philadelphia. In 1834, **Prudence Crandall** was forced by arsons and vandals to close her Connecticut Academy when she accepted a black student.

could pass the rigorous entrance examinations. Her school, Mount Holyoke Female Seminary, opened in Massachusetts on November 8, 1837. By the second year, the school actually had to turn away applicants. At Mount Holyoke, girls helped to earn their keep by performing domestic chores. In another dramatic shift, the school discarded "ornamental" classes and replaced them with ones similar to those at men's colleges. Soon many of Mary Lyon's students would also forge out into the world as well-trained teachers.

Little did Willard and Lyon know that among their students were two women who would attempt to turn the world upside down in their pursuit of women's rights. **Elizabeth Cady (Stanton)** graduated from the Troy Female Seminary in 1836. At that time few would have guessed that she would become one of the most controversial women of her generation. Mary Lyon may have glimpsed Lucy Stone's radical leanings when the student secretly left antislavery tracts in the Mount Holyoke reading room. Lyon, who felt the abolition movement was too controversial, caught and reprimanded the young activist. Stone left the school in the spring of 1839. She chose instead to attend the newly opened Oberlin College in Ohio, which admitted female, male, black, and white students. Forever after, she would oppose sex-segregated education and did not allow her own daughter to attend a women's school.

The irony of expanded education for women was not lost on observers. More than one European visitor to America remarked on the transformation women seemed to undergo at marriage. Of the unmarried girl, Frenchman Alexis de Tocqueville noted, "She has scarcely ceased to be a child when she already thinks for herself, speaks with freedom, and acts on her own impulse...she is full of reliance on her own strength, and her reliance seems to be shared by all who are about her." He went on to observe, however, that *"In America the independence of woman is irrecoverably lost in the bonds of matrimony."* Girls understood that "the amusements of the girl cannot become the recreations of the wife."

AT HOME
A NEW DOMESTIC IDEAL

CHANGING FAMILIES AND SEPARATE SPHERES
Between 1780 and 1830 there was a fundamental shift in the way that family members related to one another. Home began to be viewed less as a place where individuals worked together and more as a center for meeting emotional needs. With the coming of the Industrial Revolution, women and men's daily lives increasingly went in different directions. Fathers became less domineering but also less involved. Post-Revolution ideals, which had celebrated women for their ability to raise faithful citizens, gave way to a downright celebration of domesticity, emphasized in popular literature and across church pulpits.

Women and men had long worked at different tasks. What was new was the belief that they should be carried out in separate and distinct locations. While men's opportunities expanded, the changing economy

Examine this 1848 image for signs of the Industrial Revolution and the idea that men and women should inhabit different spheres.

made women more dependent. The world where a woman's bartering was crucial to her family's survival was disappearing. Keeping house and rearing children earned no money. It is little wonder, then, that women looked for power in their assigned roles. According to one women's newspaper,

"The man bears rule over his wife's person and conduct. She bears rule over his inclinations; he governs by law; she by persuasion. . . . The empire of woman is an empire of softness . . . her commands are caresses, her menaces are tears."

Women were promised a kind of authority over husbands and children if they would only retreat into their homes.

The ideal woman was portrayed as her husband's moral and religious superior. She was charged with quietly and submissively civilizing her household while finding utter contentment in domestic duties. She was kind, religious, gentle, utterly selfless, and kept her opinions to herself, or if possible, rooted them out altogether. This perception was a considerable departure from early colonial generations who viewed women as naturally lusty and sinful.

Sarah Hale dressed in mourning black for more than fifty years after the death of her husband.

What One Woman Did

"Nothing in the Slightest Degree Objectionable"

The ideal found its greatest champion in the person of a thirty-four-year-old widow. When **Sarah Josepha Hale**'s husband died in 1822 leaving her with five small children, her relatives set her up as a hat maker. However, what she really wanted to do was write. The eventual publication of her poetry and a successful novel, *Northwood*, allowed her to leave hat making and take a most unusual job. Sarah Hale became the first female editor of a ladies magazine, the popular *Godey's Lady's Book*. Under Hale's leadership, *Godey's* became the first periodical to publish American writing. Everybody who was anybody, both male and female, in the

"The fact that Mrs. Hale presides over its columns is an assurance that nothing in the slightest degree objectionable will ever be found there, and that the magazine may be safely put into the hands of readers of every description."
—*Godey's Lady's Book,* February 1848

American literary world appeared in her pages. Hale edited the magazine until she was ninety years old.

At the peak of its success in 1860, *Godey's* had 150,000 subscribers, a notable amount for

> ## Did you know?
>
> By the end of her life Sarah Hale would write two dozen books, convince the president to declare Thanksgiving a national holiday, raise funds to preserve Mount Vernon, write "Mary Had a Little Lamb," and devote energy and money to numerous causes.

the time. Hale became the voice of authority in American homes on topics ranging from current events to the latest fashions. But her passion was education. Regretting that as a child she had been taught at home while her brother went to college, she tirelessly promoted equal education for women and girls. Having gained her readers' trust, she took on a whole range of issues having to do with property rights, fairness under the law, and equal professional opportunity. Hale's solidarity with her readers allowed her to say what few others could and get away with it. Yet, in spite of the fact that she herself was a career woman, and advocated opportunities for women, Sarah Hale was one of the most dedicated promoters of the domestic ideal.

"AN EMPIRE OF SOFTNESS": WIVES AND MOTHERS

A reader curling up with her newest copy of *Godey's Lady's Book* would have found the ideal reinforced in short stories like "Wives and Sweethearts," published in 1841. In this tale, adoring groom William Fairfield discovers that his bride Agnes does not intend to do housework or allow him to make decisions for her. He tries to ignore Agnes's lack of housekeeping skills and then to gently steer her. She weeps and wonders why he seems to no longer love her.

As their joint misery escalates, William explains that spouses each have their assigned jobs: he his business, she the house. *"Your error lies in the false idea . . . that your happiness was to come somewhere from out of your domestic duties, instead of in the performance of them—that they were not part of a wife's obligations, but something that she could put aside if she were able to hire enough servants."* He also reminds her that men are strong and wise, while women are affectionate. Combined, they make a happy marriage. Humbled, Agnes throws her arms around Will's neck and vows, *"hereafter I will strive to find my delight in what I now perceive plainly, to be my duties."* When she does, the story draws to a happy close. The moral is clear: as Agnes embraces housework and allows her husband to make the real decisions, she will find great joy and increased influence in her home and marriage.

MARRIAGE Love continued to gain importance as a basis for marriage. *"Let your love advise you before you choose,"* advised *Godey's Lady's Book* in 1832. *"Remember the happiness or misery of your life depends on this one act, and that nothing but death can dissolve the knot. . . . Marriages founded on affection are the most happy."* However, love did not change the fact that a woman still lost all legal status at marriage. As the century wore on, she was also less likely to wield any economic clout to balance her husband's legal and financial power. Southern women referred to marriage as "resigning her liberty." In many states inheritance laws became even less favorable to women than before the Revolution.

Wedding customs varied from place to place. Wealthy Americans held large, elaborate celebrations. (There was no such thing, however, as a white wedding dress. Those did not come into vogue until the end of the century.) In New England there was little fanfare. Having announced the engagement in church several weeks before, the family gathered for a dinner. Afterward, the bride and groom remained with their own parents for another couple of weeks before "going to housekeeping." On the Pennsylvania frontier, where many settlers were of Dutch and German descent, the host family captured live

Have you ever heard of . . . Betsy Patterson?

Witty, fashionable, and fluent in French, this eighteen-year-old Baltimore socialite captured the heart of Napoleon Bonaparte's youngest brother, Jerome Bonaparte. Although both of their families strongly opposed the relationship, the couple wed on Christmas Eve 1803. Napoleon was furious. After repeated summons, the Bonapartes sailed for Europe. Despite Betsy's advanced state of pregnancy, Napoleon annulled the marriage. She gave birth in London even as Jerome was pressured to remarry a German princess. Although she never again saw her husband, Betsy Patterson spent much of her life unsuccessfully trying to gain official recognition of their son.

While in the late 1700s as many as one-third of all brides were already expecting their first child at marriage, female virtue received new emphasis in the early 1800s. In popular literature, the loss of chastity was often portrayed as leading to insanity and even death. In reality, it ruined a woman's reputation for life. It was a girl's responsibility to hold the more "naturally" sensual young man at bay. "Sit not with another in a place that is too narrow; **read not out of the same book; let not your eagerness to see anything induce you to place your head close to another person's**,*" advised* The Young Lady's Friend.

HARMONY before MATRIMONY.

These 1805 illustrations depict idealized courtships. Would-be lovers are singing and sharing poetry in their homes. How might current courtship practices be portrayed?

An 1828 newspaper notice in English and Cherokee states that William McConnell will no longer pay the debts of his wife, as she has left him. With no legal standing apart from her husband, this would make it difficult for her to survive on her own.

rabbits to set loose when the many guests arrived with their dogs. After a ceremony and feasting, the bride's friends whisked her away to her new cabin and put her to bed. The groom's friends placed the husband beside her. The raucous party continued downstairs all night with drinking and singing.

Motherhood became the ultimate symbol of womanhood, celebrated in verse, art, and song. With men increasingly away earning money, child rearing became almost exclusively a female job. For the first time books and periodicals aimed their advice at mothers instead of fathers. What's more, children began to stay with their parents longer—into their teens and twenties. The model mother was utterly devoted to her offspring, spoke softly, and never got angry. She also lovingly shaped their characters: "When our land is filled with pious and patriotic mothers, then it will be filled with virtuous and patriotic men," concluded minister John Abbott in 1833.

Of course, people's real lives were more complicated than the ideal. Not everyone could, or perhaps even cared to mold themselves to

Eight-year-old **Sarah Elizabeth Haines** stitched this sampler in 1848. It says, "By this work the world may see what care my parents took of me." How many children do you know who could do handiwork like this today?

expectations. Many husbands and wives maintained loving relationships in spite of the imbalance of power. However, it appears from letters and diaries that women often felt lonely and disappointed in marriage, and weary with their responsibilities.

CHORES Though both men and women worked hard, men's tasks were more varied and gave them opportunities for trips and recreation away from home. A husband could escape to town on business, or head to the woods with his fishing rod and gun. More locked into repetitive chores that left her rare time to herself, **Christian Barnes** of Massachusetts echoed her peers when she complained, *"A constant sameness reigns throughout the year."* Whether in towns or on farms, women's days revolved around caring for children, husbands, animals, gardens, houses, and orchards.

As in the past, mothers relied heavily on the help of their daughters, whom they trained to run their own future households. Together they sewed all the bedding, towels, and clothing for the family. Virtually every little girl learned to sew. When eleven-year-old **Marcy Jones** stitched the words, "Modesty is an ornament of the female sex" in 1810, she joined thousands of other children

who embroidered colorful and lively designs on "samplers" to practice their sewing skills.

Samplers combined a vital homemaking skill with character improvement. Girls as young as five embroidered the alphabet, Bible verses, advice, lists of family members, or poems about death. Bordered by flowers or vines, many samplers depicted intricate scenes of people, houses, animals, and trees. Families hung them on their walls and passed them down to subsequent generations. It is likely that girls took great pride in their work. Others might have agreed with **Patty Polk**, who embroidered, *"Patty Polk did this and she hated every stitch she did in it. She loves to read much more."*

Wealthier Southern daughters, less likely to receive training in housekeeping, were often overwhelmed by the job thrust upon them at marriage. To be successful, a plantation mistress needed to be capable in multiple ways, at once an organized manager, a public relations expert, nurse, and whatever else came her way. She had to coordinate what needed to be done in her home, kitchen, dairy, and chicken house, and to ensure that tasks were completed correctly and with a minimum of conflict or wasted resources. She was also expected to nurse ill slaves and neighbors, help deliver their babies, and see to the education of her own children.

COOKING In 1800 most Americans heated their homes with fireplaces, and virtually all cooked there. Open hearths were so inefficient that ice could form in the same room where a fire was burning. They were also dangerous. More than one toddler died as a result of falling into the flames. Fireplace cooking required strength, not to mention increasingly expensive firewood. People began experimenting with cast iron stoves, although some worried that warm, dry air in a house might cause illness.

Between 1835 and 1839, 102 cook stoves were patented. Designed by men who did not cook, they were rarely what homemakers needed. *Godey's Lady's Book* passed on one woman's reaction to her husband's attempt, *"You don't pretend to call that monstrous thing a cooking stove?"* Still, as models improved, and prices dropped, families tried this new method of cooking and heating. "We do all our cooking by stove," wrote New Hampshire wife **Faith Hubbard** in 1837. "Thus far I am much pleased with it, and think it saves a great deal of work."

Though a stove had to be regularly cleaned and oiled, and required a great deal of practice to use, an experienced cook could more easily prepare several dishes with less effort. Author **Sarah Orne Jewett** noted that while men often remembered fireplaces with fondness, women "knew better than their husbands did the difference this useful invention had made in their everyday work." By midcentury, most families who could afford them owned cook stoves.

In addition, as the technology for milling grain spread, more families could also have flour without growing wheat or grinding it themselves. Though baking required the cook to chip sugar off a block (those who couldn't afford sugar used honey, molasses, or syrup), milk the cow, churn the butter, and gather the eggs, women regularly made pies and cakes. A French visitor to America remarked, *"Nowhere is the stomach of the traveler or visitor put in such constant peril as among the cake-inventive housewives and daughters of New England."* Liberation from fireplace cooking resulted in more elaborate food preparation.

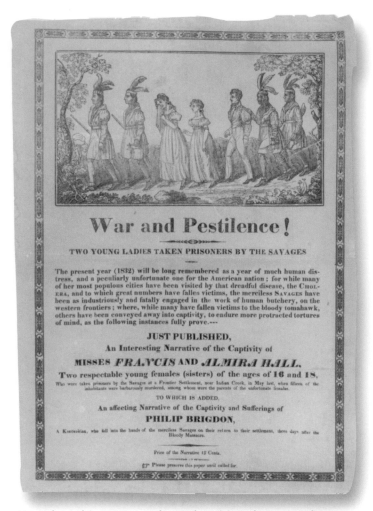

How does this 1833 woodcut advertising the story of "two young ladies taken prisoners by the savages" fail to tell the whole story?

OUTSIDE THE DOMESTIC IDEAL

"THEY OUGHT TO MIND WHAT A WOMAN SAYS": THE CHEROKEE

New notions of womanhood affected Native American groups in complex ways.

After the Revolution, representatives of the new U.S. government had been somewhat taken aback by the presence of Cherokee women at their treaty negotiations. More unsettling still was the obvious command and prestige accorded to the middle-aged **Nan'yehi**, who did not sit quietly by, but actually addressed the group. Nan'yehi, known as Nancy Ward to whites, was what Cherokees called a "Beloved Woman." Having led her clan to victory after her husband died in a battle with the Creeks, she had been awarded this most honored calling.

"Beloved Woman" was not just a title. Beloved Women participated as full members in councils, prepared warriors for battle, acted as judges, and helped in negotiations with other groups. It seemed natural to Cherokees that the women who bore warriors should have a voice in peace and war. For Cherokee women, motherhood was not a sentimental notion, but the source of their greatest power. Nancy Ward assumed the same for white women when she told U.S. commissioners, *"Let your women's sons be ours; our sons be yours. Let your women hear our words."*

shield their children from growing up too fast. They could teach their girls to fend off amorous slave boys, but had little power to protect them from the advances of masters and overseers.

Whites believed and perpetuated the idea that black women were extraordinarily lustful and sexually available. This seemed to be proved by the way that their bodies were frequently exposed, clad in rags and publicly stripped to be whipped or sold. At a time when the strongest field hand went for $1,600, exceptionally beautiful slave girls were sold for as much as $5,000 at the "fancy-girl markets" of New Orleans.

Slave women who were singled out for male attention had little choice about their sexual involvement with masters. Those who refused could be flogged or sold. Yet those who gave in and bore children to their owners might still endure the same fate, especially at the hands of the mistress. To white women, every light-skinned child born in the quarters demonstrated the disloyalty of their husbands, sons, and neighbors. Powerless to control

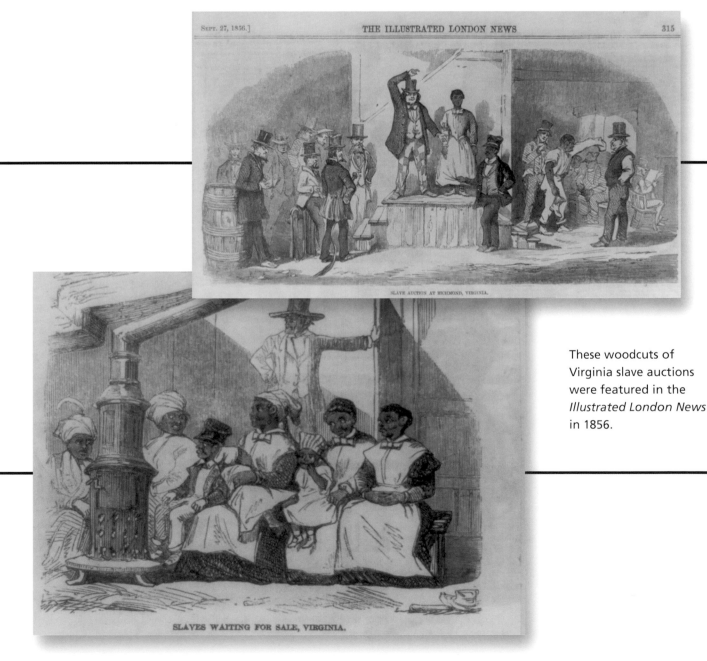

These woodcuts of Virginia slave auctions were featured in the *Illustrated London News* in 1856.

Slave **Annie Burton**'s father was a wealthy neighbor. When Burton was small, her mistress would haul her out to the road to embarrass him. She would exclaim, "Stop there, I say! Don't you want to see and speak to . . . your darling child? . . . See what a bright and beautiful daughter she is, a perfect picture of yourself." The man would hurry past as fast as possible.

their men's behavior, white women often took revenge on the hapless slave mother.

Female slaves were not exempt from flogging, torture, and other abuse. One boy, Henry Lewis McGaffey, remembered that when his master beat his mother, "de blood run down her bare back, an' den he put salt on it. I cried and he sed 'iffen I didn't shut up he would beat me,' den I went behind de kitchen ter cry." Though not all masters were this cruel, most felt justified in using at least some physical force to control their slaves.

SOUTHERN SOCIETY Southern society rested on a rigid hierarchy. At the top was the wealthy white man who presided over his household—white and black. A master's word was law, with both family and slaves expected to defer to his authority. He, at least in theory, was to provide for the needs of his dependents. Everyone knew that it was the master and not the mistress who wielded absolute power.

Regardless of age, slaves were required to obey the commands of even the youngest white child. In this photo taken in 1855, the baby is probably the owner of the child holding her.

Masters had occasion to be out and about, but mistresses and their female house servants were confined to the intimate and mutually confrontational space of the household. Mistresses had complicated feelings toward their house slaves. Unprepared to admit that black women and girls shared the same emotions and needs as they, many mistresses nonetheless became attached to the servants who waited upon them and genuinely mourned their passing. However, physical closeness did not necessarily result in affection. It just as often led to a simmering battle of wills in which mistresses tried to compel, and slaves resisted as much as they dared. The fact that all were subject to the same master did not lead white and black women into a shared sisterhood.

THE BIG HOUSE Division of labor depended upon the size of a farm or plantation. On smaller farms slave women worked a variety of jobs. One slave remembered, *"Marse would blow dat hour every mornin' an' we had to git out right now an' start dat wuk. My mammy had to cook, milk, wash, iron, spin, weave, and do de wuk in de fiel' lak de others."* Larger plantations could afford to divide their slaves into field and house servants.

"Any lady is ready to tell who is the father of all the mulatto children in everybody's household but their own. Those she seems to think drop from the clouds." —**Mary Boykin Chestnut**, slave owner

House servants lived in the midst of their white families, tending to their most basic needs: dressing and bathing them, preparing their meals, suckling their babies, raising their children, cleaning their houses, and nursing them in old age. One slave recalled, "On the same day I was born, my ole Mistis had a baby girl. . . . So they brung my mammy in de house and my mammy give one breast ter de white baby an' de udder breast she give ter me." Though living in more comfortable circumstances than field slaves, house slaves were under the constant watchful eyes of whites, expected to be up earlier and go to bed later than those they served. Some slept at the foot of their mistress's bed or near the door so as to be available around the clock. In these close quarters, slaves learned to mask their true feelings.

THE SLAVE QUARTERS AND FIELDS The majority of slaves lived in "the quarters." Slave houses differed considerably from place to place, though more often than not they were crowded, drafty cabins with dirt floors and sparse furniture. According to one former slave, *"You could take a dog by de heels an' throw him through de cracks in our house."* Sometimes more than one family would share a cabin. It was here, away from prying eyes, that they could create community, fall in love, and teach their children how to survive. **Chanie Mack** recalled her mother telling them stories of her life. "We chillun would set round de fire and listen to her talk." Slave communities also nurtured individuals separated from their loved ones by sale.

Loving someone was always a risk. When **Emily Dixon** reached adolescence she went to dances with slave boys. *"I thought a heap o' times I*

A South Carolina senator detailed his instructions for running his plantation in this book. These pages show that nursing slave mothers were to leave their homes at sunrise, returning home from the fields three times a day to nurse their babies. At the time of weaning, the child was removed from her or his mother for a full two weeks.

"Lots of times she's so tired she go to bed without eatin' nothin' herself."

—Harrison Beckett speaking of his mother's life as a slave

was in love but was fraid ter git married, 'cause I feared one or tother of us might be sold." Yet in spite of the potential loss, most slaves married. Some invited a preacher; others held hands and jumped over a broomstick together, followed by a celebration with dancing and eating.

Masters offered powerful incentives to encourage childbearing. Expectant mothers were often assigned less strenuous work and given better food. Others were allowed extra time off if they bore a certain number of children. Often women who did not conceive within the first year of marriage were sold.

Some masters allowed new mothers time to nurse their infants. Others insisted that women take babies to the fields with them. **Hanna Clay** never rested more than three days after bearing any of her eight children. Her son recalled, *"When she go back in the field she carry the baby in a red blanket tied to her back. When it get hungry she just slip it around in front and feed it and go right on picking or hoeing."*

Though childbearing increased a woman's value and possibly protected her against sale, it also gave her more to lose. Infant mortality among slaves was twice that of white children. In addition, masters frequently threatened to sell family members to control behavior. In fact, 20 percent of slave marriages ended in sale, and one in three children was sold away from his or her parents. Though some slave owners took pains to keep mothers and small children together, husbands and adolescent children were considered more expendable. This meant that adolescent girls were often torn from their mothers just when maternal protection and guidance was most essential.

Motherhood did not earn a slave the same exalted status as it did a white woman. Though society deemed white mothers tender and frail, black women were put to work in the fields at the same hard labor as men. The primary crops, tobacco, cotton, rice, and sugar cane, required long, demanding hours in withering heat and humidity. Rice cultivators stood knee-deep in mosquito-infested muddy water. In the winter, women as well as men mended fences and tools, dug ditches, and prepared fields. Many parents could only see their children late at night or on weekends.

Returning exhausted from the fields at dusk, women still had to care for their families. "De Negro women had to cook befo' daylight an' after dark," observed **Henrietta Murray**, "'cause long as they could see they stayed in dat field." Women prepared meals from rations that owners handed out once a week: usually corn meal, molasses, and salt pork. Getting enough to eat required energy

Slave resistance took many subtle forms: slowing down work, secretly sabotaging tools or buildings, stealing food, running away for short periods, and pretending to be ill, to name a few. But sometimes individuals reached **a breaking point**. Harriet Jacobs described one woman whose owner kept selling her children when they were a year or two old. "When her fourth baby was about two months old, she just studied all the time about how she would have to give it up, and one day she said 'I'm not going to let Old Master sell this baby; he just ain't going to do it.' She got up and give it something out of a bottle, and pretty soon it was dead."

and creativity. If allowed a garden, slaves cooked seasonal vegetables. Many also supplemented with fish or wild animals they could snare.

Slave women also frequently spun, wove, and sewed the rough cloth that would make up their family's meager yearly allotment of clothing. On **Mollie Watson**'s plantation, "De women had two work dresses a year an' two changes o' underwear. De white ladies give 'em dey old dresses. . . . When de everday clothes nearly wore out dey took 'em an' made baby clothes outen 'em." Everyone went barefoot through the summer months and sometimes in winter too.

Seventy years after the Revolution, four million slaves lived and toiled in America. The constant hard work, abuse, lack of rest, and poor diet and clothing, compounded by exposure to diseases such as malaria, aged them quickly and often killed them young. Life expectancy for slaves was between 28 and 36 years. In spite of this, the slave population in America continued to grow. Unable to throw off the shackles of bondage, slave women and men asserted their humanity and created their own distinctive culture.

HEALTH

After 1800, the birthrate began to decline from an average of seven children per woman. Even so, most women spent at least two decades of their lives pregnant or recovering from pregnancy. Unlike the previous century, even when a woman's expectant condition was obvious, it was impolite to discuss or acknowledge it. **Mary Scott** was not unusual. She bore children in 1790, 1792, 1794, 1796, 1798, 1799, 1801, 1803, 1805, 1807, and 1809. Three of her children died as infants.

Virtually everyone knew someone who had died giving birth. After a friend perished in childbirth in 1828, **Maria Bryan** wrote to her

Have you ever heard of . . . Mary Gove?

As a child, she secretly pored over any medical book she could get her hands on. Convinced that women's profound lack of knowledge about their bodies was as dangerous as it was ridiculous, Gove scandalized many by sharing what she had taught herself. In the 1830s she traveled the East Coast giving lectures on anatomy, physiology, and hygiene to female audiences. Gove went on to experiment with a number of alternative health practices, including celibacy and water cures.

Before the invention of photography, most families had no images to remember their loved ones by. Pennsylvania schoolgirl **Susan Winn** embroidered this picture in memory of her infant sister who died in 1806.

Many women employed **trusty home remedies** *when family members became ill. It is hardly surprising that they were willing to try just about anything to relieve the suffering of someone they loved. Treatments ranged from useful to downright poisonous. One remedy for treating intestinal worms suggested: "Take a half-pint of live angle worms, put them in a thin linen bag, and sew them up. Then put them, while yet alive, on the child's stomach. There let them remain for six hours . . . the child will never be troubled with worms again."*

sister, *"Poor Horace and his little boy look so sad and desolate that it grieves me to see them, and it would have made your heart ache to have gone there while she was dead in the house, and seen how neat everything looked, and the yard and garden and kitchen so clean, and all so snug and comfortable in their little way."* Expectant mothers lived in the shadow of death, dreading childbirth and planning for possible death.

It was perhaps this fear of death that drove more urban wives to call male physicians to their deliveries. Though only recently interested in obstetrics, doctors gained a reputation for formal training and for having delivery tools at their disposal. In fact, due to strict social codes of modesty, most young doctors had never examined a female patient or delivered a baby. True, they had a new tool: forceps, a large metal clamp that could be attached to the baby's head to pull the baby from the birth canal. But used prematurely or blindly under a blanket, the forceps could result in as much harm as good. Doctors who did not wash their hands between deliveries spread a deadly infection called puerperal fever. Given their ignorance of female bodies, it is unlikely that physicians were able to be more helpful than midwives when a delivery went awry.

Nevertheless, the number of midwives (especially in cities) declined in the coming decades as physicians set professional standards that excluded midwives and convinced patients that doctors were the experts on childbirth. In 1832, the Boston Lying-In Hospital became the first obstetric hospital in the United States.

PAID WORK

FROM HOME TO INDUSTRIAL PRODUCTION

In 1800, most families lived and worked on small farms. Even the largest towns were not big by European standards. Wives and daughters played a central role in the barter economy, trading services and homemade goods to meet their family's needs. Husbands and sons farmed or ran family mills and artisan shops with the help of apprentices.

Though different, the work of women and men was complementary and equally important to a family's economic survival.

However, this was changing. Expanding markets and the birth of industry began to permanently alter the ways that families earned their livings. During the first half of the nineteenth century, new mechanized factories and mills were able to produce goods at a faster rate. Factories replaced family workshops and businesses, and machines and machine operators replaced laborers making things by hand. This change has been called the Industrial Revolution. As a result, husbands left the home in search of uncertain wage work at the same time that wives lost their primary means of contributing to the family's economic well-being. Children became less an economic asset and more a drain on resources—consumers rather than producers. Father became the official breadwinner, mother, the domestic genius, and children, the dutiful dependents.

The change, reinforced by the ideal of separate spheres (men in the world, women at home), limited women and placed enormous pressures on men. Society's belief that women should rely on men for their support also did not consider the plight of abandoned wives, widows, and orphans. A single woman could barely earn enough wages to live, even if she was healthy and hardworking.

In cities, a growing number of poor women (often with children) survived by washing clothes, taking in boarders, or by selling food, produce, or sex. Free black women, more numerous than free black men, had the fewest options. They made up armies of street peddlers, vending merchandise from baskets. A small handful of female trades provided a more steady, if meager income: dressmaking, hat making, shoe binding, and shop keeping. Many women and girls worked as domestics, or "helps," at some time in their lives, though by 1840 their employer was unlikely to work side by side with them or treat them as part of the family.

MILLWORKERS In 1823, prospective industrialists set out to find a reliable work force to run the machines in their newly built, water-powered textile mills. Cheap labor was scarce, and local farmers and artisans couldn't spare their sons. What, they wondered, about farmers' daughters? Young women seemed to be precisely the meek, inexpensive labor force industrialists sought.

So, for the first time, young women would leave the safety of their local communities to work in factories. Recruiters set out to convince rural girls that working in a textile mill was the chance of a lifetime. They also reassured concerned parents that their vulnerable daughters would be properly cared for. Mills would simply be a temporary home away from home—one where a hardworking person could earn cash. There were a number of mills from which to choose, though the largest and best known were in Lowell, Massachusetts.

In the years that followed, thousands of Yankee farm girls between the ages of fifteen and twenty-five eagerly packed their homespun dresses and set off to seek their fortunes. For those who had never ventured far from home, the chance to see new

Have you ever heard of... Betsey Metcalf?

At the age of twelve Metcalf invented a new way of weaving straw hats. Her method led to a thriving cottage industry in which women across New England made hats at home. In 1824 one newspaper wrote of hat making, "There is, perhaps, no manufacture of its amount that can be regarded as so important to the welfare in the United States. . . . for the females, if not so employed would be idle or doing worse."

places, meet new people, and earn a wage seemed an adventure—a temporary interval before marriage. Just as appealing, the wages were better than those of a servant.

Often traveling to the mills with sisters or cousins, workers lodged in boarding houses, four to six girls to a room. In keeping with promises to parents, an older woman closely supervised each house, ensuring that employees practiced good manners, cleaned up after themselves, hung up their bonnets, went to church, and followed the 10:00 PM curfew.

Mill girls worked from 5:00 AM to 7:00 PM five days a week with a half-hour break for breakfast and lunch. On Saturdays they worked until 1:00 PM. Jobs were determined by skill level; a young woman might work at carding, spinning, dressing, or doffing (replacing full bobbins of thread with empty ones). Lit by whale oil lamps, the rooms were hot and humid in the summer and cold in the winter. Workers constantly breathed cotton lint. Machines were deafening and sometimes dangerous. *"It is very hard indeed and sometimes I think I shall not be able to endure it,"* wrote worker **Mary Paul** to her father. *"I never worked so hard in my life, but perhaps I shall get used to it."* Those who weathered the initial fatigue and confusion gained a sense of confidence and competence. Just as important, they were paid in cash at the end of the week.

Although workers sometimes became homesick, they also enjoyed the hustle and bustle

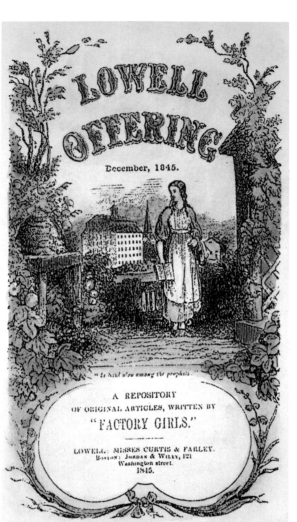

Some millworkers started a newspaper called the *Lowell Offering*, which featured their writing and poetry.

of mill towns. In their spare time, mill girls became fast friends, took walks by the river, attended concerts and lectures, and began their own sewing groups. Surrounded by their peers, workers taught one another how to dress, talk, and behave, applying social pressure to encourage appropriate conduct.

Bosses discovered that mill girls were not so easy to push around. As working and living conditions worsened, workers scandalized some by staging protests and "turn-outs." **Harriet Robinson**, who was a ten-year-old doffer in 1834, later recalled that when the other workers in her room were "uncertain what to do," she announced, "I don't care what you do, I am going to turn out, whether any one else does or not." She then marched out of the mill, and the others followed her. Though the various protests were largely unsuccessful, and eventually most farm girls ended up quitting the mills altogether because of deteriorating conditions, many felt that their working experience made a difference in their lives.

WORK AND THE DOMESTIC IDEAL Remarkably, even as farm girls experimented with wage labor, legitimate female job options narrowed. While industry was changing the physical landscape, the new ideas about womanhood were also altering the female relationship to work. The ideal defined a woman's only true labor as being that which she did

ARTS IN THE SPOTLIGHT

Would it surprise you to know that until the 1830s, almost all teachers were men with no formal teacher training? As often as not, they were individuals who had failed at other jobs, or who viewed teaching as a stepping stone to something better. As public education expanded and more girls went to school, some argued that women, who were more accustomed to dealing with children, would make better teachers. During the following decades, teaching became increasingly a female occupation. Schools could pay school mistresses a third less than men and free their male colleagues for better-paying, more prestigious work.

It is easy to imagine what would have happened if James Peale Jr. had shown any interest in art. As the son of a painter by the same name, he would have taken his place in what came to be the "first family" of American artists. However, it was not James Jr. who wanted to paint, but his three younger sisters, **Anna**, **Margaretta**, and **Sarah Peale** As part of a sprawling, affectionate family of artists, including famous Uncle Charles and cousins named after European painters, the girls grew up surrounded by canvases, paintbrushes, and pigments. Even their mother's father was an artist. James Sr. had already established himself as a painter of miniature portraits when his daughters were born in 1791, 1795, and 1800. Yet that they would follow in his footsteps was hardly likely. Serious art was considered a masculine domain.

For whatever reason, though, their father and their uncle taught the three girls to paint. In their father's studio they helped him paint designs on shawls. Uncle Charles, also a naturalist, politician, and inventor, believed girls should be educated like boys, and he encouraged his nieces. Portraits, landscapes, and still lifes were particularly in style. Anna, Margaretta, and Sarah became expert at painting fruit that looked real enough to eat, and flowers with dew sparkling on their petals. Even more than these, the public clamored for miniature portraits of loved ones small enough to be worn or kept in a pocket.

Sarah (called Sally by her family) was a particularly talented portrait painter. Watercolor miniatures on ivory required great patience and skill. As they were usually the only likeness a person would ever have, it was important that the portrait truly resemble the subject. Sally began her career at the age of sixteen and became the first American woman to make a solid living as an artist. Never married, she had her own studios in Baltimore and St. Louis and for sixty years successfully jockeyed with male artists for clients. She was also the first woman to be accepted into the Pennsylvania

within the walls of her house. Her ability to remain at home came to be a measure of her respectability, making the differences between her and those who had to work for pay more glaring. An educated woman who was forced to support herself might join the growing numbers of female teachers or writers. But for most women, especially those of the middle class, paid work was a fate to avoid if possible.

"During all my girlhood I saw no pictures, no art gallery, no studio, but had learned to feel great contempt for my own efforts at picture-making. A traveling artist stopped . . . and painted some portraits; we visited his studio, and a new world opened up to me. Up to that time painting had seemed as inaccessible as the moon."

—JANE SWISSHELM, newspaper editor

A miniature self-portrait by Sarah Peale.

Academy of Fine Arts, an honor that established her as an expert in her field.

Over the years, the Peales moved in an out of one another's studios and lives. All three sisters showed work at the Pennsylvania Academy of Fine Arts. Sometimes Sarah and Anna collaborated, with one doing the details and the other the larger part of a canvas. Both also worked for a while at the family's natural history museum run by their cousin Rubens. Anna, who began painting for money at fourteen, did art in between husbands (both died) and painted such famous individuals as Andrew Jackson, James Monroe, and Henry Clay. At the end of their long lives, the three sisters lived together. Their sister Maria is also thought to have painted, though none of her paintings have survived. The Peale family legacy did not end there. Their cousins' daughters, **Mary Jane Peale** and **Rosalba Peale**, also went on to become artists. While the Peale men have been celebrated through the years, it has only been recently that art historians have traced the legacy of the Peale women.

AMUSEMENTS

Visiting America in 1827, a cosmopolitan Scottish woman named **Margaret Hall** attended numerous gatherings, balls, and dinners. Tired of being asked whether American hospitality measured up to European standards, she observed bitingly, *"What can I say? I can't tell people who are doing their best to amuse and please me that they are not within a hundred degrees of the polish and refinement of English society."* Dismissing American music, dancing, and clothing as second rate, she was also puzzled by the fact that women and men rarely socialized together. Even at mixed gatherings she noted that "the gentlemen divided from the ladies, whether by design or accident I do not know."

Most public entertainments, drinking, wrestling, card playing, cockfighting, bear and bull baiting, horse racing, and hunting were not considered suitable for women. Even theaters were for men. Wives and sisters were also frequently excluded from events such as Independence Day celebrations, military musters, and political gatherings. When invited, it was on the premise that they would provide an appreciative audience, and that their presence would have a civilizing effect on more rowdy individuals.

Even tamer pastimes were considered inappropriate for females. As a little girl in the 1830s, **Clara Barton** ached to ice-skate with her brothers. "I was as strong, could run as fast and ride better," she recalled. However, "skating had not then become customary, in fact, not even allowable for girls." When her father saw her trying to put on a pair of skates, he gruffly sent her into the house. After a secret, disastrous attempt, Barton gave up hope. She wrote, *"I never learned to skate. When it became fashionable I had neither the time nor the opportunity."* Instead, middle-class and wealthy daughters learned to play instruments, sing, do needlework, paint a little, and entertain polite company. These achievements, however, were as much to make parents proud and attract suitors as they were to provide pleasure for the girl herself.

Outside of these more private pursuits, women attended spelling bees, oral school examinations, graduation ceremonies, funerals, and weddings, as well as traveling wax works, circuses and "animal menageries" that displayed exotic wild animals (with separate showings for men and women). Philadelphians willing to pay 25 cents to see two touring lions in 1816 were reassured, "No person may be apprehensive of the least danger, as they are secured in a substantial iron cage."

After 1807, agricultural fairs gave farm wives a chance to exhibit produce, needlework, dairy products, and poultry. Many recreations combined work and fun. Communities came together for

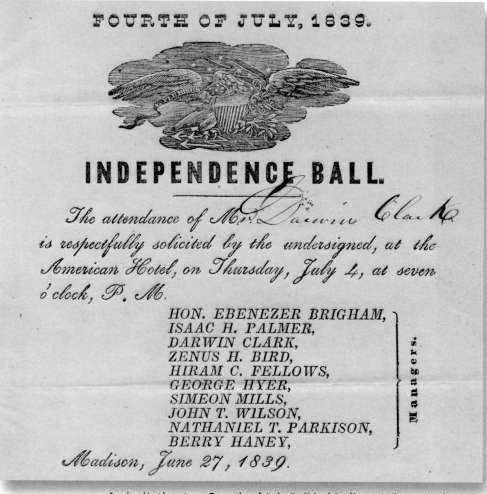

An invitation to a Fourth of July Ball in Madison, Wisconsin (1839).

As few whites knew how to swim, artist George Catlin was duly impressed with the Mandan women he met in the 1830s: "They all learn to swim well and the poorest swimmer amongst them will dash fearlessly into the boiling . . . current of the Missouri and cross it with perfect ease. They all learn to swim at an early age and women develop strong skills so they can take their children on their backs and swim across."

"All de women wore hoop skirts dat come down to de ground. Dey'd dance an' stir up de dirt an' ashes on de flo' till de dust git in de chillen's eyes an' make 'em cry an' dey'd have to take 'em home an' dis would break up de dance."
—MOLLIE WATSON, former slave

"frolics" or "bees" to help one another with tasks such as husking corn, shearing sheep, peeling apples, mowing fields, and slaughtering animals. Women enjoyed these rare opportunities to socialize, but large gatherings also meant extra work preparing food to feed the crowds.

Slaves looked forward to Sundays and holidays when they could sit under the trees and talk. "Us wuked hard in de fields," recollected **Rosa Mangum**. "But us had our past-time too; gwine ter meeting, picnics and frolics. Us had candy pullings an' watermelon cuttings on de plantation." They gathered from surrounding plantations to sing and

Sleigh riding by the light of the moon became to nineteenth-century youth the equivalent of parking in the twentieth—a chance to sit close and kiss. Groups of young people would travel from farm to farm (and in towns from neighborhood to neighborhood) in search of entertainment and refreshments, returning home late at night.

dance to fiddle, guitar, and banjo music. On **Harriet Miller**'s plantation, women knew how to dance with buckets of water on their heads.

Dancing was one of the few amusements that encouraged mingling and allowed boys and girls to get to know one another better. One particular version even allowed kissing in between numbers. Americans of all classes loved to dance—at weddings, on holidays, and after frolics. Following a corn husking in 1808, poet **Sally Hastings** wrote, "they devoted the night to dancing, singing, and other exercises . . . from the noise and discord . . . we began to fancy ourselves in the neighborhood of pandemonium."

Southern plantations were renowned for their extravagant parties, barbecues, and balls, although married ladies remained at home. In the North, on the other hand, Margaret Hall noted that it *"would be thought quite strange here that any married lady should decline dancing. They marry so very young...that they would have no enjoyment at all if they ceased to dance on that account."* In the countryside, jigs and reels were the dances of choice. Coming from Europe in the 1830s, the waltz quickly caught on in wealthier circles. Where formal minuets and quadrilles kept partners at a safe distance, the waltz allowed dancers to clasp one another close to whirl around the floor.

BEAUTY

"MUSTER ALL MY MUSLINS": CLOTHING

In January 1804, a **Mrs. Smith** shared all the juicy gossip of recent Philadelphia parties in a letter to her sister, a **Mrs. Kirkpatrick**. She reassured her sister that she spoke only the truth when she told of the "scandalous" and "strange" events at one of the balls. She began, "Madame_____ [Betsy Bonaparte, wife of Napoleon's brother] has made a great noise here and *mobs of boys have crowded round her . . . to see what I hope will not often be seen in this country, an almost naked woman."* At an "elegant and select party," "this beautiful little

What might the illustrator of this 1807 cartoon be saying about women's fashions?

A FASHIONABLE LADY
in DRESS & UNDRESS.

feathers, and jewels. Dainty, heelless, thin-soled slippers replaced shoes with any practical purpose.

It was quite a challenge to be trendy without ruining one's shoes in the mud, or freezing in winter weather. One European visitor huffed:

I have often shivered seeing a young beauty picking her way through the snow. . . . I knew one young lady whose pretty little ear was actually frostbitten from being thus exposed. They never wear muffs or boots, and appear extremely shocked at the sight of comfortable walking shoes and cotton stockings, even when they have to step to their sleighs over ice and snow.

This distinct shift set apart those who

creature" appeared in a dress of the "thinnest sarsnet and white crape without the least stiffening in it," with her arms bare, and "the rest of her form visible." Her entrance "threw all the company into confusion, and no one dared look at her but by stealth." Following the ball, several ladies sent word to Madame Bonaparte that if she wished to attend any other gatherings with them, "she must promise to have more clothes on."

Betsy Patterson Bonaparte was chastised merely for taking the new post-Revolution fashions to an extreme. Styles certainly had changed. Upper-class Americans sought to follow French fashion trends by dressing in classical Greek styles—much like ancient Greek statues. Fashionable women discarded their corsets for sparse undergarment shifts and clinging gowns made in satins, silks, and muslins. Waistlines rose, necklines plunged, and dresses became more revealing. Simple gowns were accessorized with a large assortment of headdresses, turbans, combs, bonnets, purses (called "reticules"),

During the nineteenth century, women's hairstyles usually incorporated some sort of curls. In 1800, the ringlets were on the forehead. By 1815, hair was smooth on top and curls perched in front of the ears. In an 1832 edition of the *New England Magazine*, one woman complained, "Our earlocks . . . **my ears tingle and my countenance is distorted at the recollection of the tortures inflicted on them by the heated curling tongs and crimping irons.**" By the 1830s, hair was piled higher and higher and combined with false hair to create elaborate hairdos. One stood so tall, it was nicknamed "a la giraffe."

followed the new fashions from those who didn't. For seventeen-year-old **Eliza Southgate**, it was crucial to fit in. She wrote to her mother in 1800 begging her to "muster all my muslins," for her visit with some people who were "so monstrous smart as to take no notice of any lady that can condescend to wear a calico gown." Another young woman remembered exactly the white satin bonnet with pink trim she wore while escaping a burning Washington, DC, during the War of 1812. She recalled that it was "just the style for a young lady of fifteen."

At a time when 75 percent of all clothing was still homemade, most women worked to adapt to popular styles in whatever manner they could. Women living on family farms were certainly not attired in thin slippers and muslin gowns.

After 1820, fashions changed yet again. Waistlines returned to the waist, corsets returned, and the circumference of dresses began to grow. "Leg-of-mutton" huge sleeves became popular. These new fashions were so different from previous styles that old dresses could not be remade to fit the new trends.

RELIGION AND SOCIAL REFORM

THE GREAT AWAKENING

MISSIONARIES Not everyone was worrying about what to wear. In the fall of 1819, twenty-three-year-old farm girl and schoolteacher **Lucy Goodale** received an intriguing proposal. Would she consider marrying her cousin's friend who was leaving within weeks to be a missionary in Hawaii? Without a wife, the mission board would not allow him to go. She hesitated; should she do it? After meeting Asa Thurston, Goodale decided to marry him. She had three weeks to get ready. Her preparations included cutting out and sewing twenty-two dresses, six petticoats, twenty-four nightdresses, twenty-five pairs of cotton underwear, and enough stockings, aprons, and shawls to last her possibly the rest

While many sects experimented with nontraditional marriage and communal living, **the Shakers** surpassed all others in challenging common ideas about women, men, and power. Most astonishing to outsiders was their belief that their prophetess, **Ann Lee**, was the female incarnation of Christ. Shakers, named after their ecstatic form of worship, which included frantic dancing and singing, required that members remain celibate. With the motto "hands to work, heart to God," they lived simply and communally. Women and men participated equally, and without regard to gender, in preaching and work. A sister had as much right to spiritual enlightenment as her brother. Having arrived in America from England as a small group in 1774, Shaker communities blossomed in the first three decades of the nineteenth century.

of her life. As none of the missionaries had ever been to Hawaii, and didn't know when they would return, they had to be prepared. Only eleven days after their marriage, the newlyweds joined six others (most who were also newly married) on an

The American Sunday School Union published this missionary account of Ann Judson's Baptist mission to Burma. She and her two-year-old daughter died there.

uncomfortable ship bound for Hawaii.

Surprisingly, Lucy Goodale was not so unusual. Between 1819 and 1850, eighty women, most of them married, went to Hawaii as missionaries. In the early decades of the nineteenth century a number of women accompanied missionary husbands to far away countries or to America's frontiers. Many, like Goodale, were recent brides who had married virtual strangers. **Ann Judson** followed her husband to Burma, **Harriet Newell** went to Mauritius, and **Narcissa Whitman** lived among the Cayuse Indians of Oregon. In their new homes, mission wives encountered unfamiliar cultures, new languages, and rugged living conditions while also adjusting to marriage and pregnancy. Caught up almost immediately in trying to run a household and raise children, they nonetheless tried to remain engaged in the religious work for which they had traveled so far.

What could have motivated these young women to leave everything they knew for an uncertain future? The answer lies in the new religious fervor sweeping the country. Only two decades before Lucy Goodale's decision, religious observance in America had declined. Though Protestant churches dotted the landscape (with some Catholic churches and Jewish synagogues scattered among them), many individuals no longer attended church. However, between 1800 and 1840, ministers staged traveling revivals to bring Americans back into the fold, stoking the fires of conversion in a movement that came to be called the Second Great Awakening. Religious fervor swept through frontier settlements and cities as Protestant churches competed for converts. Women, already the majority in their congregations, joined in the greatest numbers.

While religious doctrine had long taught that women were morally weak and likely to sin, ministers began shift their emphasis to that of female virtue. Women were a minister's best tool for spreading the word because once converted, they could influence their own families. They founded the first "Maternal Associations" and Sunday schools dedicated to raising righteous children.

However, tending to the souls of their families seemed inadequate when a whole world lay beyond their doors. Women did not have to look far to notice that economic upheavals were swelling cities and increasing poverty and crime. Displaced families traveled in search of work, living in squalor, misery, and despair. Caring for vulnerable members of society had long been considered a female duty. Yet, the times seemed to call for something more organized and widespread. Justifying their activities as a natural extension of their motherly roles, church ladies rolled up their sleeves and created associations aimed specifically at caring for hungry and helpless women and children.

BENEVOLENT SOCIETIES

One of the first female-run charitable organizations in America was the Society for the Relief of Poor Widows with Small Children—founded in 1797 by **Isabella Marshall Graham**, herself a widow. Graham's efforts initially drew criticism. Nonetheless, she and her co-organizers had opened a door. Women across the country—Jewish, Catholic, and Protestant, black and white, working-class and wealthy—began "benevolent" and mutual aid societies to help one another and alleviate suffering.

Many members of benevolent societies were

One newspaper short story, "Stray Leaves," written by an anonymous author, challenged the standard portrayal of the poor as passive victims. The narrator of the story, a seamstress, dismissed the judgmental help of charitable ladies who came to look over her tiny room and determine whether she went to church. She told them, "Now allow me to say ladies, that if you would do good, and save souls, your best mode of doing so is to give women work, pay them well . . . stretch your hands, extend your sympathy to their bodies."

busy married women with children like **Susan Mansfield Huntington**. She complained in 1815,

How difficult, how hopeless is the task of pleasing every body! A fortnight since a lady said to me . . . "How is it possible you can go out so much, visit your people so frequently, and be engaged in so many charitable societies, without neglecting your family?" This week . . . I am censured for . . . confining myself so much to my family. I am accused of want of interest in public charities, because I give to them so little of my time and attention. Such different opinions are formed of the same conduct!

Whether they provided shelter, jobs, or firewood, aid societies offered a rare buffer against an unforgiving world. Even so, Americans had mixed feelings about charity. They tended to believe that hard work and good morals led to success, and that

individuals became poor because of laziness and bad choices. According to this logic, only certain people were worthy of help. Aid workers felt the need to divide the "deserving" from the "undeserving." They also focused more on reforming unsavory behaviors than tackling the root causes of poverty or crime.

Nowhere was this more evident than in the temperance and moral reform movements. When a group of women began the New York Moral Reform

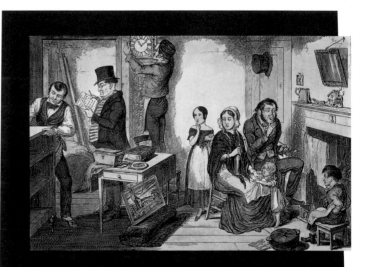

Although both women and men drank alcohol, it was estimated in the 1820s that men consumed fifteen times more alcohol than women. This may, in part, have been because, as one observer noted, "Americans traditionally found drunkenness tolerable and forgivable in men but deeply shameful in women." The social problems created by overdrinking led to **temperance organizations** committed to ending alcohol consumption. In this image, a family is losing all their possessions due to the father's continued drinking.

Illustrations of the American Anti-Slavery Almanac for 1840.

Here, abolitionists illustrate the evils of slavery to win the support of other Americans for their cause.

Society in 1834, they had no smaller goal than closing brothels and stamping out prostitution. Confronting a topic that was normally taboo, moral reformers accused men of being the main cause of prostitution, of seducing young women and ruining their lives. They shamed these "deliberate destroyers" by publishing the names of men who went to brothels. *"Why should a female be trodden under foot,"* they asked, *"and spurned from society and driven from a parent's roof, if she but fall into sin—while common consent allows the male . . . this vice, and treats him not as guilty?"*

The Moral Reform Society sought to reform victims as well as victimizers. Prostitutes and their patrons were awakened more than one early Sunday morning by praying, hymn-singing, and Bible-reading women. Convinced that prostitutes would

forsake their life of sin if given the chance, moral reformers opened halfway houses and staged rescues of runaway daughters. By 1838, the Moral Reform Society had grown to 445 auxiliaries.

Participation in associations empowered women, brought them together with like-minded sisters, and helped them gain valuable organizational skills. Collectively they were allowed rights, such as purchasing property, that did not belong to them individually. Yet, their activities did not necessarily point them in the direction of feminism. For some, charity work was a confirmation of their proper roles. For others, inequality was unbearable in any form.

"AM I NOT A WOMAN AND A SISTER?": ABOLITION

No societal ill was more controversial than slavery. The debate continued: should Americans be allowed to own other Americans? Those who thought not called themselves *abolitionists*. Some suggested that slaves should be freed gradually or sent to colonize Africa. Others insisted upon immediate emancipation. These views made some people furious enough to attack or even kill antislavery advocates.

Though it was dangerous to speak out against slavery, many abolitionists felt morally compelled to do so. Steeped in a culture that glorified motherhood, female abolitionists identified most intensely with the plight of slave mothers torn from their children. In a letter to abolitionist newspaper the *Liberator* in 1836, **Elizabeth Emory** and **Mary Abbott** wrote,

"Women's woes and women's wrongs are borne to us on every breeze that flows from the South. . . . God gave woman a heart to feel—an eye to weep—a hand to work—a tongue to speak. Now let her use that tongue to speak on slavery."

In a country where the bodies of black women were frequently stripped for public view, white women who opposed slavery were chided for being too publicly visible. Female abolitionists drew criticism for their choice of an emblem—a drawing of a half-dressed female slave, chained and on her knees, pleading. The caption read, **"Am I Not a Woman and a Sister?"** *But the image, so arresting and vulnerable, helped accomplish what words could not. It brought more women into the movement. The emblem was used on stationery, posters, and pamphlets.*

Maria Weston Chapman, **Lydia Maria Child**, and others "petticoat politicians" and accused them of "prowling about stirring up discord." Brick-wielding mobs surrounded the society's conference in 1835. When black and white delegates exited arm in arm, the enraged crowd dragged their speaker, William Lloyd Garrison, through the streets with a rope.

Free blacks had a direct interest in abolition. **Charlotte Forten** helped found the Philadelphia Anti-Slavery Society. Forten's large home in Philadelphia became a gathering place for abolitionists, and her daughters grew up to work in the antislavery cause. Black members often encountered racism from fellow abolitionists who were blind to the irony of trying to end slavery while discriminating against free blacks.

Even some free blacks did not think it was a woman's place to voice public opinion. **Maria Stewart**, a young widow, received the cold shoulder in 1832 when she began delivering speeches to Boston's African American community. Her main message was that emancipation would only come about through the efforts of blacks and that her people should work to improve their own lot: *"Daughters of Africa, awake! Arise! Distinguish yourselves."* Shunned by the community of free blacks because of her "unladylike behavior," she went on to become a teacher. Though she gave up

At first, female abolitionists helped the cause in ladylike ways: they talked to their friends and families of the evils of slavery and boycotted goods made from slave labor: rice, sugar, and cotton. However, William Lloyd Garrison, a dynamic new leader of the movement, suggested that women should take a more active role.

In 1832, only five women were present to witness the signing of the constitution for the new American Anti-Slavery Society. It did not occur to them or to their hosts that they be allowed to sign. Nevertheless, in the following years women founded dozens of their own antislavery societies. The activities of the Boston Female Anti-Slavery Society, founded in 1833, whipped some Bostonians into a frenzy. Newspapers dubbed its members

In 1837, a group of prominent New England ministers wrote an open letter condemning public speaking by women, "dangers which at present seem to threaten the female character with widespread and permanent injury." They compared lecturing women to clinging vines who were overstepping their bounds by trying to overshadow the mighty elm trees (men).

The man
over there says that women
need to be helped into carriages
and lifted over ditches, and to have
the best place everywhere.
Nobody ever helps me into
carriages or over puddles
or gives me
the best place...

...and ain't I a woman?

Look at my arm! I have ploughed and planted and
gathered into barns, and no man could head me
...and ain't I a woman?
I could work as much and eat as much as a man—
when I could get it—and bear the lash as well
...and ain't I a woman?
I have borne thirteen children, and seen most of 'em
sold into slavery, and when I cried out
with my mother's grief, none but Jesus heard me
...and ain't I a woman?

Sojourner Truth. In recent decades, her image and life story have been used to inspire people to fight for justice and equity.

lecture tour in May 1837. The following year, Angelina Grimke became the first woman to speak before a legislative session.

Two women openly discussing the most contentious subject of the era were not welcome n most towns. Though large crowds turned out to hear the Grimkes, it was difficult to find meeting places. More radical than their speeches about slavery was the way the sisters linked the oppression of blacks to that of women. Both blacks and women, they insisted, had natural rights that should be respected. *"The discussion of the rights of the slave has opened the way for the discussion of other rights,"* wrote Angelina Grimke that same year. "And the ultimate result will most certainly be the breaking

public speaking, she had set a precedent for others who wished to be heard.

A powerful voice for abolition arose in the person of a tall, dignified, former slave. **Sojourner Truth**, born Isabella Baumfree, spoke Dutch as her first language. The youngest of twelve children born to slave parents, she only knew one sibling as the rest had been sold. At the age of nine, she was also sold. Nearly thirty when she was emancipated in 1827, Truth found work as a domestic and then as an itinerant preacher. At some point, she changed her name and began to speak publicly against slavery. Truth's deep voice and message moved audiences. Accused of being a man at one meeting, she shamed the audience by baring her breasts, telling the men that they had fed many a white baby at the expense of her own five children.

Southern slaveholders were particularly enraged and embarrassed by the public condemnation of slavery by two of their own. **Angelina** and **Sarah Grimke**, daughters of an elite South Carolina family, turned heads when they became Quakers, renounced slavery, and began delivering antislavery speeches. Even most male abolitionists did not want women to address mixed audiences, but the sisters set out on an exhausting

I Sell the Shadow to Support the Substance.
SOJOURNER TRUTH.

of every yoke . . . an emancipation far more glorious than any the world has ever yet seen." No one had explicitly made these connections before.

Women's involvement in such a controversial cause only increased public outrage. In Philadelphia, female abolitionists built a beautiful three-story hall because no one would allow them to rent one. On May 14, 1838, they dedicated the building and began their convention. Mobs threw bricks through the windows as various speakers addressed the audience. The next day, crowds burned the hall to the ground. Firemen did not try to put out the flames; they merely stopped them from spreading to neighboring buildings. Rather than admit defeat, the women found another place to meet. Even violence could not quell the new ideas making their way into the public arena. Great changes were under way.

"All I ask our brethren is, that they will take their feet from off our necks, and permit us to stand upright on that ground which God designed us to occupy."
—Sarah Grimke, *Letters on the Equality of the Sexes,* 1838

CHAPTER 3

Growing Divisions
1840–1865

There was nothing very unusual about the May 11, 1840, wedding of **Elizabeth Cady** to Henry B. Stanton, except that the bride had, with great difficulty, persuaded the minister to strike the word *obey* from the ceremony. Elizabeth Cady, unlike most women of her time, was determined to have an equal relationship with her new husband. Her resolve was strengthened when, one month later, she accompanied him to the World Anti-Slavery Convention in London. There she met **Lucretia Mott**. Mott was not only an abolitionist; she also advocated equal rights for women. Stanton was captivated. She had never before met a woman who "believed in the equality of the sexes." She wrote, *"I had never heard a woman talk what . . . I had scarcely dared to think."* The need for equal rights was highlighted when male delegates refused to seat female delegates, forcing them to sit silently in a separate chamber. On that day, Mott and Stanton "resolved to hold a convention as soon as we returned home, and [to] form a society to advocate the rights of women." The seeds for an organized women's rights movement had been planted.

Many early photographs, called *daguerreotypes*, feature people whose names have been lost. This woman posed for a portrait sometime between 1847 and 1860. During this period, she would have lived through the vast changes and upheavals of her times. What might she say if she could tell her story?

The period leading up to the Civil War was one of increasing social and political divisions. In an emerging movement, women sought a measure of control over their own lives and pushed the boundaries of acceptable behavior. In so doing, they struck at core ideas about femininity and power. At the same time, many Americans left their Eastern homes seeking better lives in the West. Native American and Mexican communities resisted as white settlers encroached on their lands. Industry expanded, opening wide gaps between the worlds of work and home life. The most divisive issue, however, was slavery. Abolitionists and slaveholders clashed over states' rights, and argued about whether anyone had the right to own another human being. Tensions mounted, and Americans soon entered the Civil War, with all of its attendant challenges and horrors.

> **"In education, in marriage, in religion, in everything, disappointment is the lot of woman.** It shall be the business of my life to deepen this disappointment in every woman's heart until she bows down to it no longer."
> —Lucy Stone, 1855

WOMEN'S RIGHTS

"THE WOMAN QUESTION"

Throughout the nineteenth century, Americans debated what became known as "the woman question": did women possess the same equal, inalienable rights as men? For most, the answer was clear—certainly not! The mere thought was dangerous. What might happen if women were allowed to vote, go to college, own their own property, or keep their wages? The belief that females were naturally less capable than males was so prevalent that most women believed it themselves. Indeed, few questioned their position in society.

Ernestine Rose, a Jewish immigrant from Poland, was not one of these. Beginning in 1836, she worked for laws that gave women the right to own and control their own property. Her first challenge was to convince New York women that they should seek these rights. She later recalled that "it was a great deal of trouble. . . . *Woman at that time had not learned to know that she had any rights."* Initially, she found only five ladies who were brave enough to sign her petition.

Around dinner tables and on street corners, people took up the dispute. Since property ownership and the right to vote were closely linked, law makers were not anxious to grant women the right to own property. Who could predict how far they would take their pursuit of equal rights after that? Rose, **Paulina Wright Davis**, and others lobbied a full twelve years before the New York legislature finally passed the Married Women's Property Act in April 1848. This act set a standard for other states by giving women control over the property they brought into marriage or obtained afterward.

At the same time, a determined young woman named **Lucy Stone** was fighting her own battle for women's equality. Without family support, a determined Stone spent many years putting herself through school at Mount Holyoke and Oberlin College (the first coeducational college in America). She learned Hebrew and Greek simply to prove that the Bible, in its original form, taught that *"God loves his daughters as well as He loves his sons."* While a student, she protested reduced wages for women and opposed school rules that prevented her from delivering her own commencement speech.

Energized by some success and the encouragement of abolitionist leaders, Stone began her courageous and "unladylike" career as a reformer and public lecturer in 1847. Traveling from state to state, she worked as an agent for the abolitionists and gave lectures about women's rights on the side. Her masterful use of words, her vivid storytelling, her simple, straightforward manner, and her vigorous arguments gave her a power over her audience that became legendary. Many former opponents to women's rights were converted by her speeches. One Syracuse editor described how *Stone "threw her voice over the assembly, and swayed it with pity, and grief, and scorn, and indignation, as if it was the helpless plaything of her imagination."* When she married, Lucy Stone set a new precedent by keeping her own name. She, Ernestine Rose, and Paulina Davis would soon find themselves in good company.

THE SENECA FALLS CONVENTION In the summer of 1848, no one could have guessed that a revolution of enormous proportions was being plotted at a tea table in Waterloo, New York. The revolutionaries were five married women with children—two of whom were Elizabeth Cady Stanton and Lucretia Mott. While these friends had vowed to return from London and organize a women's convention, their intentions were eclipsed by more personal demands. By the time Lucretia Mott visited Stanton eight years later, her friend had become the overwhelmed, rural mother of a quickly growing family. She was mentally "hungry," lonely, and deeply depressed by the constant struggle to maintain a household. Yet beneath the depression lay a keen mind and tough will.

Have you ever heard of . . . Margaret Fuller?

Fuller was a poet and brilliant philosopher. When her feminist commentary *Woman in the Nineteenth Century* was published in 1845, abolitionist **Lydia Maria Child** gushed, **"It is a bold book. . . . I should not have dared to have written some things in it. . . . But they need to be said, and she is brave to do it."** Advocating equal rights, a new idea, Fuller challenged women to develop their intellects. After editing a transcendentalist journal, she traveled to Italy as foreign correspondent to the New York *Tribune.* There, she fell in love with a handsome young Italian nobleman, Giovanni Angelo d'Ossili. Returning to the United States with their small son, the family drowned in a shipwreck within sight of the New Jersey shore. Writer Henry Thoreau and others searched in vain for their bodies. Friends wanted to write her biography but asked, "How can you describe a force? How can you write the life of Margaret?"

Unlike other exhausted housewives of her time, Stanton linked her struggles to women's inequality. The knowledge of women's lack of control over their own lives "swept across" her and spurred her to action. Finally in the company of other sympathetic women, she "poured out the torrent of [her] long-accumulating discontent." In so doing, she wrote, *"I stirred myself, as well as the rest of the party, to do and dare anything."* The time had come to seek equal rights with men. The women posted signs and drew up resolutions and hoped that a few people would attend a convention to discuss women's rights. The Seneca Falls Convention, which launched a more organized women's movement, occurred on July 19 and 20, 1848, in the small town of Seneca Falls, New York.

More than 300 women and men showed up. Following a series of speeches, Elizabeth Cady Stanton stood to read the "Declaration of Rights and Sentiments." Echoing the Declaration of Independence, she stated,

"We hold these truths to be self-evident: that all men and women are created equal."

She then clearly detailed the kinds of discrimination women faced at every turn. Among other things, women were denied an education, the right to vote, and the ability to choose a profitable profession. They were bound by inequitable marriage and divorce laws, and were unable to control their own property and wages. These inequalities seemed especially pointed when at the same time the rights of the common man were expanding.

In short, women had been "deprived of their most sacred rights" by men who had worked "in every way that [they] could, to destroy her confidence in her own powers, to lessen her self-respect, and to make her willing to lead a dependent and abject life." In a series of resolutions, she then insisted that women "have immediate admission to all the rights and privileges which belong to them as citizens of the United States." Of the nearly one hundred women and men who signed the document, only one, **Charlotte Woodward**, would live to see women granted the right to vote seventy-two years later.

THE CONVENTIONS A movement had begun. Activists staged another convention two weeks later in Rochester, New York; others followed. At one, held in Salem, Ohio, in 1850, leaders did not allow men to speak. The convention recorder was thrilled:

"Never did men so suffer. They implored to say a word; but no; the President was inflexible—no man should be heard. If one meekly arose to make a suggestion he was at once ruled out of order. For the first time in the world's history, men learned how it felt to sit in silence when questions in which they were interested were under discussion."

Some scholars believe that early women's rights advocates got their inspiration from the Haudenosaunee (Iroquois) Nation. Powerful within the clan, Haudenosaunee women worked together in agriculture and owned their own property. They held authority in ceremonial and political life. When couples married, they remained with the wife's clan. Many early women's rights leaders lived in regular contact with their Indian neighbors. Just before her trip to Seneca Falls, Lucretia Mott visited the Seneca Nation, witnessing firsthand a culture where men and women were equals.

This photo of Elizabeth Cady Stanton with her sons Daniel and Henry was taken in 1848, the same year as the Seneca Falls Convention. Five more children would follow.

Elizabeth Cady Stanton's strong opinions didn't always make her popular. One young woman from Seneca Falls refused to ride in the same carriage, saying, **"I wouldn't have been seen with her for anything, with those ideas of hers."**

The first national convention in 1850 brought together for the first time many of those who had been working individually for women's rights. While conventions provided places where women could support each other, they also highlighted some of the challenges of unifying strongly opinionated leaders into one movement. Women's rights activists faced difficult questions. Should the movement include or exclude men? Who was to blame for women's inequality? What remedies should they seek? How could women best convince others of their need for equality?

One goal, however, was clear. Attendees resolved to "secure for [woman] political, legal and social equality with man," giving her the opportunity to freely choose her sphere. As word of the proceedings traveled around the world, they inspired others to action. Soon thereafter, women in Sheffield, England, made their first bid for suffrage to the House of Lords.

Women's rights advocates held national conventions nearly every year until the outset of the Civil War. Some future leaders got their start at these meetings. Twenty-six-year-old **Matilda Joslyn Gage**, one of the eventual leaders of the movement, presented her first speech at the 1852 meeting. She spoke so timidly that few could hear. Others had been honing their skills in the temperance (anti-alcohol) and abolitionist movements for years. **Abby Kelley Foster** boldly stated, *"For fourteen years I have advocated this cause in my daily life. Bloody feet, sisters, have worn smooth the path by which you have come hither."* Abolitionist and ex-slave **Sojourner Truth** commanded attention at the 1851 meeting, challenging the notion that equality was only for white, educated men and women. When she rose to her nearly six-foot stature and gave her now famous "Ain't I a Woman" speech, she left her audience "with streaming eyes and hearts beating with gratitude."

STANTON AND ANTHONY Elizabeth Cady Stanton was conspicuously missing from most of these early conventions. Following an active fall of 1848, Stanton felt her family pulling her inward. Neither her father nor her husband supported her women's rights work, and her family continued to grow and demand her attention. While others, such as Lucy Stone, kept up a grueling pace lecturing and organizing conferences, Stanton was "surrounded"

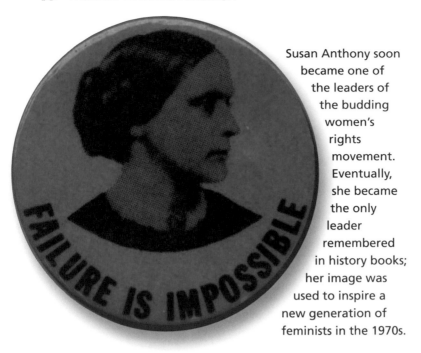

Susan Anthony soon became one of the leaders of the budding women's rights movement. Eventually, she became the only leader remembered in history books; her image was used to inspire a new generation of feminists in the 1970s.

In 1867 10,000 divorces were granted in the United States. Access to divorce depended on where a person lived. Some states opposed divorce on almost all grounds. After her husband horsewhipped and beat her, one woman took her plea for divorce to the North Carolina Supreme Court in 1862. The Chief Justice denied her, stating, **"The law gives the husband power to use such a degree of force necessary to make the wife behave and know her place."**

by her "children, washing dishes, baking, sewing, etc." On the side, she wrote letters to the editor and articles under the name of Sunflower.

Then, one fateful day in 1851, she met thirty-one-year-old **Susan B. Anthony**. Anthony, stung by discrimination against women in the temperance movement, gradually diverted her considerable energy to the cause of women's rights. Anthony emerged as a gifted organizer—Stanton, a sharp thinker. Together, they forged a formidable partnership that would last until Stanton's death in 1902.

For the next decade, Stanton was deeply immersed in running a household. She wrote to the unmarried Anthony, *"My whole soul is in the work, but my hands belong to my family."* But Anthony would not let her rest. She kept Stanton busy writing speeches, articles, and petitions that Anthony would then deliver. Shortly after Stanton had given birth to her sixth child, Anthony begged her to write a speech for an upcoming meeting. She urged, "So for the love of me and for the saving of the reputation of womanhood, I beg you, with one baby on your knee and another at your feet, and four boys whistling, buzzing, hallooing 'Ma, Ma,' set yourself about the work. It is of but small moment who writes the address but of vast moment that it be done well." Stanton responded, "Come here and I will do what I can . . . if you will hold the baby and make the puddings."

PROGRESS By 1860, women's rights advocates had made some headway. In Indiana, divorces could be granted on the basis not only of adultery, but for desertion, drunkenness, and cruelty as well. In New York, Indiana, Maine, Missouri, and Ohio, women's property rights had expanded to allow married women to keep their own wages. Clearly there was still much to be done. However, reformers had given a name to women's oppression and had set into motion the movement that would continue to change American attitudes for years to come, as they pushed for reform in everything from education to underwear.

EDUCATION

"STRONG-MINDED WOMEN"

The desire for change grew out of a deep-seated sense of injustice born of experience. When **Hannah Stone** delivered a healthy baby girl in 1819, she cried, "Oh dear, I am sorry. A woman's life is so hard." When Lyman Beecher observed his daughter's capabilities from an early age, he wrote, *"Harriet is a genius. I would give a hundred dollars if she was a boy."* When Judge Daniel Cady's only son died, he turned to his bright, energetic ten-year-old daughter and said, "Ah my daughter, I wish you were a boy." The parents of Lucy Stone, **Harriet Beecher Stowe**, and Elizabeth Cady Stanton all shared a belief in women's inferiority. As girls would grow to be wives and mothers, intelligence was often thought to be wasted on them.

While most Americans now believed that some education helped women to be better wives and mothers, most agreed with Archbishop Fenelon when he advised readers in 1847 that "there must be caution not to make females ridiculous, by making them over-learned." He continued, "Women have generally minds more weak, and more inquisitive than men. It is not proper to engage them out of their proper sphere of action." Women such as Stanton offered a different vision:

"Begin with the girls of to-day, and in twenty years we can revolutionize this nation. The childhood of woman must be free and untrammeled. The girl must be allowed to romp and play, skate, and swim. . . . Let the girl be . . . left to be, to grow, to feel, to think, to act. . . . We have had women enough befooled under the one system, pray let us try another."

To be well educated or outspoken was to risk being labeled as unfeminine and manly. Stepping too far outside the rules of conduct resulted in social isolation and ridicule. **Mary Putnam Jacobi**, who later become a prominent physician, received

When Elizabeth Cady Stanton's first daughter, Margaret, was born in 1852, she flew a flag and wrote joyously to Lucretia Mott: **"I am at length the happy mother of a daughter. Rejoice with me all Womanhood, for lo! a champion of the cause is born.** I have dedicated her to this work from the beginning. May she . . . leave her impress on the world for goodness and truth."** Stanton's second daughter, Harriot Stanton Blatch, actually fulfilled this promise and followed in her mother's activist footsteps.

In 1853, **Jane Swisshelm**, a newspaper publisher, celebrated the virtues of an equal education for girls. She advised them to "read, read—think, study, try to be wise. . . . **You should try to understand every thing you think and hear; to act and judge for yourselves; to remember you have a soul of your own to account for;**—a mind of your own to improve. When you once get these ideas fixed, and learn to act upon them, no man or set of men, no laws, customs, or combination of them can seriously oppress you."

A drawing of Dr. Elizabeth Blackwell at the age of thirty-eight.

a letter from her father reminding her: "Don't let yourself be absorbed . . . in that branch of animal kingdom ordinarily called 'strong minded women.'" Indeed, it was a smart woman's job to do all she could to avoid being labeled "strong minded."

Few were willing to risk the social stigma of becoming "overlearned." **Anna Howard Shaw**, who later became a leader in the suffrage (right to vote) movement, was one of these women. Though she had never known of a woman going to college, she determined early that despite great obstacles, she would do just that. She later recalled, *"Though my college career seemed as remote as the most distant star, I hitched my little wagon to that star and never afterward wholly lost sight of its friendly gleam."*

College was out of the question for most women. The few male institutions that began to accept women treated them as second-class citizens. They were forced to sit in the back of classrooms and denied access to classes and equipment.

Some were not allowed to graduate once they had completed their coursework. When **Antoinette Brown (Blackwell)** requested entry into a doctoral program in theology at Oberlin College in Ohio, she said, "I was reasoned with, pleaded with, and besought even with tears" not to interfere with the great harmony of life that rested on "masculine headship everywhere." Though the school allowed her to proceed with the program, she was refused her degree and ordination. Her friend Lucy Stone wondered why *"they acted as though they had rather the whole world should go to hell, than Antoinette Brown should be allowed to tell them how to keep out of it."* Brown was not granted her degree until 1908.

What One Woman Did

"The Female Student . . . Had Arrived"

Elizabeth Blackwell (Antoinette's sister-in-law) became the first "woman doctor" in America through sheer will, intelligence, perseverance, and a bit of luck. In 1847, she applied to multiple medical programs and was rejected by all. When Geneva Medical College admitted her, she had no idea that it had been a joke on the part of the student body. The moment the dean announced in a "trembling voice, that . . . the female student . . . had arrived, . . . *a hush fell upon the class as if each member had been stricken with paralysis. A death-like stillness prevailed during the lecture, and only the newly arrived student took notes."*

Striving to overcome prejudices, she graduated at the age of twenty-seven at the top of her class. Her success did little to pave the way for her younger sister's entrance to medical school. Turned down by Geneva College and others, it took **Emily Blackwell** six years to find a medical school to admit her.

Following additional training in Europe (where she befriended nurse **Florence Nightingale**), Blackwell returned to the United States to practice medicine. Her attempts again met with great resistance. Barred from practicing in New York hospitals, she opened a clinic to care for the poor women and children of the East Side of New York.

Her New York Infirmary for Indigent Women and Children was run entirely by women. Eventually, with the help of her sister, she founded the Woman's Medical College of New York. Though the medical school merged with Cornell University in 1899, her New York Infirmary continues to be staffed by women.

HEALTH

"CRUEL SUFFERING" AND REFORM

America continued to be an unhealthy place. One woman observed during this period, *"I am not able to recall, in my immense circle of friends and acquaintances all over the Union so many as ten married ladies born in this century and country, who are perfectly sound, healthy, and vigorous."* Male physicians began treating the natural cycles of menstruation, childbirth, and menopause as illnesses. Doctors blamed many symptoms, including depression, anxiety, and fatigue on the mere possession of a womb. In fact, the seeming commonness of illness in women has made historians wonder whether in some instances women were sick because they had been told they were. In some circles, ill health was almost fashionable.

Women dealt with the issues of sickness and death regularly. Cholera, malaria, measles, scarlet fever, tuberculosis, and typhoid fever plagued communities. In 1849, during a devastating cholera epidemic in Cincinnati, author Harriet Beecher Stowe wrote to her husband of the seemingly endless procession of hearses and carts removing

With death ever present and often sudden, **mourning jewelry** made with hair from the deceased became quite popular. Gold, enamel, and precious stones were offset by intricately woven strands of hair in brooches, earrings, watch chains, and other jewelry. *Godey's Lady's Book* told readers, "Hair is at once the most delicate and lasting of our materials and survives us, like love. . . . With a lock of hair belonging to a child or a friend, we may almost look up to heaven…[and] say, 'I have a piece of thee here.'" This 1868 sheet music highlights this sentiment.

the dead throughout the city. "Cruel suffering" came to her home when her baby, Charley, died of cholera. She could barely contain her grief. Midcentury letters and journals reveal women participating in the bustling activities of life—visiting neighbors, washing clothes, caring for children—alongside those associated with death—tending the sick and dying, sewing burial clothing,

Did you know?

Many Americans believed that the pain of childbirth was decreed by God and therefore should not be taken away. However, Boston Lying-In Hospital became the first to experiment with labor anesthesia in 1847.

Did you know?

Until a woman named **Dorthea Dix** came along, poor and mentally ill people were often thrown together with criminals into wretched, unheated buildings where they were beaten, chained, and barely clothed or fed. In 1841, having witnessed the misery in one prison, this schoolteacher dedicated herself to creating a mental health system that treated patients rather than simply locking them up. She told one group of lawmakers, **"I am the hope of the poor crazed beings who pine in cells and stalls and cages . . . of hundreds of wailing, suffering creatures hidden in your private dwellings, and in pens and in cabins."** Dix's untiring efforts led to the construction of at least 123 new mental hospitals, and the passage of numerous laws that promoted humane treatment of patients.

and attending funerals. When people died, women prepared them for burial.

Doctors were called into people's homes with increasing frequency. Unfortunately, many of their "cures" probably made things worse. Depending on a patient's symptoms, she might be bled, blistered, or made to vomit in an attempt to purge her body of poisons. In one situation, a doctor declared his interventions a triumph when he took nearly two quarts of blood from a laboring woman. Once she fainted, "everything appeared better."

These treatments led some to argue that there was a better way. Health reformers began to convince the public that people played a critical role in determining their own health. "Many people," wrote reformer **Mary Gove**, "seem to think that all diseases are immediate visitations from [God]. . . . Many seem to have no idea that there are established laws with respect to life and health, and that the transgression of these laws is followed by disease." Reformers promoted various solutions, from advocating a simple diet and exercise to opposing alcohol consumption and tight-laced corsets.

Those who could afford it turned to fashionable health spas for cures. Retreating from the world, women entered a place where their ailments were taken seriously. In a time when bathing regularly was still a novelty, water cures became the cutting edge of alternative medicine. There were as many as 213 water-cure establishments in America by midcentury. **Catharine Beecher**, who sought relief from her "nervous excitability," described the rigors of the cure. Patients would spend nights wrapped in wet bandages, and days repeating a cycle of taking long walks (while still wrapped in wet bandages) followed by drinking vast amounts of icy water and being plunged into baths and showers of "the coldest water."

Godey's Lady's Book's "unrivaled colored fashions" of 1855. Imagine how long it would take to get dressed if you had to put on so many clothes.

BEAUTY

"CHOKED WITH RIBBONS"

Some people blamed women's bad health on the confining fashions of the day. Young **Frances Willard** might have agreed. "This is my birthday and the day of my martyrdom," she told her journal in the early 1850s.

"Mother insists that at last I *must* have my hair 'done up woman fashion.' . . . My head aches miserably; my feet are entangled in the skirt of my hateful new gown. I can never jump over a fence again, so long as I live."

As a girl growing up in the Wisconsin Territory, Willard had great freedom to run and play. From her perch in a "tall black oak," she could "read and write quite hidden from view." Becoming a woman meant leaving all that behind. She cried "long and loud," mourning that "Now I was to be 'choked with ribbons' when I went into the open air the rest of my days."

Indeed, the fashions of the 1850s defied reason. Fashionable dresses grew to an unwieldy circumference of twelve to fifteen feet. These elaborate garments, combined with tightened corsets and layers of stiffened petticoats, restricted movement. Wealthier women spent untold hours with dressmakers who painstakingly cut, fitted, and sewed capes, dresses, skirts, bodices, and undergarments. Others pored over European fashion plates in *Godey's Lady's Book* and attempted to make their own—no small feat at a time when a basic dress consisted of twenty-five yards of material, fancy trimmings, multiple buttonholes, a lining, and a bodice made to fit "like wall paper."

BLOOMERS People turned their heads when **Elizabeth Smith Miller** began parading around her New York town wearing a curious outfit: a simple, knee-length dress over pants gathered at the ankle. Interested in reforming the way women dressed, she wore her unusual clothes for a visit with her cousin,

Bloomers even inspired music such as *The New Costume Polka*.

Elizabeth Cady Stanton. Stanton, eight months pregnant, immediately adopted the attire as a protest of "woman's clothes prison." She wrote, *"This dress makes it easier to do all these things—running from cradle to writing desk, from kitchen to drawing room, singing lullabies at one moment in the nursery and dear old Tom Moore's ditties the next moment on the piano stool. If I had long skirts, how could I accomplish all this?"*

Have you ever heard of . . . Elizabeth Keckly?

A slave who purchased her freedom from her white half-siblings, Keckly was an exceptional seamstress and businesswoman. The *New York Evening Post* called her "stately and stylish" and marveled, "Lizzie is an artist, and has such a genius for making women look pretty, that not one thinks of disputing her decrees." **Keckly was already the preferred dressmaker of Washington, DC, high society when fashion-conscious Mary Todd Lincoln hired her to make sixteen dresses.** In a time when social interaction between blacks and whites was limited, Keckly became more than the First Lady's dressmaker; she became her friend and confidante. When Mary Lincoln's son died and her husband was assassinated, she turned to Elizabeth Keckly for comfort.

It seems that every older generation proclaims that the new generation is in moral decline. Older Americans in the 1850s worried about "fast young women" who behaved in a **"laughing, giggling, romping, flirting"** manner. In New York City, young women were criticized for **"screaming** at the top of their lungs, **running** in and out of shops, spending lots of time **lounging** about in the streets." One observer thought women sporting "silks and satins at what hour of the day they please" belonged in the circus.

The clothes gained national attention when **Amelia Bloomer** wrote about them in her temperance newspaper, *The Lily*, in 1852. They became known as "bloomers." Requests for patterns poured in as women began to imagine life without heavy, dragging skirts. The interest was short-lived, however, when people realized that women's rights activists were advocating and wearing bloomers. In addition, many objected to bloomers as immoral and alluring—a woman's ankles were simply not to be seen. Distrust of the outfit was so great that the *New York Herald* predicted women in bloomers would soon "end their career in the lunatic asylum, or perchance in the state prison."

Changing what one wore was no small matter. Those who donned bloomers were mocked, criticized, stared at, and even mobbed. Stanton's sons pleaded with her not to wear her bloomers to visit them at school. Within a few years, even the most stalwart dress reformers reluctantly retired their bloomers, at least in public. Lucy Stone later lamented, "We could go upstairs without stepping on ourselves, and go downstairs without being stepped on. But useful as the bloomer was, the ridicule of the world killed it."

HOOP SKIRTS By the mid-1850s, the introduction of the lightweight, steel hoop skirt (called *crinoline*) reduced women's petticoat load, but the circumference of dresses kept right on growing. In fact, they became so huge that New York City responded by upping fares on omnibuses for women in hoop skirts. Crinolines were relatively inexpensive, making it possible for poorer women to adopt the fashion. Some slaves constructed makeshift hoops out of grapevines. One Mississippi slave recalled, ***"De white women wore hoop skirts but I neber seed a black woman with one on. Dey jes' starched deir petticoats an' made deir dresses stand out like hoop under dem."*** Imagine trying to walk through a doorway, stand close to someone, or stroll on a windy day in skirts the size of a kitchen table. Despite the fact that hoop skirts got in the way of basic activities, they remained in fashion ten years, disappearing by 1868.

Before shampoo was invented, women's magazines and books gave advice on cleaning hair and keeping it from falling out. One potion included two pounds of honey, rosemary, and tendrils of grapevines infused in milk. Others utilized egg yolks, olive oil, rum, and flowers. **Nina Larowe** recalled that in her California town, "Everybody, men, women, and children, used to oil the hair—more than oil it, literally soak it. It was put on and then the hair was brushed until it was straight . . . and smooth as satin. . . . Women often made their own [pomade]. Beef marrow, mixed with lard, was melted together, then beaten until it was like snow and highly perfumed." The hair tonic to the left promises to restore gray hair, cure dandruff, and prevent baldness.

faces,—differing widely in their graces . . . It is needful that we properly explain

IT WONDERFULLY IMPROVES & THICKENS THE GROWTH OF THE HAIR.

HOLLAND. ·AMERICA· PERSIA SPAIN.

RESTORES GRAY HAIR TO ITS ORIGINAL COLOR, CURES DANDRUFF, AND PREVENTS BALDNESS. over

. . . ped that you may scan pleasing pictures of Japan Holland Persia "dear America" and Spain.

AT HOME

THE "HEAVENLY KINGDOM"

The women who pushed society's limits by wearing bloomers, attending college, and advocating women's rights were few and far between. The vast majority accepted their limited rights and embraced society's definition of womanhood. Colonial goodwives who played a large role in family production and survival were increasingly becoming a relic of the past. Instead, the model virtuous wife and mother was devoted to "the chaste circle of the fireside" and dedicated herself to making her home a refuge from the world. With nearly 20 percent of the U.S. population living in towns, more husbands were working away from home. The home was becoming a feminine space associated with morality and

Although the law did not recognize slave marriages, enslaved women and men made commitments to one another nonetheless. Slave husbands and wives were on a more equal footing than their white counterparts because neither had access to traditional sources of power.

warmth. By 1840, this family ideal held sway even for those unable to live it.

There were few greater champions of the moral, chaste, virtues of womanhood than Catharine Beecher. For Beecher, the duties of women were "sacred," and the home, a "heavenly kingdom." She published her popular *Treatise on Domestic Economy* in 1841. In this book, Beecher elevated the work of women in the home to new heights. She presented the idea of woman as a "domestic economist," offering advice about everything from home decorating and organization to health and nutrition. According to Beecher, efficiency was crucial, not only for the happiness of her family, but for the well-being of the entire nation. She argued that only by being outside of the political process could women be a force for good.

MARRIAGE Beecher chose to remain single in a time when virtually everyone intended to marry. One philosopher of the time summed up the common attitude: "We are as truly bound to marry . . . as we are to eat, drink, sleep, labor, or pray." Yet women and men generally spent little time together. Though living in different social and emotional worlds, they still needed one another to run a household. The average woman married around age twenty and bore five or six children. However, as in the past, the decision to marry was

The daguerreotype was invented in 1839, so when this mother and child sat for this image in 1851, they were taking advantage of a relatively new fad.

fraught with peril, because married women had no legal standing, and rare recourse to divorce.

The expectations of what a woman would sacrifice in marriage made the transition traumatic for many young women. A new bride would be expected to run a more efficient household with less help than had her mother or grandmother. Half an hour before Catherine Beecher's younger sister, Harriet, wed, she confided to a friend, *"Well, my dear, I have been dreading and dreading the time, and lying awake all last week wondering how I should live through this overwhelming crisis, and lo! It has come, and I feel nothing at all."* Beecher and others had good reason to have mixed feelings. Watching their mothers, they had observed that marriage often brought suffering for women and would be "nothing but cares and forever after."

CHORES Norwegien immigrant **Gro Svendson** believed that American women worked particularly hard. She wrote in 1862, *"We are told that women of America have much leisure time but I haven't yet met any woman who thought so!* Here the mistress of the house must do all the work that the cook,

This 1869 ad promised purchasers less intense work and greater leisure.

the maid and the housekeeper would do in an upper class family at home. Moreover she must do her work as well as these three together do it in Norway."

Most women also continued to dip candles and render their own soap. **Christiana Holmes Tillson** described the "tedious" process of making candles: "From three to four mortal hours the right arm must be in constant movement. If a rest is given . . . the candles become too hard and break, and the tallow in the pot gets too cool, so dip, dip, dip, dip, six candles at a time; each time the candles grow heavier and heavier, and the shoulder more rebellious." **Martha Coffin Wright** wrote in 1847, *"How sorry I feel for Phoebe Gibbons. . . . poor child, I pity her to have to learn how to make candles &c. as much as I pity myself for having had to—and yet there is a pleasure in achieving it when you know you must."* In wealthy Southern households, white mistresses supervised slave women in these demanding, unpleasant tasks.

In rural households, women and men had their own, specific jobs. Women cared for cows and chickens, made butter and cheese, gathered eggs, grew vegetables and herbs, hauled water, and gathered wood. Men cleared land, plowed and planted corn, butchered animals, and maintained tools and buildings. If they had an orchard, they maintained it together. Men's work followed the cycle of the seasons, with stretches of intense physical exertion followed by periods of rest. Women's work, no matter the season, had no end.

CLOTHING Though most women no longer wove cloth, they still sewed all the clothing for their

The first egg beater, patented in 1857, sped up recipes that required a woman to hand beat batter for as long as 45 minutes.

families. Southern mistresses were also responsible for cutting out and sewing clothes for their slaves. When sewing machines became available in the 1850s and 1860s, women made more clothes. New, lighter fabrics made washing more necessary. For the first time, laundry became a weekly chore. Once a week, regardless of the weather, women boiled, scrubbed, rinsed, and hung the family's clothes out to dry. The following day they pressed the clothes with heavy irons heated on the stove.

PAID WORK

"A WOMAN THAT CAN WORK"

OPPORTUNITIES IN THE WEST The discovery of gold in California in 1848 placed new value on the tasks traditionally assigned to women. **Jerusha Merrill** breathlessly described the Gold Rush. While most of the prospectors hurrying to California were men, Merrill was a gold digger of another sort. She noted that people were "daily arriving from all parts by the hundreds," and that those men with "not one penny to help themselves" needed food and lodgings. *"A woman that can work will make more money than a man, and I think now that I shall do that,"* wrote **Mary Jane Megquier**.

For a time, the West expanded women's earning options. Enterprising women willing to hazard the chaotic, brawling West could make a great deal of money cooking, washing, and mending for an endless stream of rough and muddy men. Women escaped social upheaval in France to work in California saloons and brothels. Some Mexican and Chilean women opened "fandangos," or dance halls. Merrill hurried to San Francisco and started a profitable boardinghouse. She concluded, "The excited state of things cannot long exist. That large fortunes are being made it's true but in the end many must suffer…this place is not fit for anything but business."

THE NORTHEAST With so many men heading west, factory owners in the Northeast took advantage of the surplus single female workers. By 1840, women made up approximately 85 to 90 percent of the workers in New England textile mills. Work conditions deteriorated as factory owners increased profits by speeding up the work, extending workdays, and cutting pay. American-born farm girls first protested, and then abandoned their jobs to immigrants, who had little choice but to accept any working conditions. Factories cast aside any pretense of maintaining a wholesome, respectable environment.

Between 1845 and 1857, two-thirds of immigrants were either German or Irish. Like 1.25 million others, **Bridget O'Donnel** fled a long and devastating potato famine in Ireland. She had two children, and was expecting a third when her husband abandoned her. Unable to pay her rent, she was evicted from her four acres of bog land. The Irish were the poorest immigrants ever to reach U.S. shores. One in ten died of cholera or typhus en route to America. More than half of Irish immigrants were women, many of them single. While many

In 1852, **Mary Ballou** listed the chores she did in her California boardinghouse. These included washing and ironing, making mince and apple and squash pies, stuffing a ham, cooking oysters, making gruel for the sick, feeding her chickens, scaring the hogs out of her kitchen, and driving the mules out of her dining room. She wrote, "Three times a day I set my table which is about thirty feet in length and do all the little fixings about it. . . . Sometimes I take my fan and try to fan myself but I work so hard that my arms pain me."

A seamstress with her sewing machine in 1853, and a milliner (hatmaker) with her daughter in 1854.

Germans had the means to migrate inland, most Irish women settled in cities, endured anti-Irish prejudice, and took jobs that no one else wanted. Many diligently worked their way up to more skilled positions and sent money home. They tended to marry late, if at all. By 1846, almost 8,000 of the 12,000 servants in New York City were Irish. A large percentage of immigrants also arrived from England and Scandinavia during this decade.

Hedged in by numerous laws controlling their movement and actions, free urban blacks struggled to earn a living. Because slave owners tended to emancipate females more readily than males, free women

Have you ever heard of . . . Idawalley Lewis?

A strong swimmer (a very unladylike skill) and rower, fifteen-year-old Lewis and her mother began operating a Rhode Island lighthouse in 1857 after her father was confined to a wheelchair. She became so famous that after a particularly daring rescue in 1869, marriage proposals poured in and a parade was held in her honor. Lewis kept the lighthouse for thirty-nine years and is credited with saving as many as twenty-five lives.

far outnumbered free men. Whether married or not, a woman's employment was necessary for survival because men often could not find jobs. A growing black middle class obtained the education necessary to work in genteel professions such as teaching, dressmaking, or hat making, but most worked as laundresses, domestics, or seamstresses. Others earned money as flower sellers, hat cleaners, and hairdressers.

NEEDLEWORK One of the only respectable ways women could earn a wage while caring for families was by sewing clothes and the tops of shoes. In the 1840s one-third of shoe workers were women. The *New York Daily Times* estimated in 1845 that in New York alone, 10,000 seamstresses eked out a living. They labored in a "sweating" system where employers subcontracted labor by providing materials for them to cut and sew by hand at home. Though their labor was central to industrial production, they were paid very little for long hours.

The invention of the sewing machine in the 1840s proved a mixed blessing for women. They could now make clothing for their families more quickly. However, the most desperately poor of all workers, seamstresses and shoe binders, were replaced by machines. In 1850, one group appealed to the public: *"The winter is upon us and distress and want stare us in the face. By reason of the low prices for which we are obliged to work many of us are found by the midnight lamp and until daybreak at the needle laboring for a pittance."*

Unfortunately working women received small sympathy from a public who believed that a female earning wages was "tying a stone around the neck of her natural protector, man." If a wife worked for wages, it meant that she was lower class, that her husband had failed, or both.

Have you ever heard of . . . Maria Mitchell?

A teacher and librarian, she was also something much more novel at the time: a brilliant female astronomer and mathematician. Her 1847 discovery of a new comet earned a prestigious medal from the King of Denmark and opened doors into masculine scientific circles. Mitchell's lifelong work won her great respect and a job as a professor at newly opened Vassar College. Her diaries reveal a woman who constantly puzzled over scientific questions while juggling household chores. She once wrote, **"The world of learning is so broad and the human soul is so limited in power! We reach forward and strain every nerve but we seize hold of only a bit of curtain that hides the infinite."**

AMUSEMENTS

An absence of work was not license to play. In 1840, Americans thought much differently about having fun than we do today. Though willing to admit that people needed to stop working once in a while, they still frowned upon wasted time. Girls learned to use their "free time" doing something useful, educational, or uplifting. A Louisiana newspaper advocated "quiet evenings at home," and advised, *"Happy are those who find in the home circle the diversion they need. A lively game, an interesting book read aloud . . . a new song to be practiced, will make an evening pass pleasantly."* Literate girls and women wrote diaries and long, flowery letters to faraway

Young ladies should be taught that usefulness is happiness, and all other things are but incidental." —**Lydia Maria Child**, *The Frugal Housewife*, 1837

loved ones. Most read the Bible, but many also pored over historical works and an abundance of novels.

In her spare moments, a young lady might also embroider, take walks, visit friends, and attend lectures, concerts, and church picnics. For her mother, it was even less clear where work ended and play began.

Women looked forward to the regular arrival of *Godey's Lady's Book,* a periodical packed with stories, fashion plates, needlework patterns, interesting facts, sheet music, book reviews, drawings of model floor plans, and advice.

Wealthy Southern girls were allowed a short season of uninterrupted fun before marriage. Following their debut into society, daughters of the Southern elite were allowed to dress as belles and attend an endless string of social events and dances. In 1859, fourteen-year-old **Lemuella Brickell** imagined, "I shall laugh and dance and flirt. . . . am I not going to have a nice time? I will have beaux, plenty of them (that is if I can get some) and go to parties and lead a very pleasant life." The ultimate purpose of these activities was to find a suitable husband. When this goal was accomplished, a girl graduated to responsible "matron." Though now considered an adult, she would never leave home without a male escort.

"EVERYBODY TURNED OUT"

QUILTING More than any other activity, making quilts allowed mothers and daughters to combine work and fun. "We learned to sew patchwork at school while were learning the alphabet," recalled millworker **Lucy Larcom**. As she grew, a girl spent hours making squares for what would be her most important project, an all-white, bridal quilt intricately stitched with hearts, wedding rings, and vines. A common proverb cautioned, *"If a girl has not made a quilt before she is twenty-one, no man will want to marry her."*

Though quilting could be a solitary activity, women preferred to turn it into a party whenever possible. Friends and relatives gathered from miles around to sew, feast, and exchange news. "So we quilted and rolled, talked and laughed," noted one Pennsylvanian. Seated around a quilt, friends shared concerns and gave one another advice. Women also quilted when communities gathered to husk corn, shear wool, raise barns, and boil syrup. In isolated areas, quilting bees were often one's only opportunity to socialize with other women.

Adolescent girls helped one another make quilts for their hope chests. They held "calico parties" where they exchanged scraps of cloth with their friends. In 1859, seventeen-year-old **Caroline Cowles** decided to start a quilt group. *"We are to meet once every two weeks and are to present each member with an album bed quilt with all our names when they are married.* **Susie Dagget** says she is

never going to be married, but we must make her a quilt just the same." At the end of the day, young men often arrived for games or dancing before escorting quilters home.

Slave women quilted after their other work was done, creating their own unique designs. **Lucy**, a slave in Texas, remembered, *"While they were quilting . . . they would sing and have lots of fun."* Slaves on one Georgia plantation followed the quilting with dancing and sweet potato pudding and honey cakes from the mistress. "On our place, the slaves had a regular band," recalled **Cora Gillam**, who grew up in Arkansas. "They would play for the dances. The folks would give quiltings and after they got through, they would eat."

Women often stitched the phrase, "When you see this, remember me" onto their quilts. Unlike dishes washed and meals prepared, blankets lovingly made remained to tie friends and generations together, providing warmth and protection. People would be born, sleep, bear children, and die beneath these cherished works of art. Mothers passed designs

Good Housekeeping advised readers in 1888, "Each young girl should piece one quilt at least to carry away with her to her husband's home, and if her lot happens to be cast among strangers, as is often the case, the quilt when she unfolds it will . . . bring up a whole host of memories, of mother, sister, friend." This 1851 album quilt bears the signatures of many quilters.

It is easy to imagine pioneers as rugged individuals, accustomed to hard living. In fact, most gave up relatively comfortable circumstances to camp like this pioneer family, photographed in 1870.

and cloth to daughters, assigning them names that reflected their experiences—names like Rocky Road to Kansas and Arizona Cactus. A Massachusetts woman best summed it up in 1845 when she called quilts, "the hieroglyphs of women's lives."

THE WEST

"THE TIME THAT TRIED BOTH MEN['S] AND WOMEN'S SOULS": THE WESTWARD TRAIL

For women who headed west, quilts would become a physical reminder of the more comfortable lives that they left behind. Between 1840 and 1870, more than 250,000 people walked, drove animals, steered wagons, or pulled handcarts more than 2,000 miles to settle on the coasts of Oregon and California and points in between. Some hoped to strike it rich,

others to claim land. The Mormons fled to Utah and Idaho to escape religious persecution.

Prior to departure, a wife's workload doubled. It was her job to manufacture clothes, tents, wagon canvasses, oilcloths, blankets, soap, and candles and to stock up enough food to last the family for many months. When it came time to leave, it was often the belongings that she treasured most—the dishes, the feather bed, or the rocking chair—that had to be left behind.

Both men and women drove wagons. **Mary Jane Mount** recalled, "Mother drove the team . . . yoking and unyoking in addition to her other duties. One of her oxen would never learn to hold back, and when going downhill she had to hold his horn with one hand and pound his nose with the other to keep him from running into the wagon ahead of him." If the family owned a cow, they hung the cream in a barrel on the side of the wagon. By nightfall, the bouncing of the wagon had made butter. Sometimes women managed to crochet or write in their diaries while guiding the oxen. **Lucy Cooke** was proud of having rolled out pie dough on the seat next to her.

Women also walked to lighten the load, to help with the animals, and to keep an eye on their children. They gathered fuel for fires along the way. One woman recalled that on nice days, friends *"visited from wagon to wagon or . . . spent an hour walking, ever westward, and talking over our home life back in 'the states' telling of the loved ones left behind; voicing our hopes for the future . . . and even whispering a little friendly gossip."*

Wives were up before 5 AM to make fires and cook while husbands rounded up and yoked animals. Depending on the weather, the terrain, and the health of the travelers, a wagon train could cover as many as twenty miles in a day or as few as three. Though traveling exhausted everyone, women's hardest work took place while the men rested—at noon, and at the end of the day. **Henrietta Williams** wrote in her diary:

> They knew that I was no cook, but left that job for me.... I put the dutch oven on to heat...made a pie of dried apples, putting it into the oven...and turned toward the wagon...A nice cow sneaked up and helped herself to the pie and sneaked off.... I had a hard time cooking the biscuits as I was jumping in and out of the wagon, climbing over the provision box, watching my baby girl and getting what [my husband] wanted as it was his misfortune never to find anything he was looking for.

Accustomed to cast-iron stoves, most women had to learn how to cook outdoors in any kind of weather. They also tried to liven up the monotony of beans, coffee, flat bread, and salted meat with precious preserves and dried fruit.

Female relationships provided vital emotional and logistical support. On treeless plains, friends held their skirts out to shield one another while using the toilet. They also cared for one another through childbirth. One out of every five women on the trail was in some stage of pregnancy. Though sympathetic husbands did what they could, wives hoped that other women would be nearby when labor pains began. **Caroline Findley** described a birth during "a terrific storm." The wagons were flooded and, *"Within a tent...were nurses wading around a bedside placed upon chairs ministering to a mother and her newborn babe."* This scene must have worried Findley, who was expecting her first child.

While men kept the train moving and performed guard duty at night, women struggled to maintain the well-being of their families. Every week or two, trains stopped for a day to do laundry. In the meantime, mothers dried and reused soiled baby diapers. The most basic child care was challenging. **Sarah Moulding**, three years old at the time, remembered being constantly thirsty and hating the warm muddy water. Also, "The baby cried a good deal of the time from being bounced around in the wagon so much, and we two girls often cried in sympathy with him." Mothers were thankful if they had daughters old enough to help.

In 1856 **Elizabeth Stewart** wrote, *"They talk about the times that tried men['s] souls as if this were not the time that tried both men['s] and women's souls."* During the summer, nights were cold while days were scorching. Sunburned travelers breathed dust and battled biting insects. After storms or crossing rivers, wet clothes and supplies were difficult to dry. "Tis a perfect mud-hole, beds and children completely soaked," wrote **Velina Williams** in her diary.

Though guidebooks assured travelers that the trek could be done in four months, it often took as many as eight. The most treacherous part of the trail

Adolescent daughters were more likely than their mothers to see the trip west as an adventure. Allowed more freedom than at home, girls danced in the evening, enjoyed friendships with young men, and even held tea parties. Numerous young brides also headed west immediately after getting married.

Artist **Minerva Teichert** honored her Mormon pioneer heritage by painting *Washday on the Plains* in the living room of her Wyoming ranch home in 1938.

lay near the end when travelers were weary and low on supplies. Some waded through snow by the end of their journey.

Death stalked the westward trail. Accidents were common. Children fell from wagons and were run over, men drowned while guiding wagons across rivers, and women died giving birth. Already compromised by exhaustion and constant exposure to the elements, whole families succumbed to cholera, typhoid, measles, dysentery, and smallpox. On February 1, 1847, **Elizabeth Geer**, mother of seven children, noted in her journal, *"Rain all day. This day my dear husband, my last remaining friend, died."* Husbands buried wives, wives buried husbands, parents buried children, and children buried parents. Many women recorded in their diaries the number of graves and dead animals they had passed during the day, wondering when it would be their turn.

Later in life, **Mary Goble**, a fifteen-year-old member of an ill-fated Mormon handcart company, described arriving in the Salt Lake valley. She had already buried three siblings, her feet were frozen, and her mother lay dead in the wagon. A surgeon amputated her toes while women dressed her mother for the grave. Her soulful question, "Oh how did we stand it?" spoke for the suffering of thousands. Yet, perhaps the most extraordinary part of this story is that many people survived the trek and went on to live full and eventful lives in the West.

THE BORDERLANDS

By the 1840s, American families were settling in areas outside the United States. Much of what would become Texas, New Mexico, California, and other Western states was Mexican territory. Originally created as frontier missions by the Spanish, borderland settlements had by now become villages and ranches peopled by mestizos (Mexicans of mixed Spanish and Indian blood) and their Indian servants.

In this hierarchical society, men ruled their wives and children and chose husbands for their adolescent daughters. Though trained in the domestic arts, few girls learned to read or write.

This is an American artist's somewhat romantic view of mestizo women and men of California in 1850.

Even so, Mexican women were allowed to buy and sell land and cattle, and could sue for damages in court. The law also required fathers to divide inheritances equally between sons and daughters.

Married mestizo women had social freedoms that amazed settlers. They entertained in style, hosting fiestas that lasted for days. They also gambled and attended horse races and bullfights. Settlers frequently commented on the beauty and charm of mestizo women. However, settlers also mistook cultural differences for immorality. Many Mexican women, in turn, regarded the newcomers with well-founded suspicion.

Anxious to expand its territory even further, the U.S. government used a border skirmish in 1846 as an excuse to declare war on Mexico. In old age, **Maria Antonia Rodriguez Soberanes** recalled, *"We Californians in 1846 owned every inch of soil in this country, and our conquerors took away from us the greater part."*

A number of women found ways to resist the invasion. "The conquest of California wasn't liked by the Californians, least of all the women," remembered **Maria Angustias De La Guerra Ord**. After a skirmish between American and Mexican soldiers, a fellow Californio arrived in the rain asking her to hide a wounded soldier. Ord had given birth only a few days before, her husband was out of town, and her brothers were being held by the enemy—but she agreed. When Americans came to search her house that night, she hid the soldier in a couch and placed her sleeping newborn baby on top of him. The Americans left empty-handed and two days later the soldier thanked Ord for saving his life and rode away dressed like a woman.

Mexico lost the war. In 1848, the two sides signed the Treaty of Guadalupe Hidalgo, in which Mexico ceded more than one-third of its land to America. Suddenly, thousands of women who had not moved found themselves American citizens. The region was quickly overrun by "Anglo" settlers who used American law to seize property and reduce Spanish speakers to second-class status. U.S. law continued to allow Mexican women to inherit land in their own names, but in many other ways they were enveloped by a new culture that offered few rights to women of any race. Some married Anglo men, hoping that their wealth coupled with white political power would provide security. The transition to American rule initiated a gradual loss of culture for Mexican women.

"MY MOTHER'S LODGE"

For Native Americans, who had populated the West long before Anglos or Mexicanos, this loss had long been underway. Between 1830 and 1860, Indian nations were squeezed into ever smaller spaces between the frontier settlements of the West and the burgeoning population of the East. One of these was the Hidatsa. Before settlers arrived, the Hidatsa of North Dakota lived in permanent villages where women farmed and men hunted. Born in 1840, **Waheenee** described her childhood:

My mother's lodge—for an earth lodge belonged to the woman who built it—was more carefully constructed than most winter lodges. . . . I learned to cook deer skins, embroider, sew with awl and sinew, and cut and make moccasins, clothing, and tent covers. . . My father. . . helped my mothers and me when we had hard work to do. . . . For my industry in dressing skins, my clan aunt, Sage, gave me a woman's belt. . . . To wear a woman's belt was an honor.

The physical labor performed by many Native American women brought them power and respect within the community. As noted by Waheenee, the lodge a woman built was her own, as was the corn that she grew. Settlers, who thought of farming and trading as a man's job, noted with surprise that it was Indian women who were responsible for trading crops.

Though nations differed widely in their traditions, many, such as the Dakota and Delaware, allowed women to retain their own belongings at marriage, and leave husbands if they chose. According to **Sarah Winnemucca**, a Piute man was expected to do all the work during his wife's last month of pregnancy. "If he does not do his part in the care of the child, he is considered an outcast." She also wrote that Piute men listened to the counsel of their wives. "It means something when the women promise their fathers to make their husbands *themselves*. They faithfully keep with them in all the dangers they can share. They not only take care of their children together, but they do everything together; and when they grow blind. . . they take sweet care of one another. Marriage is a sweet thing when people love each other. *If women could go into your Congress I think justice would soon be done to the Indians."*

Disruption and displacement wreaked havoc on these communities. Groups that rebelled against government control and the influx of settlers—Seminoles, Sioux, Navaho, and others—were brutally repressed. Already weakened by European diseases and enslavement to Spanish-speaking colonists, California's Native American population was devastated by the Gold Rush. In only fifteen years, disease and violence claimed the lives of an estimated 115,000 Modoc, Hupa, and others.

As encounters with settlers deprived Indians of their lands, they also undermined almost every aspect of life. Whites tried to dictate the way Native American groups governed themselves, and to make Indian husbands and wives behave like whites. These efforts frequently eroded women's traditional sources of influence. In old age, Waheenee told an interviewer, *"I cannot forget our old ways. Often in summer I rise at daybreak and steal out to the cornfields, and as I hoe the corn, I sing to it, as we did when I was young. No one cares for our corn songs now."*

RESISTING SLAVERY

The movement west did more than generate conflict between settlers and the people they found there. It also added new fire to the debate over slavery and whether it should be allowed in the territories. In 1850, four million Americans were treated as property. Under this system, black families could be separated forever, girls sexually violated, and women and men maimed and killed with no recourse to law. Denied even the most basic rights, slaves continued to create meaningful lives.

DARING ESCAPES

Aside from armed rebellion, no resistance to slavery was riskier than trying to escape. Running away carried extra peril for a mother with children. According to one sympathetic observer, "None of

"My idea of slavery is, that it is one of the blackest, the wickedest things everywhere in the world. **When you tell them the truth, they whip you to make you lie.** I have taken more lashes for this, than for any other thing, because I would not lie." —**Nancy Howard,** escaped slave, 1855

The Ride for Liberty, The Fugitive Slaves, painted by Eastman Johnson in 1862. The realities of attempting escape were much harsher than depicted in this painting.

these can walk so far or so fast as scores of men who are constantly leaving." This, and the fact that female slaves had fewer opportunities to leave their plantations and learn about the surrounding areas, meant that women remained behind while husbands, brothers, and sons made the break for freedom. A few weighed the price and opted to go. While some left children behind, there is evidence that they more often took their children with them.

Mrs. John Little was seventeen when she and her husband walked from Tennessee to Chicago. "My shoes gave out before many days," she recalled. "Then I wore my husband's old shoes till they were used up. Then we came barefooted all the way to Chicago. *My feet were blistered and sore and my ankles swollen but I had to keep on. There was something behind me driving me."* Fugitives slogged their way through swamps and forests, stowed away in boats, and hid in barns and smokehouses. They faced daunting obstacles: vicious dogs, slave patrols, thorny underbrush, marshes, hunger and exposure, rivers and streams, insects and snakes, extreme temperatures, miles and miles of walking, and the constant fear of recapture.

Although an escaping slave needed courage, creativity was also useful. In 1848, **Ellen Craft** and her husband escaped from Georgia by pretending to be master and slave. Light enough to pass for white, Ellen posed as a sickly gentleman going north for treatment. With a scarf around her jaw to hide her lack of a beard, large spectacles, and a sling on her arm to mask her illiteracy, she booked passage from Georgia on various trains, coaches, and boats. William, whose extra wages paid for the tickets, pretended to be her dutiful slave. Another slave, **Lear Green**, eighteen and "in the condition of becoming a mother," mailed herself in a wooden sailor's chest from Baltimore to Philadelphia in 1857.

Some women, like **Harriet Jacobs**, fooled their pursuers by remaining nearby. Afraid for her children, Jacobs spent seven long years hidden away in the tiny attic crawl space of her grandmother's house. In her cramped cell, she wrote letters to her master and, with the help of friends, had them mailed to him from Northern states. She did not go north until she had made arrangements for her son and daughter.

What One Woman Did

"Slavery Is the Next Thing to Hell"

When **Harriet Tubman** (born Araminta Ross) was six, her owners hired her out to a neighbor who beat her severely. She later recalled that at night she would weep, thinking, "if I could only get home and get in my mother's bed." But her mother couldn't protect her or her siblings. Tubman's two older sisters were sold, one leaving her own children behind. So crossing into freedom in 1849 was a bittersweet experience for her. She had no one to welcome her because all those she loved were still in

Harriet Tubman (on the left) with some members of her family; her adopted daughter is by her side and her husband is seated next to her.

bondage. She later told audiences, *"Now I've been free, I know what a dreadful condition slavery is. I have seen hundreds of escaped slaves, but I never saw one who was willing to go back and be a slave. . . . I think slavery is the next thing to hell."* Tubman wasn't about to leave her family there.

After working for two years to earn money, she returned to Maryland not once, but at least thirteen times to rescue family members and others. Her three brothers were for sale when she stole them away on Christmas 1854. Within the year, Tubman had rescued seventeen brothers, sisters, and friends. She later successfully returned for her parents who were in their eighties.

Harriet Tubman defied many of the prejudices of her time about blacks, about women, and about education. Her quick wit, ingenuity, courage, and confidence saved her and her fellow travelers from many close calls. She hired people to take down "wanted" signs and threatened to shoot anyone in her group who tried to turn back. When traveling

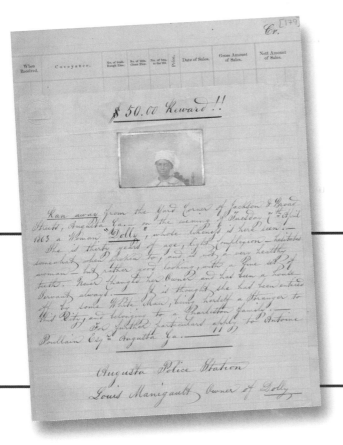

In this unusual reward poster, a Georgia slave master provided a photo of his house slave **Dolly**, describing her as thirty years old, with a light complexion, attractive, with a fine set of teeth.

with small children, she carried them in a sling and dosed them with opium so that they would not cry. Tubman also prayed constantly for guidance. In spite of a large bounty on her head, this woman who never learned to read or write outsmarted all who tried to catch her, helping an estimated 300 individuals escape slavery.

THE UNDERGROUND RAILROAD

Slaves relied heavily on free blacks to help them get away and stay away. By 1860, 225,000 free blacks lived in the North. Fugitives who could disappear into these communities stood a better chance of remaining free. Domestic workers, able to move freely about cities, became the eyes and ears of the resistance. They kept a close eye on slave owners and slave catchers. Sometimes they abducted and freed slaves who were traveling with their owners.

Free women also took part in a number of public scuffles in which fugitive slaves were rescued from heavily armed slave catchers. In Cincinnati and Boston, African American women drove slave catchers from their neighborhoods with rocks and rolling pins. Free blacks created partnerships with

THE PARTING "Buy us too."

Abolitionists used graphic images such as this 1863 collector's card to show the evils of slavery.

white allies to provide shelter and aid for fugitives. The network of people dedicated to helping escaped slaves became known as the Underground Railroad.

The resistance was carried out in the middle of people's everyday lives, and under the noses of suspicious neighbors. The Lewis sisters were more than a little amused to hear one of their proslavery neighbors remark that "there used to be a pretty brisk trade of running off [slaves] but there was not much of it done now." Only the week before, **Mariann**, **Grace**, and **Elizabeth Lewis** had moved forty fugitives through their home. In spite of neighbors who were hostile to abolition, they provided an important stop on the Delaware/Pennsylvania Underground Railroad.

It took the joint efforts of women and men to keep the Underground Railroad running. Men usually transported fugitives from point to point—an extremely dangerous activity—but women provided for their physical needs. Escaped slaves often arrived underdressed and frostbitten, starved, ill, and emotionally traumatized. On top of family responsibilities (and working outside jobs if they were free black women), women took on the extra load of feeding, clothing, and nursing escaped slaves.

Did you know?

Oral history accounts passed down in families suggest that **quilts made by black women were used to convey messages on the Underground Railroad.** Quilts could be hung in plain view, over clotheslines or out of windows, without exciting suspicion. Stories suggest that various patterns had hidden meanings that could be "read" by escaping slaves, advising them what to do next.

"NOW LET WOMEN SPEAK": ABOLITION

By 1840, the abolitionist movement was in full swing with a wide range of leaders presiding over various factions. For whites, abolition remained a lonely and unpopular stance. Many Americans regarded abolitionists as dangerously radical. Even more threatening, one antislavery faction actually encouraged the active participation of women. Abolitionists such as **Mary Ann Shadd**, Abby Foster, Lucy Stone, and Lucretia Mott toured, giving speeches.

Less visible, but crucial to the movement's success, were the ranks of rural and small-town women, both black and white, who sustained it over the course of more than thirty years. In spite of the disapproval of their communities, female abolitionists raised money, circulated petitions, voiced opinions, sewed clothes for escaped slaves, and lobbied lawmakers. Though unable to vote, they pressured political parties, went to rallies, and tried to influence their men. Some, especially middle-class blacks, threw themselves into educating African American children. Others bravely challenged church leaders who refused to take a stand against slavery.

In 1843, **Rhoda Bement** stopped her pastor on the street and demanded to know why he did not announce abolitionist lectures to his congregation. She continued the discussion in the halls of the church. As crowds gathered, Pastor Bogue became defensive, calling her "impolite" and her actions "improper." But Bement would not back down. Instead, she was excommunicated for suggesting that her minister was a hypocrite.

CAUTION!!

COLORED PEOPLE OF BOSTON, ONE & ALL,

You are hereby respectfully CAUTIONED and advised, to avoid conversing with the Watchmen and Police Officers of Boston,

For since the recent ORDER OF THE MAYOR & ALDERMEN, they are empowered to act as KIDNAPPERS AND Slave Catchers,

And they have already been actually employed in KIDNAPPING, CATCHING, AND KEEPING SLAVES. Therefore, if you value your LIBERTY, and the Welfare of the Fugitives among you, Shun them in every possible manner, as so many HOUNDS on the track of the most unfortunate of your race.

Keep a Sharp Look Out for KIDNAPPERS, and have TOP EYE open.

APRIL 24, 1851.

Elmira Swett registered her disapproval of her pastor's stance on slavery by loudly clicking her knitting needles together during his sermons. Another woman refused to pay rent on her church pew after being criticized for sharing it with a black member. Instead, she brought a stool from home on which to sit during meetings. Many abolitionists withdrew their church memberships with a letter of dissent to the congregation.

Most Americans believed that only men should express opinions in public. Women who challenged this were criticized for unladylike behavior, or worse, accused of loose morals. Yet, female abolitionists defended their actions as being supremely ladylike, arguing that women's natural goodness and sympathy made them guardians of morality. Who better than mothers and daughters to remind the nation that slavery was an abominable sin? One newspaper admonished in 1845,

"Say not that it is man's business to destroy slavery. I know man ought to do it—he should have done it a long time ago. . . . Now let woman speak, and it shall be done."

Women gained practical and organizational experience from their activities.

THE FUGITIVE SLAVE ACT Ironically, it was a law that strengthened slaveholders' powers that caused public sentiment in the North to shift in favor of abolition. The Fugitive Slave Act, passed in 1850, severely punished anyone who aided escaped slaves. Now slave catchers could cross into nonslave states to capture and return fugitives, no matter how long they had been free. The law required Northerners to help slave owners retrieve escaped slaves. Free blacks could more easily be kidnapped and sold. An estimated 15,000 fled to Canada, while others emigrated to England or Liberia. Though the harshness of the law generated new debate, it would take enormous bloodshed to finally put the question of slavery to rest.

ARTS IN THE SPOTLIGHT

"I THOUGHT OF THE SLAVE MOTHERS": HARRIET BEECHER STOWE

"Is this the little woman who made this great war?" Abraham Lincoln is said to have remarked when he first met Harriet Beecher Stowe in 1862. In a time when numerous women were writing for a popular market, Stowe was arguably the most important female writer. Her famous 1852 novel, *Uncle Tom's Cabin,* exposed the evils of slavery and caused a stir across the nation, gaining praise from Northern abolitionists and scorn from Southerners.

Harriet Beecher, born in 1811, was one of eleven children of the famous minister and abolitionist Lyman Beecher and his wife, **Roxanne Foote Beecher**. Married at twenty-five, Stowe's household eventually included seven children.

Stowe began writing out of financial necessity. Her stories and articles for magazines and the gift-book market were religious, sentimental tales and children's stories of New England life. Her subject matter changed after Congress passed the Fugitive Slave Act in 1850. Having helped a runaway slave earlier in her life, she realized that were she to do it again, she would be arrested and fined.

Isabella Jones Beecher, Stowe's sister-in-law, urged her to action, writing, *"Hattie, . . . If I could use a pen as you can, I would write something that will make this whole nation feel what an accursed thing slavery is."* One of her children recalled the effect of

In the mid-1800s, a growing number of female writers, sarcastically dubbed **"scribbling women,"** by Nathaniel Hawthorne, made a good living producing sentimental novels for avid female readers. The novels' heroines were most often virtuous young women who, through their own goodness, triumphed over the evils of the world. **Susan Warner, Elizabeth Stuart Phelps, Mrs. E. D. E. N. Southworth**, and others pursued writing careers while following social rules requiring women to stay at home.

the letter. He claimed that his mother rose to her feet, crushed the letter, and exclaimed, "I will write something. I will if I live."

With household help from her sister, Catharine Beecher, Stowe wrote amid the chaos of her young family: "a table with flour, rolling-pin, ginger, and lard on one side, a dresser with eggs, pork, and beans, and various cooking utensils on the other, near her an oven heating." She later wrote to one of her children, *"I well remember the winter you were a baby and I was writing Uncle Tom's Cabin. . . . I remember many a night weeping over you as you lay sleeping beside me, and I thought of the slave mothers whose babes were torn from them."* Reading the story aloud to her household as she wrote sent her children into "convulsions of weeping."

Uncle Tom's Cabin, published March 20, 1852, riveted the nation. Sales jumped from 10,000 in the first week to 300,000 the first year. Acting companies began putting the story on stage almost immediately. One woman wrote that she could not

LITTLE EVA CONVERTING TOPSY.

"In that moment a ray of real belief, a ray of heavenly love, had penetrated the darkness of her heathen soul."

An illustration from *Uncle Tom's Cabin.*

"restrain an almost hysterical sobbing for an hour after I laid my head upon my pillow. I thought I was a thoroughgoing abolitionist before, but your book has awakened so strong a feeling of indignation and of compassion, that I seem never to have had any feeling on this subject till now. . . . This storm of feeling . . . haunts me."

THE CIVIL WAR BEGINS

"THE MOST EXTRAORDINARY MIXTURE OF FEELING"

After Abraham Lincoln won the presidential election of 1860, South Carolina seceded from the Union, followed by other Southern states. On April 12, 1861, Confederate troops fired on a government fort in Charleston harbor, South Carolina. The Civil War had begun. Southern women encouraged their men to enlist and young belles hurriedly wed departing soldiers. Lemuella Brickell wrote in her diary, "We will conquer. God is always on the right side!"

In the North, **Jane Woolsey** noted, "There is the most extraordinary mixture of feeling with everyone—so much resistless enthusiasm and yet so much sadness." Northern streets thronged with men anxious to enlist—afraid that the war would be over if they did not hurry. In Boston, "windows were flung up; and women leaned out into the rain waving flags and handkerchiefs." Young ladies in Ohio offered to enlist and leave their bonnets and skirts for the men "who lacked the manliness to defend the flag of their country." For the next four years, Americans would kill one another with a vengeance.

DIVIDED FAMILIES The Civil War "caused the separation of hitherto devoted families," recalled **Adelaide Smith**. *"Fathers and sons were arrayed against each other, some in hate, some in sorrow; and even mothers, wives and sisters shared this unholy animosity."* Feelings of hostility ran deep and bitter. Even the first family was not immune. Though **Mary Todd Lincoln** had grown up in a slaveholding family in Kentucky, the wives of Southern congressmen

This March 23, 1861 newspaper cover displays "the superb costumes of distinguished ladies" at President Lincoln's inaugural ball, revealing nothing of the nation's brewing troubles.

Mary Todd Lincoln sometime between 1860 and 1865.

snubbed her as a traitor, packing their bags to leave Washington even as the Lincolns arrived. But Northerners also distrusted Mary Lincoln. Northern newspapers accused her of being a spy, and her sisters "the toast of southerners." When the president offered Mary's brother-in-law a commission in the U.S. Army, he refused and instead became a Confederate general. Her brother,

three half-brothers, and two brothers-in-law also joined the Confederate Army. Of the six, four died in battle. Torn between love for her family and loyalty to her husband, the First Lady managed to please no one. Though more visible than many women, her plight was a common one.

THE REALITIES OF WAR Neither side was prepared to wage war. Military hospitals and ambulance services did not exist. Because basic supplies were lacking and frequently failed to reach those who needed them, wounded soldiers often lay bloody and exposed to the elements for hours, if not days. Even able-bodied soldiers succumbed to typhoid, malaria, and dysentery as military camps became breeding grounds for illness. The public was alarmed to hear that their fathers, sons, and brothers were dying on filthy pallets of straw, too weak to cook their own food or haul their own drinking water.

"ANGELS OF MERCY"

What was a woman to do? How could she assist in a society that believed ladies were too delicate and

> *Before the war,* **Varina Davis,** *who was to become the first lady of the Confederacy, was at the center of Washington, DC's social circles. As Southerners began their exodus from the capital, she told a friend, "I would rather remain in Washington and be kicked about, than go South and be Mrs. President."*

emotionally unstable to enter the "masculine" realm of war? The answer seemed to lie in her presumed natural female compassion. Why not extend her domestic and nurturing skills into the public sphere by providing for the needs of soldiers?

BENEVOLENT WORK Soldiers' aid societies sprang up almost overnight. Women rolled bandages, knitted socks, sewed clothing, tents, flags, and blankets, raised money, and gathered foodstuffs. Two weeks into the war, "ninety-two of the most respected ladies" of New York, led by physicians Elizabeth and Emily Blackwell, founded the Women's Central Relief Association (WCRA) to coordinate groups and distribute supplies.

Though the WCRA did a brisk and efficient business, colleague Henry Bellows quietly obtained the government's permission to create the U.S. Sanitary Commission (USSC), a private organization that would do the same job. Having taken control, he and others reduced the WCRA to a branch of the Commission and dismissed the Blackwell sisters.

Bellows wanted ladies to supply homemade goods; men would do the rest. But ladies' aid societies

Did you know?

When the war began, soldiers needed uniforms, but there was no official pattern. Women made up their own designs for soldiers' uniforms, resulting in such a variety of colors and styles that it was difficult for soldiers in battle to distinguish friend from foe.

did not want high-placed gentlemen meddling in their affairs. In Iowa, one group challenged the Commission to *"roll up their sleeves and 'pitch in' . . . or get out of the way and not stand as an obstruction in the way of the women of Iowa, who would do this thing up much better without them."* During the war,

Nurses and officers of the U.S. Sanitary Commission in 1864.

women's groups produced and donated an estimated $50 million worth of goods.

Though the South never had an equivalent to the USSC, Southern women also provided aid, a task made more difficult by a blockade and the destruction of farms and factories.

> ### Did you know?
>
> The Confederate ship the *S.S. Charleston* was called "The Ladies Gunboat" because it was paid for by women's donations of jewelry and family heirlooms.

NURSES Some women wanted to help soldiers more directly. When southerner **Kate Cumming** left home to become a nurse in 1862, she wrote, *"As I had never been where there is a large army, and had never seen a wounded man . . . I could not help feeling a little nervous at the prospect of now seeing both."* Yet within hours she was bathing the wounds of soldiers who lay so close together that she was afraid she would step on them.

To be a Civil War nurse, almost all a person needed was good intentions. Women were believed to be natural caretakers; however, it was one thing to privately nurse family members, and another to venture into public to care for severely wounded strangers. Professional female nurses were a new and somewhat unsettling reality.

Though the public worried about their respectability, and military officers often balked at sharing their space with nurses, the growing volume of wounded and dying men made them vital. Charged with creating a federal nursing corps, reformer Dorothea Dix steered clear of scandal; she advertised for candidates who were at least thirty years of age, plain-looking, hard-working, and strong enough to turn over a patient single-handedly. Hoop skirts were out of the question. **Cornelia Hancock**, twenty-three and rosy-cheeked, was rejected by Dix because, *"In those days it was considered indecorous for angels of mercy to appear otherwise than gray-haired and spectacled."* Dix's nurses served in newly created military hospitals.

Cleaning wounds, changing dressings, assisting with amputations, and emptying bedpans was not for the faint of heart. Men arrived ragged, faint, caked in filth, and missing limbs. Nurses tried to buffer soldiers from the surgeons whom they felt were too gruff. Imagining their own family members in the same circumstances, they often defied doctors to make sure their patients were cared for in ways that they thought proper. Nurses offered emotional support, wrote final letters for soldiers, and closed the eyes of the numerous men and boys who expired in their care. Many also succumbed to the same illnesses as their patients.

Only Catholic nuns had nursing training and experience. In a predominantly Protestant country, nuns were viewed with curiosity, but military surgeons sought them out for their skill, adaptability, and vows never to marry. During the war, almost 600 nuns braved the horrors of the battlefield to nurse soldiers on both sides of the conflict. Surrounded by unbelievable suffering, **Sister Agatha** in South Carolina wrote, **"My heart grew sick and I was compelled to whisper to myself again and again . . . 'take it easy.'"**

Have you ever heard of . . . Mary Walker, M.D.?

Wearing trousers under a shortened dress, Walker served unofficially as a military surgeon after many battles. When she was captured as a prisoner of war in 1863, one Confederate captain sneered, **"We were all amused and disgusted too at the sight of a *thing* that nothing but the debased and depraved Yankee nation could produce—'a female doctor.'**... I was hoping that the General... would have had her dressed in a homespun frock and bonnet and sent back to the Yankee lines, or put in a lunatic asylum." Though the government never did award Walker a military commission, at the end of the war the army presented her with a Medal of Honor, which she wore every day for the rest of her life.

Some women became nurses by joining regiments with their husbands. Fifteen-year-old **Susie King Taylor**, a freed slave, signed on to wash clothes for her husband's black regiment. In addition, she nursed them, taught them to read, and even cleaned their guns. She later wrote, *"It seems strange how our aversion to seeing suffering is overcome in war,—how we are able to see the most sickening sights . . . and instead of turning away . . . we hurry to bind up their wounds, and press cool water to their parched lips."* Some women found themselves caring for strangers when the war came to them and their homes and barns were turned into makeshift infirmaries. As wounded soldiers poured into Richmond in 1862, Southern ladies created "roadside hospitals" because the hospitals were so crowded that soldiers were dying in the street.

Clara Barton, who would go on to found the American Red Cross, decided that the most crucial time for soldiers was "anywhere between the bullet and the hospital." Barton obtained permission to take wagons and supplies to the front lines so that she could step in as soon as the battle was over.

Some officers resented Barton's presence, but Dr. James Dunn wrote after one battle, "If heaven ever sent out an . . . angel, she must be one. Her assistance was so timely." She often worked for days at a stretch, stopping rarely to sleep or eat. After the battle of Antietam, Barton wrote, *"I wrung the blood*

Clara Barton, Civil War nurse, and founder of the American Red Cross.

from the bottom of my clothing, before I could step, for the weight about my feet." The soldiers loved her and often returned later to thank her for saving their lives. In addition to helping at the battlefield and gathering supplies, Barton lobbied for the fair treatment of black soldiers. When the war ended, she made herself central to the effort of accounting for the dead and reuniting the living.

Much like Clara Barton, **Mary Ann Bickerdyke** stepped uninvited into the war zone. Nominated by her town to distribute supplies to its regiment, the no-nonsense widow was appalled by what she found. Over the objections of officers who insisted that women did not belong in camp, she stayed on for the rest of the war. Bickerdyke spun like a whirlwind into camps, scrubbing, cooking, and organizing. When Union General Ulysses Grant's army moved South, she went, too. Later, she accompanied General William Sherman's troops in their march to the sea.

In a photo titled "Camp of the 31st Pennsylvania Infantry," we can only guess at this woman's role in the camp. Are she and her children (and dog) visiting their father in the camp, or are they among the great numbers of women and children who traveled with the army?

General Sherman and General Grant were her friends, but Bickerdyke's greatest affection was reserved for the common foot soldiers. When one colonel's wife complained about Bickerdyke, General Sherman told her, ***"You've picked the one person around here who outranks me. If you want to lodge a complaint against her, you'll have to take it to President Lincoln."***

Bickerdyke jealously guarded supplies for wounded soldiers. After repeatedly warning hospital staff to leave the food for her patients, she laced stewed peaches with something that would make thieves vomit. She frequently ignored orders that she felt were not in the best interest of her soldiers. Bickerdyke informed one resistant doctor, "I guess you hadn't better get into a row with me, for whenever anybody does one of us always goes to the wall. And 'tain't never me!" In 1863 she went in search of milk and eggs for the soldiers. To everyone's surprise, she returned from Illinois to Memphis with "a bizarre procession of over a hundred cows and one thousand hens."

During the war, at least three thousand women worked professionally as nurses, and many more labored unofficially. Without their intervention, the death toll from the war would have been much higher than the already 620,000 dead. Nurses earned only $12 a month compared with the $169 paid to surgeons. Some refused pay because they felt that receiving wages implied that caring for soldiers was a job rather than a selfless calling. Yet even those who did not seek to challenge their place in society were changed by the experience.

THE HOME FRONTS

THE NORTH As the war raged on, most women remained at home to manage farms, run businesses, and raise children. Confederate and Union border states experienced the conflict firsthand as battling armies sprawled across their lands. Poor women lost their breadwinners as the government enabled wealthy men to pay others to go to war in their places.

The government responded by temporarily opening a number of new jobs to widows and orphans, hiring them as clerks and copyists, money cutters and telegraph clerks. Soldiers' families flocked

Women filling cartridges and men inserting powder at the U.S. arsenal at Watertown, Massachusetts.

to factories. The sudden availability of so many new workers depressed wages. At the same time, the price of many goods doubled. Rent increased by 20 percent. It seemed to many that the conflict was "a rich man's war, but a poor man's fight."

To fight for women's rights during such a time appeared unpatriotic. Women's rights advocates Lucy Stone, Elizabeth Cady Stanton, Susan Anthony, and others turned their efforts to emancipation. While Lincoln claimed that the war was about preserving the Union, they declared that they would support the war only if it was about putting an end to slavery. Together they formed the Women's National Loyal League and collected more than 400,000 signatures petitioning for the emancipation of slaves everywhere in the United States. They hoped that this loyalty to their abolitionist colleagues and to their country would be repaid following the war.

THE SOUTH Suffering became particularly acute in the South. **Harriet Perry**'s experiences reflected those of thousands of women as she bid farewell to her young soldier husband. Perry's letters describe the antics of their two-year-old daughter, who donned her bonnet and announced that she was off to see her daddy. She drew a circle at the top of one damp page where the child had planted kisses. Soon after Perry gave birth to her second child in 1863, her lively toddler became sick and died. Within months, her two brothers were killed in battle. In the fall of 1864, Perry became a widow. Her losses, though devastating, were not unique.

Women tried to maintain a semblance of order and family life as Union blockades and the needs of the army led to shortages of food, clothing, and

On April 2, 1863, **Mary Jackson** took matters into her own hands. After the governor of Virginia refused to allow soldiers' families to buy food at set government prices, she and a group of angry women led a riot. One thin girl informed an onlooker, **"We celebrate our right to live. We are starving. As soon as enough of us get together we are going to the bakery and each of us will take a loaf of bread. That is little enough for the government to give us after it has taken all our men."** Soldiers' wives looted stores and warehouses until troops arrived to stop them.

Living behind Confederate lines did not necessarily make one a Confederate. Tucked away in a Quaker pocket of Virginia, sisters **Lizzie** (24) and **Lida Dutton** (19) and their friend **Sarah Steer** (26) engaged in the "hazardous undertaking" of writing a pro-Union newspaper. Between May 1864 and April 1865, the *Waterford News* commented on the war's effects on their community and assured readers that "from this remote portion of Dixie's land the prayers of many men and women are ascending for the army of the Potomac." The female editors juxtaposed humorous comments about the lack of eligible marriage partners and the expanding muddy pothole in the middle of Second Street with more weighty news about battles, inflation, and troop movements. Lizzie, Lida, and Sarah were delighted to have their efforts praised by much larger publications (the *Waterford News* even found its way into the hands of Abraham Lincoln), and donated the proceeds to the U.S. Sanitary Commission.

household goods—shortages that reached crisis proportions by 1863. Even the formerly wealthy went hungry. In 1864, **Sally Taliaferro** scrawled in her diary, *"Very miserable and wretched. Can get nothing to eat and no clothes for anybody. Can hear nothing from my husband."* Mothers watched their children grow emaciated as food stores dwindled. Some ate only corn bread for days on end.

The price of cloth climbed more than 100 percent in two years, sending women to their attics in search of their grandmothers' spinning wheels and looms. They fashioned shoes from old leather and animal skins or went barefoot. "Behold my tender feet," joked former socialite **Clara Solomon**, "cased in crocodile skin, patent leather tipped, low quarter Boy's shoes, No.2!" Women like Solomon learned to make candles and soap. "In present phraseology, 'Confederate' means anything that is rough, unfinished, unfashionable, or poor," complained **Sarah Morgan**.

With so many other aspects of life in disarray, slave owners monitored their slaves nervously for signs of restlessness. Mistresses wanted to believe that their slaves were like loyal children who were happy with their lot. However, with the men gone, some slaves worked more slowly and eventually refused to do anything. When appeals to their sense of duty ceased to move them, **Susanna Clay** wrote, "We cannot exert any authority. I beg ours to do what little is done." Many slaves ran away.

Meanwhile, women wrote encouraging letters to the war front. They heard news of terrible battles, then waited in suspense for news of loved ones. Casualty lists were often incomplete. Sometimes the only way to know if family members had been hurt was to wander hospital wards, scanning the faces of wounded men. Some women traveled for days to nurse their wounded, only to find upon arrival that he was dead and buried. **Lucy Breckinridge** described one Louisiana gathering: *"There were so many ladies there, all dressed in deep mourning, that we felt as if we were at a convent and formed a sisterhood."*

Plunged into destitution and starvation, women petitioned the Confederate government to discharge their husbands, brothers, and sons, or at least grant them leave. But the government,

---

Have you ever heard of . . . Zerelda Samuel?

Married at seventeen and widowed three times, her long life was never the same after her young sons joined the Confederate army and began riding with the bloody Quantrill's Raiders. In 1863, Union militiamen attacked the Samuels' Missouri farm and tortured her mild-mannered husband nearly to death. Pregnant, and with small children in tow, Samuel was jailed and forced to sign a loyalty oath. After the war, her sons did not put down their guns. Instead they began robbing banks and trains. Who were her boys? Outlaws Frank and Jesse James.

---

fighting for survival, usually dismissed the letters out of hand. Public aid for the families of soldiers was insufficient and unevenly distributed. At least 104,000 Confederate soldiers deserted.

Many women in the path of invading armies fled, seeking refuge in cities where rent was ten times what it had been before the war. Others watched numbly as soldiers destroyed their homes, burned their crops, and slaughtered their livestock. Even the homes of slaves and poor whites were rarely spared. A ten-year-old slave in 1865, **Violet Guntharpe** later recalled that soldiers "ravaged the whole countryside," and left "de air full of de stink of dead carcasses and de sky black wid turkey buzzards." She described the slaves as unsure what to do next, white women weeping in hushed tones, and "de piccaninnies suckin' their thumbs for want of sumpin' to eat . . . Lots of chillun die."

SLAVES Life for slaves during the war was particularly difficult. In Mississippi, **Ann May** "could hear the white folks talking about the war coming. I know they was scared, and when the men folks went off to war they women sure did cry. We negroes stayed home and worked, then I had to go to the field too." Often separated from their men, who were pressed into Confederate service or who ran away to join Union forces, slave women debated whether to take their children and run. Those who stayed were burdened with the extra work of those who left.

As slave owners felt their power slipping away, many became more easily provoked and more violent in the punishment of their remaining slaves. Wives of Union soldiers were especially singled out for mistreatment. A wife pleaded, *"Send me some money as soon as you can for me and my child are almost naked."* However, the Union Army paid black soldiers only half the wages paid to white soldiers. Widows had even less chance of receiving any financial recompense.

As the war progressed, more and more slave women and children fled across Union lines. In 1862, one elderly Georgia slave loaded a boat with twenty-two children and escaped down the Savannah River. Called "contrabands" by the government, the sheer number of escaped slaves overwhelmed the Union Army, who wanted no part of them. As Sherman crossed the South, their numbers swelled to 19,000. Smallpox and other infectious diseases spread like wildfire through contraband camps, where people already suffered from insufficient shelter, clothing, and food. Many died.

In some areas that had been deserted by land owners, former slaves remained and farmed for themselves. The most notable of these settlements were in the South Carolina Sea Islands. In another part of South Carolina, hundreds of women who called themselves "Combees" began their own colony where they grew peanuts, potatoes, and cotton. After the war, whites returned to reclaim the land.

"THE CHAP WHOM EVERYBODY LIKED SO WELL": SOLDIERS AND SPIES

Romance novels of the period frequently portrayed a heroine who accompanied her beloved into battle. As women sent men off to fight the Civil War, many declared that they wished they could go also. "O! If I was only a man!" insisted Sarah Morgan. "Then I could don the breeches, and slay them with a will." But ladies didn't fight wars. Or did they?

In fact, women disguised as men fought in every major battle of the war, as well as many minor ones. Though their numbers have been estimated at between 500 and 1,000, it is likely that many more took the secret to their graves. Female soldiers passed as beardless, adolescent boys. They performed guard duty, served as sharpshooters, scouted, carried messages, buried the dead, helped in makeshift hospitals, and shared other camp tasks with comrades who assumed that anything in pants must be male. Taken prisoner by Union soldiers, **Jane Perkins** informed her captors that "she could straddle a horse, jump a fence and kill a Yankee as well as any rebel."

Some women joined the army alone, but many more joined with husbands, lovers, brothers, and even fathers. **Martha Lindley**'s fellow soldiers never knew that "the chap whom everybody liked

"...they abuse me because you went away and say they will not take care of our children and do nothing but...beat me scandalously—Oh I never thought you would give me so much trouble as I have got to bear now. You ought not to have left me in the fix I am in and all these little helpless children to take care of."

—MARTHA, a slave, wrote to her Union soldier husband, 1863

In war, *contraband* usually refers to the goods that are seized by invading soldiers. During the Civil War, the term was also used for escaped slaves. This is a group of "contrabands" in Cumberland Landing, Virginia, in 1862.

so well, was not a handsome boy, but a brave and determined woman who loved her husband so well that she refused to be separated from him." Others joined out of patriotism, a desire for adventure, or to escape difficult family circumstances.

Shedding female manners allowed female soldiers the freedom to move about like a man and make more money than they could in any woman's occupation. Engaging in "manly" behaviors like drinking, swearing, fighting, and playing cards improved the disguise. **Rosetta Wakeman** wrote home, "I like to be a soldier very well," and commented in that she had marched 200 miles. In another letter, she boasted, "I have got so that I can drill just as well as any man there is in my

regiment." When she died, even the physician failed to note that she was a girl. In another case, officers were astonished when a corporal who had just been promoted for "gallant conduct" in the battle of Fredericksburg, Virginia, delivered a baby boy. One colonel joked, "What use have we for women, if soldiers in the army can give birth to children?"

Many female soldiers managed to hide their secret for years, if not the entire war. Some were found out when they were wounded, ill, or lay dead on the battlefield. One soldier noted, *"A single glance at her in her proper character leads me to wonder how I ever could have mistaken her for a man . . . except that no one thought of finding a woman in a soldier's dress."* Each time **Ella Reno** was discovered, she reenlisted somewhere else. Cuban-born **Loreta Velazquez** survived her stints as a Confederate soldier and a spy to write a best-selling, if disputed, account of her escapades, *The Woman in Battle*. Once discovered as female, the army usually sent women home. Their surprised comrades often complimented them as hard workers, good friends, and fierce fighters.

The Civil War ended with a series of Confederate surrenders in 1865. The largest of these took place in **Nancy Bennitt**'s small North Carolina farmhouse. Bennitt was nearing seventy. In a world where grown children were the only real insurance for the elderly, she and her husband had lost both sons and their son-in-law to the war. On April 17, generals Sherman and Johnson and about 400 soldiers appeared on their doorstep, wishing to use their home to negotiate the surrender of 89,270 troops. Nancy Bennitt, her grandchildren, and her widowed daughter Eliza waited out the talks in the family cookhouse nearby. Though the war was finally over, their lives, like those of so many other women in the North and the South, were forever changed. In their final years, Nancy and James Bennitt would have to labor for others, as they and their fellow Americans worked to rebuild their lives and their nation.

Society's belief that ladies were especially moral and fragile made them **the perfect spies**. Arousing less suspicion than men, they hid messages and supplies (like medicine) under voluminous hoop skirts, in handbags, and in elaborate hairdos. If caught, authorities rarely imprisoned them for long, but released them with a warning. Those who gained the greatest notoriety were Confederates **Belle Boyd**, **Rose Greenhow**, and **Antonia Ford**. Union spies included **Pauline Cushman** and **Elizabeth Van Lew**. Pictured are Rose Greenhow and her daughter, imprisoned in Washington, DC.

CHAPTER 4

New Ways of Living
1865–1890

The brutal Civil War ended with General Robert E. Lee's final surrender at Appomattox on April 8, 1865. Not only was the war over, but all slaves were free. Word of emancipation, however, took time to reach everyone. On Christmas day in 1865, **Satira Turner** accidentally learned that she was no longer a slave. The young woman had been sold three times in her life, most recently onto an Arkansas plantation where she worked in the fields and in the house. When her husband escaped north to fight in the war, Turner stayed behind with her two small children. She was in the middle of cooking Christmas dinner for her master's family when she went out into the yard to get something. A man walking by asked if she knew about freedom. He informed her that she and all of the slaves were free. Turner didn't waste any time. She ran back to the house, gathered her meager belongings into a bundle, took her children by the hand, and left . . . with dinner still cooking.

Just as Turner emerged from slavery to cope with a new set of challenges, millions of other women negotiated through the changes wrought by the war. Northern industry was flourishing. Slaves were free. The South was

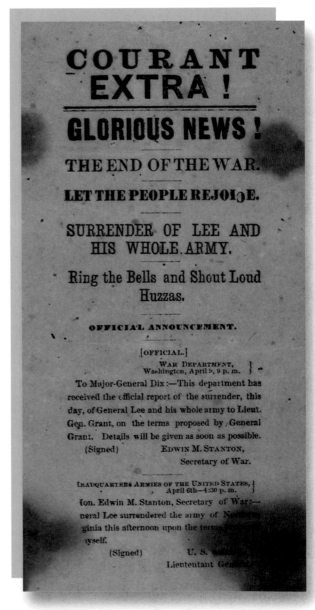

The end of the war is heralded by a Hartford, Connecticut, newspaper.

in shambles. The North had lost 360,000 fathers, husbands, and sons, the South 260,000. Southern survivors, black and white, rebuilt their lives in the midst of destitution, destruction, and disease. Thousands of war widows and their children struggled to survive in a society that believed females should not work for wages. A second wave of settlers headed west, and women's rights advocates returned to the battle for equality. War had forcibly reunited the country. Now it was time for Americans to get back to the business of living.

POSTWAR ADJUSTMENTS

THE MEANING OF FREEDOM

Across the South freed slaves celebrated with parades, picnics, and dancing. Some took revenge on cruel masters and overseers. Others, like Satira Turner, simply packed up and left. This stunned many white planters who believed that their slaves were devoted to them. As she left her plantation, a freedwoman named **Patience** explained, *"I must go, if I stay here I'll never know I'm free."* For generations black women had endured the terrible indignities of slavery: physical and sexual abuse, sale and separation from beloved family members, and toil without pay from birth to death. Now, joy of joy; they were free! But what did that mean?

For many, delight was quickly swallowed up in the battle to survive. Freedpeople desperately wanted land where they could build a house, grow food, and raise children. However, families were scattered and whites still owned the land. Seeing no other way to survive, some stayed on to work for their former owners. However, some whites evicted their former slaves. After insisting that his slaves gather the crop, **Harriet Miller**'s master "sot 'em all free and didn't give 'em anything. Dey left dar bare handed. Dey hed nothing." Without homes, money, adequate clothing, or food, these freedpeople took shelter wherever they could and foraged for food—blackberries, oysters, acorns, and even alligator meat. Many died of malnutrition, disease, and exposure.

FAMILIES Women toting children and bundles trudged the roads in search of family members. For those lucky enough to find or be found by kin, the postwar years were a time of reunion. Gus Feaster, who ran away during the war, had not seen his mother in six years. When she found him at the shop where he was working, they were overcome with emotion. *"Us was dat glad to lay eyes on one another dat we jest shouted fer joy,"* Feaster later remembered, *"and my ma tuck and smacked me wid her lips right on de mouth."*

Postwar reunions, however, could be bittersweet. Some couples, separated by sale, had

Advertisements for lost family members appeared in newspapers and magazines for years after the war. The *Afro-American,* an Ohio newspaper, reported with delight in 1885 that sixty-year-old **Ellen Johnson** had just found her mother, whom she had not seen in fifty years. The reunion not only brought together mother and daughter, but grandchildren, great-grandchildren, and great-great-grandchildren.

An 1866 *Harper's Weekly* drawing depicts soldiers returning to Little Rock, Arkansas.

remarried and started new families. **Laura Spicer**'s husband, from whom she and her children had been separated, apologized for remarrying and urged her to do the same. "I would come and see you," he wrote, but I know you could not bear it. . . . I love you just as well as I did the last day I saw you, and it will not do for you and I to meet. I am married, and my wife have two children, and if you and I meets it would make a very dissatisfied family. Send me some of the children's hair in a separate paper with their names on the paper." Even for those who managed to gather, living all together, sometimes for the first time, could be an adjustment.

Most freedpeople began establishing their new status by choosing a last name. Sorting out who was related to whom was a tricky legal business because until freedom, Southern whites had barely recognized slave families. Slave marriages did not legally exist, making all slave children illegitimate in the eyes of the law. To claim family rights,

freedpeople had to marry officially—no matter how long they had lived together. Proof of marriage was especially important for war widows seeking pensions and for women trying to wrest their children from former masters.

Planters tried to hold on to part of their workforce by labeling freedchildren orphans and quickly signing legal documents to make them "apprentices." What were children like twelve-year-old **Celia** and her siblings to do at the end of the war? Their master had sold their mother. Imagine Celia's emotions as **Mary Minor**, the mother they had not seen for five years, showed up on the doorstep. Though Minor had walked from South Carolina to Georgia in search of them, Celia and nine-year-old Henry were not allowed to leave with her—they had already been apprenticed for twenty years to their former owner. In desperation, Celia's mother wrote an eloquent plea to the President of the United States. She asked Andrew Johnson

Pastoral Visit, by Richard Norris Brooke (1881).

"if the laws of my country are such that a poor slave badly treated, and separated for years from her own children, cannot be allowed the privilege of having her children with her?" Officials declared the apprenticeships invalid. Celia, Henry, and two younger children returned to Georgia with their mother. Many former slaves were not so lucky.

WORK CONTRACTS The collapse of slavery did not herald an end to backbreaking work. After the government pardoned former slaveholders and returned their land, many refused to sell or rent to blacks. Instead, officials forced freedpeople to sign labor contracts or be arrested. The contracts resembled slavery, controlling former slave's decisions and keeping them from owning land. However, unlike slavery, workers could not be sold and could leave at the end of a contract, if they chose.

Only single women could contract for themselves and their children. The law required husbands to sign for their wives. Females also received lower wages, regardless of the work performed. Many freedwomen openly resisted doing jobs that were not specifically in their contracts. When possible, they also spent more time at home growing their own gardens and taking care of their families. Angered by this choice, many whites accused them of laziness.

ASSERTING FREEDOM African American women asserted their newfound freedom in public ways. White commentators didn't know what to think of these outspoken females who were fed up with being abused and ordered around. White journalists frequently described them as loud, boisterous, and disrespectful. Although

Single mothers often migrated to cities where they could labor as domestics or laundresses— jobs that could be more easily combined with parenting. A typical yearly contract for domestic work often read like this one between J. M. Simpson and Judy in 1866:

> In consideration of the foregoing services (cook, washer, ironer and general house servant). . . . the said Simpson promises to feed and cloth the said Judy and her three children Samuel (7), Shepard (3), and Mary (6 month) and also give said Judy next fall one pare of shoes.

Contracts like this made it difficult, if not impossible, for women to save money to improve their situations.

fashionable dresses, hats, ribbons, and parasols, and to go for carriage rides.

Public displays of pride and will came at a price. Former slave owners frequently beat or murdered women who challenged their authority. Some freedwomen were punished for simply working hard enough to become independent of whites. Returned Confederate soldiers organized the Ku Klux Klan in 1866. The Klan terrorized black communities, pulling people from their homes at night to be flogged, tortured, and even killed. Former slave **Betty Chessier** later recalled, "I laid in my bed many a night scared to death." Rape was common, although it wasn't prosecuted because in many white minds, only white women could be sexually assaulted.

In 1868 one Georgia freedwoman reported that her employer had "ordered her to the field early in the morning before she had time to properly take care of her child. She refused to go at that time and…told him she was just as free as he. On this he kicked her in the head and knocked her down seriously injuring her."

only black men were allowed to vote starting in 1867, freedwomen attended political rallies and parades, and went to the polls with their men. One Georgia reporter described them as "wilder than the men....seen everywhere, talking in an excited manner, and urging the men on. Some of them were almost furious, showing it to be part of their religion to keep their husbands and brothers straight in politics."

Wearing new clothing became another way for freedwomen to advertise that they were no longer slaves. Some used hard-earned wages to purchase

By the late 1870s, the chaos experienced immediately after the war began to abate. The contract system had evolved into a new farming arrangement. *Sharecropping* was still a kind of bondage in which poor farmers—black and white— worked other people's land for a small cut of the proceeds. Sharecropping women worked sunup to sundown in the fields, then late into the night for

This 1872 *Harper's Weekly* illustration depicts the threat of the Ku Klux Klan.

their families. The daily round of domestic work, in addition to work in the fields, made many old before their time. Life expectancy for blacks in 1870 was 23 as compared to 40 for whites.

"ALL THE FLOWERS WERE GONE"

Southern whites struggled to make sense of the changes brought by war. Those who were modestly successful or poor at its outset were now destitute.

Many became sharecroppers or found jobs in the new Southern cotton mills. Before the conflict, a small elite group of white landowners had held the bulk of Southern wealth. Now they too faced an uncertain future.

Sarah Pryor, the wife of a Confederate general, waited out the war in Petersburg, Virginia, with her four young children. She tried to remain brave when bombs fell in her yard, food was scarce, and she was informed that her husband was a

"We found it almost impossible to take up our lives again."
—SARAH PRYOR, wife of a Confederate general

prisoner of war. She later wrote that the surrender of the South "was an awful blow to us. All was over. All the suffering, bloodshed, death—all for nothing." Pryor gathered her children and returned to her farm. "A scene of desolation met my eyes," she recalled. "The earth was ploughed and trampled, the grass and flowers were gone, the carcasses of six dead cows lay in the yard, and filth unspeakable had gathered in the corners of the house. . . . As the front door opened, millions of flies swarmed forth." Parts of the South had been laid waste by armies who had destroyed buildings, bridges, and railroads, and carried off livestock and food. One-fifth of white Southern men had died, wiping out a whole generation of young men and severely narrowing the possibility of marriage. Many returned physically and emotionally scarred. Even areas that had not actually seen battle felt the effects of war and the end of slavery.

Raised in a world where slaves had performed the difficult and menial work of farm and household, formerly wealthy white women were now forced to take on new responsibilities. Some continued to manage the financial affairs of husbands who had died during the war. Others moved into more modest homes in town, or took in financially strapped relatives. Virtually all had to adjust to new relationships with the people who had recently been their property.

Angry at her slaves for leaving, **Ann Pope** wrote in 1865, *"I live in dirt, eat and sleep in it. I want the power of annihilation. I get so mad I don't know what to do—but I grin and endure it."* White women had difficulty adjusting to the idea that freedpeople could now negotiate contracts and choose whom to work for. They wanted servants to willingly put up with the same conditions as they had under slavery. Unprepared to recognize the aspirations and feelings of blacks, whites were offended when servants refused the terms of their work, or quit altogether.

Reduced resources and "servant problems" forced women to do some, if not all, of the work themselves.

Many were surprised by how much effort it took to cook and clean. Their role had always been managerial. **Ann Hairston** regretted having to answer her own door: "As much experience as I have housekeeping I never can bear to open doors."

An 1865 view of the "Burnt District" of Richmond, Virginia.

In most Southern households, the cooking had taken place in a building outside the house, so few women knew how to cook. **Jane Meares** sometimes ate only bread and milk for breakfast when she did not have domestic help. She wrote to her daughter, "You would have laughed to see Cousin Rosa and me trying to cook some biscuits and make some coffee for breakfast."

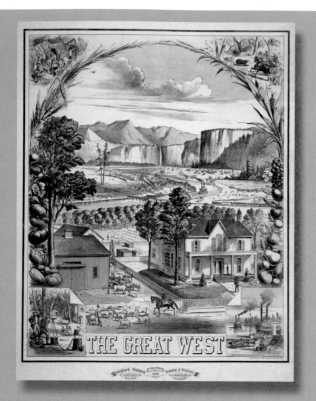

Literature often portrayed the West as a sort of Garden of Eden. Territories encouraged farm families to move west, luring them with cheap land and promises of bounty.

THE WEST

"WE WERE JUSTLY PROUD OF THE WORK": SETTLERS ON THE FRONTIER

Women in other parts of the country faced different challenges. **Angeline Mitchell**, a settler in Arizona, began her 1880 diary entry, *"My goodness—but this is a lively place to live—only it's a bit wearing on one's nerves."* This was more than an understatement—over the course of six months this young schoolteacher survived encounters with rabid skunks, a hungry cougar, stampeding cattle, and hostile Apaches. As she rode home for Christmas, her stagecoach nearly crashed over cliffs—twice. Mitchell's sentiments were echoed in the experiences of thousands on the American frontier.

By the end of the Civil War, much of the prairie had ceased to be frontier, and was now dotted by respectable houses and growing towns. Parts of the West Coast were also settled into towns. Those in search of opportunity and adventure made use of the newly installed railroad lines to take advantage of the great expanse in between. Women of all ages, races, and classes journeyed to the frontier. Although most were married, those who were divorced, widowed, and never married also joined the throngs. If they felt discomfort at displacing Native American and Hispanic communities, few noted it.

WHY GO WEST? Reasons for going west were as varied as the women themselves. Though some reluctantly followed husbands or fathers, diaries and letters show that many viewed the move optimistically. After moving to Kansas in the 1880s, **Flora Heston** put a positive twist on her new, reduced circumstances: "We have the best prospect of prosperity we ever had and believe it was right for us to come here. . . . I have a great deal more leisure time than I used to have it don't take near the work to keep up one room that it does a big house."

Before 1862 females could not independently purchase land. However, the new Homestead Act offered free government land to anyone who could "prove up" their claim—including single women. To "prove up" a claim, a settler had to build a house and work on the property for a set amount of time. Many footloose singles seized the opportunity. In 1886, youthful buddies **Mary Anderson** and **Bee Randolph** settled adjoining land in Colorado. They built a shack that crossed the property line, so that each could sleep on her own property and thus "prove up" without being alone and expending too many resources in the process.

Owning land offered a rare form of economic power for women. Some claimed land near family members. Others increased their holdings by marrying the man on the next claim while retaining their own land. Records show that the percentage of those who completed the difficult process of proving up a claim was the same for women as it was for men.

Southern blacks calling themselves "Exodusers" also jumped at the chance to own land. Beginning in 1877, thousands packed up their "poor, battered and tattered household goods" and caught steamboats down the Mississippi River. One observer found "every road leading to the river filled with wagons loaded with plunder and families who seem to think anywhere is better than here." The largest group settled in Kansas. Arriving in newly settled Nicodemus with her husband and six children, **Willianna Hickman** wondered where the town was. She recalled, "My husband pointed out various smokes coming out of the ground and said, 'That is Nicodemus.' The families lived in dugouts. The scenery to me was not at all inviting and I began to cry."

*Before moving to Nebraska, **Luna Kellie** imagined that a sod house would be "kind of nice … green and grassy," but "the sight of the first one sickened me." Her impatient father responded, "Well, it is dirty looking because it is made of dirt."*

LIVING CONDITIONS Hickman was not the only person to weep at the sight of her new home. In areas with few or no trees settlers began their Western sojourn in rough log cabins, shelters dug out of the side of a hill, or houses built from sod (soil and plant roots) bricks stacked one on top of the other. Soil houses were cooler in the summer and warmer in the winter, but nearly impossible to keep clean. One Montana woman complained that when it rained, water would drip into the house for days. Settlers often shared the space with insects, rodents, and snakes that burrowed through walls and

The **Chrisman sisters**, Harriet, Elizabeth, Lucie, and Ruth, all took adjoining land to increase their family's land allotment. Ruth later recollected that in an 1888 blizzard, they were out of fuel and burned corn stalks and some old chairs to keep warm.

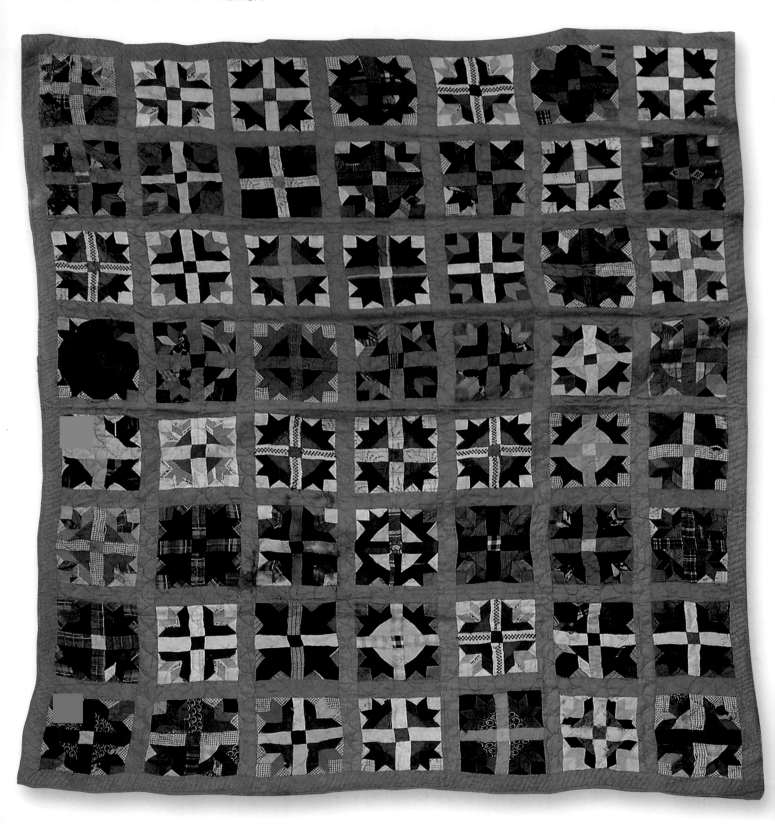

Experience Hack Smith began this quilt in Vermont and finished it on her homestead in Nebraska. She entered the quilt, "Goose Tracks," in the county fair in 1881.

ceilings. Even so, women decorated these makeshift homes with knickknacks, flowers, rag rugs, and newsprint wallpaper. Some took apart precious outfits to make curtains. As soon as they could, they built more comfortable houses.

ROLES On the plains, as in the East, men had more freedom to explore and try new things. Most people agreed that a woman's place was at home. But what if that home was in a wild, lonely place? Frontier women continued to manage all the needs of house, garden, and family—except that on the frontier, these jobs were more difficult. Husbands and brothers provided scant help, as often they were occupied with their own work, or were gone altogether. In Kansas, **Jennie Marcy** lamented, *"Why were the men always away when terrible things happened?* It was then that the coyotes were more neighborly, or the Indians were following the trails from the Reservations to the Territory, or the prairie grass mysteriously caught fire." Settlers got tough and resourceful, or returned to the East.

The realities of frontier life often led women to do traditionally male jobs. They worked alongside their fathers, husbands, and brothers in the fields and barns and replaced the men if they died or went away. Showing they could work as hard as men gave women a feeling of accomplishment. **Mary Alice Zimmerman**, who helped her father clear his land for planting, preferred plowing to cooking. The five Mitchell girls helped their father build their log cabin and dug out the root cellar by themselves. **Margaret Mitchell** recalled, "We were justly proud of the work, for no one in our neighborhood had a better one."

CHORES It is not surprising that when sunburned newlywed **Sadie Martin** arrived at her new home in the Arizona desert she gratefully welcomed "a long cool drink of delicious water." The scarcity of water was the biggest hardship for most frontier women. In arid, dry places, clothes and diapers still had to be washed, gardens watered, meals prepared, and houses and children kept clean. Until water could be located and a well dug, they caught rare rainwater in cisterns, and trekked daily to the nearest running stream. Many helped dig

wells. Once a well was completed, pulling numerous buckets of water from a depth of as much as 65 feet required strength. Settlers learned to make the most of the water they had, reusing bathwater for washing clothes or floors, and dishwater for watering gardens.

Have you ever heard of . . . Laura Ingalls (Wilder)?

Born in 1867, Ingalls's childhood was similar to others with homesteading parents. She worked hard at chores and farm work, and became a teacher at the age of fifteen to supplement the family income. As an older woman, with the help of her daughter, Ingalls rewrote her childhood journals into the *Little House on the Prairie* series.

Getting enough to eat was also a challenge. Women improvised with whatever was on hand, and worked to fill their larders with preserved meats, vegetables, and fruits. The survival of many frontier families depended on the additional income that women could bring in through the home production of clothing, soap, candles, and food. Without wood to burn, women reluctantly turned to fuel that lay all around them—buffalo chips (manure) or "prairie coal." Baking bread, like washing clothes, could be an all day affair. One woman wrote that after baking pies and cookies, "The fronts of my dresses would be scorched, the toes of my shoes burned, and my face blistered."

MOTHERING Married women carried out these daily tasks in the midst of bearing and raising numerous children. During the winter before **Malinda Jenkins** bore her second child, she "spun and wove four blankets. And made up all the clothes, the jeans and the flannels for the whole family, knitted all the stockings and everything." She also wove a rag carpet. Jenkins later recalled, *"Sunday I cleaned the house and got ready. Monday, after dinner I had an eleven pound baby."* But even with a new baby on hand, plenty of other work still had to be done.

Parents could not constantly supervise children and rightfully worried that their children could fall into creeks or abandoned wells, be bitten by snakes, or be carried off by wild animals. When **Bessie Wilson** was small, she encountered a rattler while making mud pies. She remembered that her mother "came running, catching me by the arm and ruthlessly snatching me from my perilous position. By the time she had finished killing this snake with the garden hoe, she was ready to collapse."

Many settlements became towns almost overnight. Women sometimes moved to town so their children could go to school, or to escape farming. But frontier towns were rough, dirty, loud places, frequently filled with drunken, fighting men. Long dresses dragged in the muddy streets and the lack of streetlights made walking alone at night dangerous. Ladies viewed themselves as a moral, civilizing force and as the guardians of culture. In many communities they formed churches, schools, and other public institutions. They taught their children manners, sustained holiday traditions, and tried to bring refinement into the lives of those around them.

Emma Leadbetter Rawding, her husband, daughter **Bessie,** and sons pose in front of their Nebraska sod house. Might they be showing their good humor to have their cow on the roof for the photograph?

Mary Hallock Foote, a professional book illustrator and writer, noted in 1888, **"Whoever has lived in the West must have observed that here it is the unexpected that always happens."** Battering rain, hailstorms, tornadoes, brush fires, grasshopper plagues, and disease epidemics could wipe out a person's dreams in mere hours. Foote documented from experience the toll this kind of life took on women. Her popular magazine articles portrayed women (rather than cowboys and miners) as central to the Western story. She noted wryly that young frontier men "always pick out the pretty girl, when a less expensive choice would be so much more serviceable and fit the conditions of their lives so much better." She concluded, "Between them both, the girl who expects to have a good time, and the young man who is confident that he can give it to her, there will probably be a good deal to learn."

"REAL COURAGE": NATIVE AMERICAN WOMEN

Though seemingly desolate to settlers, the plains, deserts, and mountains of the West were already occupied by thousands of American Indians. Some were newcomers who had already been pushed out of their homes in the East. From the farmer Navaho in the Southwest to the nomadic Sioux of the plains to the hunter-gatherer Madoc of California, each nation had its own language, culture, and way of life.

APACHES Apaches lived a roaming life, keeping their possessions spare and easy to transport. Expert at preparing meals with wild desert and mountain plants, women also wove beautifully decorated willow baskets to carry and store belongings, food, and water. They dressed and preserved meat and tanned animal hides.

Did you know?

While Americans of European descent considered house construction a manly activity, in most Native American tribes, women made the houses, a job for which they were honored.

Girls learned the same skills as the boys—to hunt wild animals, shoot with a bow and arrow, escape an enemy, and mount an unsaddled horse without help. They wore bright cotton skirts, buckskin shirts with fringe, and bead necklaces. Their knee-high moccasins contained a pouch in which to store a knife. A girl was eligible to marry at puberty. When she married, her husband gave her gifts and came to live with her family. Her parents called him "he who carries burdens for me."

A Mescalero Apache woman, with her baby safely bundled onto a cradle board, would teach her young child to survive in the desert.

PUSHED OUT Apaches and other Western tribes reacted with alarm as settlers arrived in droves, killed wildlife, and seized water and land. In numerous instances, government soldiers rode into villages and brutally murdered anyone they found there. When attacked, Apache women knew how to fight back. Government soldiers imperiled their own lives when they dismissed the battle skills of Apache females. In 1868, one officer warned: "They ride like centaurs and handle their rifles with deadly skill. . . . No account is taken of the fighting women, who are numerous, well trained and desperate, often

exhibiting more real courage than the men."

Some groups retaliated by killing white settlers. The government took this as proof that Indians and settlers could not live side by side—Native Americans would have to go. In 1868, Congress decided to stop making treaties, and to remove all Indians to reservations formed from undesirable lands. Farming was nearly impossible. Tribes were not allowed to leave the reservations, but were given insufficient, substandard government rations. Many people died of hunger and sickness.

Have you ever heard of . . . Lozen?

Lozen was a fearless and respected Apache warrior who grew to mythical status. Normally, only married women accompanied men into battle, but Lozen, who never married, fought alongside the men until the bitter end. Tall and athletic, friends later remembered that "she was magnificent on a horse . . . could handle her rifle as well as any man, most of whom she could outrun on foot." Lozen was so amazing that legends grew up around her, making it difficult for historians to separate fact from fiction. It is known for certain, however, that she was captured with one of the last resisting groups of Apaches and sent to prison in Florida. She died of tuberculosis in the late 1880s.

Soldiers take Chiricahua Apache women and children captive in 1885.

Deprived of their livelihoods and their homes, some Indian groups took up arms. Others fled, preferring the hardships of eluding government troops to life on a reservation. Over the next two decades, U.S. soldiers chased numerous groups of Cheyenne, Sioux, Apache, Navaho, Comanche, Piute, Nez Perce, and others through canyons and across deserts and mountains.

Life on the run was especially difficult for women with small children and elderly parents. A crying baby could give away the location of a whole group. As a little girl, Piute **Sarah Winnemucca**'s mother hid her by burying her up to her head in the sand because she was not fast enough to run away. One Apache boy remembered that as he and his mother, **Gouyen**, were fleeing a battle on horseback, they saw his

Government Indian School, Swinomish Reservation, La Conner, Washington. What stories might these children tell of their assimilation into American culture?

baby sister on the ground. *"My little sister cried to my mother and [held out] her arms. But my mother could not get close enough to pick her up."* She begged a nearby relative to save her baby. "He swooped down and picked my little sister up from the ground and rode off. And we never saw her again. We think they were both killed." Hurried flight forced them to leave behind precious belongings and food stores. Some watched in horror as soldiers burned their animal skins, cooking utensils, and lodge poles. In addition, women lost husbands, fathers, brothers, and sons who were trying to protect them.

LOSING NATIVE CULTURE In the end, whether friendly or hostile to settlers, all tribes lost the right to live where and how they desired. Just as devastating, well-intentioned whites insisted that Indians leave their traditions behind, thinking they would be better off if they could learn to speak, look, and act like whites. To this end, they took numerous Indian children away from their parents and sent them to boarding schools far from the reservations. The loss of native culture and language would devastate future generations.

In 1884, eight-year-old **Zitkala-Sa**, a Dakota Sioux, was taken to a missionary school where students dressed like white children and were only allowed to speak English. In order to cut her long hair, her teachers tied her, kicking and scratching, in a chair. She later wrote,

"I cried aloud, shaking my head all the while until I felt the cold blades of the scissors against my neck, and heard them gnaw off one of my thick braids. Then I lost my spirit. . . . in my anguish I moaned for my mother, but no one came to comfort me."

MUI TSAI, PROSTITUTES, AND WIVES: CHINESE WOMEN

As Americans expanded west, building railroads and mines, they looked for inexpensive labor. Thousands of Chinese men answered the call, leaving their wives and families behind in China. By 1880,

A photo simply titled "Fishdealer's daughter."

Chinese men in the United States outnumbered Chinese women by more than ten to one. Chinese immigrants faced hostile racism and were frequently beaten or killed with no recourse to law. While marriage with Caucasians was outlawed, it was nearly impossible to bring a Chinese woman to the United States to marry. This resulted in a black market where girls were kidnapped or purchased from their families in China to be servants or prostitutes in America.

Wu Tien Fu was six when her father gambled away the family's money and decided to pay his debts by selling her. She later remembered, *"mother was crying. . . .* She gave me a new toothbrush and a new washrag in a blue bag when I left her. When I saw her cry I said, 'Don't cry, Mother, I'm just going to see Grandma and be right back.'" But Fu's "worthless father" took her onto a ferryboat and locked her in a cabin while he sold her. *"I kicked and screamed and screamed,"* she recalled, *"And they wouldn't open the door till after some time.* . . . I went up and down, up and down, here and there, couldn't find him." The little girl was taken to a brothel in America where she worked as a *mui tsai,* or indentured servant.

PROSTITUTES AND MISSIONARIES Chinese American prostitutes were alone and nearly friendless. Unable to speak English, they were at the mercy of their captors. While some managed to escape or to be purchased as wives of laborers, many lived short, tragic lives.

Protestant missionaries and Chinese reformers became the only real allies of Chinese prostitutes, establishing "rescue" houses to which they could flee. Escaping prostitution was expensive and dangerous. Rescue homes offered these women a chance at respectability by educating them and helping them find eligible marriage partners.

WIVES A small number of Chinese women immigrated as merchants' wives. They lived secluded, pampered lives. Chinese customs required that a woman be quiet, submissive, and literally confined to the home. In China, the centuries-old practice of binding feet had been one way to ensure

that a woman wouldn't wander far. The feet of elite young girls were wrapped tightly with bandages until the arches broke, the toes bent under, and the whole foot was only a few inches long. A number of wealthier women who came to the United States had bound feet and needed servants to take care of all domestic affairs. They entertained themselves with needlepoint projects, playing cards, worshiping at the family altar, and other in-home activities. Some did not leave their homes for years at a time. Fortunately for their daughters, they did not continue the practice of binding feet in America.

In 1882, Congress passed the Chinese Exclusion Act, suspending the immigration of laborers from China. This slowed Chinese immigration, especially that of women, to a trickle.

PAID WORK

NO CHOICE BUT TO WORK

After the Civil War, most jobs that had been briefly available to women were returned to men. A newspaper columnist commented, "To hear some very proper persons discourse upon woman's sphere . . . one would imagine that all women are blessed

An 1870 illustration of a German immigrant ragpicker in New York City.

Have you ever heard of . . . Nellie Bly?

An expressive young newspaper reporter, she refused to write society columns. Instead, Elizabeth Cochran (Bly's real name) went undercover to experience firsthand the dire state of America's slums and factories and expose them to the public. In 1889, she circled the globe in less time than it took in the novel *Around the World in 80 Days*. Traveling alone, something a respectable woman never did, Cochran visited places most Americans had never heard of, and returned in 72 days. She was an instant celebrity.

with comfortable homes, having nothing to do but cultivate amiability and gladden . . . hearts." Comfortable in the belief that females should be cared for financially by men, many Americans turned a blind eye to conditions that forced immigrants, widows, and poor women to work for

wages. Alabama alone had 80,000 widows at the close of the war. A severe economic depression from 1873 to 1877 increased the number of working women and children by 38 percent. Most toiled as domestics, laundresses, seamstresses, or factory workers.

NEW PROFESSIONS Sometimes even educated, middle-class mothers and daughters needed to earn money. For them, working as teachers, librarians, nurses, or writers was an acceptable way to earn a living. As public education expanded, the number of female schoolteachers skyrocketed. People believed that teaching was the perfect training for motherhood. In addition, female teachers could be hired much more cheaply than men.

Some teachers stayed in the East, but others traveled south to teach freedchildren, or west to educate frontier children. Arriving in Colorado to teach, **Ellen Pennock** found that the school was "undisciplined . . . dirty, window lights broken, blackboards nearly paintless, and almost every pupil has a different kind of book." It was a challenge to keep order while working with children of all ages. A young woman teaching freed slave children in Georgia compared her classroom experience with trying to keep "so many marbles in place on a smooth floor." Teachers usually stayed with students' families, although some lodged in the school. In addition to teaching, a teacher's job included cleaning and heating the school, obtaining equipment, and protecting her students from possible harm. Many persisted, in spite of hardships and low pay. By the 1880s, two-thirds of public schoolteachers were women. The turnover, however, was high, because they were required to quit when they married.

An enthusiastic male librarian noted in the 1870s that female librarians *"soften the atmosphere, they lighten our labor, and . . . they are infinitely better than equivalent salaries will produce of the other sex."* Hardworking and willing to earn less, educated women were now in demand as librarians. As with teaching and medicine, men filled the top spots, and women took the lower-paid posts.

The service of volunteer nurses during the Civil War had helped to legitimize nursing as a

A teacher and her students in front of their one-room schoolhouse in Juneau, Alaska (1887). What challenges might she have faced trying to educate children of such varying ages?

profession for women. As a result, the first nurse training schools opened in New York, Boston, and New Haven, Connecticut, in 1873, followed by thirty-five other programs. That year, **Linda Richards** became the first nursing school graduate.

WAGES Women's meager wages continued to be based on the premise that they were supplementing those of a male family member. Worse still, dishonest employers found it easy to cheat female employees.

Reformers focused not on increasing wages, but on training female workers in "appropriate" jobs so they could earn money at home and not mix with unsavory characters. Others discussed ways to get husbands for women so they wouldn't have to work. Women especially outnumbered men in the Southern states. Based on the war death toll and the number of men heading west, the *New York Times* predicted in 1869 that some 250,000 females on the eastern seaboard would never marry.

GOING ON STRIKE Many attempts to control work conditions were local and short-lived. The first national women's union, the Daughters of St. Crispin, organized a number of successful strikes for shoe workers, but soon fizzled. However, in 1881, a new union, the Knights of Labor, took the unprecedented step of extending membership to workers of all races, genders, and skill levels (except Chinese men). The Knights chose sixteen women to attend the 1886 national assembly. In the nine years the Knights held sway, female workers participated in decision making and strikes with their male colleagues.

Between 1866 and 1881, black laundresses in Texas, Mississippi, and Georgia staged strikes to increase their wages. Washing, drying, and ironing clothes was backbreaking labor, but it was one of the few jobs open to African American women. Many chose it over domestic labor so they could work at home near their children. In Atlanta, they went on strike just before the city's big cotton exposition. The group, calling itself the "Washing Society," grew

Have you ever heard of . . . Fredericka Mandelbaum?

This immigrant wife and mother became the queen of the New York underworld between 1860 and 1880. A shrewd businesswoman, Mother Mandelbaum earned great wealth by deftly selling stolen goods for career criminals. She successfully eluded arrest by bribing police and officials. She also gained a reputation as a good person and an "honest crook." People referred to her as "a wonderful person" and claimed that she was "a business woman whose honesty in criminal matters was absolute."

By 1875, young women who took the unprecedented step of traveling alone to cities to look for work had a friend in the Young Women's Christian Association (YWCA). Concerned that girls "adrift" would fall into evil ways, the YWCA established boardinghouses and helped them find suitable jobs. YWCA houses eventually included libraries, gyms, auditoriums, and classrooms.

Many women who had served faithfully during the Civil War felt dismissed and forgotten. Nurse **Adelaide Smith** opined, "How few, even of the army veterans, remember the sacrifices of the women of the war. . . . never have I heard a chaplain or minister give a thought of the women workers by whose faithful care many of these brave soldiers were nursed back to life, and restored to their anxious families." Women who had deviated even further from female propriety by fighting as soldiers were written out of history altogether, dismissed as crazy, misguided, or simply lower class. The government did not grant pensions to Union nurses until 1892.

Employers justified paying women less by hiring them only for unskilled positions. This was impossible in the case of cigar makers from Bohemia. Women were the experts. A war in Europe led thousands to immigrate to America in the 1870s. Arriving with their own tools, these skilled workers quickly earned enough money for their husbands and children to join them.

Have you ever heard of . . . Margaret Knight?

Next time you visit a grocery store, sing her praises. Among other things, she invented and patented a machine that made brown paper shopping bags. Knight got an early start, inventing a safety device for factory looms when she was only twelve years old.

from 20 to 3,000 members in three weeks. After a month, the laundresses wrote to the mayor, saying, "We mean business this week or no washing." In spite of arrests, taxes, raised rents, and threats to replace them with commercial laundries, they refused to wash clothes for two months. Atlanta's white citizens panicked when their cooks and other household workers threatened to follow suit. Their ability to cause such a commotion highlighted the continued dependency of whites on black labor. The strike was only part of ongoing attempts by those who were most vulnerable to exploitation to negotiate fair working conditions.

WAGES IN THE WEST Some women tried to get ahead financially by going west, where the demand for services meant increased wages, even for domestics. Resourceful women were able to transform traditionally female tasks into income-generating activities, opening hotels, boardinghouses, and brothels in the growing towns.

Postmistresses delivered mail out of the fronts of stores to settlers who were far from homes and families. **Jessie Stratford**

remembered that on "many bitterly cold winter mornings," her mother and grandmother "arose when the stage arrived at two o'clock a.m. and distributed mail by the light of a coal oil lamp." Economic success gave many women leverage in their relationships with men, even if it did not change underlying assumptions about proper roles.

AT HOME

WEALTHY WOMEN It remained the ideal, however, for women to dedicate their efforts to home and hearth. In the years following the war, the large, beautifully decorated mansion became, more than ever, the outward symbol of social and financial success. Industry made a small minority of American families outrageously rich.

The wealthy enjoyed parading their wealth, staffing their ornate homes with armies of servants. Many also owned summer cottages by the sea or in Europe. They traveled regularly, carting home expensive treasures, and frequently sending their children abroad to study. A wealthy woman was expected to entertain guests regularly and lavishly. Large windows enabled passersby to gaze upon

Women and children doing laundry in 1900.

Have you ever heard of . . . Mary Fields?

This tall, strong, gun-toting, cigar-smoking, hard-drinking freed slave moved west to help and protect a group of Ursuline nuns in Montana. Fields became widely known as "Stagecoach Mary" in her sixties when she and her mule Moses delivered mail through blizzards and heat alike.

windows, stenciled wallpaper, and picket fences. These homes were increasingly filled with beautiful lace curtains, pianos, and overstuffed furniture. Most middle-class housewives were able to hire a servant or two to help, but even so, their duties were, as one advice writer put it, "as numerable as the stars." Servants merely enabled women to divide up the labor. Middle-class wives were rarely idle. Most still did their own baking—an all-day affair—and canned quarts and quarts of fruit, berries, and vegetables.

POOR WOMEN Urban workers and rural sharecroppers lived in cramped, unsanitary shacks or tenement buildings where cooking, eating, sleeping, and bathing often took place in the same space. Most owned a little furniture, a washtub, and some cooking and eating implements. Poor women toiled long hours, leaving little time or energy for housekeeping. Even so, many did what they could to make their homes more inviting by hanging magazine pictures or whitewashing the walls.

COURTING, MARRIAGE, AND DIVORCE

For wealthy and middle-class Americans, courting was a closely supervised ritual meant to pair young people of similar backgrounds. Before a girl came of age, she spent little time with males other than her own relatives. Once she could

the party and see what they were missing. While the servants did the real work, it was the lady of the house who ensured that they did it right. To be seen working would tarnish a wealthy woman's reputation.

MIDDLE-CLASS WOMEN The wives and daughters of a growing number of office workers and professional men aspired to the lifestyle of the upper class. Though less wealthy, many were still able to move to newly built suburbs, with handsome two-story homes with elaborate entryways, stained-glass

Housewives and domestics alike were thrilled by the invention in 1873 of the **carpet sweeper**, *two revolving brushes attached to wheels and a pan. The carpet sweeper rescued women from the heavy labor of dragging rugs outside to be beaten.*

A woman works in a well-equipped 1874 kitchen. Not all women were quite so lucky.

Carrie Williams, the young wife of a Nevada miner, wrote in her diary in 1849: "How tedious and tiresome pass the hours, now days to me. Wallace's [her husband] whole time and attention are directed here lately to practice music to play with the band. No persuits in common between us anymore, no more pleasant readings together, no more evenings spent talking and making plans as we used to. **We go on day after day, without speaking a dozen of words to each other some days.** I feel more and more evry day that this is not what it should be, but Wallace does not seem to think. What is going to become of our happiness at this rate?"

become respectfully acquainted with young men, she followed a strict set of rules. If she was interested in a boy, she might pay an official, chaperoned visit and leave a calling card. At various dances and balls, she would schedule dances on a program card, attempting to leave spaces for those she most hoped to dance with. In all her interactions, she would keep a formal distance by addressing possible suitors not by their first names, but as Mr. _____. Girls carefully guarded their reputations, as even rumors of wrongdoing could destroy the opportunity to marry well. Engagement was signaled by a ring, worn by the young woman on the third finger of her right hand.

While society continued to promote an ideal of "separate spheres" for men and women, a new generation of women, influenced by popular literature, began envisioning the possibility that husbands and wives could also be friends. These new ideas set the stage for possible disappointment. Brides were often surprised to find that when the honeymoon trip ended, their husbands were no longer so attentive. Many men were not looking for a friend, but rather for a caretaker who would create a haven where they could retreat from the rigors of the world. Books and magazines illustrated the vices into which a husband might fall if his home was not sufficiently nurturing.

FEMALE FRIENDSHIPS Once married, most women and men went their separate social ways. It was to other females—mothers, sisters, aunts, and friends—that most girls and women turned for intense, meaningful friendships and emotional support. Many mothers and daughters were fast friends who found it difficult to be separated by marriage. Within these female circles, friends rarely competed, but fostered one another's children, wrote adoring letters spanning great distances and lifetimes, and supported one another through times of births, deaths, and other crises. When **Nannie Alderson**, a settler in Montana, lay ill in the 1880s, someone suggested calling a doctor from a nearby city. Alderson responded, *"I don't want a doctor. I want a woman!"*

DIVORCE When marriages were unsuccessful, it was becoming more possible, if not respectable, to divorce. New states and territories passed less stringent divorce laws, making Illinois or Iowa, followed by the Dakotas and Oklahoma the destinations for those seeking to be free of a spouse. "Mental cruelty," a broad, new provision allowed individuals to leave unhappy unions. Women who could prove that their husbands were unfaithful or abusive were more regularly awarded their children in custody disputes. By the turn of the century, the United States claimed a divorce rate of one in twelve, the highest in the world.

Female friendships flourished in the 1870s as women joined study clubs. After **Jane Cunningham Croly** was excluded from a New York Press Club dinner in 1868, she formed what is believed to be the **first women's club in America**. She called it Sorosis, a term referring to plants with fruit-bearing flowers, and invited a group of friends to study literature, art, drama, and music. Previously, most avenues for such study were closed to females. The idea was so popular that soon others began organizing and joining women's clubs. Though attending club meetings seemed unconnected to their family duties, ladies justified their actions by insisting that they were educating themselves to better care for their families.

HEALTH
"OCEANS OF PAIN"

SICKNESS Ill health continued to plague women after the Civil War. One influential doctor warned the country that if American women continued to be so sickly, men would have to travel to Europe to find healthy wives. Tight corsets and infrequent exercise led to physical problems for middle- and upper-class women. Lower-class women endured poor nutrition, overwork, and terrible living conditions that bred illness. Tuberculosis, influenza, scarlet fever, pneumonia, and other diseases made life tenuous for women everywhere. In 1865, more than one in twenty would die from tuberculosis before turning thirty. When medical intervention was sought, many doctors probably made matters worse because of their ignorance of the female body. As a male doctor examined his female patient, he was expected to preserve modesty by never looking at her body.

CHILDBIRTH Multiple, life-threatening pregnancies and deliveries challenged women of all classes. Despite a decline in overall birthrates, most women still bore four or more children. Smaller families led to more indulgent, child-centered parenting. Minority, immigrant, and frontier families, however, still tended to be large, with as many as seventeen children. Of the delivery of her third baby in 1885, one woman wrote, *"Between oceans of pain, there stretched continents of fear; fear of death and dread of suffering beyond bearing."* Even a woman in good health had to confront the reality that she or her baby might die in childbirth.

While male physicians increasingly attended deliveries, they still had to negotiate with female friends and relatives who gathered to support the laboring woman. Though not actively delivering the baby, other women around the childbed offered comfort and ensured that the doctor acted in the best interest of his patient. Doctors could now administer chloroform to ease pain. However, they also continued to practice bloodletting (taking blood, often to the point of fainting) while women were in labor.

Midwives remained a fixture in rural communities. In southwestern Hispanic villages, the midwife, called a *partera,* was honored. Although strict rules governed the interactions between the sexes, a *partera* was allowed to travel alone with men. She stayed until the mother and child were settled after a birth. The grateful family paid whatever they could afford: a chicken, or perhaps some garden produce.

Recovery from childbirth could be as dangerous as the birth itself. Many women endured (and sometimes died from) childbed fevers brought on by infection. Others suffered from fallen uteruses and vaginal tears. Alone on the frontier, one woman recalled, *"So here I was, inexperienced and helpless, alone in bed, with an infant a few days old. . . . I struggled along, fighting against odds; how I ever got well at all is a wonder."*

MEDICINE With few available cures, many doctors simply tried to make their patients more comfortable by treating them with opium and morphine. Laudanum, a form of opium, was often used to take the edge off depression. These drugs were legal, freely available, and frequently prescribed. Alcohol use by women was frowned upon, but use of opiates, often referred to as "taking something," was socially acceptable. One druggist said in 1876, "Young women cannot go to a ball without taking a dose of morphine to make them agreeable."

Doctors failed to understand the addictive nature of these drugs. During this time, an estimated 200,000 to 400,000 Americans became addicted. The majority were older, middle-class women who had been given the drug by their doctors. One woman told the harrowing story of her friend's addiction: "When she first commenced the use of it to relieve her mind after the loss of her son, little did she think future existence and tolerable comfort would render its use absolute necessity."

Top 10 girl's names of the 1880s: Mary, Anna, Elizabeth, Margaret, Minnie, Emma, Alice, Bertha, Florence, and Rose.

Have you ever heard of . . . Lydia Pinkham?

If you opened any family medicine cabinet in the late 1800s, you would surely have discovered a bottle of Lydia Pinkham's "Vegetable Compound." A remedy brewed from roots and strong alcohol, Vegetable Compound was called a "sure cure" for "women's complaints." Pinkham originally concocted the compound for herself and her friends. But when times got hard in 1873, Pinkham's sons convinced her to sell her medicine. Its great popularity continued long after her death.

As they had for centuries, women shared secret homemade beauty recipes among themselves, mixing and applying such items as horseradish and sour milk or lemon juice and sugar to improve their skin. In addition, they began to add ingredients available from druggists, including paints and powders. Items such as cold cream, cologne, lotion, and hair oil began to appear in drug stores, as well as tongs to curl the hair and silver and gold dust to sprinkle on the skin for special occasions.

Though criticized for their vanity, some women whitewashed their faces with a kind of paint to make their complexions seem perfect. Commercially made cosmetics were often toxic, and included ingredients such as mercury, arsenic, and lead. One twenty-four-year-old St. Louis woman, "Mary C.," began using Laird's Bloom of Youth to lighten her complexion. In 1877, her arms became paralyzed. At first denying and finally admitting use of cosmetics to her doctors, she was admitted to the hospital where she died of lead poisoning.

FASHION Of hoop skirts, devout churchgoer **Nancy Williard** huffed, *"Take care, for they are so large you can hear them strike the seats and scrape the door casings."* With multiple layers of fabric and an amazing array of frills, drapes, and fringes, ladies' fashions took up a great deal of space and were

BEAUTY

LOVELINESS AT ALL COSTS

COMPLEXION In the last decades of the nineteenth century, a woman's clear, light complexion continued to be her greatest asset, a standard of beauty difficult for poor and rural working women to achieve or maintain. One photographer noted that on the frontier, *"people are all sunburnt and roughskinned, and even the pretty girls are sadly tanned by exposure to the weather."* For others—black, Indian, and Hispanic women in particular—this standard was impossible. Racist notions that women with darker skin could not be beautiful helped maintain class and race distinctions.

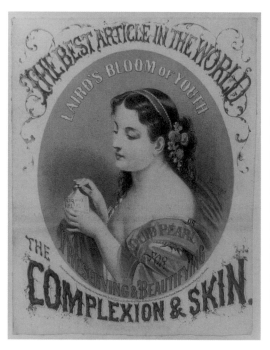

This 1863 Laird's ad doesn't tell the whole story. Are there any hidden dangers in using today's beauty-enhancing products?

This 1872 *Harper's Weekly* illustration criticizes the hazards of the day's fashions. What might such an illustration poke fun at today?

anything but practical. Even "swimming costumes" were so heavy a woman could easily drown. Bell-shaped skirts gave way to skirts with trains and bustles on the back. By the 1880s, women wore steel bustle hoops that lifted dresses up to two feet in the back. With each shift in fashion, corsets changed shape.

Faster travel made it possible to keep abreast of changing Paris fashions. Despite tightly laced corsets cinching women in and bustles tugging at their spines, it was so crucial to be fashionable that one man observed, the *"average woman can no more deviate from the dress of the day than an animal can choose to change its skin or its spots."*

Women who moved west carried their beliefs about beauty with them. The younger generation sometimes rebelled when their mothers attempted to protect their fair complexions with large, stiff sunbonnets "as uncomfortable as a football mask." With their sunbonnets thrown back, some gave in to freckles and tanned skin. Others sewed seams up the middle of their dresses for ease in horseback riding.

AMUSEMENTS

As in other times, what a woman did for fun was dictated by what was considered socially appropriate. But it also depended on where she lived, and how much money she had.

"THIS PURSE-DESTROYING VICE": SHOPPING

Middle-class New York housewife **Harriet Richards** reported in her diary that she shopped six days out of eight in May 1885. Taking the trolley to the new and dazzling world of downtown department stores, she wandered through aisles and floors of gorgeously arrayed merchandise—everything from tropical fruit and children's toys to home goods and lion cubs. She was not alone. By the 1870s, shopping had become both the occupation and the main recreation of urban, middle-class women.

Although a few stately emporiums catering to female customers opened before the war, stores were generally a male province, staffed by men. Store owners kept their limited goods out of reach of customers and made little attempt to market their wares. Prices were not set, and most purchases were considered final. As industry produced more goods, and cash became the main medium of commerce, merchants experimented with new ways of selling. They quickly realized that their most profitable market was not men, but women.

Department stores are so common today that it is hard to imagine that they were ever a revolutionary idea, but almost everything about the early department stores was novel and remarkable, and women adored them. They loved the beautiful stained-glass skylights, carpeted floors, chandeliers, and marble staircases that went up as many as seven stories. They also loved the electric lights, the elevators, and the fact that they could not only touch the merchandise, but exchange it if necessary. Merchants strategically planned their stores to ensure that customers walked past as many displays as possible.

> *The new job opportunities as sales clerks held status for working girls, even though employees were frequently fined for mistakes and could be expected to work as many as 112 hours in a week—on their feet for the entire time.*

Even those who could not afford to buy were encouraged to look. Store employees were to be "polite and attentive to rich and poor alike." Poorer women who normally shopped from the open stalls and pushcarts of the streets could walk around the department store, then go to the basement for bargains. Crowds gathered before another marketing innovation: beautifully illuminated picture windows filled with artistically displayed merchandise.

By the 1880s, stores included other services to delight customers. Shoppers loitered in comfortable libraries, powdered their noses in ornate lavatories, mailed packages at store post offices, and ate lunch

In the 1870s, police noted a new kind of criminal: middle- and upper-class women shoplifters. Observers were baffled. Doctors concluded that shoplifters suffered from an illness called "kleptomania," a state of insanity that caused them to steal. This rested on the belief that women were weak and irrational. Doctors blamed stores for tempting women beyond what they could bear. "Women," they concluded, "couldn't help it." Many shoplifters bought into this message, insisting to police that they didn't even remember taking the items. One shoplifter declared that she was "physically unable to resist the temptation to steal . . . she could no more control the action of her hands than she could fly."

with their friends in restaurants or tearooms. They could check their coats at the door, and have their purchases delivered to their homes free of charge. Shopping was a way for women to be domestic (buying for their families) in a fun and public way.

Far from urban centers, in small towns and on isolated farms it was now also possible to shop with the help of mail order catalogs. By the late 1890s, Sears and Roebucks and Montgomery Ward reached more than six million customers with their beautifully illustrated catalogs. Nannie Alderson, a settler in Wyoming, said of the Montgomery Ward catalog she began receiving in 1885, "it was impossible to exaggerate the importance of the part played by this book of wonder."

Although merchants and husbands needed women to link industry and home, at the same time they condemned them for being frivolous. In 1881 an editorial in the *New York Times* complained that *"the awful prevalence of the vice of shopping among women is one of those signs of the times which lead the thoughtful patriot almost to despair of the future of our country.* Few people have any idea of the extent to which our women are addicted to this purse-destroying vice."

OTHER PASTIMES

VISITING As in earlier generations, women of all classes passed the time making calls on friends. Wealthier society ladies visited one another almost unceasingly, following an elaborate set of social rules. For even the poorest, the pleasure of talking with friends provided a relief from work. In Kansas, **Mary Lyon** later insisted, "Don't think that all our time and thoughts were taken up with the problems of living. We were a social people. We never waited for an introduction or invitation to be neighborly, any day or any night."

On the frontier, women longed most for the company of like-minded members of their own sex, especially in areas where they were far outnumbered by men. Husbands were no substitute for girlfriends. **Nellie Wetherbee** summed it up in her journal: *"I have been very blue, for I cannot make a friend like mother out of Henry."* One Arizona woman recalled, "If the loneliness was at times so intense that even dogs, horses and chickens seemed to take on a personality, to encounter a human being of any description assumed the proportions of an adventure." To meet the need for female camaraderie, frontier women combined their heavy workload with their need to socialize—visiting and letting children play together while they quilted, husked corn, or preserved meat.

MUSIC AND MAGAZINES Mothers who could afford it made sure that their daughters learned to play the piano. Many viewed the possession of a piano as proof of good breeding. A surprising number of families hauled their pianos or small parlor organs west, even when they had no other furniture. Women also enthusiastically read books, magazines, and newspapers. A favorite was *Godey's Lady's Book,* filled with fashion plates, recipes, and stories. *Harper's Bazaar* appeared in 1867, followed by *Cosmopolitan* in 1886, and *Ladies' Home Journal* in 1889.

When **Louisa May Alcott**'s novel *Little Women* was published in 1868, reviewers called it "delightful," "charming," and "sprightly." *Putnam's Magazine* reported, "We gave it to a girl of twelve to read, for whose opinion we have great respect, and she pronounced it *just the nicest book,* **'I could read it right through three times, and it would be nicer and funnier all the time.'** And to our certain knowledge, she read it twice in one week, and would have read it again, had not the book been carried off."

TRAVELING SHOWS Life in many communities was relatively quiet (punctuated by visits with friends and occasional lectures, debates, or concerts), so nothing could quite match the excitement when the circus came to town. Families gathered to admire processions of elephants and giraffes, rhinos in gilded

Born Helen Louise Leonard, this Iowa girl became the superstar love goddess of her age. Radiant and blonde, her mesmerizing stage presence launched her into a theatrical career at the age of seventeen. She traveled in numerous musical productions and soon became a household name. The adoring public forgave her excesses, including four husbands, several lovers, a large appetite, and expensive living (her dog "Mookie" had a diamond-studded collar worth $1,800). Russell's increasing poundage did nothing to diminish her popularity— fat was beautiful. She was well known for her openhanded generosity to everyone she met and was as likely to be seen playing poker backstage as dining in the most expensive restaurants of the world.

cages, acrobats on bicycles, turbaned dancers, dwarfs, and ornate wagons filled with oddities. Irish nannies, black laundresses, and middle-class housewives alike squeezed onto narrow benches inside tents to witness strange and exotic sights.

STEPPING OUT Although society had long frowned upon physically active females, the public began to accept some forms of physical recreation. Well-to-do women took up croquet and archery, and after 1873, they played lawn tennis, wearing huge hats, corsets, and bulky skirts. Roller-skating became popular. Many towns built maple-floored roller rinks where couples could circulate with skates attached to their shoes. Freed from some of the conventions that ruled their urban sisters, women in rural areas enjoyed gathering berries, fishing, hunting, horseback riding, camping, and sleigh riding.

In most places, dancing was a community affair, and dances were attended by people of all ages. People looked forward to church meetings, holidays, and special events such as weddings so they could dance. Whole families traveled miles in their Sunday best to kick up their heels. Young children and babies dozed on the sidelines as dancers reeled, polkaed, square danced, and waltzed, often until three or four the next morning. **Mary Hopping**, an Idaho settler, remembered a woman who was anxious to dance but had a baby in her arms. She spotted a bachelor in the corner, "plumped her baby down in his lap and said, *'yer—Hold this youngin' while I dance and if he cries, you wallop 'im.'*" It was up to the ladies to serve coffee and fresh baked goods at midnight, and sometimes breakfast in the morning.

Hispanic communities also celebrated baptisms, weddings, saints' days, and holidays with fiestas and dances that lasted for days. Women prepared huge feasts of tamales, roast pig, and baked tantalizing cakes and breads. In California, it became popular to break egg shells filled with gold and silver confetti, colored water, or cologne over peoples' heads. **Mary Barnard Aguirre** described one wedding in Las Vegas where men shooting guns and playing fiddles accompanied the bride and groom to a "fine breakfast." There everyone

Acrobats and trapeze artists in an 1890 circus ad.

visitors did not. "I got perfectly enraged," wrote Thomas, when some men "said that they didn't see any good of a woman's learning Latin or Greek it didn't make them any more entertaining to their husbands. A woman had plenty of other things to do sewing, cooking, taking care of children dressing and flirting." They spoke of *"woman being too high too exalted to do anything but sit up in perfect ignorance with folded hands and let men worship at her shrine."*

Dr. Edward Clarke, a retired Harvard Medical School professor, added his voice to those against educating females. His best-selling 1873 book, *Sex in Education,* argued that studying upset the delicate balance of women's bodies. According to Clarke, thinking used up the limited energy that was meant to keep the "female apparatus" healthy. This rerouting of energy from the reproductive system to the brain could severely damage a woman's ability to bear children. In short, he insisted that girls who pursued higher education risked sterility, mental breakdowns, and even premature death.

On January 1, 1872, M. Carey Thomas confided in her journal, *"What I want almost more than anything else in the world is to go to Vassar. When I go to bed I think about it, and when I get up I think about it."* Vassar College was part of the great experiment of educating women. Opening in 1865, it was founded on the belief that women could take the same difficult courses as men without becoming ill or insane. While some colleges had reluctantly opened their doors to female students before the war, few had welcomed them with open arms. Despite heated opposition, Vassar succeeded so well that other colleges in the northeast followed suit.

Within a few years, women's colleges known as the "Seven Sisters"—Vassar, Wellesley, Smith, Mount Holyoke (though founded in 1837, it wasn't officially a "college" until 1893), Radcliffe, Bryn

danced, and the musicians made up verses about the wedding guests.

EDUCATION

"SOMETHING SPLENDID AFTERALL"

HIGHER EDUCATION On January 1, 1871, fourteen-year-old **Martha Carey Thomas** began a journal that she hoped to keep "from the public gaze." In it she resolved, "I'm going to study my lessons a great deal harder, especially Latin and Greek." This desire alone placed her in the middle of the continued debate about whether or not girls should study and aspire to higher learning. One hundred years after the Revolution had opened more doors of education to females, Americans still resisted attempts to teach girls the same way they taught boys.

Lively discussions on the subject took place in Martha's own living room. Her Quaker parents believed in female education, but many of their

"I don't see why the world is made so unjust and I don't see why all unjustness should be turned against girls in general and me in particular."

—M. CAREY THOMAS, October 1, 1871

The faculty and student body of Bryn Mawr College in 1886. Notice how many of the professors of the women's college are men (one of them is Woodrow Wilson, future president of the United States).

Mawr, and Barnard—were established. These colleges trained many future leaders. In addition, a few private and public universities (primarily in the West) began to accept female students. By 1872, there were ninety-seven coeducational colleges in America. For the first time in U.S. history, many middle-class young women found a period of independence between living with their parents and marriage. Between 1870 and 1900, the number of female college students increased from 11,000 to 85,000.

In 1877, M. Carey Thomas boldly entered Cornell University in the first class to accept females. The first women to enter classes with men were barely tolerated, and alternately stared at and ignored. Cornell fraternities made rules that forbade brothers to even speak to coeds. Following her "fiery ordeal" and graduation, Thomas struggled against ongoing prejudice. At Johns Hopkins University, she was not allowed to attend classes with men; at a foreign university she had to sit behind a screen, out of sight of her male colleagues. Nonetheless, she forged ahead, earning a Ph.D. and becoming the president of one of the newly created women's colleges, Bryn Mawr. In doing so, she fulfilled her hope "of doing something splendid afterall."

EDUCATION FOR FREED SLAVES Unfortunately, Thomas, who was otherwise so advanced for her time, joined with many others in believing that whites were inherently superior to blacks. Thus, she did not believe nonwhites should have the very educational opportunities she sought for herself. By

In 1870, there were only five female lawyers in the United States. **Myra Bradwell** was refused admission to the Illinois bar in 1869 because she was married. The Illinois Supreme Court declared that work as a lawyer would destroy femininity. The U.S. Supreme Court agreed that women were too delicate and timid for such work. Bradwell was finally admitted to the bar in 1890.

After the Civil War, **female physicians** were rare. In 1869, when a few brave women attempted to attend a clinical lecture at Pennsylvania Hospital, they were greeted with taunts, pelted with "missiles of tinfoil," and spat upon with tobacco juice.

1890, a survey of colleges found that only thirty-one college degrees had been granted to black women.

But just as Thomas had defied the men who told her she was unfit for education, so too did many freed slaves. Freedwomen were adamant about educating their children. Although most did not have the time to go to school themselves, they contributed their meager resources and time to build schools and hire teachers for their children. It was a significant sacrifice to send children to school instead of to the fields where their labor was needed to help the family survive. *"Dem chillen know a heap more'na me,"* one freedwoman confided to her children's teacher, *"When they come home they talk so smart, I ain't know what they say, but I is proud all the same."*

Despite great opposition and violence, by 1869, 600,000 blacks attended elementary schools. One man wrote, "The colored people are far more zealous in the cause of education than the whites. They will starve themselves, and go without clothes, in order to send their children to school." Middle-class blacks founded colleges and institutes to train the thousands of teachers needed to meet the demand. **Fannie Jackson Coppin**, a Philadelphia principal, mirrored the sentiments of her community when she declared that "knowledge is power." Writing to Frederick Douglass in 1877, she described her desire "to see my race lifted out of the mire of ignorance, weakness and degradation . . . crowned with strength and dignity" that true education would bring. Dedicated women such as **Lucy Laney** and **Charlotte Hawkins Brown** helped to bring that true education to the South by establishing schools for black women.

SUFFRAGE
"EXISTING PUBLIC SENTIMENT ON ANY ISSUE IS WRONG"

THE NEGRO'S HOUR When the war ended, many women's rights activists felt their time had finally arrived. During the Civil War, leaders such as **Susan B. Anthony** and **Elizabeth Cady Stanton** had put aside their pursuit of equality to support the war effort. Now they were ready to take up the fight again, forming the American Equal Rights Association in 1866. With many of their old abolitionist friends in positions of power, they were poised to reap the rewards for their loyalty, and the reward they sought was suffrage, or the right to vote. They were bitterly disappointed when previous supporters counseled them to wait their turn once again.

"This is the Negro's Hour," declared their old allies. Postwar abolitionists sought to secure black men's voting rights by passing the Fourteenth and then the Fifteenth Constitutional amendments. Backers of the amendments worried that linking their cause with that of women would doom the amendments in Congress. In fact, they abandoned women's rights advocates so thoroughly that they actually defined citizens as "male" within the Constitution for the very first time. Outraged, Susan Anthony fumed, *"I would sooner cut off my right hand than ask for the ballot for the black man and not the woman."* Elizabeth Cady Stanton prophesied, *"If that word 'male' be inserted as now proposed, it will take a century to get it out again."*

SUFFRAGISTS DISAGREE The issue of whether or not to support the amendments caused a great rift in the women's movement. While Stanton and Anthony raged against the injustice of excluding females, other suffragists, such as **Lucy Stone**, were willing to wait.

Old friends found themselves on opposite sides at the annual meeting of the American Equal Rights Association in 1869. Stanton and Frederick Douglass, longtime friends, spoke out against each other. Lucy Stone urged patience. She spoke of the "ocean of wrongs that cannot be fathomed" faced by both black men and women, and concluded, "I thank God for the Fifteenth Amendment, and . . . *I will be thankful in my soul if* any *body can get out of the terrible pit."* Former allies turned into bitter enemies as each side accused the other of failing to see the bigger picture.

The united suffrage movement split into two factions. The division between the two groups was painful, deep, and wide. Stanton, Anthony, and other radical suffragists formed the National Woman Suffrage Association (NWSA) in May 1869. Stone and her husband, Henry Blackwell, countered that November by creating the American Woman Suffrage Association (AWSA).

The National Woman Suffrage Association embraced controversial issues. In fact, Stanton stated,

"It is a settled maxim with me that the existing pubic sentiment on any subject is wrong."

Members of NWSA questioned many of society's ideas about women and continued to shock the nation by proposing reforms on issues such as divorce, abortion, prostitution, equal pay for equal work, marital relations, and birth control. They worked to pass a sixteenth amendment for women's suffrage to the Constitution.

At the same time, the American Woman Suffrage Association continued to work through less controversial means to seek female suffrage. They sought male leadership, continued relationships with former abolitionists, and worked to obtain the vote state by state. Less radical, they made it possible for more conservative women to support the vote.

An 1873 petition in which Susan Anthony, Matilda Joslyn Gage, and Elizabeth Cady Stanton "respectfully ask Congress to enact appropriate legislation . . . to protect women . . . in their right to vote."

Elizabeth Cady Stanton and Susan Anthony in their later years.

During a lecture in Nebraska, an angry man rudely interrupted Elizabeth Cady Stanton. He said, "Don't you think that the best thing a woman can do is perform well her part in the role of wife and mother? My wife has presented me with eight beautiful children; is not hers a better life-work than that of exercising the right of suffrage?" Looking him up and down, she responded, **"Frankly sir, I know of few men worth repeating eight times."**

YEARS OF UNCEASING EFFORT Despite major setbacks, suffragists continued to win over new supporters. They sold their cause by lecturing all over the United States in churches, schools, and halls, all the while enduring rutted roads, bad food, and the anger of those who disagreed with their message. For eleven straight years Stanton toured, "stirring up the women generally to rebellion" from California to New York. She actually put her children through college with the proceeds. No one, however, could rival the travels of Anthony, who crisscrossed the country relentlessly, only canceling two lectures in her twenty years on the circuit. In Walla Walla, Washington, one suffragist wrote, *"Miss Anthony made scores of converts, and frightened the few old fogies in the city almost out of their wits."*

SUFFRAGE IN THE WEST Territories in the West proved more responsive than the rest of the country to the idea of female voters. In a place where the living was as hard on women as it was on men, it was not so easy to argue that they were too delicate to vote. The efforts of **Esther Morriss** and others led Wyoming to become the first state to grant suffrage

in 1870. Seventy-year-old **Louisa Swain** was the first woman to vote in the new territory. One man later recalled, *"No rum was sold, women rode to the polls in carriages furnished by the parties, and every man was straining himself to be a gentleman because there were votes at stake."*

The other territory to grant females the vote in 1870 was one that had been accused by many of trampling on women's rights. Utah, settled by members of the Church of Jesus Christ of Latter-day Saints (or Mormons) in the 1840s, did not seem a likely place for suffrage. The Mormon practice of polygamy (a man marrying more than one wife) shocked and offended many Americans. Yet Mormon suffragists, actively involved in their communities from the very beginning, played a crucial, if less visible part in their enfranchisement.

Many Americans hoped that after women in Utah were given the vote, they would outlaw polygamy. When this did not happen, the federal government attempted to end women's suffrage in the state. Although at least 75 percent of Mormons did not practice polygamy, even monogamous women defended the practice. Prominent Mormon leaders such as **Eliza Snow** and **Sarah Kimball** argued that polygamy was misunderstood and that it was "the only reliable safeguard of female virtue and innocence; and the only sure protection against the fearful sin of prostitution and its attendant evils." The issue divided suffragists both within and outside Mormon ranks. When the AWSA became outspoken in its opposition to Mormons and polygamy, the NWSA again proved its willingness to address controversial issues by inviting polygamist suffragists to the 1879 Convention. Prominent suffragist **Sara Spencer** rose to defend the Mormons, stating that "the difference between Mormons and the Christian statesmen is that the Mormons marry their mistresses, the congressmen don't." The Mormon Church officially ended the practice of polygamy in 1890.

Portraits of twenty leaders in the Mormon Church in 1883.

Have you ever heard of . . . Abigail Scott Duniway?

Duniway was an outspoken suffrage leader in the Pacific Northwest. Despite persecution, she dedicated much of her life to spreading the message of women's equality. When a farmer's wife wrote that her husband would no longer allow her to receive Duniway's newspaper, the *New Northwest,* Duniway responded, "You shall have your paper." She sent it to the woman's neighbor and encouraged her to "manage" her "pig-headed" husband. When Oregon granted suffrage in 1912, the governor arranged for Duniway to be the first female in the state to register.

NEW TACTICS

Over and over again, women's rights advocates invented new battle tactics to further the cause. **Matilda Joslyn Gage**, one of the great radical thinkers of the movement, masterminded many of the arguments that fueled the suffragists' actions. Her ideas led women around the country to test state laws by attempting to register and vote in their local elections. The most publicized story that emerged from this tactic was that of Susan Anthony voting in the 1872 election.

CIVIL DISOBEDIENCE *"Well I have been & gone and done it! Positively voted the Republican ticket,"* wrote Anthony to Stanton after the election. She wrote that fifteen other suffragists had followed suit and called it a "fine agitation in Rochester." On Thanksgiving Day, a U.S. Marshal showed up on her doorstep with a warrant for her arrest.

With Anthony's trial date set, she and Gage traveled the county speaking out for women's rights as citizens. They succeeded so well that her trial had to be moved to another county. Undaunted, Anthony and Gage simply took their lectures to the next county. At her trial, the judge (described by Gage as a "small-brained, pale-faced, prim looking man") refused to allow Anthony to testify and then ordered the all-male jury to find her guilty.

Just before sentencing Anthony, the judge made the tactical error of asking her if she had anything to say. Rising to her feet, she took the day with a long, impassioned speech accusing the court of "trampl[ing] under foot every vital principle of our government." Though the frustrated judge persistently ordered her to sit, she continued, *"My natural rights, my civil rights, my political rights, my judicial rights are all alike ignored."* When the judge finally broke in, he sentenced her to a fine of $100. Anthony shot back, "I will never pay a dollar of your unjust penalty." In addition, she assured him that she would continue to "rebel against your man-made unjust, unconstitutional forms of law, which tax, fine, imprison and hang women, while denying the right of representation in the government."

Virginia Minor, an NWSA officer, was one of the 150 women who, like Anthony, attempted to vote in 1872. Unlike Anthony, she was not even allowed to register. Consequently, her husband (as a married woman, she lacked the legal right to sue) sued the registrar. The outcome of her case, *Minor v. Happersett*, struck a great blow to the hopes of suffragists. The U.S. Supreme Court decided unanimously that their right to vote was not protected under the Constitution. This decision had far-reaching consequences. States now held the absolute authority to determine who could and could not vote, and Southern states began to deny black men the right to vote.

When New York Governor Lucius Robinson vetoed a bill granting females the right to serve on school boards, Matilda Joslyn Gage and fellow suffragists worked tirelessly to defeat him in the next election. The governor who replaced him signed the new bill in 1880. Gage gloried in the victory and pointed out that **"when men begin to fear the power of women, their voice and their influence, then we shall secure justice, but not before.... We must be recognized as aggressive."** The next school board election in her hometown produced an all-women slate of officers, including Gage's daughter Helen.

Matilda Joslyn Gage

Victoria Woodhull, "Mrs. Satan," in 1872.

What One Woman Did

"Mrs. Satan"

Amid this flurry of activity, a stranger to the suffrage movement caught the nation's attention. In 1870, fifty years before women could vote nationally, the beautiful, captivating **Victoria Claflin Woodhull** announced her candidacy for president of the United States. It wasn't only her gender that made her an unlikely candidate. Woodhull had grown up in a poor family of questionable reputation. As a girl she had acted as a spiritual psychic, fortune-teller, and clairvoyant in her father's traveling medicine show, often avoiding arrest by skipping town. Through a series of strange events, she and her sister **Tennessee (or Tennie C.) Claflin** came into contact with and charmed the millionaire Cornelius Vanderbilt. With his financial backing, they became the first women to operate a New York brokerage firm. Their success, wealth, and strange family situation (a large assortment of freeloading, swindler relatives and ex-husbands lived with them in their mansion) made them the talk of the town.

Coming from such a colorful background, Victoria Woodhull challenged all sorts of social rules. She questioned dress standards and believed in legalized prostitution. She promoted something called "free love," saying, *"I have the inalienable, constitutional and natural right to love whom I may...to change that love every day if I please."* She sought to bring attention to the issues of women's rights and suffrage through her candidacy. As it turned out, neither the country nor the suffrage movement was quite ready for such radical ideas. The press dubbed her "Mrs. Satan." And though she was initially quite taken with Woodhull, Susan Anthony would not allow anyone to do damage to the suffrage cause she cared about so passionately. When Victoria Woodhull attempted to address a June 1872 meeting of NWSA, Anthony stormed backstage and had the lights put out. The first woman to run for president had few followers among suffragists.

CREATING HISTORY Even during their lifetimes, Matilda Joslyn Gage, Elizabeth Cady Stanton, and Susan B. Anthony knew that their work was historically significant. As a result, they wrote a history of the suffrage movement even as it unfolded. Stanton pointed out, *"Men have been faithful in noting every heroic act of their half of the race, and now it should be the duty as well as the pleasure, of women to make for future generations a record of the heroic deeds of the other half."* The

Susan B. Anthony hated writing. She found it a "perfect prison." While working on *The History of Woman Suffrage,* she complained, **"O, how I long to be in the midst of the fray and here I am. . . . I love to make history but I hate to write it."**

women eventually produced a three-volume work: *The History of Woman Suffrage.* The first volume was printed in 1881. While Stanton and Gage did most of the writing and editing, Anthony worked to get it published. Once it was completed, they distributed copies to libraries around the country.

DIVERGING PATHS As the years passed, advocates for suffrage moved further and further away from their early radical roots in an attempt to gather support. Suffragists felt the need to make their demands seem unthreatening in order to attract the greatest number of supporters. Anthony, in particular, was increasingly single-minded in her pursuit of suffrage to the exclusion of all other women's issues. She became a regular fixture in Washington, leading conventions and lobbying endlessly for an amendment that would give females the right to vote. As Anthony grew increasingly conservative, she amassed a group of loyal followers, younger women whom she referred to as her nieces.

At the same time, Stanton and Gage grew more radical. They went so far as to attack Christianity as a source of women's oppression. Their unconventional ideas increasingly isolated them from the movement. At one point, Stanton told Anthony, "Don't speak to me of conventions. *I can't bear having to hold my tongue for fear of offending someone."* As she aged, she was less and less willing to withhold her controversial opinions. Suffrage leaders feared that their ideas would alienate an already uncertain nation. What had earlier been a movement to gain equal rights became a movement solely to gain the right to vote. There was no longer room for those who saw the larger picture of women's inequality. Yet even with this narrowed focus, the right to vote would elude them for decades.

To a certain extent, it was Susan Anthony's more conservative, dedicated following that carried on the suffrage cause and eventually won the vote in 1920. Because they were the victors, for decades it appeared that Anthony had fought for the vote single-handedly. Because of their radical ideas, Stanton and Gage were virtually written out of history, only to be revived in recent years.

WOMEN'S CHRISTIAN TEMPERANCE UNION

In April 1874, the *New Northwest* newspaper described a scene that had become familiar in towns across America. A group of about twenty women gathered on the sidewalk to protest alcohol use by singing and praying before a Portland, Oregon, saloon. The owner, Mr. Moffett, and his followers responded loudly with whistles, "gong-beaters, organ-beaters," and "bell-ringers." They "used insulting language and committed insulting and violent acts in the presence of the ladies." Abigail Scott Duniway reported, *"The ladies, surrounded by an excited crowd, remained hour after hour, silently or inaudibly praying."* Soon the men began quarrelling. In the end, two men "were knocked down, one man stabbed, chairs thrown about, etc. Mr. Moffett himself brandished a pistol." The women were charged with "making a loud noise" and engaging in "violent and disorderly conduct." They refused to pay a fine and chose to be jailed instead. However, the police captain would not put them in jail, and the ladies held a grand reunion at the local church.

Many families endured poverty, desertion, and violence because of alcohol abuse. As a result, the "temperance" movement that had begun earlier in the century picked up steam across the Midwest. Women who had previously kept quiet about the problem of alcoholism decided to speak up. Soon, saloon owners across the country faced throngs of pious sisters intent on their destruction.

These women formed the Women's Christian Temperance Union (WCTU) in 1873 to fight against alcohol companies and their interests. By 1879, **Frances Willard** had emerged as the crusading leader of the WCTU and one of the most famous, loved women of her time. Her stated goal was to "make the whole world homelike." By 1890, the WCTU boasted a membership of 160,000—the largest of the era's women's groups.

"Pleading with a saloon keeper…Woman's Crusade Against Intemperance." An 1874 *Harper's Weekly* illustration.

Frances Willard led the WCTU to expand its reform agenda. Under her leadership, the WCTU pushed to require prayer in schools, outlaw public activities on Sunday, and change the Constitution to make Christ the author and head of government. By 1882, she had decided that women needed the right to vote in order to push Christian reforms. Though many suffragists feared an alliance with the WCTU, the association brought suffrage from the fringes of society and lent it the respectability of middle-class values.

Frances Willard was famous for uttering memorable mottos, one of which stated, "The sweetest words are mother, home and heaven." Matilda Joslyn Gage disagreed. Her tombstone in Fayetteville, New York, reads, **"There is a word sweeter than mother, home or heaven. That word is Liberty."**

ARTS IN THE SPOTLIGHT

At art museums, you will notice that men created much of the art on display. Why is that? Are men just naturally more artistic? Is it possible that only men have wanted to draw, paint, and sculpt? Or are there other reasons that fewer women have become famous artists? Women often lacked the encouragement, training, time, and resources to embark on artistic careers.

ALONE AMONG THE IMPRESSIONISTS: MARY CASSATT

In spite of many obstacles, there were still women who managed to become professional artists. One of the most famous was **Mary Cassatt**. Cassatt's parents were well-to-do Pennsylvanians who believed that travel was an important part of a child's education. When Mary's parents took her to see art museums in Europe, they probably did not expect her to love them enough to want to be an artist. But love them she did, and in 1861, her parents allowed her to begin studying art at the Pennsylvania Academy of the Fine Arts.

American, and one of only three women, ever asked to exhibit with them. As they experimented with light, bright color, and perspective, the friends influenced one another. Degas, a notoriously ill-tempered man, once said of Cassatt, "I will not admit that a woman can draw so well." People admired Cassatt's tender pastels, paintings, and prints of women and children depicted in everyday activities. She was able to support herself on the money she earned from these.

Later in life, she became interested in the suffrage movement and painted a mural in the Women's Building at the World's Fair in Chicago in 1893. Cassatt never married and painted until she lost her eyesight in 1915.

Other female artists of the time included sculptor **Harriott Hosmer**, **Lilla Cabot Perry**,

Mary Cassatt in 1914.

Five years later, when Cassatt wished to continue her training in Europe, her father responded, "I would rather see you dead." In time, he relented, and she traveled to Paris to study. At the time Cassatt arrived in France, the art world was in a whirl. A group of young artists calling themselves "Impressionists" were challenging traditional ways of painting. Artists were expected to follow rules set by the artist's "salon," and those who did not comply were not allowed to show their work. The Impressionists banded together and staged their own exhibits. Cassatt, who was bored with conventional painting, saw the art of Edgar Degas in a window. She later wrote, "I used to go and flatten my nose against that window and absorb all I could of his art. It changed my life."

She struck up a friendship with Degas and other Impressionist artists, becoming the only

A study created by Mary Cassatt for her 1893 mural for the Chicago World's Fair.

When **Ellen Day Hale** exhibited her *Self Portrait* in 1887, one critic attempted to compliment her by saying that she displayed "a man's strength." Hale, who was related to the accomplished Beecher family, trained in Boston and in Paris and continued painting throughout her life.

who was in France at the same time as Cassatt, and **Edmonia Lewis**. Lewis, the daughter of an African American father and Native American mother, rose to prominence as a sculptor in the 1860s and 1870s. Many of her works drew a connection between bondage in biblical times and American slavery. Six of her sculptures appeared at the 1876 centennial celebration in Philadelphia.

LADY LIBERTY: A LIGHT TO THE WORLD?

In 1886, the Statue of Liberty, a gift from France, was unveiled in New York's harbor. To help pay for the pedestal, poet and immigrant **Emma Lazarus** penned the words that would eventually define the statue's meaning for many Americans:

"Give me your tired, your poor,
Your huddled masses yearning to
*   breathe free,*
The wretched refuse of your teeming
*   shore.*
Send these, the homeless, tempest-
*   tost to me,*
I lift my lamp beside the golden
*   door!"*

For Lazarus, the colossal woman lifting a torch to the sky represented the ideal of democracy, freedom, and hope. For others, the Statue of Liberty was a reminder of the empty promises of life in America. Suffragists protested with a water parade during her dedication. They announced, "The Statue of Liberty is a gigantic lie, a travesty, and a mockery. It is the greatest sarcasm of the nineteenth century" to portray liberty as a woman "while not one single woman throughout the length and breadth of the Land is as yet in possession of political Liberty." Matilda Joslyn Gage declared, *"Ah women, I wish I could fill your hearts with a desire for liberty like that which boils in my heart."*

Women had fought for nearly forty years for liberty and still they lacked many of the rights of citizenship, including the right to vote. Immigrants and minority groups continued to battle with racism and prejudice. Native Americans continued to lose their homes. The next generation would face many challenges as it strove to obtain the liberty the statue symbolized.

CHAPTER 5

Wider Paths

1890–1920

On October 4, 1911, twenty-seven-year-old **Elizabeth Dierssen** couldn't make up her mind. Should she buy new silk gloves or use the fifty cents to join the town's "Wednesday Club"? Though a seemingly insignificant decision, her choice to join the club linked her to a larger movement of women who were challenging and influencing American society. Dierssen kept a lively diary of her club's meetings. One account described Mrs. Himmelberger's suggestion that they become more than a social "study group":

"What I want most of all is for the Club to do something for this town. It's time we were. Why, this body of women can do anything they make up their minds to—anything at all!" She sat down flushed. . . .

Mrs. Bell squared her shoulders. "I agree perfectly. It is time this Club was doing something about this town. . . . Up to now we've been just a study club. It is time we add something else."

One felt the atmosphere of transition from culture to crusading, lady-like, a shade militant.

Elizabeth Dierssen was swept up in the atmosphere of transition that marked the thirty years from 1890 to 1920. Change was everywhere. Cities swelled with immigrants and migrants in search of a better life. In the West, Mexican Americans and Native Americans engaged in a monumental

An 1897 photograph entitled *The Readers.*

struggle for autonomy. Industries grew larger, more mechanized, and more impersonal. Technology offered opportunities but also made new demands. While these changes meant hope and opportunity for some, for others they meant oppression and inequality. The progressive movement was born out of a desire to care for the needs of all Americans. As progressives, Dierssen and other women forged sisterly organizations and collectively reached out to improve conditions in their communities. In response to the many injustices they saw, women of varied classes and races stepped across their thresholds to become crusaders—"lady-like" and "a shade militant."

> *"When I arrived in America, I was surprised to find out that the streets were not paved with gold. In fact, I found that they were not paved at all, and I was expected to pave them."*—an Italian American lament

IMMIGRATION

"WE HAD COME A LONG WAY"

The United States has long been a land of immigrants, but between 1890 and 1920, they poured into the nation in unprecedented numbers. While most came from Eastern and Southern Europe, others journeyed from other parts of Europe as well as Asia and Mexico. Like earlier immigrants, they came in search of a better life, often fleeing war, poverty, or racism. Many challenges of being a new arrival in America have changed little in the last 100 years. Immigrants then, as now, were subject to prejudice, low-paying jobs, changes in diet, conflicts between generations, differences in gender roles, and distance from family—all while trying to learn a new language and understand strange new customs.

By 1900, up to one-half of the populations of Baltimore, Philadelphia, Chicago, and Boston were immigrants. Few families could afford to sail to America all at once. Usually fathers or sons made the trip first. Wives and children followed, sometimes years later. After a long, uncomfortable ship voyage, those from Europe stopped at Ellis Island in New York Harbor to be checked by doctors and registered before going ashore.

Rahel Mittelstein, a Jewish immigrant from Eastern Europe, later recalled,

Ellis Island in Russian is called the "Island of Tears," and in every way it merited the name. We all cried.... *We cried because of fear and disappointment.* We had come a long way: we had sold everything we had and spent every cent, and now we were afraid of being sent back. . . . All the way to America, we were scrubbed, cleaned, and examined by physicians and *now dirt and squalor seemed everywhere*. . . . As for the people in charge of us, *they seemed to regard us as some sort of inferior beings.*

An Italian immigrant family at Ellis Island, about 1910.

THE TOLL ON FAMILIES Sometimes after years apart, families struggled to become reacquainted. Women who had never worked for wages now needed to earn money. Doing contracted factory work at home made it possible for a woman to combine home chores with earning a wage, but it also isolated her and made it more difficult for her to adapt.

The strain of making a new life took its toll. Divorce, desertion, and death left many women alone with the double burden of raising children and making a living. Job options for women were extremely limited. Some mothers were forced to leave their children in orphanages and go find work. **Jenni Herbst**'s father died of tuberculosis. She said, *"What was my mother to do?"* There were no jobs for women. She cooked at weddings, she plucked chickens, took in boarders. My oldest brother dropped dead three weeks after his wedding in 1911 when I was eight.... *She became a janitress* in the Hebrew school...scrubbing the classrooms and halls, making up the stoves to heat the offices." Many immigrants hoped that their sacrifices would provide their children with opportunities.

JAPANESE IMMIGRANTS

Between 1900 and 1920, more than 20,000 Japanese women entered the United States at Angel Island, in the San Francisco Bay, as "picture brides." Having seen only photos of their future husbands, these young women got off boats to marry Japanese men they had never met. Often brides were shocked to discover that their new husbands were much older than the photographs they had sent. One woman described the reactions of her new friends as they saw the men waiting at the dock: "A lot of people I came together with said, 'I'm going back on this very boat.' I told them, 'You can't do that; you should go ashore at once. *If you really don't like him, and you feel like going back, then you have to have a meeting and then go back.'"* Far from fulfilling dreams of wealth and romance, these arrangements were often difficult.

Picture brides wanted to fit in. On arrival in California, one woman recalled, *"I was immediately outfitted with Western clothing*....Because I had to wear a tight corset around my chest, I could not bend forward....I wore a large hat, a high-necked blouse, a long skirt, a buckled belt around my waist, high-laced shoes, and of course, for the first time in my life, a brassiere and hip pads."

Try as they might, Japanese immigrants faced great prejudice. Picture brides arrived in the United States at a time when anti-Asian sentiment was high, especially in the West. In 1906, the same year as the great earthquake and fire, schools in San Francisco required that Japanese children go

Amid urban squalor, a young, middle-class woman named **Crystal Eastman** made a different observation. In 1907, she wrote,

The city is really marvelous on a summer night. Everyone is out. Mothers and fathers and babies line the doorsteps. Girls with their beaux, standing in the shadows, or gathered in laughing groups on the corners....Let someone only strike up a common dance tune on a wheezy street organ, and though it be the hottest, dirtiest street, and the weariest people in the land—you'll see the eyes light up and the feet begin to go—there'll be humming and singing here and there—and the little ones will dance their legs off.

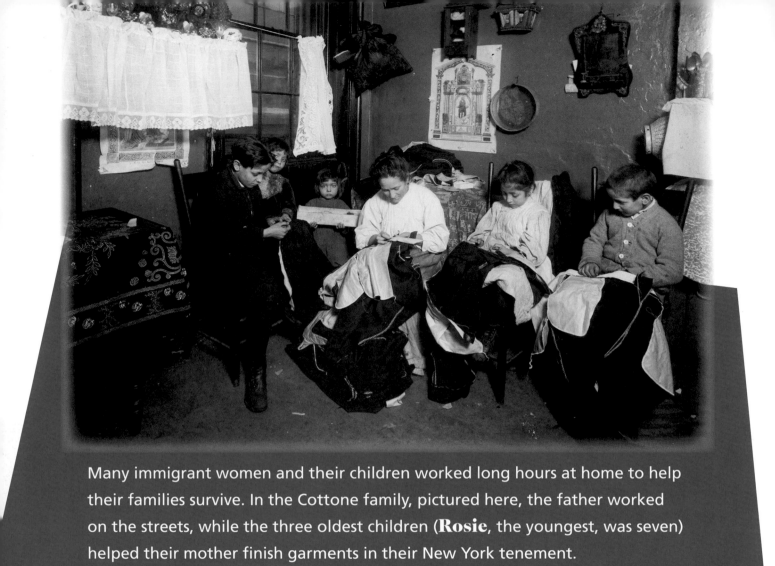

Many immigrant women and their children worked long hours at home to help their families survive. In the Cottone family, pictured here, the father worked on the streets, while the three oldest children (**Rosie**, the youngest, was seven) helped their mother finish garments in their New York tenement.

to segregated schools. In 1913, the Alien Land Act made it impossible for Asian Americans to buy land because even those born in the United States could not be citizens.

Women who could not remain at home worked in laundries, restaurants, and other small Japanese-owned businesses such as plant nurseries. Many also took positions as servants in middle-class homes. Although the constant struggle to make a living could be hard on a marriage, the traditional belief in duty and obligation kept many couples together.

"POVERTY OOZED FROM EVERY CORNER": LIFE IN THE TENEMENTS

Large numbers of immigrants and native-born Americans settled in urban slums that were awash in filth and pollution. One woman described Chicago in these words: "The Streets are inexpressibly dirty, the number of schools inadequate, sanitary legislation unenforced, the street lighting bad, the paving miserable and altogether lacking in the alleys and smaller streets, and the stables foul beyond description." Garbage and waste lay everywhere.

As wealthier Americans moved out to newly constructed suburbs, they left crowded, disease-infested, crime-filled cities to immigrants and the poor. Families lived crammed into urban apartment buildings (known as tenements) and no longer had gardens or animals to supplement their meager earnings. Immigrants tended to settle near others from their own country, creating small ethnic communities.

What One Woman Did

"The Falling of a Lily in the Mud"

In the 1800s, there were few programs in the United States to help the poor. Many current programs originated with those begun by progressives at the turn of the century. Progressives had many ideas about how middle-class women could improve the lot of the working poor. **Jane Addams** was a progressive. College educated and single in the 1880s, Addams found herself without any appealing outlets for her knowledge and skills. She was not alone. She pointed out later, *"We have in America a fast-growing number of cultivated young people who have no recognized outlet for their active faculties."* Addams's family assumed that if she wasn't going to marry, she would help raise nieces and nephews. Her career choices were limited to the small list of reputable professions available to educated middle-class women: she could choose to be a teacher, librarian, or nurse. Addams had other ideas.

While worrying about her future, she visited Toynbee Hall in London. Toynbee Hall was the first settlement house (a place that provided welfare services) in the world. This experience inspired her to start her own settlement house in the United States. She would use her education and resources to bring culture, hope, and money to poor communities. In 1889, Addams and a friend, **Ellen Gates Starr**, bought a neglected mansion in a tenement neighborhood in Chicago and turned it into a kind of community center they called Hull House. This was a brand-new idea at the time.

Hull House provided a gathering place for community meetings, classes, and cultural events. At Hull House, poor immigrants could learn how to become part of middle-class America. Staffed with educated volunteers who lived in the settlement, Hull House sponsored social clubs, after-school activities, a nursery, and a kindergarten. Volunteers organized a chorus, a debate club, and an art gallery. They also created the first public playground in Chicago.

Addams and her volunteers offered aid when people had nowhere else to turn: they nursed the dying, protected battered wives, and cared for unwanted children. In time, the Hull House complex took up a whole city block. Addams's idea was so popular that within a year, there were more than one hundred more settlement houses in cities around the country. Although the majority of

Jane Addams was known as the "mother of the world" for her tireless work for peace and for the underprivileged. In 1931, she became the first American woman to win a Nobel Peace Prize.

settlements were white, by 1910 there were also ten settlement houses for blacks.

Volunteers often worked outside jobs to support themselves while living and helping at Hull House. The public worried about middle-class young women mingling with the working classes. One paper likened their work among the poor to the "falling of a lily in the mud." Although more women were educated than ever before, society regarded women who went to college and became too smart as unlikely candidates for marriage. In fact, many women college graduates did not marry. Settlements and women's schools became communities where educated single women could band together for mutual support rather than living as burdens to their families.

Settlement houses provided a space for middle-class women to learn valuable skills and lobby for legislation. They worked for safer working conditions, laws to protect children, and pensions for working mothers. Many important progressive reformers got their start as workers and found lifelong friends at Hull House. These included **Florence Kelley**, **Lillian Wald**, and **Julia Lathrop**.

By embracing the popular belief that women were naturally pure and self-sacrificing, progressive women could defend their public work nurturing the young, the sick, and the poor. Their efforts evolved into the new fields of social work and public health.

Not all reform-minded individuals agreed with the kinds of education taking place at settlement houses. **Emma Goldman**, a self-styled revolutionary, told a friend, "Teaching the poor to eat with a fork is all very well, but what good does it do if they have not the food. **Let them first become masters of life; they will then know how to eat and live.**"

Have you ever heard of . . . Alice Hamilton?

With only two years of formal schooling, Hamilton was tutored by her father and went on to get a medical degree at the University of Michigan. She lived and worked at Hull House for twenty-two years. At the time, Americans did not know that there were often poisonous fumes in factories or that the lead used in making many products was toxic. **Hamilton's research made her effectively the creator of industrial medicine in the United States and led to laws protecting workers from industrial poisons.** In 1919, she became the first female professor at Harvard University.

When a factory worker was asked in 1915 why more girls didn't want to become domestic servants, she answered, "Intelligent people set no stigma on factory workers who are well-bred and ladylike. These girls are received in good circles anywhere. Many women of wealth and standing are interested in these girls and even invite them to their homes. **But no one has ever invited someone's maid or cook to their home for afternoon tea or any other social affair."**

PAID WORK

WASHERWOMEN TO FACTORY GIRLS

Now that American industry produced one-third of the world's goods, factories needed more workers than ever. By 1910, one in four women worked for wages. Most worked out of necessity, not because it brought them great fulfillment. Paid work went against the middle-class ideal of mother as homemaker. This ideal was not an option for most black women, who worked their entire adult lives. Chinese immigrant women also labored long hours as washerwomen, seamstresses, gardeners, fisherwomen, storekeepers, and laborers. Others rolled cigars, made brooms, or took jobs as domestics. Poor white immigrant and native-born girls worked for a few years before they married. After marriage, they were more likely to take in home work or boarders for income.

The kinds of work a woman could do, and remain respectable, were increasing but still severely limited by today's standards. Fifty percent of women continued to live in rural communities and work on farms. Among urban laborers there was a hierarchy, with the office jobs offered to American-born workers providing the greatest status, and domestics and waitresses receiving the least. Clerical workers looked down on department store workers, who looked down on factory girls. Factory girls in turn disdained servant girls.

DOMESTIC WORKERS "There is no need to say to anyone in this country that housework is the last occupation the intelligent American working girl will seek," stated reporter **Mary Trueblood** in 1902. Despite undesirable working conditions, one-third of working women toiled as domestics, cleaning, cooking, and watching children for wealthier families. The reasons for avoiding paid domestic work become clear in the story of a middle-aged African American woman who had begun working as a servant when she was ten years old. As a mother of three and a widow of fifteen years, she described her life:

"I frequently work from fourteen to sixteen hours a day.... I am allowed to go home to my own children, the oldest whom is a girl of 18 years, only once in two weeks, every other Sunday afternoon—even then I'm not permitted to stay all night.... I see my own children only when they happen to see me on the streets.... *[E]very day in the week I am the slave, body and soul, of this family.* And what do I get for this lifetime bondage? The pitiful sum of ten dollars a month! And what am I expected to do with these ten dollars? Pay my house rent, which is four dollars per month, for a little house of two rooms, just big enough to turn around in; and...feed and clothe myself and three children."

The town photographer of Black River Falls, Wisconsin, took this 1890 photograph of one family's household staff (probably all Norwegian immigrants). Can you figure out who did what kind of work?

the home provided women with opportunities to be with other young people, make friends outside their own neighborhoods, and hear new ideas. In spite of the long hours, or perhaps because of them, working girls and women created a work culture of their own. They read dime novels about working girls marrying millionaires, and recounted the plots over the hum of the machines. Some made up fictional names for themselves and practiced being ladies by copying genteel speech. They sang, argued about politics, and discussed their personal lives.

FACTORY WORKERS By the turn of the century most of America's ready-made women's clothing was manufactured in New York. The newest craze was the shirtwaist, a woman's shirt that could be worn to work in offices and stores. Shirtwaists were made solely in factories, and mostly by women. A third of working women found jobs doing repetitive, nonskilled labor in factories. Cotton mills became the largest industrial employers for Southern women. Highlighting the terrible working conditions in many of these factories, one young shoe stitcher said, *"The stitching room will take the bloom out of any girl's cheek."*

Though conditions were poor, factory workers had some freedom. Jobs outside

SALESCLERKS The creation of department stores opened up another line of work for women. By 1890, 100,000 young women, primarily native-

These wooden-box factory workers pose with a woman identified as **"Mrs. Graham,"** probably the wife of the factory owner. How would these women's lives have differed from hers?

born Americans, worked as salesclerks. While the pay was not any higher than factory work, salesgirls enjoyed greater social status among the working classes. The trade-off was that they spent long hours on their feet, were not paid for overtime, and found it difficult to save money because they had to buy clothes for the job.

CLERICAL WORKERS About 12 percent of women held the most coveted and well-paying jobs as clerical workers. Today, working in an office as a secretary is stereotyped as women's work. But that hasn't always been the case. Until the 1870s and 1880s, clerical work was considered a man's job. However, as business firms grew, they needed more people to keep records and manage production. More goods and better transportation opened new markets and increased demand for clerical workers. Besides, employers believed that women's piano-playing skills would make them superior typists. As women moved into office work, men shifted up and out.

Have you ever heard of . . . Williamina Stevens Fleming?

Fleming worked as a domestic servant for Harvard astronomer Edward Pickering. Fed up with his male lab assistant, Pickering fired him, saying that his maid could do a better job. Indeed, she could. Fleming became a professional astronomer. In 1890, she published a catalog of "stellar spectra." Her success paved the way for other women. When she died, a younger woman took her place as curator of astronomical photographs at the Harvard College Observatory.

"A MIGHTY ARMY, RISING OUT OF THE NIGHT AND DEMANDING TO BE HEARD": UNIONS

As women increasingly joined the ranks of wage earners, they needed the protection that membership in a union could provide. Factory workers relied on union leaders to negotiate with employers for better working conditions and higher wages. When talks broke down, unions helped organize strikes. However, many male union organizers snubbed female workers. The largest union refused them membership. Other unions made the dues too high or held their meetings at night or in saloons. Rather than recognizing a joint cause with female laborers, many men believed women workers took their jobs. They also viewed women as temporary laborers who brought down wages. Undaunted by the lack of male support, women formed their own unions, such as the Women's Trade Union League (WTUL) and the International Ladies Garment Workers Union (ILGWU).

THE SHIRTWAIST STRIKE

Female workers had staged strikes before with limited success. This changed in 1909 when many women and a minority of men working in New York's textile factories decided they'd had enough. Workers began to walk off their jobs. Those brave enough to picket their factories were locked out, harassed, and arrested by the police.

In a union meeting on November 22, mostly male union leaders discussed whether to call a general strike. After listening to long speeches, **Clara Lemlich**, a twenty-one-year-old worker, pushed her way to the podium. Speaking in Yiddish, she declared, *"I am tired of listening to speakers who talk in generalities. What we are here for is to decide whether or not to strike. I offer the resolution that the strike be declared now."* The crowds cheered wildly and took an oath. Within a week, 30,000 garment workers had left their jobs.

The strike spread to other cities and brought production to a standstill. One onlooker observed,

"From every waist-making factory in New York and Brooklyn, the girls poured forth, filling the narrow streets....It was like a mighty army, rising out of the night and demanding to be heard." The public and the employers were amazed. No one thought that women could manage a large-scale strike. Striking women and girls sang while they marched with picket signs, and threw rotten eggs at those who crossed the line to work.

The WTUL had a new weapon that helped to turn the tides: the support of sympathetic wealthy society women. Though this alliance was strained at times, it proved to be invaluable during the shirtwaist workers strike. It was no small thing to have **Anne Morgan** (sister of millionaire banker J. P. Morgan) or **Alva Belmont** (activist, extravagant party thrower, and owner of many mansions and cars) on their side. Called *"uptown scum"* by factory owners, wealthy women held rallies and invited working girls to explain the strike to elite clubwomen. They also picketed, posted bail, attended court hearings, and provided food for strikers and their families.

Americans were horrified in the fall of 1911 to hear of the fiery inferno that swept through one New York garment factory. The upper floors of the **Triangle Shirtwaist Company** caught fire and 146 women and girls died because there was no way out—the doors were locked and there were no fire escapes. What made the deaths particularly awful was that many of these girls had only recently and unsuccessfully participated in a large-scale strike over these very safety issues.

Some joined picket lines and were arrested. When one policeman discovered that the woman he had arrested was **Mary Dreier**, the president of the league, he scolded, *"Why didn't you tell me you was a rich lady? I'd have never arrested you in the world."* But the factory owners held out. Women provided cheap labor, and they wanted to keep it that way.

The WTUL tried to ensure the story of the strike reached the English-speaking public. Newspapers had a field day. They wrote articles about the poor but undaunted strikers, creating an outpouring of public sympathy. In Chicago, elderly women sewed quilts to keep strikers warm. Children in Wisconsin donated the money for their Christmas dinners to the strikers' treasury.

The strike ended in February 1910 with various settlements that improved conditions for some, but not all, workers. Factory owners refused to acknowledge unions, but women needed to go back to work. The Triangle Shirtwaist fire a year later was tragic proof of the danger female factory workers faced.

What One Woman Did

"Pray for the Dead, and Fight Like Hell for the Living"

An unlikely leader emerged out of this battle between employers and workers. **Mary Harris Jones**, known to most as Mother Jones, was a little old lady. She was best known for her battle cry, "Pray for the dead, and fight like hell for the living." Well past seventy, barely five-feet tall, and weighing less than one hundred pounds, Mother Jones was fearless. Having watched her husband and four children die one by one in a yellow fever epidemic in 1867, and losing her dressmaking business in the

Chicago fire of 1871, she devoted the remainder of her life to improving the lives of mine and factory workers.

Conditions for those working in the coal and copper mining areas of Appalachia, Colorado, and Arizona were bleak. Workers and their families risked their lives daily for exhausting, unhealthy, low-paying jobs. In order to survive, mothers sent their boys to work as young as six or seven years old. Many died or were permanently disabled by accidents. Miners' wives fought an unceasing battle with grime, poverty, illness, and premature death. Mother Jones was their ally.

Mother Jones believed that *"no strike has ever been won that didn't have the support of women."* After one seemingly hopeless strike in Pennsylvania, she told the men to stay home with their children. She then created an army of miners' wives wielding mops, brooms, and washtubs, and marched them to the entrance of the mine. The women knocked down the guard, scared the mine mules, chased strikebreakers, and created pandemonium. They stood guard over the mine for a number of days and nights. The strike was a success.

Mother Jones repeatedly placed herself at the center of labor conflicts. When she was seventy-four years old she was thrown out of Colorado for helping with a strike. She dashed this letter off to the governor:

Denver, Colorado, March 26, 1904

Governor James H. Peabody:

Mr. Governor, *you notified your dogs of war to put me out of the state. They complied with your instructions. I hold in my hand a letter that was handed to me by one of them, which says "under no circumstances return to this state." I wish to notify you, governor, that you don't own the state.... I am right here in the capital, after being out nine or ten hours, four or five blocks from your office. I want to ask you, governor, what in Hell are you going to do about it?*

Mother Jones

Mother Jones, pictured here at the age of ninety-four with President Calvin Coolidge.

Undaunted, Mother Jones led workers until she was nearly 100 years old.

For her 100th birthday, her friends and supporters threw her a huge party. John D. Rockefeller Jr., the son of one of her old archenemies, sent her a friendly birthday telegram. So many cards and messages arrived that she complained she couldn't get any sleep. When she died later that year, thousands of people, many of them miners, came on buses to attend her funeral. She is buried beside her "boys" in the Union Miner's Cemetery in Mt. Olive, Illinois.

The 1912 Women's Metropolitan Golf Championship, Nassau Country Club, Long Island, New York.

AMUSEMENTS

Until the late 1800s, society severely restricted the leisure activities in which women were allowed to participate. With the dawning of a new century, this began to change.

"WE NO SOONER TRIED IT THAN WE LIKED IT": SPORTS

When a Boston lady like **Eleonora Sears** played polo and won squash championships with gusto, she raised more than one eyebrow. Though many women performed demanding household labors, most Americans still believed "ladies" were frail and unable to withstand intense physical exercise. To sweat was considered lower-class or manly. But by 1890, Sears and others challenged the standard. She scandalized club members by wearing trousers to ride her horse and organizing a football team on which she played fullback. Sears's enjoyment of sports was infectious. Wealthier women began to swim, golf, and play tennis.

THE OLYMPICS People around the world were becoming interested in physical fitness. In 1896, when Pierre de Coubetin reintroduced the Olympics, there was controversy over women's participation. Ultimately, female athletes competed unofficially in tennis, golf, and archery until the Olympic committee made these sports official for the 1908 London games. When figure skating was added as a women's event in 1904, the U.S. Olympic Committee did not allow U.S. women to participate, because they insisted that women should only play sports in which they could wear long skirts.

BASKETBALL Forward-thinking educators began to introduce sports into women's schools. **Senda Berenson**, a physical education teacher at Smith College, wrote, "I read in a small magazine that an indoor game was invented called Basket Ball. We no sooner tried it than we liked it." They played their first match on March 23, 1893. In keeping with the prevailing beliefs about girls, Berenson altered the rules to make sure the game was not too strenuous. Although critics worried that competitions between colleges might be too much to handle, girls soon played the game on numerous U.S. college campuses.

Ice skaters in Washington, DC.

FIELD HOCKEY In 1901, physical education teachers at Vassar and a number of other women's colleges learned another new game. **Constance Applebee**, a visiting student from England, taught them to play field hockey, a very popular sport in Britain. Field hockey was then introduced to girls in their physical education classes. Applebee stayed in the United States, where she promoted the sport and founded the American Field Hockey Association with Senda Berenson. She also started the *Sportswoman,* the first sports magazine for women.

Sterling Cycles.

⟶ Built like a Watch. ⟩

"A WOMAN AWHEEL IS AN INDEPENDENT CREATURE": BICYCLING

In the 1890s, bicycles seemed to be everywhere. Manufacturers began to produce bikes in great numbers, and ambitious individuals opened academies to teach people to ride. Academies in New York City hired "bicyclettes," fashionably dressed girls who promoted the sport by riding conspicuously around the city. To attract female customers, riding schools also conducted training sessions that began with a tea.

As women took to the roads, the public discussed everything from whether females should be allowed to ride bikes to where and how women should ride. Some individuals argued, for example, that when a man and woman rode a tandem bike, the woman should sit in front in order to better see the view. As this also allowed her to steer—a job thought to be too difficult for a woman—others

Have you ever heard of . . . Fanny Bullock Workman?

She loved to climb mountains with her husband, a hobby they began in 1898 when she was thirty-nine and he was fifty-one. They went on seven different climbing expeditions that made them famous. **Workman climbed higher than any woman on record** and had her picture taken on a mountain holding up a newspaper that read, "Votes for women." The Workmans also wrote books about their adventures biking across Algeria, Spain, and India.

Have you ever heard of . . . Ann Taylor?

The first person ever to go over Niagara Falls in a barrel was a woman. In 1901, Taylor, a childless widow, took the plunge while crowds watched. Although bruised and bleeding, she survived to tell onlookers, "Nobody ought ever to do that again."

suggested that perhaps a woman should sit in back where manly shoulders could protect her from the chilling breeze.

Some doctors worried about new biking ailments they called "bicycle face," and "bicycle wrist." One doctor wrote about a particularly female illness, "bicycle twitch"—a condition of downcast eyes accompanied by a nervous twitching of the head caused by tight bloomers. If doctors were at first concerned, most soon became convinced that bike riding could treat almost every ill. Twenty-eight doctors in Chicago advised women to take off their "murderous corsets" and strengthen their muscles through cycling. The corset industry reacted by developing lines of bicycle corsets.

Over time, debate shifted from whether riding a bicycle was healthy for women to whether it was moral. The bicycle allowed women a new freedom, as expressed in this 1894 Minneapolis newspaper article: *"Cycling is fast bringing about this change of feeling regarding woman and her capabilities. A woman awheel is an independent creature, free to go whither she will."* Not everyone thought this freedom was a great idea. Stories abounded of young girls eloping and married women running away with lovers on bicycles.

Critics of the bicycle were right in one regard: they did bring change. More than anything,

bicycling helped revamp women's clothing. Women began wearing bloomers—billowy, bunched-up pants that dress reformers had advocated since the 1840s. In an era when ankles were still considered sexy and were always covered by layers of long skirts, women wheeling around town and country streets in bloomers were heart-stoppers.

The fears of those who saw bloomers as a sign of female revolt were realized when some women began to experiment with wearing the bloomers away from their bicycles. **Ada Coleman**, an organist for the Methodist church in Mason, Ohio, scandalized her congregation by playing the organ in bright red bloomers. Many thought she should be excommunicated. Toward the end of the decade, the bloomers craze faded; what remained were other clothing reforms such as shortened skirts and less-confining corsets.

"Bodily contact has been conventionalized to an unprecedented degree....Couples stand very close together, the girl with her hands around the man's neck, the man with both his arms around the girl or on her hips; their cheeks are pressed close together, their bodies touch each other." —JUVENILE PROTECTIVE LEAGUE OF CHICAGO

DOING THE "SLOW DRAG" AND THE "FUNKY BUTT": DANCING

In the 1910s, working-class Americans danced like crazy. Dancing had always been a part of American life in various forms, but until the 1890s, dancing in public places such as dance halls and saloons was often only for "bad girls." With the construction of large, more reputable dance spaces, and an increasing acceptance of unchaperoned mingling by single women and men, many young working women became enthusiastic dancers.

After long workdays, young women hurried to dance halls, where they found festive, milling crowds, bright lights, and loud ragtime music. Dances lasted until one or two in the morning on weeknights, and most of the night on Saturdays.

Dance styles changed. No longer did dancers perform a formal set of steps while keeping a respectable distance from their partners. Now, dancers held each other tight and made up steps. One popular dance consisted of clutching couples wheeling wildly around and around the dance floor. "Tough dancing," which began in the brothels of San Francisco, pushed the envelope of acceptable behavior and was a hit by 1905. It included steps called the Grizzly Bear, the Bunny Hug, Shaking the Shimmy, and the Lover's Two-Step.

Dance halls varied according to the ethnic make-up of the neighborhood. Most dance halls were segregated by race. In black dance places, called "jook joints" or "dives," dancers dimmed the lights and swayed to the blues. New dances included the Slow Drag, the Funky Butt, and the Grind. These dances offended middle-class blacks because they wanted to improve the way that whites viewed African Americans. They also worried about the ill effects of dance halls on young women.

A 1917 report by the Juvenile Protective League of Chicago stated that in some halls "obscene language is permitted" with the "less sophisticated girls" standing around "listening, scandalized but fascinated." It was hoped that sending out policewomen as "municipal chaperones" might help, but even that didn't stem the tide of change. T. A. Faulkner, in his book *The Lure of the Dance,* warned "poor little girls" of the temptations of dancing that came in the "form of a polite, well-dressed young vampire in human form." He cautioned that by going to dance halls young women would lose their souls. Many working girls adored dancing, and try as they might, reformers were unable to dampen their enthusiasm.

"WE THOUGHT THEY HAD REALLY DIED": MOVIES

The moving picture was another popular new escape. In 1910, working girls who could not afford new outfits to go dancing or to go to amusement parks could usually muster the five cents it cost to attend a show. Leaving behind the cramped quarters of tenement housing, they poured into makeshift movie theatres to catch up on the latest gossip and watch the newest movies.

Movies had special appeal to immigrants. Because they were silent, anyone could follow the story line without speaking a word of English. One

Movie Stars

In the beginning of the film industry, there were no movie stars. Actresses and actors were paid a small salary ($5–$15 a week) like everyone else on the lot. They were also expected to help out with odd jobs when not being filmed. When actress **Florence Lawrence** was fired by her movie company, her enraged fans did not even know her name to demand her return. When they did finally determine her identity, she became the first movie star known by her own name. By 1914, things really changed when actress **Mary Pickford** signed a record-breaking contract that paid her $104,000 a year.

Italian woman later remembered, *"We'd go to the movies, the silent pictures, but . . . we didn't know that these stories weren't true. So we would cry and cry, if somebody died. We thought they had really died."* Immigrant parents were more likely to allow their daughters to attend movies than other youthful activities.

Ruth Roland stars in *The Timber Queen* in 1922. Adventure serials with names like *What Happened to Mary* and *Hazards of Helen* featured heroic women toting guns and jumping from buildings onto moving trains. Many told the stories of common people. *The Girl Strike Leader* and *How the Cause Was Won* portrayed women workers who pushed successfully for improved working conditions.

BEAUTY
MAKING THE CHANGE

HIGH FASHION In 1890, women had quite a job keeping up with the day's fashions. Hairdos were puffed and built over pads along the front of the head. This was frequently topped with an enormous hat, often covered with feathers, flowers, and plumes. A large bust could be achieved with the use of a few well-placed handkerchiefs. Layers and layers of underclothing (including a corset, chemise, drawers, and multiple petticoats) supported skirts laden with ribbons, bows, and bobbles. The ensemble was completed with various accessories: boas, stoles, pillow-shaped muffs, and parasols. As a London fashion writer stated in 1902, "Women of fashion require many parasols during a London season."

This would begin to change. The thirty years from 1890 to 1920 saw radical changes in women's dress. As the decade wore on, the Gibson Girl (a look based on drawings by Charles Dana Gibson)

entered the scene with her hair piled high and her shirtwaist tucked neatly into her long skirt. As well-to-do women began to play tennis and golf, and ride bikes, styles had to adapt. Women went from wearing an abundance of layers, high-necked collars, and heavy clothing to the free-flowing, shortened dresses associated with 1920s flappers—quite a dramatic change for such a short period of time.

WORKING GIRLS' FASHION Many photos of working girls in the early 1900s show them as poorly dressed, somber individuals. These photos were often taken to protest horrendous working conditions in factories, but they don't tell the whole story. In fact, working girls often rejected the appearance of poverty and went to great pains to appear fashionable. While they worked, young women chatted with friends about "swell evening pumps and lace petticoats." Historians have begun to explore the ways that dressing up helped working women to feel more powerful and more political. Working women didn't want to look poor; they

The brassiere was mentioned for the first time in a 1907 issue of Vogue.

Three young women sporting the Gibson Girl look in 1915.

wanted respect. As one young woman simply stated, *"We want to be treated like ladies."*

Sold from street pushcarts, small stores, department stores, and catalogues, ready-made clothing made fashionable clothes more accessible to the working girl. Available in only a couple of sizes, the back seam of dresses was left undone to fit various body sizes. When one working girl finally bought a suit from an actual department store, she said, "You see, I have always had my suits from a pushcart....I wish I could wear the label [of the department store] on the front."

Middle-class Americans felt that working girls should not put on airs by dressing above their station. Girls who dressed in finery and feathers did not fit the picture of the "deserving poor." Reformers worried that dressed-up workers did not appear to need help. They also thought that working girls could not possibly pursue cheap popular culture and be serious about unions and social reform. Working-class women disagreed.

Girls at a Georgia cotton mill (1909).

In 1905, a single page of the Sears, Roebuck catalogue offered seventy-five different styles of ostrich-feather decorations. With feathers adorning just about everything, many species of birds faced extinction. A group of Massachusetts women were dismayed and decided to take action. Forming the **Massachusetts Audubon Society**, they actively championed the cause of birds by convincing women not to wear clothing made with bird products. Their petition and letter-writing campaigns also led to laws protecting birds. Efforts like these led to the environmental movement of the twentieth century.

"We're human, all of us girls, and we're young. We like new hats as well as any other young women. Why shouldn't we?. . . Sometimes a girl has a new hat. It is never much to look at because it never costs more than fifty cents, but it's pretty sure spoiled after it's been to the shop."

—**Clara Lemlich**, GARMENT WORKER, 1909

Thorsten Veblin, in his 1899 book Theory of the Leisure Class, *described the* **corset** *as designed "to impress upon the beholder the fact (often indeed a fiction) that the wearer does not and can not habitually engage in useful work."*

In rural North Dakota there was yet another set of fashion rules and expectations. **Ella May Stumpe** remembered,

Girls were girls until the age of sixteen, when we became "young ladies." We wore longer skirts and blouses with higher necks. Braids circled our head and "buns" decorated the lower back. We used hairpins and fancy combs of colored shell. **At sixteen, young ladies were eligible for marriage.** *By eighteen, you had better be looking. And at twenty-five, well, you were an "old maid" and on the shelf.*

"THE RELIGION OF BEAUTY, THE SIN OF UGLINESS": WOMEN BEGIN TO MAKE UP

At the turn of the twentieth century, a woman wearing makeup was considered morally loose. The times, however, were changing. Here and there, women braved society's disapproval to powder their faces or put some color on their cheeks. Their challenge met with resistance. One upright woman declared, "I have seen women going along the street with their cheeks aglow with paint,

As in earlier times, white women were held up as the norm for what was considered beautiful. A 1915 article from *Leslie's Illustrated Weekly* newspaper highlighted this sort of racism:

China's Perfect Girl: *Miss* **Yarlock Lowe,** *a Chinese student at the University of California, enjoys the distinction of being* **the only physically perfect girl among 500 female students.** *She underwent a careful examination and was declared to be perfect not only in health, but to be the most symmetrical of the entire class. The examining physicians were amazed at this, since, they say, a Chinese woman who even approached physical perfection has never before been recorded.*

everyone twisting their necks and looking." A Macy's department store manager joined other bosses who hoped to stem the tide by firing made-up employees. He stated that he "was not running a theatrical troupe but a department store." Many women began to ask if it was possible to wear makeup and remain socially acceptable.

The cosmetics industry, which was just beginning, had an answer. In the 1890s, a diverse group of "beauty culturists" emerged. They helped to distinguish between wearing makeup and being immoral. One culturist, **Madame Yale**, dedicated her life to the "benefit of her Sister Women" by delivering lectures around the country on "The Religion of Beauty, the Sin of Ugliness." Many women promoted beauty through "scientific" means.

Significantly, many of the new cosmetic entrepreneurs were women from the margins of society—disadvantaged immigrant and African American women with few employment options. With little to lose, they invented, manufactured, promoted, and distributed cosmetics. **Elizabeth Arden**, **Martha Matilda Harper**, **Madame Le Fevre**, **Annie Turnbo Malone**, **Marie Juliette Pinault**, **Helena Rubenstein**, **Ida Lee Secrest**, and **Sara Spencer Washington**,—the list of beauty crusaders is long. **Madam C. J. Walker** was another of these women. A glimpse into her life shows the richness of the stories behind the names.

What One Woman Did

"I Am Not Ashamed of My Humble Beginning"

Madam C. J. Walker (born **Sarah Breedlove**) found that selling beauty empowered her, as well as others. Born in 1867 to newly freed slave parents, Walker was orphaned at age six, married at fourteen, a mother at seventeen, and a widow at twenty. Her early life was filled with the hard labor of a servant and washerwoman. After she began to lose her hair at the age of thirty-eight, she claimed that she had a dream in which she was visited by "a big black man" who told her "what to mix up" for her hair. He told her that she would beautify and uplift her race, and she set out to do just that. Madam C. J. Walker became the first self-made female millionaire in the United States.

In 1906, Walker began to promote her products in earnest, selling her Wonderful Hair Grower. She developed a new way to sell various products: she outfitted hundreds of female selling agents in tidy uniforms and sent them to sell her products door-to-door. With the scarcity of jobs available to black women, it is significant that by 1917 Walker employed nearly 300,000 mostly female employees.

Madam C. J. Walker viewed her products and business as a way to empower black women, to help them achieve dignity and aspire to a better life. In a 1913 speech delivered to the National Negro Business League, she stated, "I am not ashamed of my past; I am not ashamed of my humble beginning. *Don't think because you have to go down in the wash-tub that you are any less than a lady!*" An active philanthropist in the black community, she donated great amounts of money to black organizations and charities. She organized her workers into "Walker Clubs," awarding prizes to the clubs that did the most for the community.

THE CLUB MOVEMENT
"LIFTING AS WE CLIMB"

Toward the close of the nineteenth century, American middle-class black and white women were better educated and had smaller families than earlier generations. For some women in urban areas, electricity and gas made day-to-day living easier. With servants to help cook and clean, many upper- and middle-class housewives had more time on their hands for other pursuits. Those with high school and college educations were eager to put their knowledge and skills to good use outside their homes. As a result, large numbers of women joined clubs where they studied and discussed history, art, music, and literature. Club members soon moved from self-improvement programs to serving and reforming society. In doing so, they joined settlement house volunteers and other reformers as active participants in the progressive movement.

Despite a common interest in many of the same causes, black women were blatantly excluded from white women's clubs. So they started their own clubs and went to work. The National Association of Colored Women (NACW) became the umbrella organization for numerous clubs that sprang up in communities around the country.

In the eyes of NACW leaders, "a race could rise no higher than its women," so they addressed not only the plight of black women, but of the entire race. According to **Mary Church Terrell**, the organization's first president, "We have to do more than other women. Those of us fortunate enough to have education must share it with the less fortunate of our race. *We must go into our communities and improve them; we must go out into the nation and change it.* Above all, we must organize ourselves as Negro women and work together." Using the slogan "Lifting as We Climb," club endeavors varied, but their purpose was the same: "racial uplift" for all

Madam C. J. Walker.

"A social club of self-supporting young women (teachers, stenographers, and bookkeepers) who have made good." From the 1916 book *American Civilization and the Negro: The Afro-American in Relation to National Progress.*

blacks. Some clubs offered classes on motherhood, sewing, and buying and building houses; others opened orphanages, hospitals, and homes for the elderly or for wayward youth, all funded and run by volunteers.

Everywhere clubwomen turned, they encountered social problems such as poverty, alcoholism, illiteracy, and sickness that begged for their womanly intuition and care. By the turn of the century, corseted crusaders dotted the land, intent on improving not only themselves, but also the world around them. They assumed that like an untidy house needing order, society needed women's homemaking skills and nurturing instincts.

The consequences were profound and far-reaching: public kindergartens; school lunch programs; money for public playgrounds, parks, and libraries; improved conditions in hospitals, mental institutions, and prisons. Members lobbied for sewer systems, clean water, and public health legislation and saw that child labor laws were passed. Chinese immigrants in California raised funds for disaster relief after news of floods and famine in China. Crusading in "lady-like" ways, using their influence and power for good causes, clubwomen joined progressives in improving the way Americans lived, worked, and played.

Did you know?

Mother's Day in the United States began when **Anna Jarvis** sought to honor her dearly departed mother by paying tribute to the nation's mothers. She campaigned first in West Virginia, and then across the country for a nationwide Mother's Day. On May 9, 1914, President Woodrow Wilson issued the first presidential Mother's Day proclamation, asking for flags to be flown on that day in their honor (Father's Day would not be official until 1935).

U.S. EXPANSIONISM

"A BIG UNTILLED FIELD": MISSIONARIES

Many women looked beyond problems in the United States and strove to "civilize" and Christianize the rest of the world. As during the earlier part of the

This image from a Singer sewing machine booklet speaks volumes about America's interest in spreading its ideas and goods throughout the world.

century, religious missions abroad were popular. With nearly three million women belonging to religious societies, thousands of young women went forth as missionaries. They intended to use their feminine goodness and education to "enlighten" individuals in Africa, China, Syria, India, the Pacific Islands, Latin America, and other foreign lands. Missionaries engaged in many of the same activities as their progressive sisters; they just worked overseas.

One of these young women was **Azalia Emma Peet**. Peet, a farmer's daughter from Webster, New York, confided in her journal on March 12, 1912, that since her graduation from college, "the problems of the country do interest me greatly. The people need much that the college-educated woman has to give."

Azalia Peet was twenty-four years old and at a crossroads. Following her graduation from Smith College, she felt lonely and confused. She considered joining a settlement house, attending a YWCA training school, or going to live with an aunt in Oregon. Instead, after much soul searching, she applied to become a missionary. The following October she wrote, ***"Indeed I am in Japan.... At last I have broken all ties of friendship and home to come over here and for what?... [I] believe that there is a big untilled field here among the girls of fair Japan."*** Peet stayed in Japan for thirty-seven years. There she ran schools, social centers, day-care centers, and health clinics.

Like most Americans, Peet had absorbed prevailing ideas about civilization. Science was used to "prove" that social, racial, class, and gender hierarchies were natural. In this way of thinking, some people and cultures were considered naturally superior to others. Americans used these ideas to justify expansion into places like the Philippines, Panama, Cuba, and the Dominican Republic as right and necessary.

Women did not put on uniforms and fight foreign wars, but like Peet, they were influenced by U.S. expansionism. They set out to spread Western culture in their own ways. Some believed it was possible to Christianize without changing people's culture; others were absolutely convinced that to Christianize and change people's culture were the same project.

Missionaries Azalia Peet and **Alice Finlay** in Japan (1918).

"QUILTS, DRAPERIES, NEEDLEWORK, AND OTHER WOMEN'S RUBBISH": THE CHICAGO WORLD'S FAIR

In 1893, the United Stated hosted an enormous fair to display its great strength, industry, and civilization to the rest of the world. The Chicago World's Fair attracted at least 20,000 people a day. The layout of dazzling white buildings modeled the hierarchy many Westerners believed existed in the world. Exhibits from other parts of the world were separated from those of America and Europe, and women's work was set off to the side completely. Though women attempted to join the planning committee, the message was clear: women's contributions to U.S. progress were different from men's and so small they would fit in one building.

Chile-born **Sophia Hayden** designed the Women's Building and **Bertha Palmer**, a wealthy Chicagoan, took on the task of "lady manager." She asked the famous impressionist artist **Mary Cassatt** to paint a large mural. Sculptor **Anne Whitney**, who felt that women's art should be exhibited with men's, told the committee that she did not care to show her work with "quilts, draperies, needlework, and other women's rubbish." In the end, she did allow a fountain and a number of her statues to be displayed with women's work. Forty-seven countries accepted Palmer's invitation to set up exhibits in the Women's Building. African American women, who repeatedly requested to be included, were rebuffed. Male organizers were surprised when the Women's Building successfully drew crowds.

QUEEN LILIUOKALANI OF HAWAII

In 1891, a queen sat on the throne of Hawaii. **Queen Liliuokalani** was a regal, intelligent woman with many interests. As a young woman, Liliuokalani loved riding horses and had a good ear for music. She learned to play the organ, ukulele, zither, piano, and guitar. She also composed music, writing the well-known Hawaiian anthem "Aloha-Oe." Americans who seized control of Hawaii shortened Queen Liliuokalani's rule.

By the 1880s, U.S. plantation owners had gained great political power in Hawaii. Queen Liliuokalani was troubled by the strong U.S. influence in her islands and attempted to regain authority that had been lost before her rule. Wealthy planters and cabinet members, including pineapple kingpin Sanford Dole, were not about to give up power. With U.S. troops floating offshore, they staged a takeover of Hawaii in the name of public safety. When some of Liliuokalani's followers hid weapons in the garden of her home, this was used as an excuse to imprison her in her palace. After

EX-QUEEN LILIOUKALANI

announcing that Liliuokalani was no longer queen, the planters sent an application to Washington requesting the annexation of Hawaii.

Although Liliuokalani was later released and made a trip to Washington to speak to the president, Hawaii was annexed in 1898. It became a U.S. territory in 1900. In the hearts of many Hawaiians, Liliuokalani remained the queen, though she lived out the rest of her days as an American subject.

TRANSITION AND MIGRATIONS

HISPANICS IN THE BORDERLAND

Not everyone in America lived in an Eastern city or had emigrated from another country. However, the industrialization, urbanization, and expansion that characterized the turn of the century also had a ripple effect on those living in the vast stretches of rural America. Like women all over the country,

Mexican, Indian, and black women worked hard, kept houses, and raised children.

Yet these mothers faced the added challenge of maintaining their dignity and preserving their culture in environments that were often hostile to both. Whether they chose to migrate, like many Southern blacks, or adapted like Crow Indians, they worked to find their own solutions. Half a century after the United States had annexed large parts of the West from Mexico, more remote Hispanic villages in New Mexico, Texas, Arizona, and Colorado still managed to hold on to their way of life.

In the borderlands, a girl was allowed to run and play like the boys until she was eight and had her first communion at church. Then she was expected to help her mother. **Rosalia Salazar** was born in Arizona in 1904. In her family, the children helped both parents. Salazar got up at 4:30 AM to bring in kindling and milk the cows before school. She ground flour by hand, washed clothes on a washboard, and in the summer picked vegetables and fruit. She also helped her father with the cattle. Salazar recalled, *"All of us girls . . . learned to saddle and ride a horse at a very young age. But in those days one didn't wear pants; we wore skirts and rode sidesaddle."*

The Catholic Church was central in village activities. Girls participated in religious life by attending services, cleaning the church, cooking for religious festivals, and walking in religious parades. Girls and women looked forward to the month of May, when they celebrated Mary, the mother of Jesus.

Girls and boys met at village dances. Girls usually married between the ages of fifteen and twenty-one. Boys married between the ages of nineteen and twenty-six. When a love-struck young man wanted a girl to marry him, he proposed with the help of family members and godparents. A girl was free to accept or decline. When she accepted, the young man paid for the wedding party and purchased the items needed to set up housekeeping.

Once married, women kept gardens, raised animals, and prepared meals. They also built their own fireplaces and ovens, and were responsible for plastering their adobe houses each fall. "The buildings were mostly adobe, clean inside and out," wrote one visitor. "Often against the white walls on the outside of the dwellings we would see long strips of red pepper, the chili pepper." Village women took pride in keeping a clean and beautiful house.

Life changed at the turn of the century, as English-speaking Americans, or Anglos, poured into the Southwest, building railroads and putting up fences. When the U.S. government took their communal lands, Mexican families no longer had space to herd animals or farm. Men were forced to go in search of wage labor. Women were left in the village to raise children and run farms. Some moved to mining towns. Soon they were joined by refugees fleeing the Mexican Revolution. Between 1900 and 1914, the Hispanic population in the United States tripled.

NATIVE AMERICANS

White migration had long intruded on Native Americans. On December 29, 1890, the 7th U.S. cavalry, armed with automatic guns, massacred a group of cold and starving Lakota Sioux at Wounded Knee Creek in the Badlands of South Dakota. The "battle" began accidentally and mainly

A 1901 portrait of a Native American mother and child from the Great Plains region.

consisted of soldiers shooting Sioux, even wounded women and children trying to crawl away. **Louise Weasel Bear** later recalled, *"We tried to run, but they shot us like we were buffalo."* When the fighting was over, an estimated 300 Sioux and 25 soldiers lay dead in the snow.

The events at Wounded Knee symbolized for many Americans the final subjugation of Indian peoples. By the time of the massacre, the majority of Native Americans lived on reservations—often low-quality land far from their original homelands.

COMPLICATED CHANGES Reservation life was complicated as communities struggled to maintain dignity and tradition in the face of white control. Changes forced upon Indians affected groups differently, based on their original culture and individual circumstances. Changes also often affected men and women in different ways. White Americans continued to push Indian men to take over farming—traditionally a woman's job and source of power. Also, white Americans' ideas on morality and male authority influenced relationships between men and women, often in negative ways. On the other hand, becoming involved in the American economy sometimes provided Indian women more opportunities than their spouses to earn money. One unifying theme of reservation life was the attempt to remain Indian in a white-dominated country.

The words of **Agnes Yellowtail Deernose**, a Crow Indian from Oklahoma, reflect the tensions between white and Indian cultures. Agnes Deernose was born in 1908, the same year that Henry Ford introduced the Model-T Ford.

Childbirth: "I began my life in a tent.... There was a hospital across the way, but in those days Crows didn't like to go to the hospital.... Once I was on the way, my mother put herself under the guidance of her mother, as old people knew what to do."

Men and women: "Food was hard to get after the government stopped giving out rations. Men brought in meat seasonally when hunting elk or deer in the Big Horn Mountains, and women continued to prepare the food, dress the skins, and make clothing as in the old days. The idea that women should put food on the table was carried over, and women had to dig deep into their money purses and work hard at drying fruits and Indian turnips to keep hunger away."

Housing: "In my time, when you passed a house, there was a wall-type tent or a canvas-covered tipi pitched nearby. People didn't like to live in houses and spent as much time as possible outside in tents. The air was fresher, and tents were cooler during the day."

Family relations: "I never did learn much from my mother. She was too busy tanning hides, making clothes, doing household chores, and helping with the haying to find time to teach me.... In the Crow way it is not just your mother and father who teach you, but also grandmothers and grandfathers and women of your own clan who are 'mothers' to you."

Marriage: "I met my boyfriend at a Fourth of July celebration when I was fifteen. He wanted to marry me, but my folks wouldn't let me, so he married someone else. My parents picked out a husband for me and made me marry in the old way."

BLACKS IN THE SOUTH

The 1890s were an explosive time in black and white relations, both in the North and the South. Although slavery was thirty years past, a strict social code required people of color to "stay in their place." Laws restricted blacks' access to hospitals, libraries, parks, theatres, schools, and hotels. In addition, there was a rise of white on black violence. Even so, African Americans continued efforts to better their lives. Threatened by rising levels of black education and confidence, many Southern state governments passed laws restricting voters' rights and black rights in general. These so called Jim Crow laws put into writing the second-class position of blacks in U.S. society, dictating that the races should be "separate but equal."

What One Woman Did

The Antilynching Campaign

Ida B. Wells carried a pistol for protection. Born a slave during the Civil War, she went on to become a college graduate and teacher. From the beginning of her career, she opposed segregation. After biting the conductor of a train who tried to remove her from the ladies' car, she sued the railroad for their practice of segregated seating. Although she initially won, the Tennessee Supreme Court overturned the ruling. She also lost her teaching job when she protested the unequal treatment of black students. After that, she became a journalist for the *Memphis Free Speech*, an African American newspaper in Memphis.

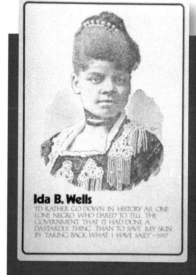

Ida B. Wells
"I'D RATHER GO DOWN IN HISTORY AS ONE LONE NEGRO WHO DARED TO TELL THE GOVERNMENT THAT IT HAD DONE A DASTARDLY THING THAN TO SAVE MY SKIN BY TAKING BACK WHAT I HAVE SAID" -1917

This poster from the 1970s reveals that Ida B. Wells provided inspiration for later activists.

In 1892, three prominent black businessmen, friends of Wells, were shot to death by a white mob. She put her own life in danger when she spoke out against the murders in the *Free Speech* and suggested that blacks use economic pressure to seek justice. Although Wells had not put her name to her writing, whites determined who the author was and she had to flee for her life. She went north, and it was thirty years before she dared return to the South.

In Chicago, Wells began a one-woman campaign to stop lynching. Her tactics were those of a progressive reformer. She gathered facts, then worked to raise public awareness. White Americans largely ignored her pamphlets, but she was determined to be heard. In 1893 and 1894 she launched popular speaking tours in England. She convinced the English to pressure white Americans to stop lynching. When a committee from London sent a delegation to the South to investigate, Americans were angry and told the British to mind their own business.

Wells was not able to stop lynching all by herself, but her efforts brought violence against blacks into the public eye, where Americans were forced to acknowledge it. The number of lynchings began to decline, from 161 in 1892 to 62 in 1912. While continuing her involvement in efforts for racial equality and women's rights, Wells married and settled in Chicago, where she raised four children.

"AND SAY, HONEY, I GOT A BATH TUB!": THE GREAT MIGRATION

In 1910, nine out of ten black Americans lived in the South. The racism they faced included low wages, violence, and unfairness under the law. Times were getting worse. Jobs were scarce, cotton prices were falling, and boll weevils were destroying crops throughout the deep South. This coincided with a labor shortage in the North. Consequently, Northern industries began recruiting African Americans. Blacks needed little persuasion. Between 1914 and 1920, an estimated half a million African Americans moved from the South to the North in what came to be known as the Great Migration.

When asked why they chose to migrate, many blacks spoke of wanting to be in a place where women could be safe and respected, and children could get an education. In the South, there were no provisions in the law to protect a

black woman from rape. Black men who defended their wives, girlfriends, and daughters were likely to become victims of violence themselves.

One man who spoke to Southern audiences about migrating told them:

> *So many of my folks are leaving that I thought I'd go up and see whether or not they had made a mistake. I found thousands of old friends up there making more money than they'd ever made in their lives. I said to one woman in Chicago, "Well, Sister—, I see you're here."*
> *"Yes, Brother—, I'm here, thank the Lord...."*
> *"But you expect to return, don't you?"*
> *"Don't play with me chile. What am I going to return for? I should say not. Up here you see when I come out on the street I walk on nice smooth pavements. Down home I got to walk home through the mud. Up here at nights it don't matter much about coming home from church. Down home on my street there ain't a single lamp post. And say, honey, I got a bath tub!"*

This migrant family had just arrived in Chicago from the rural South in 1922, when this picture was taken. What challenges might they have faced in their new urban life?

The North turned out to be a mixed bag for black migrants. They continued to face prejudice. In addition, moving from rural to urban areas was an adjustment. Women had to learn how to use new household technology and how to manage resources in a cash economy.

Being a mother in Northern cities presented new problems. With pool halls, saloons, and brothels located near black neighborhoods, unsupervised children could easily get into trouble. Women who worked as domestics began to insist on living with their own families, although they were still gone much of the time. Although black women traded one set of problems for another when they chose to migrate, life in the North provided them opportunities that they did not have in the South. Women sent their children to school, and after 1920 they could also vote.

ARTS IN THE SPOTLIGHT

"AT ONCE STRONG AND FINE": EDITH WHARTON

Little in **Edith Wharton**'s early life would have predicted the Pulitzer Prize in literature she would receive in 1921. And yet, everything about her aristocratic upbringing was central to her writing. Edith Newbold Jones was born into the idle luxury of New York City's elite. Brought up in New York and European society, she gathered the experiences, sights, and sounds that would fill her novels for the rest of her life. Though she privately published a book of poetry by the time she was sixteen, she spent the next decade living the life she had been raised to live. She debuted in society in 1878, attended parties and balls, made social calls, had many suitors, and married a wealthy Bostonian (whom she later divorced).

In 1889, with family money to support her lavish lifestyle, Edith Wharton began to write again. She first published poetry, then short stories, and eventually a series of novellas and novels. *The*

House of Mirth, Custom of the Country, and *The Age of Innocence* are peopled with the manners, prejudices, and attitudes of New York's old aristocracy and set in Madison Avenue mansions and large country houses. Wharton's more than fifty volumes extended beyond her New York upbringing to another familiar landscape—the countryside of Western Massachusetts. This writing included short tragic novels *Ethan Frome* and *Summer.*

Wharton's work was critically acclaimed. One contemporary hailed *The Age of Innocence* as "a masterly achievement." The characters were "as real as their actual lives would ever have let them

Have you ever heard of . . . Kate Chopin?

Most critics panned her 1899 novel, *The Awakening,* for its exploration of a woman's growing independence and rejection of traditional values. Though they admitted her writing was good, they said it committed "unutterable crimes against society," and labeled it "poison." Who could this risqué author be? Chopin was the widowed mother of six children. When her husband died of "swamp fever," she turned to writing to support her family. She became a moderately famous writer. Following her death, however, *The Awakening* fell into obscurity. Recently, Chopin's work has become required reading for many university and high school students.

> "I think that most of the basic material a writer works with is acquired before the age of fifteen. That's the important period: when one's not writing. Those years determine whether one's work will be poor and thin or rich and fine." —**Willa Cather,** BEST-SELLING AUTHOR OF *O Pioneers!* and *My Antonia*

be." Another writer praised her in 1925, saying it was a "matter of pride that such [a] rare flower could grow on American soil."

In addition to her writing, Edith Wharton was recognized for her extensive aid to French and Belgian refugees during World War I.

Have you ever heard of . . . Isadora Duncan?

Duncan's life was dramatic. At a time when ballet was the official style of classical dance, she improvised a new way of moving. Many consider her the founder of modern dance. Her dance style liberated other dancers and gave them courage to try new things. She wore flowing costumes and danced stories from ancient Greece set to classical music. She became the toast of Europe where she mingled with the rich and famous. In 1916, she toured South America. She died tragically in a car accident.

Elizabeth Shippen Green painted *Life Was Made for Love and Cheer* in 1904. The painting celebrates life at the Red Rose Inn, where Green lived with her friends and fellow artists **Jessie Wilcox Smith** and **Violet Oakley**. Green became the first female staff artist for the popular magazine *Harper's Weekly.*

SUFFRAGE
THE ANTHONY AMENDMENT

On January 10, 1918, many women who had worked doggedly for woman suffrage crowded into the visitors' galleries of the U.S. House of Representatives, anxious over the impending vote on "the Anthony Amendment" or woman's right to vote. It was a crucial moment. Every prosuffrage vote was needed for the nineteenth amendment to pass. Imagine the women's relief at seeing one of their backers who was ill carried in on a stretcher to cast his vote, and another who waited to have his broken shoulder cast in order lend his support. Picture the wife of a New York representative sending her husband to vote for women's suffrage though she lay dying. When the final vote was tallied, the amendment passed with exactly the number of votes needed. The women, silent at first, broke out in jubilant song.

It was a significant victory, and yet the suffrage crusaders could not rest. First the amendment had to pass in the Senate. Next they had to push for ratification by the necessary thirty-six states. By 1920, all eyes were on the state of Tennessee, where the fight for suffrage hung in the balance. Would Tennessee be the thirty-sixth state to ratify the amendment? Opposition raged. The suffragists needed one more vote to win. Twenty-four-year-old Harry Burn, the youngest legislator, was undecided. He received this letter from his mother only hours before the vote:

> Dear Son,
>   *Vote for suffrage and don't keep them in doubt. I notice some speeches against. They were very bitter. I have been watching to see how you stood, but have not seen anything yet. **Don't forget to be a good boy and help Mrs. Catt put "Rat" in Ratification.***
>
>   *With lots of love,*
>   Mama

Burn voted "yes," and women officially won the vote on August 6, 1920.

"Young people think that all the privileges, all the freedom, all the enjoyments which woman now possess always were hers. They have no idea of how every single inch of ground that she stands upon today has been gained by the hard work of some little handful of women in the past."

—**Susan B. Anthony**

THE DEBATE It had taken seventy-two years of unrelenting labor to achieve the vote for women nationally. Why did it take so long? What ideas did people have about women and their roles that made them so fearful of women's enfranchisement? One might think that the greatest battle would be convincing men that women should vote. That was often the case; surprisingly, however, much of the time women themselves had to be convinced.

THE ANTI-SUFFRAGISTS Annie Block was an anti-suffrage activist. In 1913, she told U.S. senators why women should not vote. She declared:

- "Suffrage robs women of all that is gentle, tender, attractive."
- "Woman suffrage in California brought women into too familiar contact with men. . . . Where previously men were generally courteous, now they are rude."
- "Women voting interferes with the great plan of God."
- *"Woman is impulsive; she does not inform herself; she does not study; she does not consider the consequences of a vote. The ballot in her hands is a dangerous thing."*

She concluded, "Hark! The suffrage parade advances. . . . Men, awake! Rouse from your

By 1915, women in Kansas and many other Western states had won the right to vote. In this illustration, women in the East reach out for the same right.

Opinions about women's suffrage were as varied as women themselves. The following newspaper article from the February 15, 1911, *Lawrence Journal World,* reveals how women in the university town of Lawrence, Kansas, felt about the debate.

Horror of horrors. The women of Lawrence, the Athens of Kansas, are not rampant suffragettes. Among thirty-five University and Club women whom *The World* phoned today, only eleven confessed to being wildly enthusiastic over "Votes for Women." More than a third of those queried in reference to their position were indifferent or neutral on the question. They had no objections to their more masculine sisters casting ballots if they wished, but personally they themselves, were not immensely gratified at the boon the legislature had cast at their feet. . . .

Among thirty-five women phoned, eleven were for suffrage, ten were opposed to the movement, and fourteen were coldly indifferent to the entire matter.

Here are some of the one minute interviews Lawrence women gave:

Mrs. Frank Backmar—"I'm not one of the women who worked for suffrage, but if it is passed, I believe I'll go and vote because they need me."

Mrs. E. Hawerth—"I'm opposed to it. **I believe voting belongs to the men**. They have run the government successfully and women have house duties. . . ."

Mrs. A. J. Griffin—"Oh, I believe they will all flock to the polls when it becomes fashionable. I guess I'm in favor of it. . . ."

Mrs. E. H. S. Baily—"I can see two sides to the question. I'm not inclined to be radical, the men in my family have always voted right anyway. . . ."

Mrs. S. D. Alford—"I believe women really need the ballot."

Anti-suffrage images played on people's fears. What dangers lurked for men if they chose to support suffrage?

THE CASE FOR SUFFRAGE Jane Addams and others wanted to convince the public that voting was simply housework on a bigger, more public scale. Problems such as unsanitary housing, sewage and contaminated water, infant mortality, crime, prostitution, and drunkenness could not be solved without "the human welfare point of view" of women. Indeed, Addams argued that cities were failing because women, who, she maintained, were naturally charitable, virtuous, and moral, were not allowed to do the jobs they were so aptly prepared for.

The older generation that had fought for suffrage had been far more radical in their ideas. The Seneca Falls Convention in 1848 had focused on the broad issues of women's inequality, with the right to vote as only portion of the larger problem of society's attitudes toward women. **Elizabeth Cady Stanton** had told a convention of suffragettes in 1890, *"We don't want to limit our platform to bare suffrage and nothing more. . . . Wherever a woman is wronged her voice should be heard."* As

lethargy. Do you not already see the streets flowing with blood? I pray to God you will not help to bring a curse upon us."

Reactions like these irritated suffragists. Writer **Dorothy Dix** said of the anti-suffragists, *"The only real argument against suffrage is the Anti herself.* That there could be a woman with no desire for political freedom in her soul and with so little self-respect she does not object to being classed with idiots, the insane and the criminal almost makes one doubt that women are prepared for the ballot."

Did you know?

The word **feminist** first appeared in print in 1895 describing a woman who "has in her the capacity of fighting her way back to independence."

Women in the New Jersey suffrage campaign..

the decades wore on, issues of women's inequality and oppression in marriage, family, employment, education, and religion were addressed less and less, and the right to vote received more and more attention.

The new century brought a new wave of leadership in the suffrage movement. These leaders single-mindedly pursued enfranchisement. They worried that they could lose precious ground by making further demands. But as the movement became less radical, it gained greater popularity among the middle classes. If women weren't trying to be equal with men, but simply trying to make the world a better place for their children, maybe it wouldn't signal the end of the world if women got the vote.

> *"While our men seem thoroughly abreast of the times on almost every other subject, when they strike the woman question they drop back into sixteenth century logic."*
>
> **—Gertrude Mossell**
> JOURNALIST AND EDUCATOR

Rose Schneiderman, a union leader, said of her working-class sisters: "Women in the laundries stand for thirteen and fourteen hours in the terrible steam and heat with their hands in hot starch. **Surely these women won't lose any more of their beauty and charm by putting a ballot in the ballot box."**

BLACKS IN THE SUFFRAGE MOVEMENT In order to be popular with the masses, suffragists didn't always make the best decisions. Not only did the movement shift away from its original radical roots; it also rejected some of its former friends. Sometimes, white suffragists resorted to racist arguments to gain support. They claimed that white, educated women could outvote those who were foreign-born or black. Henry Blackwell told listeners that "in every state save one there are more educated women than all illiterate voters, white and black, native born and foreign."

Leaders of the suffrage movement who had once counted blacks as their allies now backed away fearing that Southern voters and legislators would abandon the movement if it included black women. One Mississippi suffragist claimed that "the enfranchisement of women would insure immediate and durable white supremacy, honestly attained." Because of arguments like these and the fact that the suffrage movement largely ignored black women, the main suffrage organizations were made up of primarily middle- and upper-class white women.

Still, racist attitudes and segregation didn't keep black women out of the fight for the vote. In 1913, Ida Wells-Barnett, suffragist, journalist, and antilynching crusader, stood for her right to be heard. When told that she must march at the end of the National American Suffrage Parade in Washington, DC, she waited until the Illinois delegation passed her by, then slipped between two white women and marched to the Capitol. When black women like writer and activist Mary Church Terrell worked for suffrage, they did so primarily in their own groups and clubs. **Adella Hunt Logan**, of the Tuskegee Woman's Club, argued that, *"If white women needed the vote to acquire advantages and protection of their rights, then black women needed the vote even more so."* On the other hand, **Margaret Murray Washington**, a clubwoman and educator, said, "Personally, woman suffrage has never kept me awake at night."

Alice Paul in 1913, and her Woman's Party members holding a banner in front of the White House in 1917.

THE BATTLE IS FINALLY WON

Also on the margins of the suffrage movement were the women of the more extreme National Woman's Party (NWP), with young **Alice Paul** at the head. As **Carrie Chapman Catt** and the National American Woman Suffrage Association (NAWSA) fought for suffrage with conventional methods and pursued the vote state by state with an organized strategic plan, Alice Paul and her militant supporters took another route. They kept women's suffrage constantly in the papers using radical tactics and demanding a national amendment.

President Woodrow Wilson found it difficult to ignore them. During his first address to Congress after the 1916 election, the NWP unfurled a banner from the balcony that demanded, *"Mr. President, What Will You Do for Woman Suffrage?"* On his inauguration day, one thousand women marched around and around the White House. Following that, they kept a constant vigil outside the White House for months. It was the first time in American history that any group had attempted such a thing. Some of the women were arrested and went on a hunger strike. The public was so outraged by the terrible jail conditions, forced feedings, and other treatment the women received, that the movement gained many supporters.

It was through the concerted efforts of hundreds of these women, both conservative and radical, that women finally won the vote. Carrie Chapman Catt wrote,

> **"To get the word male out of the Constitution cost the women of the country . . . years of pauseless campaigning. *Hundreds of women gave the accumulated possibilities of an entire lifetime,* thousands gave interest and such aid as they could. It was a continuous, seemingly endless chain of activity. Young suffragists who helped forge the last links of that chain were not born when it began. Old suffragists who forged the first links were dead when it ended."**

Indeed, just days before her death on March 13, 1906, Susan Anthony had told her dear friend **Anna Howard Shaw**, *"Just think, I have been striving for over sixty years for a little bit of justice no bigger than that, and yet I must die without obtaining it. . . . It seems so cruel."* As she drifted in

"True emancipation begins neither at the polls nor in court. It begins in a woman's soul."—**Emma Goldman,** ANARCHIST AND FEMINIST

and out of consciousness, she mumbled the names of the suffragists with whom she had worked. Shaw remembered her saying, "They are still passing before me, face after face, hundreds and hundreds of them. . . . I know how hard they have worked. I know the sacrifices they have made."

Did you know?

There was a time when a woman virtually ran the presidency of the United States. In September 1919, President Woodrow Wilson had a stroke. For the next eighteen months, his wife, **Edith Bolling Galt**, quietly assumed control of the White House. Galt adored her husband and was determined that he would finish his presidency, so she kept his condition secret from the country. She sorted through his papers to decide what was important, and with the help of his doctor, propped the president up so he could sign them. In this way, a woman with two years of formal education and a determination to be a good wife, a woman utterly opposed to the female vote, assumed many of the powers of the presidency.

A young telegraph messenger brings news of the Tennessee ratification to the National Woman's Party headquarters in Washington, DC.

HEALTH

A small percentage of women had managed to become physicians by the first decades of the twentieth century, but in the face of male opposition their numbers were about to decline again. Medicine, as a profession, was soon firmly in the hands of male professionals who employed all the newest scientific knowledge in their diagnoses and treatment of patients. Physicians were beginning to understand the effects of poor nutrition and the importance of sanitation, as well as the origins of tuberculosis, syphilis, yellow fever, and malaria. Even with this new knowledge, life expectancy for a woman in 1900 had only risen to forty-eight years.

Doctors continued to believe that men's bodies were the norm; women's bodies were the exception. Because of this, many of the rational ideas used in treating men's diseases were cast aside when it came to women. Older notions about the inferior nature of women mixed with new

The health of the child
is the power of the nation

APRIL 1918 **Children's Year** APRIL 1919

UNITED STATES CHILDREN'S BUREAU AND WOMAN'S COMMITTEE OF THE COUNCIL OF NATIONAL DEFENSE

The U.S. Children's Bureau was created out of the grassroots efforts of Lillian Wald and Florence Kelly, who had begun their careers in settlement houses. The Bureau sought the welfare of all American children.

scientific information to create medical literature that often sounds insane today.

In 1870, a doctor addressing a group of medical experts stated that it appeared *"as if the Almighty, in creating the female sex, had taken the uterus and built up a woman around it."* Indeed, medical experts insisted not only that women's ovaries were at the core of most women's ailments, but that they controlled women's personalities and made them emotionally unstable. Decades later, this belief continued to influence the medical treatment of women. In 1906, an estimated 150,000 women had their ovaries removed for a wide range of problems, including overeating, suicidal tendencies, and depression. Some husbands even hoped to use this surgery to cure their wives of "difficult" behavior.

EDUCATION AND HEALTH *The Household Physician*, a widely read book of medical advice, insisted that the health of adolescent girls was particularly vulnerable. It counseled mothers of young women to keep them from too much activity. *"The nervous system [is] unduly developed by excitement.* . . .It is hastened by high living; by the whirl and bustle and excitement of city life; by reading novels which are full of love-incidents; by *attending balls, theatres, and parties;* and by

mingling much in the society of gentlemen." Instead, young women were supposed to eat an "unstimulating diet" and have "a large amount of exercise in the open air."

The book also cautioned girls against trying to stop their periods. "Girls sometimes, in their utter thoughtlessness or ignorance, dip their feet in cold water, when their courses are upon them, and bring on a suppression of a most dangerous character.

When **Helen Hamilton Gardener**, author, feminist, and government appointee, died in 1919, she willed her brain to Cornell University for researchers to study **a thinking woman's brain.** Gardener sought to refute the claim that women's brains were smaller than men's, and thus inferior. She pointed out that she had used her brain to try to "better the condition of women." She assumed her brain would be superior to the brains of "less fortunate women" previously studied.

The most lovely and innocent girls have done this for the purpose of attending a party; and, in some instances, *the stoppage induced has ended in death within a few hours."*

As women began to venture farther from the home for unladylike activities, some doctors predicted dreadful consequences. One doctor advised young women in 1899, "Women beware. *You are on the brink of destruction.* You have hitherto been engaged in crushing your waists; now you are attempting to cultivate your mind. *Beware!! Science pronounces that the woman who studies is lost."* Illness in women, it was often believed, stemmed from these unwise choices. Therefore, most cures required staying home and being domestic.

When **Charlotte Perkins Gilman** suffered a breakdown following the birth of her only child, her doctor told her to *"never touch pen, brush, or pencil...have but two hours intellectual life a day,"* and *"live as domestic a life as possible."* She defied his advice and went on to write *The Yellow Wallpaper,* becoming one of the most important feminist theorists of her time.

PREGNANCY AND CHILDBIRTH If women were already considered weak and fragile, a pregnant woman was more so. *A Nurse in Every Home,* published in 1913, instructed the family of an expectant mother to help her "avoid large gatherings such as church or theatres, on account

During World War I, physician **Josephine Baker** pointed out, "It's six times safer to be a soldier in the trenches in France than to be a baby born in the United States." In 1900, one in ten white children—and one in five black children—died before the age of one.

of the mental impressions to which they subject her.... *Great allowance should be made for the whims and irritability of the pregnant woman* as she is often not responsible for her altered temper. She should be humored and shielded, her peculiarities should be gently overlooked."

Thanks to a better understanding of the role of germs in infection, fewer women died in childbirth. Midwives still delivered 50 percent of all babies. Some women who were admitted to hospitals had the option to try a new delivery technique—"Twilight Sleep." A woman was given an anesthetic that made her unconscious during delivery. She would wake hours later to meet her new child. Twilight Sleep was used through the 1960s.

In this 1890 *Life* magazine cartoon, domestic life is about to attack a sleeping scholar. The caption reads, "For the benefit of the girl about to graduate."

BIRTH CONTROL

At the turn of the last century, many American women had a very incomplete knowledge of how to prevent pregnancy. This case of massive ignorance was due in large measure to legislation passed by Congress in 1873. The Comstock Act labeled all information about contraception (or birth control) "obscene," placing it in the same category as pornography. The consequences of the act were far reaching.

Not only did the Comstock Act make selling contraception illegal, it made giving out information on birth control a crime. Even doctors were prevented from giving their patients information. Moreover, newspaper editors censored material on reproduction. Newspapers that disobeyed were shut down. With little or no information about birth control available to the masses, women had little choice but to keep having babies.

What One Woman Did

"Mothers Whose Miseries Were Vast as the Sky"

Margaret Sanger, a nurse and activist, was almost alone in her fight for women's right to birth control. Sanger believed that until women could control what happened to their own bodies, other changes for women (like gaining the vote) would have little meaning. She preached "joyous voluntary motherhood," and coined the phrase "every child a wanted child."

Personally witnessing the desperate condition of women, she wrote, "These were not merely 'unfortunate conditions among the poor' such as we read about. I knew the women personally. They were living, breathing, human beings, with hopes, fears, and aspirations like my own, yet their weary, misshapen bodies . . . were destined to be thrown on the scrap heap before they were thirty-five." One night, after watching helplessly as a young Russian immigrant named **Sadie Sachs** died from complications of a botched abortion, Sanger reflected on the "pains and griefs" of these women. She recalled, "It was the dawn of a new day in my life also. . . . I was resolved to seek out the root of evil, to do something to change the destiny of mothers whose miseries were vast as the sky."

Margaret Sanger sought the support of other progressives. However, Carrie Chapman Catt, Jane Addams, Charlotte Perkins Gilman, and others engaged in feminist struggles failed to appreciate her vision. Sanger remembered her frustrations, ***"How were mothers to be saved? . . . Progressive women whom I consulted were thoroughly discouraging.*** 'Wait until we get the vote. Then we'll take care of that,' they assured me. . . . 'Wait until women have more education. Wait until we secure equal distribution of wealth.' Wait for this and wait for that. Wait! Wait! Wait!" Sanger was not willing to wait.

In 1913, she published information about women's bodies and sexually transmitted diseases in an article entitled, "What Every Girl Should Know." The U.S. Post Office refused to deliver the paper and Sanger was threatened with arrest. Undaunted, she traveled to Europe to research birth control methods. Returning with greater knowledge, she founded the National Birth Control League and published *The Woman Rebel.* This time, Sanger was arrested and indicted. She avoided punishment by leaving for Europe again.

Returning to America in 1916, Sanger and her sister, **Ethel Byrne**, opened a clinic for working-class women in Brooklyn, New York. During the ten days the clinic was open, almost 500 women came to get information and contraceptives that Sanger had smuggled from Europe. Then she and Byrne were arrested.

> "You can almost tell people's age now by their attitude towards birth control. To the young it is merely one of the accepted facts; if questioned, they assume the whole matter must have been settled long ago."
>
> —Margaret Sanger, 1938

Mothers with baby buggies line up in front of Margaret Sanger's birth control clinic.

Sanger was jailed for thirty days, but this did not stop her. She battled in the courts, attempting to discredit the crucial legal connection between obscenity and birth control. It wasn't until 1936 that the Comstock Act was struck down and doctors were able to prescribe contraceptives. Sanger continued to lobby for reproductive rights internationally. She traveled around the world, and raised funds for birth control research.

In 1960, the birth control pill went on the market. By the time of Sanger's death six years later, millions of American women were using this revolutionary form of contraception. Writing of her life's work, Sanger concluded,

"My life has been joyous and exulting and full because it has touched profoundly millions of other lives. It is ever a privilege to be a part of something unquestionably proved of value, something so fundamentally right."

AT HOME

"MY HOUSEWORK? OH THAT'S ALL DONE"

Most women were neither radicals nor missionaries, factory workers nor suffragettes. The average woman married around the age of twenty-two and then raised children, cleaned house, and participated in the community where she lived.

The 1910s saw the invention of a number of new appliances, though they were used most often in homes that could already afford servants. Some well-to-do families also enjoyed indoor running water and gas lamps for the first time. Cast-iron stoves, while improved, were still fueled by coal.

RURAL WOMEN Few of these technological advances eased the burdens of rural and urban poor women. Electricity and the new accompanying gadgets were costly—the first mechanized home refrigerator, which appeared on the market in 1916,

"Yes, drive over right away? I'll be ready. My housework? Oh that's all done. How do I do it? I just let electricity do my work nowadays. I have an electric dish washer,...electric clothes washer,...electric iron,...electric vacuum,...toaster stove,...coffee percolator."

—ad for Western Electric Co., 1915

"My mom could . . . make a washboard sing, just sing. She had a knack. . . . She had a rhythm, just like someone a-strummin' his guitar for a rhythm."

—**Edna Winter,** INDIANA FARMWIFE

At the turn of the century, **divorce** was becoming more common. Reformers took a long, hard look at marriage and family to see if there were things that could be done to help. Their efforts led state and federal governments to become more involved in regulating family matters. Among other things, they raised the legal age at which a person could marry and established family courts to moderate divorces.

cost $900—more than twice as much as a new Model T. Ford. As late as the 1930s, only 10 percent of farms would have electrical power.

Consequently, for the first decades of the new century, farmwives lived lives similar to those of their mothers and grandmothers. **Ella May Stumpe** of North Dakota remembered growing up on a farm in the 1910s:

> There was no telephone on the farm for years.... There was no plumbing. Water was carried in from the well in a bucket for the family needs...There was no washing machine. The wash boiler, washtub, washboard and homemade soap were every Monday morning necessities...There was no refrigeration, no ice maker, no ice.

Washing clothes still took an entire day and was done in all kinds of weather. Women then pressed the clothes with heavy irons that were heated on the stove. **Vivian Jefferson** of Arkansas recollected, *"We thought then that everything had to be ironed. I even ironed the dishtowels and the baby's diapers...I don't know why I didn't have sense enough to use them without it, but I didn't."*

Southern sharecroppers were the least likely to benefit from new technology. Poor and often in debt to landlords, sharecropping women worked in the fields, took in other people's laundry, and then returned to their long list of domestic duties. One mother of nine told an interviewer, *"I worked many hours after they [her husband and children] was in bed. Plenty of times I've been in bed at three and four o'clock and get up at five, the first one in the morning."*

DOMESTIC SCIENCE MOVEMENT The discovery that invisible agents called *germs* were responsible for diseases added to a woman's daily workload. The introduction of germ theory convinced people that dangerous germs and invisible poisons lurked everywhere. Who better to fight for the health of her loved ones than the wife and mother? It was up to her to banish ill health from her home by scrubbing it top to bottom. But she was not left alone to fend off disease and disorder. She had scores of household management experts at her fingertips

A 1916 photo of a rural mother nursing her baby, entitled "Cornstalk Madonna."

"It is woman, the dainty, the beautiful, the beloved wife and revered mother, who has by common consent been expected to do the chamber-work and scullery work of the world," wrote Charlotte Perkins Gilman. "All that is basest and foulest she in the last instance must handle and remove. Grease, ashes, dust, foul linen, and sooty ironware—among these her days must pass." Gilman, a grandniece of Harriet Beecher Stowe and Catharine Beecher, felt that many problems would be solved if women were less financially dependent upon men. She focused on *economics,* not home economics, as the means to female empowerment. Gilman envisioned apartments and households with common kitchens and eating areas where families could eat together or have the food delivered. Professionals would clean, cook, and care for children, freeing women to work for pay.

in the form of cookbooks, mother's manuals, home economics textbooks, women's magazines, and etiquette guides.

In pursuit of the germ-free house, experts informed women that particular attention should be given to the size and cleanliness of the bedroom. Doctors worried that breathing the same air all night caused illness. Consequently, advice books such as **Helen Dodd**'s *The Healthful Farmhouse By a Farmer's Wife* counseled women to throw open all the doors and windows of the house (imagine doing this in North Dakota in the winter) and "sun the night clothes, pillows, and other bedding out of doors." Dodd urged women to "keep a high standard" despite the never-ending stream of work a germ-free house required—a near impossibility for poor women working long hours.

The stakes were high. Domestic scientists (echoing the words of Catharine Beecher) warned that the very nation was at risk if women failed in their household duties. *"Is it not pitiful, this army of incompetent wives, whose lack of all knowledge of domestic science is directly and indirectly the means of filling our prisons, asylums, reformatories and saloons,"* lamented one. Home economics were soon emphasized in university, high school, and community classes across the country.

SCIENTIFIC PARENTING Domestic scientists also pressured parents to raise children more "scientifically." They tried to convince mothers that they were too sentimental and that their parenting instincts could be damaging. Children, they insisted, needed rigid schedules and discipline to become productive citizens.

Parents of babies born in 1900 were warned against such foolishness as kissing and playing too much with their infants. In fact, according to one expert, *"Babies under six months old should never be played with, and the less of it at any time the better."* Toilet training was to begin by three months and thumb sucking was to be discouraged by using aluminum mittens or pinning sleeves shut over the "offending hand." Women were told that while the new ideas might "seem hard," without them, mothers might unwittingly drive their children to delinquency.

Not all parents had the luxury of worrying whether or not they should play with their children. Many poor mothers struggled just to keep their children clothed and fed. Even so, most probably felt pressure to conform on some level to modern "scientific" parenting ideas. After all, children were a yardstick by which women were measured.

Between 1900 and 1920, the most popular girl's name year after year was **Mary**. *The second most common name was* **Helen**. *Following these, the top girl's names included Anna, Margaret, Ruth, Dorothy, Mildred, Esther, Florence, Marie, and Gladys.*

THE GREAT WAR

"WAR AND PEACE"

Though women's lives are profoundly altered by war, women are often overlooked in historical accounts of military conflict. Because men have traditionally been the combatants, war is considered their story alone. Yet, it has been, in large measure, women who have raised the sons who go to war. It is they who have received notices of the deaths of sons, husbands, and fathers. Women have taken care of business at home and raised children at times of reduced resources. When war has come to them, women have often been singled out for violence. Consequently, during any war, there are women who are not convinced of the necessity of armed conflict. This was the case in 1915.

THE PEACE MOVEMENT With World War I already raging in Europe and the United States debating whether to become involved, three thousand women, including Jane Addams, Carrie Chapman Catt, and Charlotte Perkins Gilman, joined together to form the Women's Peace Party in 1915. The party called for arms limitation and mediation in the war. They declared:

"As women we are particularly charged with the future of childhood and with the care of the helpless and unfortunate. We will no longer endure without protest that added burden of maimed and invalid men and poverty-stricken widows and orphans which was placed upon us [in past wars]....We demand that women be given a share in deciding between war and peace."

In April of the same year, a small group of American delegates traveled to the International Congress of Women held in the Netherlands. Jane Addams, the chair of the meeting, said, *"The great achievement of this congress is . . . the*

An anonymous soldier and two women. Who were these women and what might they think about sending this young man off to war?

getting together of these women from all parts of Europe when their men folks are shooting each other from opposite trenches." **Emily Green Balch**, who attended the conference, was moved by "the beautiful spirit of the brave, self-controlled women who dared ridicule . . . to express a passionate human sympathy."

Women around the country debated whether the United States should enter the war. Some felt that those who opposed the war were "reds" or traitors. Jane Addams, whom the country had previously adored for her work among the poor, was now denounced and hated by many.

SUPPORT FOR THE WAR When the United States declared war against Germany and its allies on April 6, 1917, many women in the peace movement put their pacifism aside and chose to

Have you ever heard of . . . Jeanette Rankin?

Rankin was another woman who worked for peace. Rankin, from Montana, was the first woman elected to Congress. In that capacity, she voted against entering the war in Europe. On April 6, 1917, the *New York Times* read, "On the second roll call Miss Rankin's name was again called. She sat silent as before. The eyes of all the galleries were turned on her. For a moment there was a breathless silence. Then Miss Rankin rose. In a voice that broke a bit but could be heard all over the still chamber she said, **'I want to stand by my country, but I cannot vote for war. I vote no.'**" During her second stint as a member of the House of Representatives, she was the only member to cast a "no" vote against entering World War II. Still a pacifist at the age of eighty-seven, she led a 1968 march on Washington, DC, to oppose the Vietnam War.

join the war effort. Women showed their support for the troops in various ways. They grew gardens, canned produce, and ate more simply to save resources. They even gave up their corsets. The U.S. War Industries Board declared, "American

American delegates (Jane Addams is second from the left) on their way to the Netherlands for the International Congress of Women.

women's sacrifice of their [corsets] during the war released 28,000 tons of steel—enough to build two battleships." Women gathered to organize war-bond drives, roll bandages, and prepare supplies for soldiers. Others ran farms and family businesses while their husbands were away.

Thousands of women took a more active role in the war as well. Many served at home and abroad as aides, clerks, social workers, support staff, and army nurses. Eleven thousand women enlisted as Navy "Yeomanettes," 305 became Marine Corps "Marinettes," and more than 20,000 served as Red Cross nurses.

SHIFTING POSITIONS IN THE WORKPLACE: THE LABOR CRUNCH

As the first military draft called more than one million men to service, American manufacturers began to hire women and black workers, who had previously been considered less-desirable laborers. Increased wage opportunities led to a radical reordering of positions. In New Jersey, it was reported that *"Negro women are leaving the kitchen and laundry for the workshop and factory . . . [taking jobs] made vacant by the shifting of Hungarian, Italian, and Jewish*

girls to the munitions plants." Each group along the socioeconomic spectrum stepped up the social and pay ladder when possible. This is how it worked:

Domestic Servants: Southern black women escaping agricultural and domestic work in the South took the least desirable domestic servant jobs in the North. Though still at the bottom of the economic ladder, Northern domestics could often make twice that of Southern domestics.

Dangerous, Unskilled Factory Jobs: Until the war, black women were a rare sight in U.S. factories. Once admitted, they were given the most hazardous, monotonous, exhausting jobs. A belief that black women could withstand more danger, heat, heavy lifting, and grime than whites got them hired in places such as glass factories, bakeries, and fur-dying operations. They were paid substantially less for doing the same jobs as white women (who were already making less than white men for doing the same work).

Unskilled Factory Jobs: Many white women moved from domestic service into the better unskilled factory jobs; some Northern black women moved

"REMEMBER WE MUST FEED DADDY TOO."

Joan of Arc Saved France

W.S.S.
WAR SAVINGS STAMPS
ISSUED BY THE
UNITED STATES
GOVERNMENT

WOMEN OF AMERICA
SAVE YOUR COUNTRY
Buy WAR SAVINGS STAMPS

UNITED STATES TREASURY DEPARTMENT

Women were called upon to support the war effort in a number of ways. These government posters represent a fraction of the messages being sent to American women during the war.

Sow the seeds of Victory

plant &
raise
your own
vegetables

WRITE TO
NATIONAL
WAR GARDEN
COMMISSION
WASHINGTON
for free books on
gardening, canning
& drying.

"Every Garden a Munition Plant"
Charles Lathrop Pack, President

CAN
Vegetables
Fruit AND
the Kaiser too

Tomatoes

Peas

Monarch Brand
Unsweetened

Write for Free Book to
National War Garden Comm
WASHINGTON, D. C.

Charles Lathrop Pack ~ President   P. S. Ridsd

STAGE WOMEN'S
WAR RELIEF

into these factory jobs as well. These jobs were repetitive and didn't require much training. For example, women stuffed life jackets—the filling often irritated ears, noses, and throats, so men claimed the job of stitching the life jackets together.

↓

Skilled Factory and Office Jobs: Some unskilled native and immigrant factory workers moved into higher-paying, more-skilled jobs—working in munitions and aircraft plants, shipping yards, steel mills, and offices. In a few cases, black women moved into the more-skilled jobs as office workers and government clerical workers.

Men who did not go off to war had mixed feelings about working with women. While some praised the work of female colleagues in their factories, others refused to work with them and did all they could to make women's working lives miserable. They even resorted to what would now be considered sexual harassment: changing their clothes in front of embarrassed women and refusing to close bathroom doors while using the facilities.

"THIS SHALL BE THE LAST WAR": THE WAR ENDS

Throughout the conflict, women kept the home fires burning—a crucial contribution because soldiers needed something worthwhile to return to.

On November 11, 1918, the armistice was signed with Germany, signaling the end of World War I. **Elizabeth Stearns**, who worked for the Red Cross in France, wrote to a friend:

"Just think, tonight everybody says that the Armistice has been signed with Germany and that there will be peace. . . . It doesn't seem possible that the war can really be over. I keep thinking of the infinite joy of the people whose men are at the front. After the strain of the four years I should think the joy would almost kill one. . . . It has all been so horrible. Do you suppose people ever could start up another? Did the world have the same feeling of nightmare, the same exhaustion in 1815 and have we merely lost the experience through the generations in between? I pin my faith to the idealistic, youthful—naïve, if you like—determination of the American people that this shall be the last war."

The next year, Elizabeth Stearns died of bronchitis. Many of her friends would live to see the next world war.

CHAPTER 6

Pushing the Limits

1920–1930

When **Louise Rosine**, a tourist from Los Angeles, refused to roll her stockings up on a sweaty Chicago beach in 1921, a police officer moved in to arrest her. After all, proper bathing attire included a wool swimsuit and rolled-up stockings. Rosine informed the officer that it was nobody's business whether her stockings were rolled up or down. When he tried to apprehend the large woman, she punched him in the eye, broke his glasses, and bit him on the wrist. Once in jail, Rosine took off all her clothes and announced that she would remain naked until freed. The embarrassed warden pinned blankets around Rosine's bars so that no one could see her.

Before this time, women were expected to swim in layers of fabric, stockings, shoes, and sometimes even hats. Outfits that exposed more female flesh and showed off the contours of the body were viewed by many as an indication of a downward spiral to moral decay. As more women went to beaches to swim, and bathing suits got smaller, city governments passed ordinances regulating what was appropriate.

In her own way, Rosine took part in a national debate about women's place in society. Should women

In some cases, beaches hired swimsuit patrols that ventured out with measuring tapes in hand to provide "first aid to the inadequately clad mermaid." Officers in one town were also encouraged to take action against "bald-headed men who came to the beach to stare." This policeman is ensuring that women follow the order that women's suits not be more than 6 inches above the knee at the Washington, DC, Bathing Beach.

be allowed to dress and act as they pleased? Women could now vote, but should they be allowed to shed traditional standards? Americans looked to the future with a mixture of excitement and apprehension. Increasingly prosperous and interested in leisure, fewer women pursued progressive reforms. The great swimsuit debate of the twenties in many ways typifies the challenges of a nation attempting to deal with radical changes in the ways people lived.

LIFE AFTER SUFFRAGE

Clearly this was a new time with different opportunities and challenges for women. After they gained the right to vote on August 26, 1920, people waited to see how life would change. Many suffragists predicted the dawning of a great new day when women would help bring an end to many of society's problems. The anti-suffragists anticipated a near-collapse of civilization. Who was right? How did the country react to this shift in politics?

Initially, there were some promising signs that women's votes would make a difference. In the first elections, politicians felt obliged to pay attention to female voters and the issues they might care about. As a result, in 1922 they passed the Sheppard-Towner Maternity and Infancy Protection Act, which provided the first federal money ever designated for health care. At the time, 250,000 U.S. infants died every year and poor families lost one in six children in the first year of life; this act intended to improve prenatal and infant health by funding maternity clinics.

However, victories for women were few. Politicians and suffragists alike soon discovered that all forecasts of the outcome of women's suffrage were overblown. The truth was that women did not vote very differently from their husbands and fathers. As **Emily Blair** wrote in 1925, *"There is no woman block. . . . The women who have mated with men and borne men-children for countless ages have not decided to go off and wage political war against husbands and sons."* In addition, there wasn't a particularly rousing female voter turnout. While some women were elected to high political offices (two women were actually elected as state governors in 1924), women remained primarily political outsiders. With a few exceptions, the voices of women in politics were heard less and less as the decade wore on. By 1929, even the Sheppard-Towner Act lost its funding.

So what happened to the many women who had toiled for women's suffrage? At the end of their long battle, many reformers were weary. For years they had picketed, campaigned, written letters, and delivered lectures. They had done so not only for the right to vote, but for child labor laws, better living and working conditions for the poor, and other noble causes. Women such as **Lucy Burns**, a dear friend of radical suffragist **Alice Paul**, had led suffrage marches and endured jail and hunger

Did you know?

Native American women did not get the vote in 1920 because the U.S. government did not consider them citizens. Congress finally offered citizenship to all Native Americans in 1924.

In 1920, women of Yoncalla, Oregon, secretly plotted to oust all male city officeholders and elect women in their places. In what was called a **"feminist revolution,"** they rose "in their wrath, to take over city hall." They kicked out inefficient officers to elect **Mrs. Mary Burt** as the new mayor, with **Mrs. Laswell**, the wife of the exiting mayor, as one of the newly elected officials. Apparently, Mr. Laswell was "much surprised."

strikes. After winning the vote, Burns retired permanently from public reform. Another suffragist voiced the feelings of many: *"I no longer work in movements,"* she stated. *"My energies are bent on achieving income."* These reformers and many others stepped out of the women's movement and back into their clubs once the vote was achieved.

For those who remained, there was a tough road ahead. The campaign for suffrage had drawn women together with a single, achievable goal. Once that goal was attained, women found that they disagreed greatly on what should happen next, and they splintered into many smaller groups that had a difficult time attracting attention to their causes.

EQUAL RIGHTS AMENDMENT AND PROTECTIVE LEGISLATION

One of the biggest sources of conflict between women's groups was a potential Equal Rights Amendment (ERA) to the Constitution. The ERA, authored by suffragist Alice Paul, and first introduced in Congress in 1923, said, *"Men and women shall have equal rights throughout the United States and every place subject to its jurisdiction."* With this amendment, Alice Paul and others sought to erase the more than 1,000 state laws that discriminated against women. In many states, a woman's earnings still belonged to her husband and she had no legal rights over her children. Other state laws kept women from serving on juries. Supporters of an ERA felt that women and men should not be treated differently under the law.

On the surface it seems like an equal rights amendment would be something that suffragists

Many concerns about the morality of bathing suits were tossed aside when it was confirmed that pretty, scantily clad women could be real moneymakers. This "Bathing Girl Parade" was held on California's Balboa Beach in June 1920, two months before women won the right to vote nationally. The annual Miss America Pageant was begun in Atlantic City in 1921 as a way to keep summer patrons around for a few extra days in September.

Nina Allender's political cartoon (published by the National Woman's Party in 1923) opposed protective legislation and showed its dangers. The sign on the door reads, "Protection—Motherhood is the noblest profession in the world. Therefore you must be given inferior jobs, the lowest pay, and your hours for work shall be limited. (Except in the HOME)."

required to work to regulating the amount of heavy lifting expected of women workers. Other laws forbade hiring women to work at night. For years, many progressive women had lobbied for these laws to create better working conditions for poor women. Passage of an equal rights amendment would have negated the many laws that were enacted to protect women. Consequently, most progressive feminists who had fought for these laws were decidedly against the ERA. ERA advocates are working for passage to this very day.

Those who supported an equal rights amendment argued that protective legislation was bad for women. **Harriot Stanton Blatch** (daughter

Posters such as this one issued by the Milwaukee County League of Women Voters urged women to use their right to vote.

would support, and yet, the vast majority of women's groups opposed it. Why? Arguments against the ERA revolved primarily around something called "protective legislation." These were laws that protected women because of their special status as mothers and potential mothers. Laws ranged from limiting the number of hours a woman could be of Elizabeth Cady Stanton) and others believed the laws "crowded [working women] into lower grades of work." Working women were split in their support for protective legislation. While it did save them from being exploited in some ways, it also made it impossible for women to be hired for many jobs they might have wanted. One female union member argued that those seeking protective legislation were *"trying to make our legislators believe that we women in industry are a class of weaklings, a special class of creatures devoid of both moral strength and physical stamina, totally unfit, mentally, morally and physically, to decide for our selves, to judge between right and wrong."* Despite the efforts of ERA advocates, it failed to gain momentum and languished in Congress for many years.

Other groups had different plans to further the cause of women. One major group, the League of Women Voters, educated female voters and promoted laws that were beneficial to women and children. They reported on the number of women being elected to office, numbers that declined over the course of the decade. One of the major problems women's groups faced was an aging membership without young people to take their places.

YOUTH CULTURE

"LET THE WORLD AND MORALS ALONE"

Few young women in the next generation were interested in progressive causes. In 1920, Cornell University's student paper declared, *"The American public is weary of persons who seek to better the world . . . and sometimes wishes that among all the efforts at uplift and betterment some comfortable souls would get together and organize a society of down-pullers, to even things up a little."* In 1927, it stated, "let the world and morals alone." Reform was out of vogue. To be concerned about the common good was passé, something associated with bitter old ladies—too boring, serious, stuffy, and old-fashioned.

The younger generation, unconcerned with how long and wearisome the journey had been, cared little for those who had worked for women's rights. Writer **Dorothy Dunbar Brumley** pointed out that young women associated feminism with old "fighting feminists who wore flat heels and had very little feminine charm," and those "who antagonize men with their constant clamor about maiden names, equal rights, woman's place in the world, and many another cause." Young women in the 1920s certainly were not going to give the best years of their lives to fight for causes. They were going to have a good time.

The old reformers didn't sit back and take this criticism lightly. In 1923, **Charlotte Perkins Gilman** declared, "It is sickening to see so many of the newly freed abusing that freedom in a mere imitation of masculine weakness and vice." After having labored so long, the indifference and frivolity of the next generation was hard to bear.

"SHIMMYING TO THE MUSIC OF THE MASSES": FLAPPERS

> "The myth of the pure woman is almost at an end."
>
> —writer, V. F. Calverton, 1927

Who was this new generation? In 1920 two-thirds of the population was thirty-five or younger and the median age was twenty-five. Youth became a force in American culture like never before. This was the first generation to have wide access to movies, radio, cars, and telephones, all of which helped to

"My generation didn't think much about the place or problem of women. We were not conscious that the designs we saw around us had so recently been formed that we were still part of the formation."

—playwright **Lillian Hellman**

Did you know?

The term *flapper* was first used in Britain, where adolescent girls made a fashion statement by wearing their rain boots, or galoshes, open and flapping.

Shocking their elders, young women defied traditional standards. They cut their long hair, shortened their skirts, lowered their necklines, and tossed out their corsets. Many took up dancing, smoking, driving cars, and going to movies. They wore cosmetics and went on dates. In every way that women of the previous generation had gone out of their way to prove they were morally superior to men, many of the new generation set out to confirm just the opposite. Young women showed the world that they could partake freely of the same vices that had been available to men. H. L. Mencken observed that the flapper "seldom blushes; it is impossible to shock her."

Flappers were not the first women to participate in these activities. Young women from the working class had been pushing the boundaries for some time. In 1900, the middle class had looked down on working-class girls and declared their unchaperoned music, dances, and dates disgraceful. Imagine their alarm when their own daughters and sons took up those very vices. It was then that the nation took notice. The flapper and her male counterpart were now the center of attention.

Middle-class daughters and sons discovered jazz (which had originated in black communities) and joined a national dance craze. Parents looked on

change their perceptions of the world. Many were better educated than their parents had been. They were growing up in a different world, and they were ready to be independent, experiment, and push the envelope of respectability. Young women, previously the least powerful members of society, burst into public consciousness. V. F. Calverton, a writer and editor, alerted the nation: *"Cigarette in hand, shimmying to the music of the masses, the New Woman and the New Morality have made their theatrical debut upon the modern scene."* People called these girls "flappers."

It is thought that author F. Scott Fitzgerald based the character of Daisy in *The Great Gatsby* on his wife **Zelda Fitzgerald**, the personification of flapperhood. She wrote that the flappers "flirted because it was fun to flirt and wore a one-piece bathing suit because she had a good figure, she covered her face with paint and powder because she didn't need it and she refused to be bored because she wasn't boring."

Flappers at a football game in Washington, DC, and Winnebago flappers: **Florence**, **Mary**, and **Ann** with their mom, **Rachel Whitedeer Littlejohn** in Wisconsin.

Middle-class white girls were not the only flappers. Flapperhood cut across racial and economic lines. Writer **Eunice Hunton Carter** described schoolgirls in Harlem:

> A group of school girls, bright felt hats perched jauntily on sleek bobbed heads, with short fur coats from which bright scarves fluttered in the night, passed by linked arm in arm, chattering as they went home from a late moving picture. To me, from my high perch, they looked like school girls the town over, but a passerby would have seen skins of olive, tan and copper beneath the bright felt hats.

in dismay as their children did the fox trot, tango, cakewalk, and kangaroo dip. Colleges, parents, city officials, and women's clubs all tried to put a stop to what they viewed as an immoral fad. One professor decried the evils of jazz, declaring that it "expresses hysteria, incites idleness, revelry, dissipation, destruction, discord and chaos." Middle-class parents were at a loss in dealing with their unmanageable youth. Certainly *they* had never danced like that.

As the new flapper fashions made a boyish figure the ideal, women became preoccupied with losing weight. Smoking was advertised as a way for women to stay thin. One well-known ad encouraged women to "Reach for a Lucky instead of a Sweet." For women, smoking had always been associated with "bad girls." Suddenly, it became a symbol of equality. Women could enjoy the same bad habits as men. College administrators tried to halt the trend by expelling girls who smoked, but advertisers employed celebrities to convince women that smoking was socially acceptable. Lucky Strike hired fashion designers to promote dark-green clothing that was the same color as Lucky Strike packages so that a girl's cigarette pack could match her outfit.

This 1926 *Life* magazine cover captures a multitude of fads.

EDUCATION

PEER PRESSURE IN THE "PARADISE OF THE YOUNG"

By 1920 more than 85 percent of Americans aged five to seventeen were enrolled in school. Adolescents were spending more time together doing sports, driving, going to school proms and bonfires, "parking," and going to the movies and the soda shop. The percentage of students attending college doubled from 8 to almost 16 percent between 1920 and 1930. Princeton's dean, Christian Gauss, observed that students had forgotten college's original purpose: "[College] has unfortunately become a kind of glorified playground. It has become a paradise of the young." This was the first American generation to be more influenced by their peers than by the adults around them.

Thus, while young people were undertaking what seemed to be a daring rebellion against tradition, they did so in a massive group, experiencing enormous pressure to fit in with their peers. With movies, magazines, advertisements, and advice books to lead the way, there never had been a generation so unified in its likes and dislikes. Conformity was mandatory for popularity. Numerous fads helped youth determine who was in and who was out. It was vital to wear the right clothes and be able to do the new dances. To fit in, young people swore and used slang terms like "queer birds" and "wet smacks" to describe those who were eccentric or unpopular. It was unfashionable to appear too responsible or serious-minded. Rather, the objective was to appear dashing, cynical, witty, and unconcerned.

As growing numbers of young women flocked to coeducational state colleges, the focus of college life was increasingly on social activity. Whereas women's colleges of the previous generation had turned out an abundance of unmarried reformers, coed colleges primarily produced wives. The new college girl was more interested in joining a

Younger girls imitated the attitudes and styles of women in magazines and movies. **Yvonne Blue** had the flapper requirements figured out by the age of fourteen. She confided her dieting woes in her diary as she desperately tried to achieve a necessary thin, lanky figure. She also wanted to adopt the temperaments of the flapper. She wrote on October 11, 1926,

"Here are ten little things I should like to have, even tho they may not all be good: Self possession, Superiority, Cynicism, Will power, Silentness, Differentness, Subtlety, Immense range of knowledge, Supreme indifference, Great independence."

sorority, getting a date, and finding a husband than in spending time in the company of other women working to reform society. Consequently, she often saw other girls as competition. She was going to make it in life, not with, but despite the other girls around her. She was determined to be a *"good dresser, a good sport, a good pal,"* so guys would ask her out.

BEAUTY

"A GOOD DRESSER"

Everyone, it seemed, had an opinion about the new fashions. In 1922, an Atlanta newspaper quoted a churchman as saying, *"Young men like to have the girls remove their corsets. . . . This makes dancing a thing of passion. Corsetless dancing is nothing but passion."* When one Mexican American girl asked her mother to buy her a bathing suit, her mother replied, "No, you can bathe at home. I will educate you . . . but [I will] not buy a bathing suit. You can wait till I'm dead and buy it then." A Japanese American man wrote to his hometown newspaper to complain about "these slick, knock-em-dead sheiks and these painted, red-hot shebas that strut about the streets of Little Tokyo." He described the young women as "short-skirted baby dolls with their artificial rosebud lips and their languishing, mascara'ed eyelashes" who "arrogantly displayed" their "knock-kneed bowshaped, overgrown limbs."

According to critics, the problem was not just what women wore, but the accompanying attitude.

Women, including Miss America, spent hours waving or curling their hair. They were aided by a permanent wave machine patented in 1928 by African American **Margorite Joyner.**

Some protested that the new styles would be too distracting to men in the workplace. According to one male writer, working men "cannot stand having about them women who are obviously women and not imitation men."

Many women, however, did not give long underwear, huge hats, and ankle-length skirts a backward glance. Forty-year-old **Mrs. H. Fletcher Brown** quickly adopted the new styles. She wrote, "Skirts can't be too short for me, now that at this age I am climbing in and out of automobiles, and gardening in the mud, and playing golf in all weather." Of corsets, she simply stated, *"with bones digging in and garters pulling at every move. No wonder the modern athletic girl wants them off."* **Nina Wilcox Putnam** summed it up in a magazine editorial: "In the dress of the over-criticized flapper I see much that is good. Not only has she had courage to do what I merely dreamed but she got away with it in spite of clacking tongues."

So what were the changes that drew so much comment?

Bobbed hair: Once a source of pride, long locks were clipped into a jaw-length hairdo. Bobbed hair may have been lighter, but it was not necessarily easier. Beauty parlors appeared across the United States even as women were fired from their jobs for cutting their hair.

Have you ever heard of . . . Ida Rosenthal?

Did you know that brassieres are a relatively new item on the clothing scene? Rosenthal, a Russian immigrant, and **Enid Bisset** owned a clothing store in New York. Rosenthal designed a bra meant to improve her customers' appearance and gave one to each woman who bought a dress. Bras were so popular that the Rosenthals founded Maidenform, a company that still exists. Of her life's work, Rosenthal said, **"Nature has made women with a bosom, so nature thought it was important. Who am I to argue with nature?"** By the end of the decade her company had sold more than one million bras.

Makeup: Cosmetics were no longer only for "racy" women. The "Egyptian look" became popular, with eyeliner smudged around the eyes. This, of course, meant that women needed stylish bags in which to carry their makeup. Brand new nail polishes were popular but impractical—the polish ran when wet.

Knee-length dresses: Dresses were straight and low-waisted. Silk was the fabric of choice because so many French cotton and wool mills had been destroyed during World War I. Some dresses were sleeveless—another indication to critics that America was in moral decline.

Accessories: Simpler dresses were spiffed up with accessories. Women wore deep crown hats, dangling earrings, costume jewelry, and head scarves. The Japanese discovery of the cultured pearl process made pearl necklaces more affordable.

Stockings: A stocking ad in 1927 proclaimed, *"A focal point of the world's attention is now the revealed knee."* Stocking sales increased more than 100 percent during the decade. When skirts were long, baggy stockings were acceptable, but now that women were exposing their legs, they preferred formfitting silk stockings with a seam. Garters attached to a girdle held them up.

Underwear: Shocking but true, females needed less underwear with their new attire. A woman's choice to keep the corset and a cotton union suit, or to try the new peach-colored silk teddies and chemises indicated to many where she stood on the new styles.

AMUSEMENTS

"A GOOD SPORT"

Women grew increasingly interested in sports during the 1920s. They competed in track and field events and set new records. Many women and girls swam and played tennis and golf, though participation was limited to those who could afford memberships at clubs. But unless one was a star, attitudes toward women in sports continued to be condescending. Female athletes were often dismissed as less capable than men. One magazine article called the participants in a New England golf tournament "battalions of babbling women." Of the young women at the fore of sports stardom, Gertrude Ederle and Helen Wills attained heights that wowed Americans.

Gertrude Ederle swam the English Channel in 1926. The daughter of German immigrants, Ederle was twenty and already held numerous world records when she stepped into the cold waters of the channel. She sported goggles, a swim cap, and one of the first two-piece swimsuits ever worn in public. Slathered from head to toe in lanolin, she battled rain, high waves, shifting tides, and seasickness as

Lillian Cannon offers her best wishes to Gertrude Ederle as Ederle sets out to swim the English Channel.

she swam. She sang songs to keep herself going: "Let Me Call You Sweetheart" and "Yes, We Have No Bananas." Ederle swam from 7:09 AM until 9:40 PM, becoming the first woman to cross the channel and beating by two hours the times of the five men who preceded her. One reporter called it "the greatest athletic feat by a woman in the history of the world." Crowds in Europe celebrated, and Ederle returned to one of the biggest ticker-tape parades ever held in New York. President Calvin Coolidge dubbed her "America's best girl."

Helen Wills was a powerful tennis player. Magazines and newspapers frequently wrote about her successes. Children taped pictures of her to their walls, Herbert Hoover recruited her to work on his presidential campaign, and Charlie Chaplin said that Wills playing tennis was the most beautiful thing he had ever seen. Competing against both men and women, she won tennis titles in the United States, France, and England, never lost a singles set between 1927 and 1933, and earned nearly three times as much as Babe Ruth.

"A GOOD PAL": DATING

Have you ever heard adults get sentimental about the good old days, when times were simpler and people somehow got along better? Would it surprise you to know that parents in the 1920s idealized the past in similar ways? During this time, young women and men began slipping out from underneath their parents' watchful eyes to go on dates. It was a revolutionary change in the way that girls and boys got to know one another better. Parents spoke fondly of their youthful years, when young men came to call on young women. Back then, courting took place in the home, in the presence of hovering parents and other chaperones.

The old system of courtship had actually given girls and their families a measure of control over the courting process. A young man would never call without first being invited; the young woman would play hostess with the help of her family. There was an underlying code of manners that dictated the roles and behaviors of everyone involved. Dating changed this. On a

In this 1920 journal entry, eighteen-year-old **Marion Taylor** wrote about a "blind date":

JUNE 24—*Well, Mr. Trevor called. I must admit I was disappointed. He is short, and has a little bullet head and stiff yellow hair closely cropped, and a red face.....He sprang at me to help me on with my cloak, and I didn't want it on in the least and got so flustered. And he edged around for the outside of the sidewalk, and I forgot that the gentleman is supposed to do that and I nearly knocked him off because I started to walk on the outside too.* **At last he fell all over himself and I knew my family was enjoying the spectacle immensely from the window!***...I was embarrassed half to death when we reached the house.....I made various lame remarks and there were several harrowing pauses. He asked for my phone number and said he would call me up some evening. I breathed a sigh of relief when he was gone. I hope to goodness he doesn't call.*

date, it was up to the young man to decide whom to ask out, where to go, and how much money to spend. A date was an invitation into the man's public sphere, where he acted as host and assumed control.

Cars played an important role in the emerging dating scene. The family battle for car keys is not a new one. Youth quickly learned that cars could whisk them far from the front porches and parlors of their parents. Adults worried about this new freedom. There was no good way to monitor kids' activities once they were out of sight. Dances could be chaperoned; cars could not. One judge voiced the concerns of many when he declared the automobile to be "a house of prostitution on wheels."

Youth all across the United States sought this new freedom; however, some parents fought harder than others to keep a watchful eye on their children, especially their daughters. This was particularly true in Mexican American communities. **Maria Ybarra** remembered, "When we would go to town, I would want to say something to a guy. I couldn't because my mother was always there. She would always stick to us girls like glue. . . . She never let us out of her sight." In a culture where a girl's purity was crucial to her family's honor, chaperones were a reality that Mexican American youth simply had to accept.

Young women and men were not left on their own to discover the new rules of dating. They could look to movies for clues (the first feature-length "talkie" appeared in 1927). **Kate Simon** remembered that "the brightest, most informative school was the movies. . . . *We learned how tennis was played and golf, what a swimming pool was and what to wear if you ever got to drive a car . . . and of course we learned about Love, a very foreign country like maybe China or Connecticut.*" One girl said that she learned to close her eyes while kissing. She admitted, "I always thought it rather silly until these pictures, where there is always so much love and everything turns out all right in the end." Movies shown across the country taught people the same lessons about life and romance whether they lived in urban New York City or rural Kansas. One lesson was loud and clear: women were in open competition with each other for men's attentions. Ultimate success lay in capturing the best and richest man to marry.

AT HOME

"FRIENDS AND LOVERS": MARRIAGE

The ultimate goal of dating, as it had been with courting, remained marriage. The rebellion of 1920s youth was often short-lived and not quite as wild as observers believed. In actuality, young college women married in ever-greater numbers and at earlier ages. Once she had lived it up a bit, the young flapper, and those aiming to be like her, married and worried more about buying kitchen appliances than about learning the steps to the new fad dance.

What had changed dramatically were people's expectations of marriage and family life. Many believed that romantic love was "the only basis" for a happy modern marriage. Women hoped to share "joys and sorrows with a mate" who would be "not merely a protector and provider but an all round companion." The new modern families were supposed to provide a place where everyone could find affection, contentment, and personal fulfillment. Wives and husbands were to be "friends and lovers" with each other and "pals" to their children. For the first time, marriage counseling programs came into being.

Beyond maintaining this nurturing environment, new pressure was placed on women to "keep the thrill in marriage." As movie star **Dorothy Phillips** reminded, *"marriage is a competitive game in which **getting** a husband is merely the first trick."* Women's calling to be "special custodians of romance" was a complicated one. They were supposed to continue to be exciting to their husbands while at the same time acting as domestic goddesses and doting mothers. It was up to the wife to figure out how to be both efficient and alluring. The result of their failure to do so was illustrated in more than three hundred movies that told the stories of cheating spouses.

Advertisers, a new power in society, capitalized on this concern by offering women items guaranteed to keep them young and desirable. As one woman advised,

"a woman who is properly gowned can rule nations, while a misplaced hairpin has caused more tragic mistakes than a misplaced commandment."

Advertisements reassured women that they might save their marriages by purchasing the right products.

Did you know that Baby Ruth candy bars, which went on the market in 1921, were named after President Grover Cleveland's daughter Ruth, who died at the age of thirteen?

A postcard of Mary Pickford and Douglas Fairbanks in front of their home.

MARRIAGE AND THE MOVIES Movies, now a multimillion dollar industry, also shaped attitudes toward marriage. During the 1920s, one-third to one-half of Hollywood's screenwriters were women, many of whom were college educated and saw themselves as morally emancipated. It is interesting then, that although women in films were frequently portrayed as free-spirited and seeking equality with men, the ultimate message for women was that they could have their wild moment, but in the end would return to their traditional roles.

The public was also very interested in movie-star marriages. When "America's Sweetheart" **Mary Pickford** tied the knot with handsome star Douglas Fairbanks, people felt they were observing the "most successful and famous marriage the world has ever known." The couple seemed to personify the joys of a modern marriage. She was youthful and sweet; he was manly and athletic. In 1920, Pickford told newspapers, "Married life is an art. It is something that must be carefully attended to." Like many film stars to follow, they basked in the luxury of their elite lifestyle and praised the home as the place where they found true happiness. They appeared to have the perfect formula for the happy, modern marriage: youth, beauty, romance, and a charming home filled with elegant things.

Their marriage didn't last, however. By the end of the 1920s, one in six marriages ended in divorce. Some blamed the "restlessness" of the new woman, who increasingly worked outside the home; others

The public health crusades of earlier decades resulted in a heightened interest in personal hygiene. People were encouraged to bathe more and use soap, toothpaste, shampoo, and mouthwash. How important does the ad make it seem that this woman buy the right kind of soap for her family?

pointed to the slackening of the nation's morals and rising premarital sex rates. One thing seems clear: with so much at stake, and expectations for marriage so high, many couples were disappointed with the realities of married life. Romantic dating relationships didn't always lead to romantic, ideal, modern marriages. Once marital happiness was declared essential, it became difficult to make people stay in unhappy relationships.

ADVERTISING AND CONSUMERISM For many, the 1920s were a time of plenty. Advertisers began using psychology to sell products. According to them, a woman's most important job was to buy, buy, and buy some more. Few families still employed maids, so magazines, ads, and advice books reassured the housewife that the most important way for her to show love for her family was to buy the right products, clean her own house, and prepare tasty, nutritious meals. Ads celebrated modernity and ease: "Where women once climbed cellar stairs, we now have only to open the pantry or refrigerator. . . . How much we have learned that they did not know, not only about saving labor, but about better food for our families!"

Shopping was easier. Many stores offered credit. Others made it possible to purchase food in one place instead of going to specialized shops. These new stores were called "supermarkets." Customers loved the newest sales gimmick that allowed them to put their merchandise in a basket and pay in the front of the store instead of filling out an order with a supply clerk. The store even delivered the groceries.

Problems such as body odor, which had long been considered inappropriate to talk about, found their way into ads: "Shall we discuss it frankly? Many a woman who says, 'No, I am never annoyed by perspiration.' . . . does not realize how much sweeter and daintier she would be if she were entirely free from it." This new openness offended some women and caused them to cancel their magazine subscriptions. Most simply tried the new products.

Women who could afford them bought newly available appliances such as electric irons and vacuum cleaners. Other new household gadgets

Have you ever heard of . . . Lupé Velez?

Americans called her "The Wild Cat of Mexico." A redheaded actress from Mexico, she made a name for herself in Hollywood playing beautiful, intense characters. Her personal life, including her speeding tickets and her off-screen romance with actor Gary Cooper, was reported in the newspapers. Velez and other Hispanic actresses such as the regal **Delores del Rio** had a difficult time making the transition to talking films because moviemakers were convinced that audiences did not want to hear Spanish accents. To see Velez in action, look for the 1927 film *The Gaucho.*

included electric waffle irons, heating pads, toasters, food mixers and grinders, coffee makers, and curling irons. Although only prosperous families had indoor bathrooms, everyone wanted one. Refrigerators were expensive and unreliable, so many people continued to use an icebox. Each week the iceman delivered

Have you ever heard of . . . Louise Boyd?

Boyd, a wealthy California debutante, arctic explorer, and geographer once said, "I powder my nose before going on deck, no matter how rough the sea is. There is no reason why a woman can't rough it and still remain feminine." She visited the Arctic for the first time in 1924 and loved it so much that she returned numerous times. Boyd began by hunting polar bears, but went on to gather scientific data on plants, animals, and sea depths. She did all this while traveling with a maid and wearing a flower. Her photographs and charts were considered so valuable that the United States classified them during World War II.

a large block of ice intended to last the week. While washing machines reduced some labor, the less expensive ones still required a woman to carry the heated water and put the clothes through a wringer by hand.

Treated water, pasteurized milk, and a new understanding of the role of vitamins and minerals in good health led to better, more varied diets. Women were reminded that the family's health was their responsibility. Numerous companies marketed their foods as health products. Even candy and ice cream were promoted as "wholesome, nutritious food." Fortified breakfast cereals replaced country-style breakfasts for many Americans. With increased access to canned vegetables, fruits, pork and beans, noodles with tomato sauce, and soups, women spent less time preparing food. In case they felt guilty for cutting corners, they were reassured by ads that promised "on the word of the greatest scientific authorities, that food in cans is as safe as food can be." Salads and casseroles were popular, and most urban women now bought bread instead of making it themselves.

Advertisers assured housekeepers that by purchasing their products they could have "hours of leisure and recreation." Yet, in reality, as the tools for preparing meals and doing housework increased, so did social expectations. People expected a woman's house to be cleaner than in the past. One study showed that in the 1920s, women spent between 48 and 61 hours a week on housework—roughly the same amount of time their mothers spent doing housework. The nature of the work had changed, but the number of hours spent performing the work was the same.

FARMWOMEN Some could not afford to participate in the nation's raging buying spree. Although the "roaring twenties" was a time of prosperity and glamour, dance contests, and cigarette smoking flappers for some, a full 40 percent of U.S. families still lived at the poverty level.

For the first time in American history, people in rural communities were outnumbered slightly by city-dwellers. Those who farmed for a living struggled more than most through this supposedly prosperous decade. Families who had to make the

PAID WORK

Middle-class married women were the new workers of the 1920s. Some, like their working-class sisters, worked out of necessity, but an increasing number worked because they wanted to; they enjoyed the sense of fulfillment and liked earning extra money for their families. Although working-class and black women had combined wage work and family responsibilities for some time, the idea that it might be possible to do both was a new one for the middle classes. Middle-class women worked primarily in jobs that involved service, and used the same skills needed by wives and mothers. These included office jobs, education, nursing, and social work and paid approximately half of what men earned at comparable jobs. By 1925, 90 percent of all clerks and typists were women.

Working-class women who wished to pursue jobs in male-dominated fields faced steep

tough choice between buying a new tractor and farm equipment or having electricity or running water chose the farm tools.

Annie Greenwood was one of these rural women. She and her husband homesteaded in Idaho. She wrote of women on farms, "The reason mentally deranged farm women are not in the insane asylum is because they are still on the farms. I do not write this to make you smile. The sanest women I know live on farms. But the life, in the end, gets a good many of them—that terrible forced labor, too much to do, and to little time to do it in, and no rest and no money."

While there were doubtless happy moments on farms, the underlying reality was that, in the 1920s, many farmwomen lived difficult lives. Unfortunately, conditions for rural communities would only get worse in the coming years.

For many, such as this Wisconsin farmwoman, a woman's workload was no different than it had been in the past.

Did you know?

New York created a Policewomen's Bureau in 1926. Policewomen were specifically assigned cases involving women, children, and shoplifting.

opposition. When World War I ended, many were pushed out of the "masculine" jobs they had filled while the men were away. Although women's foray into new occupations turned out to be mostly temporary, their sense of opportunity was not. The experience had changed them. Women wanted more options and better-paying jobs. They wanted to be able to earn a living and have time left over for other activities. **Anzia Yezierska**, a working woman and immigrant, spoke for many when she wrote, "Women who have known the independence of earning their own livings before marriage are the ones who feel most poignantly the humiliations they have to live through while being supported."

Half of women workers still earned their wages in factories, as servants, or in agricultural labor. Black, Hispanic, and Asian American women continued primarily to occupy the worst jobs among these. New protective legislation ensured that hours and conditions were better than in the past, but there was still much room for improvement.

DECADE OF ISOLATION

Strangely enough, a decade that was wild and innovative for some was also profoundly conservative. Americans reacted to immigration, the great migration, World War I, and the rapid growth of industry and science by turning inward. During the 1920s, the government passed laws restricting immigration and the right to teach evolution in the schools. Unions and women's groups were accused of being Communist. Race riots destroyed black communities, and foreign-born individuals were accused of un-American activity and deported. The tendency toward isolation is also evident in two well-known movements that rocked the country.

"GIVE PROHIBITION ITS CHANCE"

"Ever since the days of Noah there has been a drink problem," wrote **Ella Boole**, president of the Women's Christian Temperance Union (WCTU). By the time the Eighteenth Amendment prohibiting the production and sale of alcohol went into effect on January 16, 1920, crusaders had been lobbying for nearly a hundred years to outlaw drinking. Temperance arguments were valid ones: "It was the home that suffered. . . . the women and children who did without necessary food and clothing because of money spent for drink . . . It was the wife and mother who listened until morning for the staggering footsteps of her drunken husband or son." Boole suggested that America "give Prohibition its chance" by following the law "from home to home."

But much of America did not go dry. The violence and illegal activity that followed prohibition are legendary. Women as well as men frequented hidden bars, or "speakeasies." Manufacturers made

Mrs. Graze Knippen, of Zion City, Illinois, helps get rid of 80,000 pints of beer.

special alcohol flasks that could be strapped to a woman's leg under her dress. College youth drank on the sly. A fiery preacher named John Straton went undercover to a number of dance halls in 1925 and saw "tipsy girls" and "young women who were raving drunk, some of them surging out of the hall on to the street outside, with their loud talking."

Women were instrumental in creating prohibition, and, interestingly, just as instrumental in repealing it. Out of the ranks of temperance crusaders came a group as conservative as the WCTU, the Women's Organization for National Prohibition Reform (WONPR). Like the WCTU, the WONPR believed that homes should be protected, and that alcohol did great damage to society. But their conclusions about prohibition were different. They saw the results of the Eighteenth Amendment as being far more damaging to society than the original problems of alcohol consumption. They also decided that temptation would always exist and that self-control, in the case of alcohol, must be a personal effort. Temperance Union members felt betrayed by these women, whom they had believed were their allies. Nonetheless, the WONPR worked to end prohibition. In 1933, the Eighteenth Amendment became the first and only amendment ever to be repealed.

SELF-APPOINTED GUARDIANS OF MORALITY: THE KU KLUX KLAN

Participation in suffrage politics, missionary work, and the temperance movement led hundreds of thousands of white Protestant women down an unexpected path in the 1920s. When the Ku Klux Klan (KKK) was resurrected, these women used their acquired skills to further white supremacist goals.

Although the new Klan was the brainchild of William Simmons, it was **Elizabeth Tyler**, the woman he recruited to be his publicity manager, who effectively sold it to the public. She was so successful that the Klan became huge overnight, with as many as half a million female members by the middle of the decade. They had their own organization, Women of the Ku Klux Klan (WKKK), and did not want men to tell them how to run it. Their charitable deeds, church dinners, Klan

Have you ever heard of . . . Celia Cooney?

Although she didn't look the part, Cooney was a bank robber. She and her husband Edward held up ten banks for a total of $1,600 in the early 1920s. People called her the **"bobbed-hair bandit."** When the Cooneys were captured in 1924, they were given ten to twenty years in prison but were paroled seven years later.

weddings and baby baptisms masked the underlying belief that Catholics, blacks, Jews, immigrants, and other minorities were a threat to the United States.

The WKKK picked up where the KKK left off and was just as effective. Determined to reform schools, influence local politics, and rid their communities of unwanted individuals, members circulated falsehoods, boycotted businesses, and spearheaded social exclusion campaigns. They also turned names of people they thought needed physical punishment over to the male Klan. These activities had especially disastrous results in towns with small and very visible minority populations. WKKK members were unmoved by the damage they did to individual lives because they were convinced of the moral correctness of their actions. When interviewed years later, many WKKK members remembered the experience as a wonderful community affair. After a series of scandals in 1929, the Klan fell apart as quickly as it had begun. Its remnant struggled on, but without a large membership or widespread public support.

ARTS IN THE SPOTLIGHT

THE HARLEM RENAISSANCE

When half a million African Americans migrated north between 1914 and 1920 they hoped to escape the blatant racism of the South. Unfortunately, it followed them. Many settled in the upper Manhattan neighborhood of New York City called Harlem. Harlem became home to a wide range of poor, middle-class, and wealthy blacks, West Indians, and Hispanics. Treated nearly everywhere as second-class citizens, blacks found in Harlem a place where they could express themselves. Between the two world wars, this population's pent-up energy and desire spilled over in an unprecedented flood of creativity that came to be known as the Harlem Renaissance. As the movement spread to other cities and even to the Caribbean and Europe, Harlem became more than a place; it became a state of mind. During this time, African American writers, musicians, and artists challenged the indignities of white prejudice.

Writers published books and newspapers and gathered in salons such as the "Dark Tower," owned by **Madam C. J. Walker**'s daughter **A'Lelia Walker**, to debate issues of race. Even this haven from outside prejudice had its own pecking order of color, class, and gender. To be uneducated, too dark-skinned, or too poor placed one at a disadvantage. Women, however talented, suffered the gender bias of their husbands and male colleagues.

Writer Langston Hughes recalled that after Zora Neale Hurston moved into an apartment with no furniture or money, "friends gave her everything, from decorative silver birds, perched atop the linen cabinet, down to a footstool. And on Saturday night, to christen the place, she had a hand-chicken dinner, since she had forgotten to say she needed forks."

WRITING IN HARLEM

Zora Neale Hurston was funny and smart—the life of the party. She told fabulous stories, published numerous books and essays, and was well-known by both blacks and whites in the literary community. A fellow writer said of Hurston, "She seemed to know almost everybody in New York . . . and had met dozens of celebrities whose friendship she retained." Yet when writer **Alice Walker** put a tombstone on Hurston's grave in the 1970s, few people remembered that Hurston had ever existed.

Hurston, the daughter of a poor Florida minister, left home after her mother died and worked as a domestic and a servant in a traveling theater group. Through sheer ingenuity and will she managed to get a college degree and do graduate work. Her first short story was published when she was thirty. She then traveled around the South and Caribbean and published her observations in a book entitled *Mules and Men.*

Hurston's writing gave voice to a group to whom few people paid any attention—rural black women. She portrayed relationships within black communities and depicted women who were capable and determined. The work of her own she loved most was *Their Eyes Were Watching God* (1937). She described it as the "untold story" inside her. Her

Zora Neale Hurston beating a drum.

Battling great odds, women such as **Jessie Redmon Fauset**, **Nella Larsen**, **Dorothy West**, and **Helene Johnson** wrote at a time when white publishers were rarely interested in their work, and their own community was sometimes patronizing.

While their works explored universal themes such as aging, marriage, parent/child relationships, community, and violence, these women frequently showed how such topics were complicated by race and class. They also provided windows into the double bind of being both female and black in a society that placed little value on either.

SINGING THE BLUES

Other women found Harlem fame by singing the blues—a uniquely black American style of music

Bessie Smith.

colorful characters and her use of black dialect were controversial among her colleagues, who feared that she reinforced negative racial stereotypes. Hurston insisted that race was not her central concern:

"From what I had seen and heard, Negroes were supposed to write about the Race Problem. I was and am thoroughly sick of the subject. My interest lies in what makes a man or woman do such and such, regardless of his color. It seemed to me that the human beings I met reacted pretty much the same to the same stimuli."

The rediscovery of Hurston led historians to wonder about other black women who wrote between 1900 and 1945. Researchers turned up more than one hundred writers of poetry, children's books, short stories, novels, plays, and essays.

that was born in the slave quarters of the American South. African American women performing on stage and cutting records in the 1920s first introduced the blues to a wider audience. **Bessie Smith**, **Ethel Waters**, and **Alberta Hunter** were all born to poor parents in the South. Bessie Smith was raised by relatives after her mother died and Alberta Hunter by her mother after her father abandoned the family. Ethel Waters felt like she never really had a family at all.

Each woman had her own style and first made her name in the South. They also occasionally viewed one another as competitors. Waters remembered that "people everywhere loved [Smith's] shouting with all their hearts," but the crowds who nicknamed Waters "Stringbean," also adored her "low, sweet" way of singing the blues. A friend of Hunter's recalled that that when she sang about being jilted, "you felt so sorry for her you wanted to kill the guy she was singing about."

Singing was an unreliable way to earn a living, so each woman in turn experimented with film, stage, musical extravaganzas, and radio broadcasting. But white Americans had limits to what they would allow from a black woman. Waters eventually accepted roles playing caring black domestics in Hollywood films. Smith died in 1937 from the injuries she sustained in a car wreck (**Janis Joplin** would place a tombstone on her grave in 1970). Hunter returned to the stage as an elderly woman after having spent most of her adult life caring for her mother and working as a nurse. Their musical accomplishments, however, lived on to inspire and sustain a new generation of blues and jazz singing women.

WOMEN IN FLIGHT

Flying above Harlem and above the debate on the female's place in society was a new woman—the woman aviator. Before World War I there had only been seven licensed female pilots, but in the 1920s

Grace Hurd, **Evelyn Harrison**, **Corinna DiJiulian**, and **Grace Wagner** (under the car) learn the art of auto mechanics at Central High School in Washington, DC (1927).

The attention given to women pilots was not always positive. A 1925 *Time* magazine article quipped:

Because of the impaired co-ordination of their nerves under pressure, the liability of their hearts to variation, and their general inclination to giddiness, women seldom function as airplane pilots. Occasionally, in flying circus outfits, women have capitalized the fact that their sex is, in the air, a freak, and accepted large sums of money to perform comparatively safe flights.

women aviators became increasingly visible. Some used their skills to dazzle people and earn money by traveling the country with flying "barnstorming" circuses. Crowds were amazed to see women flying upside-down or jumping out of airplanes. **Marie Meyer** performed flying stunts at state fairs. She also stood on the wings of the airplane her husband flew between buildings in St. Louis.

Other female pilots saw flying as a means of helping people. **Florence Barnes**, a movie stunt pilot, was one of a number of woman aviators to create a disaster assistance corps. To prove their

effectiveness, they dropped a crate of eggs from 7,000 feet without breaking one. **Phoebe Fairgrave Omlie**, the first woman to earn a professional air mechanic's license, patrolled for forest fires with her husband.

Although trained as a hairdresser, **Bessie Coleman**'s dream was to open a flight school for blacks. This daughter of sharecroppers went to France for training because no U.S. flight school would admit a black woman. As the first African American pilot, she returned to the United States to perform in air shows. Her career was cut short in 1926 when she was killed while rehearsing for a show in Florida.

Because airplanes were still relatively new, women had many opportunities to experiment

Mary Fechet in flying gear.

and set records. **Amelia Earhart**, who had worked as a telephone operator, bought her own airplane and flew solo across the United States and back in 1928. The next year, women pilots began their own organization, the Ninety-Nines, with Earhart as president. Member **Katherine Sui Fun Cheung** told reporters, "I don't see any reason why a Chinese woman can't be as good a pilot as anyone else. We drive automobiles—why not fly planes?" The first women's cross-country air derby from California to Ohio was also in 1929. Fifteen of the twenty "sweethearts of the air" finished the race.

For the sweethearts of the air, flappers, and others, America seemed full of opportunities in the 1920s. Expectations of women's capabilities appeared to be expanding. Women, as individuals, could aspire to work and play as never before. There seemed to be nothing that could stop the progress of a modern society. In 1920, **Edna St. Vincent Millay**, a young poet, actress, and playwright, penned this quatrain that for many has come to describe the era:

My candle burns at both ends;
It will not last the night;
But ah, my foes, and oh, my friends—
It gives a lovely light!

Making It Through
1930–1945

Dressed in a flowing cape, uniform, and hat, **Ellen Church** became the first airline stewardess in 1930. On her first flight for what became United Airlines, she attended to the president's son, Herbert Hoover Jr., and fifteen other passengers. Her duties included serving box lunches and coffee, hauling luggage, handling emergencies, fueling the plane, and pushing planes into hangars. Church's innovation of placing women on flights to care for passengers caught on as competing companies quickly followed suit. Airlines had strict requirements for stewardesses, or "hostesses" as they were called: they had to be registered nurses, single, white, younger than twenty-five, attractive, and weigh 115 pounds or less. A pleasant personality was also a must. The 1920s had seemed full of new possibilities for women in and out of aviation. But when women began serving cookies and coffee on airplanes, the message was clear: a woman's place was not in the cockpit, but in the kitchen.

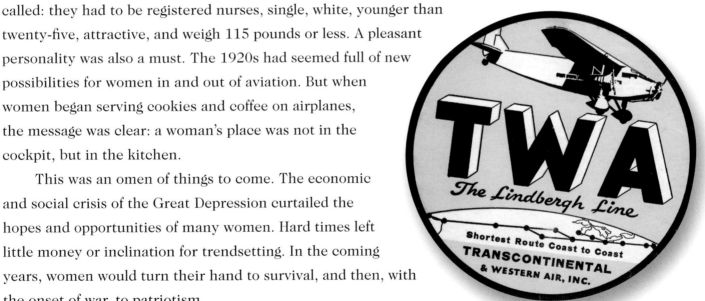

This was an omen of things to come. The economic and social crisis of the Great Depression curtailed the hopes and opportunities of many women. Hard times left little money or inclination for trendsetting. In the coming years, women would turn their hand to survival, and then, with the onset of war, to patriotism.

THE GREAT DEPRESSION

What would you do if your family's income stopped one day? How long would your family be able to make it before you lost your home and ran out of food to eat? What would you do if local charity organizations ran out of money and there were no government-sponsored programs to feed and clothe you? Such was the fear

We often only see images of the Great Depression in black and white. This 1940 photograph of the Whinery family of Pie Town, New Mexico, shows the hardscrabble lives of homesteaders.

and desperation of millions of Americans during the Great Depression, which officially began with the stock market crash on October 29, 1929.

The stock market had been wildly profitable during the 1920s, creating millionaires overnight. Americans had begun borrowing money to purchase stocks. Banks had invested people's deposits in the stock market. When stock prices suddenly plummeted, people panicked and sold their stock for a pittance. Americans rushed to the banks, but banks were in disarray. Thousands closed for good without returning money to customers. The stock market declined nearly 90 percent from 1929–32. Reactions to the crash had a domino effect. People stopped buying and businesses closed.

As the economy slowed to a crawl, middle-class women and men lost their jobs and homes and slipped into poverty. The poor got even poorer and struggled to survive. In 1931, longtime reformer **Jane Addams** said of the poverty in Chicago, *"I have watched fear grip the people in our neighborhood.* . . . men and women who have seen their small margin of savings disappear; heads of families who see and anticipate hunger for their children before it occurs. *That clutch of cold fear is one of the most hideous aspects."*

As the decade wore on, unemployment climbed from less than 3 million in 1929 to 12.5 million in 1932, when one-third of households lacked even one wage earner. In Toledo, Ohio, 80 percent of workers were out of jobs. In Charleston, South Carolina, 70 percent of African Americans couldn't find work. With no safety net to support them, it is believed that more than 90 percent of children in West Virginia suffered from malnutrition. Reporter **Lorena Hickok** wrote, *"The chief trouble with people in South Dakota . . . is sheer terror.* They are afraid of the future." For many, it was this overwhelming sense of uncertainty that defined the era.

THE NEW POOR

In 1928, President Herbert Hoover had announced, "We in America today are nearer to the final triumph over poverty than ever before in the history of any land." During the twenties even the poor had hoped for better days. The middle classes had felt immune from poverty and purchased large ticket items on credit. The Depression delivered a huge financial blow. For many it also resulted in the loss of hopes and dreams, and an embarrassing decline in status. Once-prosperous middle-class families lost homes, cars, and businesses and struggled to live on greatly reduced resources. They became members of a new class: the new poor. **Bernie Weaver** was sixteen when her parents lost their family grocery store in Ohio. After allowing desperate families to

The authors' grandmother, Cora Pearson, before and after the stock market crash. Pictured right, between **Lucille Fiksted** and **Xenia McKanlay**, and below in 1937 with their father as an infant.

"We went to the forest and cut logs, peeled them and built our own [two-room] log house. . . . All we had were the log walls and a roof over our head. It was quite a change for me, having been raised in a house with four bedrooms, a bath, living room, dining room, kitchen and a lovely back porch. . . . It wasn't easy. I had so much pride that I would go hungry rather than tell my mother I needed something. I can remember saving the last bit of butter so if my folks came I could serve butter for their meal."

purchase groceries on credit, her parents could no longer meet their own debts. Weaver had never seen her parents cry, but on the day the store closed, she recalls that they lay on their bed and wept.

One of the nine million families who lost their life's savings in 1929 was the Pearson family. Before the crash, **Cora Pearson** had grown up on a thriving, affluent Idaho farm in one of the "nicest homes in the surrounding area." She recalled, "I can't remember Mom ever having an empty purse because it was my dad's pride and joy to keep money in it." At that time, she said, "There were good reasons for working hard, being ambitious and setting high goals. We viewed the future through rose-colored glasses."

Then one morning they "got word that the banks all over the country were closed. Dad had money in both banks in town and lost every cent." As part of the graduating class of 1930, Pearson's life suddenly changed and her dreams of going to college were "shattered." She wrote that *"Grover [Hemming] and I were married during the Depression and so we learned first hand what the word depression meant."* In order to strike out on their own, she recalled,

Pearson joined millions of others in adapting her life and expectations to meet the realities of a world much changed.

THE OLD POOR

The Depression was a startling experience for the middle classes, but for poorer Americans who had already struggled through the "prosperous" twenties, poverty was nothing new. Although conditions were difficult for poor white people, racial discrimination had long insured that regardless of educational level or ability, minorities would live in the worst housing, have the least desirable job opportunities, and toil in the lowest paying jobs. For them, hard work and careful budgeting did not ensure financial security. When times got bad, they were the first to be fired.

Even before the Depression, Mexican Americans were often the poorest people in their

Mexican American children in San Antonio, Texas, in 1939.

towns. Real estate restrictions forced all Mexican Americans, whether middle-class or poor, first or fifth generation, to reside in "barrios" or Mexican neighborhoods. Housing was overcrowded, substandard, and lacking in comforts. Babies died at alarming rates, and many people suffered from tuberculosis.

Carlotta Silvas, of Arizona, was twelve when the Depression began. She lived with her grandmother, aunt, uncle, and thirteen cousins. Her parents and siblings also lived nearby. It took the wages of most of the adults—her grandmother was a seamstress, her uncle a gravedigger, and her father a miner—to keep the family afloat. Her Aunt Armida was responsible for feeding everyone on one dollar a day. And yet, Silvas's mother would fill little bags with flour, sugar, and potatoes to hand out to people in need. Silvas observed the Depression up close. She watched "people in their rickety old cars, their clothes in tatters, escaping the drought and the dust bowls." She later explained to her grandchildren that she had never learned to ride a bike because she would not have thought to ask for one when her family barely had money for food.

Many immigrant families were poorer than Carlotta Silvas's but were afraid to request charity for fear of being deported. To make matters worse, angry Americans blamed Mexicans and other minorities for the job shortage. Between 1931 and

In America today we are taught to **"reduce, reuse, recycle,"** but how much do we really do it? How would your habits change if your family's resources were drastically reduced? What if you found yourself in a position where you needed to sew your own clothes, grow your own garden, and can your own food? Would you have the skills to survive or would you need to learn them really quickly?

Top ten girl's names in the 1930s: *Mary, Betty, Barbara, Shirley, Patricia, Dorothy, Joan, Margaret, Nancy, and Helen.*

1935, the U.S. government deported one out of three Mexican Americans, even those who were American-born. Immigration agents carried out surprise sweeps of neighborhoods and hauled people to the border. Mexico was also in the midst of a depression and deportees had a difficult transition. Some died of exposure or starvation because they had no family or home to which they could return.

AT HOME

"A LITTLE WORSE EACH DAY"

Just as many of the nation's wives had grown accustomed to the idea that they should bring their families happiness by buying things, they were thrust back into the role of family producer. America's motto was no longer "Buy! Buy! Buy!" It was "Make do or do without." The first line of defense against the ravages of the Depression involved stretching depleted family resources. Women adapted their lives to the emergency by returning to traditional ways—the days of home production.

With or without resources, the job of running a home was women's work. During the Depression, women had to learn many of the skills that had been abandoned by their own mothers and grandmothers: gardening, canning, making soap, remaking old clothing, and baking bread. Numerous publications offered advice on "how to keep a budget, how to make your own clothes, how to conceal the wear in old chairs, restore old pictures, paint shabby walls, make a tasty meal of leftovers, and glue together furniture." Indeed, it took creative management to keep a family housed, fed, and clothed.

FOOD AND CLOTHING During this time, the price of food increased dramatically as family incomes declined. Even the thriftiest mother could not make food appear out of nowhere to feed her hungry children. The choices facing poor mothers were grim. One woman told a reporter of "her hungry babe whimpering in the night and growing children tossing in their sleep because of gnawing plain hunger." The poorer a woman was, the more likely she was to fill empty bellies with less expensive and less nutritious starches—corn bread, wheat bread, and potatoes. Formerly middle-class moms bought cheaper cuts of meat and got

When a teacher in West Virginia told an inattentive student to go home and eat, the little girl informed her that she couldn't because it was her sister's day to eat. These children were photographed in Red House (top) and Omar (bottom), West Virginia, in 1935.

Did you know?

Chocolate chip cookies were invented by accident in 1933. **Ruth Wakefield**, the owner of the Toll House Inn in Massachusetts, thought she could save some steps in the cookies she was making by adding pieces of a broken up candy bar. The result was so tasty and the cookies so popular that, in 1939, Nestlé's bought the rights to the Toll House name and began selling chocolate chips.

Writer Studs Terkel interviewed many ordinary people who endured the Depression. Dynamite Garland told him, "I finished high school and got sort of engaged. I thought maybe if I got married I could eat hamburgers and hot dogs all night, have a ball, play the guitar and sing. I was singing with a hillbilly band and married the guitar player. Anything would be better than coming home and sleeping on the floor."

creative with the sparse ingredients on hand.

Clothing presented another problem. Children could go barefoot in the summer, but when the school year started, they needed shoes. Women took apart old adult clothes and made them into outfits for children. The cut-off legs of men's trousers became pants for little boys. Farmwomen made shirts, dresses, and underwear from cotton animal feed sacks. Theo Hammond from North Carolina later remembered that feed sacks came "in very pretty colors at that time . . . we'd buy two sacks of the same color because it would [be enough] to make a garment." Some women bleached the brand names off of the cloth so their kids would not have "Pillsbury on their seat." During winter months mothers sent their children to school or the library to keep warm. As the assigned breadwinner, the husband also needed passable clothes, either to find a job or to keep one. For most women, this meant putting aside their own clothing needs for another year, and then another.

Poor nutrition and inadequate clothing led to illness, but people who couldn't afford basic necessities did not have money to pay a doctor. Many women nursed sick family members and delivered their babies at home. An Oklahoma woman wrote, *"The unemployed have been so long without food, clothes, shoes, medical care, dental care, we look pretty bad—so when we ask for a job we don't get it and feel a little worse each day—when we ask for food they call us bums."* Though life expectancy for women had risen to sixty-three years in 1931, it dropped back to fifty-nine by 1936.

These struggles were compounded by a continuous flow of strangers appearing on doorsteps needing to be fed. America's byways were clogged with scruffy, unwashed, and hungry wanderers looking for work. "There were many beggars, who would come to your back door, and would say that they were hungry," recalled **Kitty McCulloch**. With no money to give, she took them to her kitchen and fed them. When **Emma Tiller** saw "tramps and hobos" picking up castaway items along the railroad tracks she gave them old clothing. She remembered, *"Many times I have gone into my house and taken my husband's old shoes—some of 'em he needed hisself, but that other man was in worser shape than he was."*

Tiller listened to their "hard luck" stories, then sent them on their way with a cloth sack full of corn from her garden.

RELATIONSHIPS Economic hardship placed tremendous stress on relationships among spouses, relatives, and friends. The Depression brought families together or tore them apart, depending on the strength of those relationships. Families who did not get along or who were already poor had fewer resources to buffer them during difficult times. Divorce rates declined during the Depression, not because more couples stayed together, but because many men who couldn't afford the application fee for the legal paperwork just left and never came back.

"You don't know what it's like when your husband's out of work," one migrant told a reporter. *"He's gloomy and unhappy all the time. Life is terrible. You must try all the time to keep him from going crazy."*

When families lost their homes, they often moved in with relatives. For a woman this meant seeing her "workplace" overrun by extra bodies to feed, clothe, clean up after, and find sleeping places for. It could also mean being the "guest" in someone else's house. Even in such situations, women often found strength in working together and sharing each other's company. Sharing limited space was nothing new to families who were already poor at the outset of the Depression. These women had long pooled resources to survive. **Mary Owsley** said, *"A lot of times one family would have some food. They would divide. And everyone would share. Even the people who was quite well to do, they was ashamed. 'Cause they was eatin', and other people wasn't."*

BEAUTY

Women's styles in the 1930s reflected the country's somber mood. Tailored jackets emphasized squared, broad shoulders as if to show that women could bear the burdens they carried. Many women stopped

Unemployed husbands felt humiliated for being unable to provide for their families, and wives were unsure how to relieve their despair.

Women and girls were among the drifters who traveled from place to place, but the belief that no respectable woman would live on the street meant that few provisions were made to help them. A graduate student who traveled around with "tramps" reported that most of their time was spent trying to find food. He wrote, "A boy can steal. . . . A girl can offer her body, but likely as not she will find nobody in the market with desire and a dime. The usual course is to remain hungry until breakfast at a mission for a boy, or until breakfast can be begged by a girl."

Did you know?

Bra cup sizes A–D were introduced in 1935.

buying hats. Hairstyles and skirt hems lengthened and waistlines returned to the waist. One study discovered that the "dark shadows cast by the Depression" had changed clothing worn by college students. College girls tended to wear simple, sporty sweaters and skirts, ankle socks, and comfortable shoes. Advertisers, aware of the shrinking American pocketbook, appealed to buyers with ads like one for "Warm . . . Dependable Coats . . . for Small Budgets." Evening wear, by great contrast, represented a form of escape from real-world problems. Sumptuous slinky silks and satins with low-cut backs were paired with an abundance of jewelry and furs for the few who could afford them.

Trends moved away from the boyish flapper figure to women with curves. The *Washington Post* wondered if women might help the nation's economy by gaining weight and buying longer skirts. *"A little plumping of the ladies at this time might rescue the farmer. A new deal in contour might whirl the wheels of the great textile industry."* The idea was that farmers could prosper by producing enough food for each American woman to gain five pounds, which would result in a national total of 300 million pounds.

PAID WORK

"WHICH MEN WANT TO TAKE THEIR PLACES?"

The American Woman's Association declared in 1934 that working women were "the employment casualties of the Depression." Many working women had come from a generation of women that "stressed and exulted in the importance of jobs for women." They had aspired to better jobs for better wages.

The Association reported that *"during the Depression years they have had to meet doubt and distrust and fear, loss of morale and disturbance of established ways of living."*

As employment opportunities dwindled, everyone seemed to agree that men should hold the few remaining jobs. Men gladly stepped into occupations that women had increasingly held—as social workers, teachers, bookkeepers, and insurance agents. The Economy Act, passed by Congress in 1932, prohibited more than one family member from working for the government. This caused many women to lose their office positions. Most school districts refused to hire married women and fired those who got married.

Unemployed men, however, shunned the more menial jobs that were considered "women's work" and showed little interest in becoming laundresses, domestics, telephone operators, store clerks, typists, or secretaries. As one commentator put it, "Approximately 3,100,000 women are employed as domestics. Which men want to take their places?" Men's disinterest in the lowest rungs of female employment allowed at least some women to retain their jobs.

It was no longer popular for a woman to aspire to independence and a career. The dean of Barnard College told her students that *"perhaps the greatest service that you can render to the community . . . is to have the courage to refuse to work for gain."* Striving for a career was condemned as an antisocial act that deprived another family of income. In 1936, 82 percent of those polled opposed women working.

At many factories, women hid their marriages for years to keep their jobs. Factory worker **Irene Young** said, "I have worked in plenty of shops in Detroit, and I have lied to get into them and I have lied to stay there."

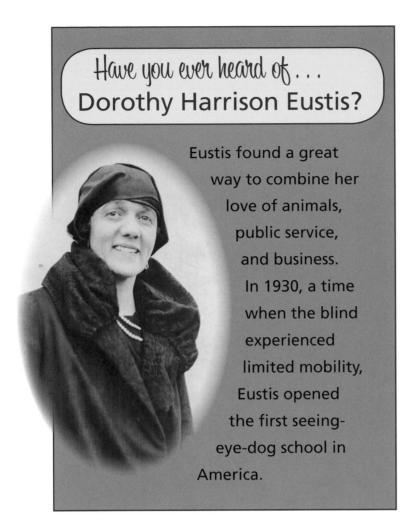

Have you ever heard of . . . Dorothy Harrison Eustis?

Eustis found a great way to combine her love of animals, public service, and business. In 1930, a time when the blind experienced limited mobility, Eustis opened the first seeing-eye-dog school in America.

Depression. They were less likely to lose their jobs than their husbands, because they worked as domestics, seamstresses, shopkeepers, and secretaries. For them, this shift in responsibility inspired new confidence and independence.

OUT OF WORK For many single and minority women, the Depression was catastrophic. Many Mexican American and African American women were already barely subsisting when they lost their jobs and couldn't get public aid. Black women in New York lined up in the Bronx, ready to clean people's houses for as little as fifteen cents an hour. This became known as the "Bronx Slave Market." These women were virtually invisible to those who created programs for the poor. Programs were initiated under the assumption that women had someone to care for them. As one worker observed, women without family support lived where *"no one helps but God in heaven."*

Journalist **Meridel Le Sueur** wrote of women's quiet desperation: "It's one of the mysteries of the city where women go

Working women became easy targets for public disdain. Public officials referred to married working women as *"undeserving parasites."* One man wrote to his congressman, "Woman's true place is her home . . . and I do not believe we are again going to have normal and prosperous times until women do return to their homes." This hostility put women into a double bind, because their labors were often necessary for their family's survival.

Chinese American communities also suffered from economic hardship, but ironically, the prejudice that had segregated them from other parts of the population worked in their favor during the Depression. Because they were forced to depend mainly on themselves and imports from China, their economy was generally not closely tied to the national economy. Strong community networks also helped individuals survive. Surprisingly, there is evidence that, on the balance, Chinese American women in San Francisco benefited from the

In 1938 **Yuri Kochiyama** recalled that "Japanese could not find jobs except in Japan Town and China Town. Even when I finished Junior College, I was one of the only Japanese Americans who was working in San Pedro. . . . I heard that it was the first time that a five-and-dime hired Japanese. Woolworth hired me where other five-and-dime stores wouldn't even let me make out an application."

During the Depression, many women participated in successful strikes and negotiations with employers for the first time in their lives.

UNIONS The Depression breathed new life into labor unions. Female membership, which had waned in the 1920s, tripled in the 1930s. Tired of unfair work situations, women joined the Congress of Industrial Organizations (CIO) as well as trade unions that would accept them. They also joined organizations like the Communist Party, which recruited women and minorities. African American women led campaigns to boycott businesses that would not hire black workers. Mexican American fruit canners joined with their white coworkers to press for better working conditions. The help of women also proved to be critical to the success of a number of men's strikes. Women's auxiliaries enabled the men to hold out by providing a continual supply of food, blankets, and first aid. In truth, this was the role for women that most male workers continued to prefer.

when they are out of work and hungry. There are not many women in the bread line. There are no flop houses for women as there are for men." She continued, *"I've lived in cities for many months broke, without help, too timid to get in bread lines. I've known many women to live like this until they simply faint on the street from privation, without saying a word to anyone."*

She described what it was like for women waiting for work at the Minneapolis employment bureau: "We sit here every day, waiting for a job. There are no jobs. Most of us have had no breakfast. . . . We look away from each other. . . . It's too terrible to see the animal terror in each other's eyes." When one homeless girl entered and became hysterical, the woman in charge screamed back. "So they stood there the two women in a rage, the girl weeping and the woman shouting at her. In the eight months of unemployment she had gotten ragged, and the woman was shouting that she would not send her out like that. *'Why don't you shine your shoes,' she kept scolding the girl, and the girl kept sobbing and sobbing because she was starving."*

IN THE DUST BOWL

"A WAY OF LIFE DESTROYED"

Perhaps the most dramatic effects of the Depression were seen in the farming heartland of America, where drought and massive windstorms created what came to be known as the dust bowl. **Ann Marie Low**, the sixteen-year-old daughter of a North Dakota farmer, began a diary in 1927, "the last of the good years before the Depression." The eldest of three kids, Ann Marie was her father's biggest help. She knew how to ride, raise livestock, herd sheep, mend fences, and cultivate crops. Over the next ten years, Low shared with her diary experiences that were similar to those of many young women living in the dust bowl: the hard work, the deferred hopes, and also the continuing belief that things would get better.

When the stock market crashed in 1929, Low noted that farmers were already well ahead of the rest of the country in hard times. What began as difficulty turned to disaster as a relentless drought was followed by hot windstorms that blew away the topsoil. Low wrote that *the air was full of dirt "coming, for literally hundreds of miles. It sifts into everything. After we wash the dishes and put them away, so much dust sifts into the cupboards we must wash them again before the next meal.* Clothes in the closets are covered with dust." This dust lasted not for weeks, but for years, and was a constant nightmare for women trying to maintain homes for their already suffering families.

Low's parents wanted education for their children, so at great sacrifice, they sent her to the local college with the understanding that she would then help to pay for her sister and brother to attend. She worked at the school library to help pay the bills. She also hurried home often to help her parents. Her diary mentions numerous young men who took her to movies, dances, and roller-skating. When they proposed marriage, which many of them did, she "pointed out the impossibility." Their own family responsibilities combined with hers made getting married seem irresponsible. With this decision, she joined hundreds of thousands of other young women who delayed marriage and having children. As **Ella Ponselle** later said,

"Do you realize how many people in my generation are not married? . . . There were young men around when we were young. But they were supporting mothers."

Around the country, families lost their farms. Low wrote that her grandmother turned off her hearing aid when government agents came to discuss buying her farm. She also described crops that cooked in the ground for lack of water, chickens that stopped laying eggs, and animals that were shot for lack of money to feed or transport them. Bud, her younger brother, lost the herd that was to help pay for his college education, placing even more pressure on Low to help him. After he had to kill his favorite cow, she wrote, "Somehow, to me, *the look on his face when he shot Isabelle stood for this whole tragedy of a land laid waste, a way of life destroyed."*

When Low graduated and got a job teaching school, she frequently went stretches without pay because the school district had no money. When she had money, she sent almost all of it home. In spite of this, the Lows lost the farm that had been in the family for two generations.

Families such as Ann Marie Low's, although struggling, at least had the resources of education and land. Sharecroppers, farmers who worked someone else's land for a portion of the returns, were even more devastated by the Depression. With no safety net, thousands found themselves jobless, homeless, and on the road.

What One Woman Did
Documenting the Dust Bowl

Dorothea Lange never intended to be famous, and yet the picture she took of a worried and tired-looking migrant mother and her children in 1936 has become the image most often associated with

Did you know?

Lange's famous photograph almost never happened. On that August day in 1936 she drove past a sign for the pea pickers' camp but had gone another twenty miles before she decided to go back. Lange later recalled, "I drove into that wet and soggy camp and parked my car like a homing pigeon. I saw and approached the hungry and desperate mother, as if drawn by a magnet." **Florence Owens Thompson** was huddled in a tent with her seven children (see previous page). Nearby lay the car whose tires she had just sold to buy food. She told Lange that the only thing they had to eat were small birds and frozen vegetables from the fields. Lange's photo was published in two national magazines and raised sympathy for the plight of migrants. Unfortunately, it did nothing to ease the plight of its actual subjects. As a matter of fact, Thompson, a strong woman and union activist, was sorry the picture had ever been taken. She did not like being the poster child for the Depression.

the decade. Lange did more than just take pictures. She talked with the people she photographed and recorded what they said about their circumstances. Many of her subjects were refugees from the dust bowl states—migrants making their way to California with all their children and earthly possessions packed into old cars. Lange, a mother of two, was moved by the plight of other mothers who were destitute, dirty, and desperate.

When the Depression began, Lange owned a successful photography studio. The misery she saw every day convinced her that taking studio portraits when people were starving was absurd. As soup kitchen lines trailed around the block, she closed her studio and searched for a way to help.

Lange used her skills to raise public awareness and convince the government to do more to ease the suffering of poor Americans. Hired by the Emergency Relief Administration, she and her husband, Paul Taylor, made a strong case for federal aid by combining her photos with his written reports. The powerful combination influenced government decisions. The photographs taken by Lange and others were published in newspapers and magazines, alerting the public to the breadth of the disaster. Her photos also inspired John Steinbeck as he wrote his novel of America's dust bowl, *The Grapes of Wrath*.

Despite prejudices against hiring women, a number of government programs employed female photojournalists to document the dismal conditions around the country. These included Southern author **Eudora Welty**, industrialist photographer **Margaret Bourke-White**, and dancer-educator-photographer **Marion Post Walcott**.

THE NEW DEAL

"ELEANOR EVERYWHERE"

When Depression-weary Americans elected Franklin Delano Roosevelt (FDR) president in 1932, they voted for "bold, persistent experimentation" in the form of a New Deal. The new president promised government programs to bring relief and an end to the Depression. What Americans couldn't have imagined was the bold, persistent experimentation of his wife, **Eleanor Roosevelt**, who would exert major influence over policy and life in America for decades to come.

For anyone who has ever felt awkward and unattractive, lonely and abandoned, it might be encouraging to discover that one of the most famous, beloved women in American history could relate to those fears. For most of her life, Eleanor Roosevelt dealt with the lingering pain and insecurity borne of an unhappy childhood. Roosevelt began life as a plain, shy, gawky girl who was dismissed by her mother as a "funny child, so old-fashioned, that we always call her Granny." She was orphaned at ten and raised in the "grim atmosphere" of her grandmother's house. Roosevelt wrote of her childhood, "I was always afraid of something: of the dark, of displeasing people, of failure. Anything I accomplished had to be done across a barrier of fear."

Remarkably, Eleanor Roosevelt crossed the "barrier of fear" to become a powerful force for good in the world. Despite scathing criticism and a steady stream of hate mail, she stepped into the role of First Lady like no woman before or since. Political cartoonists mocked her appearance, the media often portrayed her as someone who didn't know her place, and reporters made fun of her voice when she spoke on the radio. Consequently,

when Roosevelt said *"everyone must live their own life in their own terms and not according to anybody else's ideas,"* she spoke from difficult experience. She found that she could not satisfy everyone's expectations, and so she set out on her own path—one utterly unpaved by previous presidential wives.

"The century-old White House wore a startled air today as its new mistress took over," wrote reporter **Bess Furman** on March 4, 1933. Roosevelt signaled her unprecedented activism by holding weekly news conferences that were open only to female reporters—a tactic that helped female reporters retain their jobs during massive layoffs.

Eleanor Roosevelt served as a voice for the poor and disenfranchised. Americans looked on in wonder as she criss-crossed the country visiting downtrodden and discouraged people. The First Lady went down mine shafts, visited shantytowns, relief projects, hospitals, churches, and schools.

Eleanor Roosevelt posing with Washington, DC, Girl Scouts with a Christmas tree sent by a New Hampshire troop. A friend of hers declared that photos of Roosevelt were "very unjust." "It misses her immaculate freshness of appearance, her graciousness, the charm of a highly intelligent, forceful, and directed personality."

"You gain strength, courage and confidence by every experience in which you really stop to look fear in the face. You are able to say to yourself, 'I lived through this horror. I can take the next thing that comes along.'... **You must do the thing you think you cannot do."** —ELEANOR ROOSEVELT

Marian Anderson wrote of the day in 1939 when she performed on the steps of the Lincoln Memorial in Washington, DC: "All I knew then as I stepped forward was the overwhelming impact of that vast multitude. There seemed to be people as far as the eye could see. . . . I had a feeling that a great wave of good will poured out from the people, almost engulfing me. . . . I sang, I don't know how."

In 1933 alone, Roosevelt received 301,000 pieces of mail and answered up to fifty letters a day. During her husband's second term in office in 1939 she hosted 4,729 people for lunch or dinner, had 9,211 people to tea, had 323 overnight guests at the White House, and officially received and served refreshments to 14,056 people. In 1940, *Life* magazine dubbed her "Eleanor Everywhere." The magazine noted that since entering the White House, the First Lady had traveled more than 280,000 miles, visited every state but South Dakota, written a million words, given away over half-a-million dollars, presented hundreds of lectures, "and probably not wasted as much time as the average person does in a week."

Roosevelt won over much of America with her energy, warmth, and generosity. Writer **Martha Gellhorn** noted, "No one seeing her could fail to be moved; she gave off light." She continued, ***"With Mrs. Roosevelt, empathy reached the rank of genius."*** In an uncertain world, her "power of empathy" and "clear and constant sense of justice and injustice" was "a national asset."

When she found appalling conditions at a black reformatory school, she detailed the problems for the press and shocked Washington observers by inviting the girls to a garden party on the White House lawn. When racism kept **Marian Anderson**, a famous black opera singer, from performing a concert at Constitution Hall, Roosevelt helped organize a concert featuring Anderson at the Lincoln Memorial. At a conference in Atlanta where blacks and whites were segregated on different sides, she moved her chair to the middle of the aisle.

A NETWORK OF WOMEN

To accomplish the many things she did, Roosevelt relied on an extensive network of progressive women with whom she had associated for decades. The economic collapse in the United States created an unprecedented opportunity for them to influence government policy. Their efforts were turn-of-the-century-style progressive reform on a large scale. One of the first things Roosevelt did after becoming First Lady was to sponsor the White House Conference on the Emergency Needs of

Women. She and her trusted friend **Molly Dewson**, the chair of the Democratic Women's Committee, pressured President Roosevelt and other government leaders to appoint women to government jobs.

Roosevelt would go to her husband and say that *she "was weary of reminding him to remind the members of his cabinet and his advisors that women were in existence."* Government agencies finally began hiring women, many of whom left their mark on New Deal programs. By 1939, they comprised more than 44 percent of employees in the newly created agencies. Among these, Frances Perkins and Mary McLeod Bethune assumed particularly important positions of power.

"THE BEST MAN IN THE CABINET"

When **Frances Perkins** went to college, it was not politics that interested her, but science. Her focus changed after a history teacher assigned her to tour a factory and observe working conditions. The injustices she witnessed and the needs she perceived altered her plans considerably. She decided to work in industrial reform.

On March 25, 1911, she had another life-changing experience. Hearing horse-drawn fire engines outside where she and some friends were having tea, she ran to the scene of the emergency. Perkins watched in horror as women and girls threw themselves from ninth-story windows in an attempt to escape the burning Triangle Shirtwaist Factory fire. She later said that "Out of that terrible episode came a self-examination of stricken conscience in which the people of this state saw for the first time the individual worth and value of each of those 146 people who fell or were burned in that great fire.... *Moved by this sense of stricken guilt, we banded ourselves together to find a way by law to prevent this kind of disaster."* Her investigation helped lead to legislation to protect workers.

Having gained reform experience volunteering in Chicago's Hull House, she went on to work as a labor lobbyist and an industrial commissioner for New York. Thus, when Franklin Roosevelt was elected in 1932, Molly Dewson lobbied hard for appointing Frances Perkins to head the Department of Labor. When Perkins expressed doubts about taking the job,

"I never pass that little white meeting hall without remembering Mrs. Roosevelt—the First Lady—coming in there in a gingham dress and mud on her shoes one night to square dance with the settlers. . . . That was real democracy."

—JAMES MANCHIN OF ARTHURDALE, WEST VIRGINIA.

The New Deal consisted of government programs that tried to bring people relief from the ravages of the Depression, as well as help the country recover economically from the Depression.

Average Americans felt as if they knew Mrs. Roosevelt and wrote to her as if she were a friend. She received the following letter from a twelve-year-old South Carolina girl:

Dear Mrs. Roosevelt,

Mrs. Roosevelt will you send me and my sister, Ruth, a pair of ball bearing roller skates? Our friends have skates and we are not able to buy them. We sure will thank you if you will.

yours truely, L. L.

"Imperceptibly we have come to recognize that government has a responsibility to defend the weak."

—ELEANOR ROOSEVELT

Perkins's appointment was attacked on many fronts. Not everyone was thrilled to have a woman in a powerful cabinet position. Eleanor Roosevelt wrote to a friend about Perkins: "How men hate women in a position of real power." Ralph A. Horr, Republican Congressman from Washington, dismissed her appointment as "a widespread gesture" made for the benefit "of the mothers and sweethearts of the nation." Others thought she was perfect for the job. One man referred to her as "the best man in the cabinet."

Dewson urged, *"Don't be such a baby, Frances. You do the right thing. I'll murder you if you don't."*

In her first meeting with the president, Perkins insisted that if she accepted the position, she "should want to do a great deal." She handed him a long list that included programs for children, the unemployed, and the elderly. These programs rested on the assumption that government should help relieve the suffering of its citizens. On one occasion, the president said to Perkins, "We are going to make a country in which no one is left out." Frances Perkins's work on the New Deal attempted to do just that.

"THE BLUE SKY OF HOPE AND PROMISE"

When **Mary McLeod (Bethune)** was a child in South Carolina, her mother, who was a freed slave, washed laundry for white families. Once, while delivering clean clothes, little Mary picked up a book belonging to one of the children. The girl said, "put that down—you can't read!" Mary decided then and there that if the big difference between white and black people was education, she was

Frances Perkins's programs were at the heart of the New Deal, which provided jobs, introduced Social Security to care for the elderly, regulated working conditions, brought electricity to rural farming areas, and created social welfare programs.

A 1925 portrait of Mary McLeod Bethune by Reiss Winold.

"I am my mother's daughter, and the drums of Africa still beat in my heart. They will not let me rest while there is a single Negro boy or girl without a chance to prove his worth."

—MARY McLEOD BETHUNE

growing number of students, and Bethune's untiring fundraising efforts, led her to found Bethune-Cookman College on the site of a cleared dump in Daytona Beach. The school, which she said was "prayed up, sung up, and talked up," became a respected and beautiful thirty-two acre campus.

Later in life Bethune became a good friend of Eleanor Roosevelt. Her many activities on behalf of racial justice led President Roosevelt to appoint her as the head of the Division of Negro Affairs for the National Youth Administration (NYA). As such, she was part of FDR's unofficial "Black Cabinet"—a group that helped advise the president on black affairs. Speaking of her accomplishments in the NYA, Bethune said that they had "dispelled the thick and oppressive clouds of despair under which Negro youth has long struggled until they now see through the rift the blue sky of hope and promise."

UNDER THE NEW DEAL

Throughout the Depression, women's organizations and charities were on the front lines in the battle against poverty. Women conducted food and clothing drives and operated soup kitchens and shelters. Female-run organizations such as La Cruz Azul Mexicana and Madrecitas were under pressure to serve their own minority populations who could not find help anywhere else. Aid resources dwindled as the Depression stretched on. In three years, the number of unemployed Americans quadrupled to 12.5 million. If the government wouldn't intervene, who would?

NEW DEAL WORK PROGRAMS When Franklin D. Roosevelt became president in 1933, all eyes turned to him and his advisors for solutions. Calling their plan "The New Deal," they created programs primarily for men. They assumed that men were the providers and if they had jobs, whole families would benefit. This prevailing image of what a family should be failed to take into account the numerous households headed by

going to learn her letters. When an African American schoolteacher opened a school in a nearby town, Bethune was the only one of her sixteen siblings chosen to attend. But she didn't keep her knowledge to herself: she taught her brothers and sisters to read.

After college, she dedicated her life to making education available to as many black children as possible. She taught in a number of states, then opened her own school in Florida with five girls and charred pieces of wood for pencils. The

women. The first projects of the New Deal only hired men, but it soon became clear that the government needed to help women as well.

The first New Deal program to directly assist women was not started until the Depression was six years old. The Works Project Administration (WPA), begun in 1935, only hired men, single women, widows, or women with disabled husbands. While men gained real job training, women were assigned "feminine" tasks that were labeled "unskilled" work and received lower wages. Still, the jobs did offer support to women who otherwise could not have provided for their families. Unfortunately, government programs such as Social Security made no provisions for domestic workers or farm laborers, the jobs most often held by minorities.

Because each state was responsible for running its own WPA, local prejudices meant that the distribution of aid was often unfair and turned eligible people away. In the South, black women were frequently given dangerous and difficult manual labor such as clearing land, working in dumps and garbage incinerators, picking cotton, and hoeing tobacco.

ARTIST PROGRAMS An unusual branch of the WPA, Federal One, gave jobs to writers, musicians, artists, and theater personnel. Under the Federal Writer's Project, writers such as **Margaret Walker**, **Zora Neale Hurston**, and **Anzia Yezierska** were paid to document folklore. Other women interviewed elderly ex-slaves and recorded their stories. In each state, writers created state guidebooks. Under the Federal Theater Project, headed by charismatic **Hallie Flanagan**, actresses and actors, technicians, writers, and directors put on stage productions. The tickets were inexpensive or sometimes free, making theater available to audiences unaccustomed to attending plays. One Federal Art Project paid 162 trained woman artists, selected by anonymous competition, to paint murals or create statues for newly built post offices and courthouses. Many of these works of art can still be seen in public buildings around the country.

THE INDIAN NEW DEAL On reservations, the Indian Reorganization Act of 1934, or "Indian New Deal," represented a big shift in government policy toward Indian nations. Well-intentioned but

READY TO SERVE
TRAINED EFFICIENT WORKERS

HOUSEHOLD SERVICE DEMONSTRATION PROJECT
W·P·A

Most female WPA workers labored in sewing rooms, producing clothing for the poor. Others taught nursery school and adult education, repaired and catalogued library books, served hot lunches to school children, canned produce for distribution, and worked as household aides to the elderly and handicapped. Some translated books into Braille. This poster was created by Cleo Sara, an artist for the WPA's Federal Art Project.

A New Deal intervention that made a tremendous difference in the lives of many women was the Rural Electrification Administration, which brought electricity to the countryside. The impact of this project was far-reaching. Farm women finally had access to electric labor-saving devices that had long been available to others. Electricity also ran water pumps, saving women the toil of lifting water from wells. "To me, Heaven arrived the day we got it," recalled **Edith Gladden** of Missouri. "I remember hearing Roosevelt on the radio making a speech, and he said, 'We are going to have electricity on every farm in the United States.' I could not imagine that man had any idea of what he was talking about."

controversial, it proposed to change the way land was distributed, restore tribal governments, and promote economic improvement. Under the Indian New Deal, women were offered new opportunities for education and employment. The act also empowered women who had been excluded from political participation in their tribes.

At the same time, the Indian New Deal undermined more traditional kinds of female power that did not fit into the American version of government. Although the act mandated that traditional culture be respected, some Native American groups believed that its ultimate goal was to turn Indians into white people. In order to receive its benefits, a tribe had to officially endorse the act. Some did, but others refused. **Alice Lee Johnson**, a Seneca-Cherokee woman, bitterly opposed the Indian Reorganization Act, while **Gertrude Bonnin**, a Sioux, urged her people to participate.

AMUSEMENTS

FUN FOR CHEAP

When hard times hit, some families tried to hide their troubles from neighbors by pretending everything was normal. It became easier to avoid seeing friends than to face the shame when those friends found out the truth. One woman complained to the president, *"We don't have no pleasure of any kind."* Still, people did find ways to forget their problems. Americans craved distraction from the dreariness of their daily lives—but those distractions had to be affordable for people with more time than money.

If you lived during the Great Depression, your list of inexpensive ways to have fun might have included:

Jigsaw puzzles For the first time, puzzles were made out of cheap cardboard rather than wood, and cost as little as 10 cents.

Board games Monopoly, created in 1935, allowed savvy players to own property and get rich. The week it went on the market, twenty million sets were

Creole girls in Plaquemines Parish, Louisiana, in 1935.

Homesteaders having refreshments in Pie Town, New Mexico in 1940.

sold. Other popular games were Sorry and Backgammon. Women also played a card game called Bridge.

Radio Millions of women tuned in daily for radio shows like "Our Gal Sunday, "The Romance of Helen Trent," and "Stella Dallas." Funded mainly by soap companies, they came to be known as "soap operas." By 1939 there were sixty-one soap operas to choose from. Listening to the radio was also a family activity. Wives, husbands, and children often listened together in the evenings. A 1937 study indicated that people listened to the radio for an average of four and a half hours a day.

Dance Sometimes people just needed to get out of the house. Young women and men jitterbugged to swing bands and danced to songs like, "I've Got My Love to Keep Me Warm." A dance marathon craze hit the country. Participants competed for cash prizes by outlasting other contestants. Dancers took turns sleeping while the other partner shuffled their feet and held them up.

Children waiting in front of a moving picture theatre on Easter Sunday in Chicago.

ESCAPING TO THE MOVIES

In spite of dire economic circumstances, people somehow found money to go to the movies. In the dark of a theater, a woman could temporarily forget that her husband was unemployed, her dress shabby, and her house shared with numerous relatives. Hollywood gave her story lines that did not resemble her life—glamorous women and men dancing and falling in love, throwing pies at each other, or riding into a Western sunset.

Actresses such as **Ginger Rogers** and **Claudette Colbert** were elevated to goddess status. Perky child actress **Shirley Temple**, with her curls and dimples, was a favorite, perhaps because she always put a positive spin on things. Hollywood replaced Paris as the fashion mecca for the few Americans who could still afford to shop. When **Greta Garbo** wore an evening suit, others followed. When **Jean Harlow** became the star of the moment, girls attempted to replicate her platinum blonde hairstyle with peroxide and other bleaches. They wore dark lipstick and nail polish, and plucked their eyebrows and penciled them back in. Women colored and permed their hair, and donned fake eyelashes. Even with a depression on, the demand for movie star clothing was so great that movie companies began to alert clothing and shoe manufacturers and retailers of the clothing that would be worn in upcoming films. One manufacturer said, *"Every time a new picture is released a new style is created and there is an instantaneous demand for it from women in all parts of the country."*

A disturbing trend in Depression-era movies was the frequency with which violence toward women was portrayed as normal and even comical. Frustrated male characters frequently put women "in their place." One movie analyst wrote, "Today, a star scarcely qualifies for the higher spheres unless she has

Jitterbugging in a juke joint on a Saturday night outside Clarksdale, Mississippi, in 1939; photo taken by twenty-nine-year-old government photographer Marion Post Walcott.

been slugged by her leading man, rolled on the floor, kicked downstairs, cracked over the head with a frying pan, dumped into the pond, or butted by a goat." No one thought it objectionable when a billboard for the 1936 film *Love Before Breakfast* pictured a beautiful blonde woman with a black eye.

Until 1934, films also pushed the boundaries of respectability with stories like *Call Her Savage, Laughing Sinners,* and *Unguarded Girls.* One movie ad winked, "If your Aunt Minnie from Duluth happens to be in town next week, *don't* invite her to *The Story of Temple Drake."* In these films, illegal, forbidden, and sinful activities did not lead to the downfall of the characters. Instead the message to audiences was that wickedness could pay. Hollywood's antics offended so many people that in 1934 movie codes were born. Many movie board rules regulated the ways that the female body could, or could not, be photographed.

One actress dared to flaunt the rules, and often got away with it—**Mae West**. With her voluptuous body and husky voice, she claimed the part of "bad girl." She wrote much of her own dialogue for movies and was famous for her witty, off-the-cuff remarks. In one well-known movie exchange between Mae West and Cary Grant, he asked her, "Haven't you ever met a man who can make you happy?" Her response: "Sure, lots of times." She was so controversial that she spent eight days in jail on obscenity charges and saw her name banned on 130 radio stations. Unconcerned, she stated,

"Personally I admire good women, but you never hear about good women in history. The only good girl to make history was Betsy Ross and she had to sew up a flag to do it."

SPORTS

By the 1930s, many schools had athletic programs for girls, though less strenuous and with less funding than those for boys. Talented girls had fewer opportunities to practice and compete. In spite of this, a number of U.S. female athletes qualified for the 1932 Los Angeles Olympics. They could not stay in the Olympic Village, which was built only for male athletes, but they took medals in diving, swimming, and track and field. Although **Louise Stokes** and **Tidye Pickett** qualified, they were not allowed to participate because they were black.

SPORTS HERO America's shining star, **Babe Didrikson** was the self-assured daughter of Norwegian immigrants. She excelled at virtually every sport she tried. As a child she already knew that she wanted to be "the greatest athlete that ever lived." Although she had never been to a

Babe Didrikson: golfing in Iowa in 1946; boxing in New York in 1934; running in West Virginia in 1932; and playing tennis in California in 1944.

Have you ever heard of . . . Jackie Mitchell?

She made the news when she struck out Babe Ruth, Tony Lazzeri, and Lou Gehrig during an exhibition baseball game that she pitched against the New York Yankees in 1936. She was only seventeen years old. When the baseball commissioner revoked her contract, he said, "Life in baseball is too strenuous for women."

Decked out in satin shorts, striped knee socks, and high-top tennis shoes, The All American Red Heads proved that not only could women play basketball, they could excel at it. Begun in 1935, the team traveled the country competing with men's teams. The Red Heads were wildly popular. Not only did they win nearly three-fourths of their games, they also entertained the crowds with awe-inspiring half-time basketball tricks and antics. The team, made up of ever-changing players, lasted until 1986.

track meet, at fourteen she began training for the Olympics by hurdling the hedges in her neighborhood. In high school she played every sport except football, from which she was excluded. A little over five feet tall, she ran circles around everyone on the basketball court. As the only member of the Employers Casualty track team, eighteen-year-old Didrikson entered the Amateur Athletic Union championship against other teams and single-handedly won. At the Olympics a few months later, she earned gold medals in the javelin throw and 80-meter hurdles. Didrikson enjoyed competing in baseball, diving, and swimming events. When she took up golf (at which she also excelled), a reporter asked her if there was any game she didn't play. Didrikson responded, "Yeah. Dolls."

ARTS IN THE SPOTLIGHT

READING TROUBLES AWAY

Reading provided another escape. Americans loved magazines—and there were many written by and for women. Appearing in 1931, the adventures of Nancy Drew thrilled girls. Nancy was fashionable, popular, smart, and drove her own car while solving various mysteries. For others there were comic books, the first of which arrived on store shelves in 1933. Sensational news stories such as the crime sprees of **Ma Barker** and bank robbers **Bonnie** and Clyde also grabbed peoples' attention.

But popular entertainment wasn't all about escape. Some of the most popular novels of the day were about people enduring difficult times.

Americans could relate to the deprivation and hunger in the popular novel *The Good Earth*.

The Good Earth, by **Pearl S. Buck**, was published in 1931. It is the saga of a Chinese peasant family buffeted by natural and social forces beyond their control. Wang Lung and his wife O-lan work the land side by side until famine tears them from their home. American readers connected with Wang Lung's displacement and despair as he joins the faceless, starving masses of people heading south: "Day by day beneath the opulence of this city

While writing The Good Earth, *Pearl Buck maintained a household and cared for a husband and a child. She said that she felt "like a juggler trying to keep a handful of balls all aloft at once.... Were I a man, my books would have been written in leisure, protected by a wife and a secretary and various household officials. As it is, being a woman, my work has had to be done between bouts of homemaking."*

Have you ever heard of . . . Anna May Wong?

In a time when few Asians found jobs in the film industry, Wong managed to have a career in Hollywood. She acted in more than 100 films. The roles offered to her were narrow and based on racial stereotypes. She could be a helpless "lotus blossom" or a wicked "dragon lady." In either case, the characters were portrayed as exotic and not entirely trustworthy. She auditioned for the lead role of O-lan in *The Good Earth*, but the part was given to a Caucasian actress. Anna was asked to play the selfish mistress, but declined.

Wang Lung lived in the foundations of poverty. . . . There was not food enough to feed savage hunger and not clothes enough to cover bones." Wang Lung's wife, O-lan, is a courageous, industrious woman who remains strong in the face of misery. Chronicling the family's endurance and their return to the land, Pearl Buck created characters with whom readers could identify.

Buck was well acquainted with the Chinese countryside and peasants of which she wrote. Having grown up in China as the daughter of missionaries, she spoke fluent Chinese. When she returned to America for college, she recalled her wonder that her "college mates never asked about China, or what the people there ate and how they lived and whether China was like our country. *So far as I can remember, no one ever asked me a question about the vast humanity on the other side of the globe.*" Her novels exposed most Americans to Chinese culture for the first time. She succeeded in humanizing Chinese peasants, and helped her American readers feel a common bond with them.

The Good Earth won the Pulitzer Prize the year it was published and was subsequently translated into over thirty languages. Buck went on three years later to be the first American woman to win the Nobel Prize for literature.

THE MOVIE While millions of Americans were losing their jobs, homes, and farms, Hollywood spent considerable sums of money to transport whole Chinese villages to the California set of *The Good Earth.* They grew Chinese gardens and imported grasshoppers from an actual plague in Utah to eat them up. All this attention to authenticity contrasted with America's deeply engrained prejudices that caused producers to cast Caucasian actors in all the major roles.

AMERICA ENTERS WORLD WAR II

"SUCH A MOMENTOUS THING"

While government intervention helped many distressed Americans survive the Depression, it took a war to revitalize the economy. In 1941, the war in Europe was already several years old and the Germans, who had invaded numerous countries, appeared to be winning. Most Americans knew that the country might be drawn into the war, but not when or how.

THE BEGINNING On Sunday afternoon, December 7, **Delores Dudley** was washing the floor of her Minnesota apartment when she flipped on the radio to listen to music. She was horrified to hear a reporter announcing that Japanese planes had just carried out a surprise attack on the American base at Pearl Harbor, Hawaii. In addition to killing more than 2,000 servicemen, the bombs had also destroyed 21 ships and 162 planes. Dudley later said that when she heard the news, *"I was so astounded that I forgot where I was. I started to jump to my feet not realizing I was under the kitchen table and hit my head on the way up."* The next afternoon, President

WPA poster offering instructions of what to do during an air raid; created by Federal Art Project artist **Charlotte Angus**.

Roosevelt announced to the waiting country that the United States must enter the war.

Women who had been "making do" for a decade now made sacrifices for the common good. Suddenly, economically depressed America became responsible for supplying itself and its allies with goods needed for the war. War strategists realized that the only way this massive mobilization could succeed was if the public sincerely believed that what happened at home directly influenced what happened abroad. The war must be waged on two fronts and success would rely on the zealous participation of women as well as men. To this end the Office of War Information used movies, posters, magazine articles, and advertisements to remind the public that *"women by themselves cannot win this war. But quite certainly it cannot be won without them."*

Nazi persecution of the Jews began almost immediately after Adolf Hitler took power in 1933. By 1939, thousands of desperate Jewish refugees sought asylum in the United States and other countries. Though news of Nazi atrocities had leaked out, the U.S. government clamped down on immigration, allowing only a small fraction of refugees into the country. In 1939, the steamer SS *St. Louis,* carrying 930 German Jewish asylum-seekers, was turned away at U.S. ports. Those on board were devastated. Sixteen at the time, **Gerta Blachmann Wilchfort** later recalled, "So we saw the lights of Miami. We saw the lights of America and that was it. We slowly sailed back to Europe." Blachmann and her mother became refugees in Switzerland. Many SS *St. Louis* passengers, however, perished in the Holocaust.

Young women especially were caught up in the feverish excitement of the early days of World War II, as the defense industry tooled up, men enlisted, and people got married. **Dellie Hahne**, a young teacher, remembered that although she knew that "war was a terrible thing," it provided excitement in her otherwise dull life. She recalled, "Suddenly single women were of tremendous importance. . . . **When it started out, this was the greatest thing since the crusades.**" Hahne took a job as a nurse's aide. She, like many other young women, also showed her patriotism by marrying a soldier she had only

known for six weeks. **Olga Lanzione** said that she cried while listening to the news about Pearl Harbor, "then on Monday, I went out and applied for a war job with the government." During the next four years, the lives of all women were touched in some way by the war, whether as homemakers, consumers, volunteers, reporters, soldiers, nurses, or prisoners.

SOLDIERS For some time, Congresswoman **Edith Nourse Rogers** had lobbied for a corps of women "auxiliaries" for the military. A veteran of World War I, Rogers insisted that fighting men needed the logistical support that female soldiers could provide. When World War II began, her colleagues finally listened. The Women's Army Auxiliary Corps (WAACs—later WACs) was created in May 1942 and included units of black and Native American women. A navy auxiliary, the WAVES, followed in July. By the end of the war, the Army Air Corps had WASPs, the Coast Guard SPARS, and the Marines WRs. Each of the women's auxiliaries was seen as a means to free men for combat.

Have you ever heard of . . . Dorothy Thompson?

Reporter Dorothy Thompson "swept through Europe like a blue-eyed tornado." In 1934, Adolf Hitler expelled her from Germany because of her scathing reports about his government. Millions read her columns, which helped to shape America's attitudes about the war. *Time* magazine reported in 1939 that "She and Eleanor Roosevelt are undoubtedly the most influential women in the U.S."

Most Americans were uncomfortable with the idea of women in the military. The unprecedented step raised many questions about interpersonal relations between men and women as well as about what jobs were appropriate for men and women. Military officials had to decide who could date whom and what to do if a female soldier married or became pregnant. Everyone agreed that women were not to be sent into combat or posted in places where they could become prisoners of war.

> **Peggy Terry** worked in a shell factory. She said later, "I believe the war was the beginning of my seeing things. You just can't stay uninvolved and not knowing when such a momentous thing is happening."

1943 government poster recruiting women to work in factories.

Nevertheless, more than 400,000 women enlisted and participated in every part of military operations except combat. They taught male pilots to fly,

> *Movie star* **Betty Grable** *was such a popular pinup girl during the war that her movie studio insured her legs for $1 million.* **Lena Horne** *held the number one pinup spot with African American soldiers.*

Many male soldiers had doubts about female soldiers. **Frances Densmore**, a marine posted in Hawaii, recalled:

> *One day I had my head under the hood of my two-ton truck, which had stalled.... Hearing a noise, I looked up and saw I was surrounded by Marines. One of them said he'd heard about WRs working on trucks but thought it was hard to believe. They stood around and watched me check the ignition. I located the loose wire. Thank goodness the motor turned over when I stomped on the starter. The Marines all cheered when I chugged away in a cloud of dust. It made me feel really good.*

packed parachutes, ran mail rooms, operated radios, repaired vehicles, hauled supplies, made maps, worked as medical technicians, and provided numerous other support services. Most people, especially male soldiers, were surprised at how much female recruits could do when given the chance.

NURSES From the outset, nursing had a positive public image. Caring for the sick and wounded was considered a naturally female activity and good training for homemaking and motherhood. As casualties mounted, many women joined the various nursing corps. While some military nurses cared for wounded soldiers stateside, others served in the midst of the dirt and horror of the war, working behind the lines in Europe, North Africa, and the South Pacific. Next to those in combat, they came the closest to death. In 1942, eighty-eight army nurses were captured by the Japanese and became prisoners of war on the island of Bataan. Thirteen nurses shot down over Albania in 1944 walked 850 miles to safety. The tough conditions under which military nurses operated paved the way for a more rigorous and professional approach to nursing.

MILITARY WIVES As the war began, many Americans dashed to the marriage altar. Couples also decided to have children right away. Marriage and birth rates skyrocketed. Life as a military wife was hard. It was lonely, and military salaries were

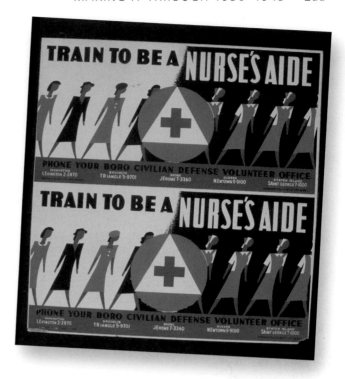

small. Some wives followed husbands from post to post until they were shipped overseas, but they had a difficult time finding housing and jobs. Newly married Dellie Hahne "felt sorriest" for "pregnant women who could barely balance in a rocking train, going to see their husbands for the last time before the guys were sent overseas. *Women . . . traveling with small children . . . trying to feed their kids, diaper their kids. . . . It suddenly occurred to me that this wasn't half as much fun as I'd been told it was going to be."* Although communities had many organizations and services for military men, there was no such help for their wives. If they wanted support, women had to create it for themselves.

Native American nurses served in integrated units, but black and Asian nurses did not. **Joan Hamilton, Geneva Culpepper, Marjorie Mayers, Prudence Burnes,** and **Inez Holmes** served in Australia in 1944.

Almost half a million American mothers lost sons in WWII. Another 670,000 sons were wounded. The woman who lost the most children was **Alleta Sullivan** *of Iowa. Her five sons all died on the same day in 1943 when their ship was sunk in the Pacific.*

HOUSEWIVES According to government publicity, everyone was a soldier, even the woman who did not enlist or send her husband off to war. One newspaper reminded its readers, "men fight the war with bayonets, long hours at defense jobs," but *"the kitchen and sewing room are the housewife's battleground."* A housewife could help by saving or gathering scrap metal, paper, bones, rags, cooking fat, bottles, rubber, and batteries. She could knit clothing for soldiers, grow a garden, can produce, or do volunteer work. The Red Cross, American Women's Voluntary Services, and United Service Organizations (USO) were among the groups that organized the service efforts of millions of women. Female volunteers staffed USO community centers as hostesses and dance partners for soldiers. Married women acted as surrogate mothers for young men who were away from home for the first time. Black women performed the same tasks at segregated USO centers.

Although people finally had money, there wasn't much to buy. As massive resources were channeled overseas,

many goods were rationed at home. Each family was issued a ration card with a certain number of points that could be "spent" for various items. Meat, sugar, vegetables, soap, and other staples were frequently unavailable. Gasoline was rationed, and the production of most household appliances was discontinued for the duration of the war. Clothing was expensive, of questionable quality, and difficult to obtain. Women were reminded that it was their patriotic duty to meet their family's needs within these constraints, even if it meant standing in endless lines to obtain even the most basic items. When new car tires could not be purchased, Native American and other rural women walked miles from their homes to buy supplies.

Women were expected to remain feminine while meeting these challenges. Corset designer

The government reminded women of their role in helping the war effort.

Women's fashions were restricted by war shortages. Official regulations restricted "the length and circumference of skirts and the width of jackets." There were to be no slacks with a cuff, no big sleeves, no zippers or metal fastenings. When women could no longer obtain silk stockings, they used eyebrow pencils to draw lines down their calves to give the illusion of stocking seams.

Ruth Merson reminded them, *"It is essential that the women of America do not let down their men. Women must keep up the morale of their men and still continue to be their guiding star. To this end they must be their trim and shapely selves."* No one seemed to notice the absurdity of linking a soldier's ability to fight with the shape of women's bodies.

WORKERS A primary reason families finally had money was that the number of working women increased 57 percent between 1940 and 1945. Though attitudes about gender roles had not changed, the war created tremendous labor shortages and higher pay for workers. The government needed to convince both women and employers that women could and should build airplanes, tanks, and torpedoes. Posters recruited women with statements like this one: *"If you've used an electric mixer in your kitchen, you can learn to run a drill press."* But Americans wanted women to retain their feminine charm and dedication to home even in the midst of welding, riveting, and heavy lifting. Hence, government ads also pictured women doing housework while wearing factory coveralls. Female workers received mixed messages—for eight hours a day they should be strong machine operators, but for the other sixteen they should be sweet and ladylike.

The war opened up a wide range of job opportunities for women. School districts lifted the ban on married teachers. Women also found new jobs in banking and retail management, and as doctors, lawyers, and chemists. Many second generation Chinese American women took war-related jobs because of the good pay and to demonstrate their patriotism. For the first time, the symphonies in Chicago and Boston accepted female musicians. Black women fled from domestic to factory work in droves, however demanding or dangerous the work might be. The government also hired a small number of African American women as clerical workers. Women worked on railroads, in streetcars, as taxi drivers, and as lumberjacks.

Nicknamed "Rosie the Riveters" by the press, many women gained satisfaction and confidence from their jobs. **Margie Lacoff**, an electrician in a navy yard, told a reporter, "I like my work so much that they'll have to fire me before I leave." This was in spite of a 48-hour week, limited promotions, and the hostility of many male colleagues. "Maybe you think it didn't take nerve for women to make that first break into the [ship]yards," said ship builder **Lily Solomon**. "I never walked a longer road in my life than that to the tool room."

A 1944 editorial cartoon.

While many Native American women left reservations to work in defense industries, Menominee women in Wisconsin managed the tribe's mill and protected its forest lands.

Railroad workers in Clinton, Iowa, take a lunch break in 1943.

These Rosies work as welders, mass producing bombers in 1942.

America's first comic strip female professional, Brenda Starr, appeared on comic strip pages in 1940. Featuring a red-haired, fearless female reporter, the strip was created by **Dalia Messick**, who had changed her name to Dale in order to make it in the newspaper world.

Esperanza Padilla worked the night shift at an airplane factory, returned home to take care of her kids and the house, and then earned extra money by washing clothes for other families. Padilla, like many other Rosies, carried the double responsibility of work and home. Most believed that this state of affairs was temporary and that soon female workers would put down their tools and gladly hurry home.

BASEBALL In 1943, Phillip K. Wrigley, the owner of Wrigley Chewing Gum, had a great idea. With Americans' love for baseball and many male athletes off fighting a war, why not hire female players? He envisioned the All-American Girls Baseball League as a temporary measure to fill the vacuum and make some money.

The league began with four teams—the Peaches, Blue Sox, Belles, and Comets—but eventually expanded to ten because the sport was so popular. While the ball and the field layout originally followed softball regulations, they soon were switched to those of baseball. Fans flocked to watch.

But audiences did not want to see masculine women on the field. Players were required to have long hair and wear skirts and makeup. They were enrolled in charm school to practice etiquette. In spite of these trappings, league players were talented athletes. The most popular was **Dorothy**

Kamenshek, who had the highest batting average, and only struck out 81 of 3,736 times at bat. She later said of the experience, *"It gave a lot of us the courage to go on to professional careers at a time when women didn't do things like that."* The league lasted until 1954 when television and the migration of major league teams to the West reduced audiences.

JAPANESE INTERNMENT CAMPS

"I LOST MY FREEDOM"

Times of crisis often make people feel vulnerable and fearful. When this happens, they are often willing to sacrifice liberty—their own or that of others—to obtain a feeling of security. After Pearl Harbor, Japanese Americans became the scapegoats.

"One hundred thousand persons were sent to concentration camps on a record which wouldn't support a conviction for stealing a dog."

—EUGENE V. ROSTOW, scholar and government official

The government labeled all Japanese Americans on the West Coast as a threat to national security. The government uprooted 110,000 people, two-thirds of whom were American citizens, and placed them in "internment camps."

Japanese Americans, none of whom were individually charged with crimes, were given less

than a week's notice to report to a civil control station. Leaving their homes, businesses, and possessions, they were put on buses and trains to "Assembly Centers." A church secretary, **Eleanor Breed** wrote of those who reported for evacuation in Berkley, California, "Among the first group was a pair of newlyweds, arm in arm, the bride with a collegiate bandanna around her head and a flower in her pompadour,

In February 1942, the San Francisco *Examiner* used a then-common racial slur to announce the forthcoming evacuation and relocation of thousands of Japanese Americans. By April, those pictured below were forced from their neighborhoods in San Francisco and sent to the Santa Anna Assembly Center. In May, evacuees (above) from Elk Grove, California, awaited a bus for an internment camp in Manzanar, Utah.

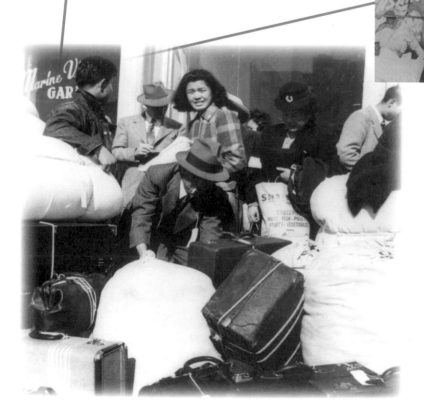

and a big American flag in brilliants on her lapel." Another woman said,

"To this day I can remember vividly the plight of . . . a young couple with four preschool children. The mother had two frightened toddlers hanging on her coat. In her arms she carried two crying babies."

Most families lost everything. One woman was given only three days to sell her hotel of twenty-six rooms, and had to settle for an offer of $500. Another woman recalled,

For those who had been born in America and viewed themselves as Americans, these events were particularly shocking. Nine-year-old **Kay Uno** was stunned when her former friends turned their backs to her saying, "There goes that little Jap!" She looked around, wondering, "Who's a Jap? Then it dawned on me, I'm the Jap." Dorothea Lange took this photo in San Francisco in 1942.

"We took whatever we could carry. *So much we left behind, but the most valuable thing I lost was my freedom."*

The assembly centers were hastily converted racetracks, fairgrounds, and stockyards where people stayed for weeks and months awaiting transfer to an internment camp. Arriving for her stay in a horse stall, **Yoshiko Uchida** remembered, "Shivering in the cold, we pressed close together trying to shield Mama from the wind. As we stood in what seemed a breadline for the destitute, *I felt degraded, humiliated, and overwhelmed with a longing for home.* And I saw the unutterable sadness on my mother's face." Sixty-four women bore children under these conditions in California's Tranforan Assembly Center alone.

THE CAMPS From the Assembly Centers, internees were moved to one of ten internment camps located in remote, deserted areas of the West. The camps consisted of dozens of makeshift, uninsulated barracks surrounded by barbed wire fences, guard towers, and search lights. Recalling the camps, one woman said, "The main thing you remembered was the dust, always the dust."

In these cramped settings, women attempted to create livable spaces for their families— hanging sheets to create some privacy and ordering material from Sears, Roebuck to make curtains. Mothers of young children had it particularly tough as they walked crying babies in the night to keep from waking neighbors. Mothers

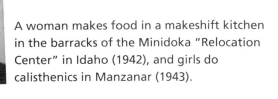

A woman makes food in a makeshift kitchen in the barracks of the Minidoka "Relocation Center" in Idaho (1942), and girls do calisthenics in Manzanar (1943).

had to watch through barbed-wire fences as their older sons were drafted and left to fight in the war. Since they were no longer buying and preparing food for their families, women had more free time than ever before. Some worked in camp mess halls and hospitals, others learned English, took up crafts, or created beautiful rock gardens.

It wasn't until October 1946 that the last of the internment detainees were released. Most Japanese Americans had to start all over. In 1983, a government war commission determined that the internment camps "were not justified by military necessity, and that the decisions were based on race prejudice, war hysteria, and a failure of political leadership."

In 1988, Congress apologized for the injustice of internment, offering $20,000 in compensation to all former internees. However, many survivors did not live long enough to receive their checks.

THE WAR ENDS

In 1945, the war ended with an Allied victory, and troops returned home to loved ones. Japanese American internees began the long process of rebuilding their shattered lives. The government now faced the job of convincing women to hand over their jobs. On one government radio ad, a woman cooed,

"When this war is over—I'll get a manicure, put on the frilliest dress I can find, pour a whole bottle of cologne over my head and THEN, I'll be GLAD to give up my union share...to some boy who comes marching home deserving it."

Women were reminded that in good times and bad, they were best suited to the home. A ration cookbook extolled the virtues of domestic life, "You have been strengthening your country's defenses as plane workers, as flyers, as members of the armed forces, as producers in war plants and homes and in Red Cross and Civilian Defense activities. *But whatever else you do, you are, first and foremost, homemakers*—women with the welfare of your families deepest in your hearts." Women adjusted their lives to fit the changing times as they had during the emergencies of the Depression and war. As women were ushered back to their kitchens, issues of women's equality were largely ignored or cast aside.

CHAPTER 8

Security at Last?
1945–1963

People around the world breathed a collective sigh of relief when World War II was over. "Ohh, the... beautiful celebrations when the war ended," recalled **Peggy Terry**. "Everybody was downtown in the pouring rain and we were dancing. We took off our shoes and put 'em in our purse. We were so happy." She celebrated her husband's homecoming by getting a tattoo on her leg "where it wouldn't show," a heart with an arrow through it: "Bill and Peggy." For many women and men long separated during the war years, both by miles and experiences, the transition back to family life would be a complicated one. *Good Housekeeping* magazine offered this advice, "After two or three weeks he should be finished with talking, with oppressive remembering. If he still goes over the same stories, reveals the same emotions, you had best consult a psychiatrist. This condition is neurotic." Suggestions such as this did not prepare women such as Peggy Terry to understand the experiences of their loved ones. Terry did not know how to deal with the changes she now saw in Bill. She recalled later that when he awoke with nightmares, she'd sit for hours and "hold him while he just shook."

The end of the war meant challenges for all. Millions of Rosie the Riveters who had worked nontraditional jobs to aid the war effort were forced to

Celebrating V-J Day, August 14, 1945, in Times Square with a passionate kiss.

return home. Japanese American women who had lost everything when sent to internment camps began to rebuild their lives in an often hostile environment. Puerto Rican immigrants poured into New York City hoping for a better life. Chinese American women who had participated in the war effort assumed a new, more public role in their communities. Native American families welcomed returning veterans who now had experience with the world outside the reservation. Finally, between 1945 and 1952, an estimated 80,000 Jewish survivors of the Holocaust made new homes in the United States. During this time, working-class whites gained access to many of the luxuries that had been reserved for the rich. African Americans who had fought for democracy abroad returned to claim equality at home. But after 15 years of depression and war, what Americans wanted most was security—economic, social, and political.

PEACETIME TRANSITIONS

WAR BRIDES

During the war, close to 100,000 American soldiers married abroad. In order to reunite soldiers with their new wives, Congress passed the War Brides Act, which made way for many women to emigrate to the United States. As a result, thousands of women from Great Britain, Australia, China, Germany, Poland, Italy, and other countries arrived in America on "bride ships" provided by the U.S. government.

One of these war brides was **Dong Zenn Ping** from China. Her story is quite different from war brides who arrived from other parts of the world. For decades, anti-Chinese immigration legislation had made it very difficult for Chinese citizens—especially women—to immigrate to America. Consequently, when Ping's husband immigrated years before the war, he couldn't reveal to American authorities that he left a pregnant wife back in China. He lived and worked in America posing as a bachelor and was one of the 12,041 Chinese American men drafted into the war. Following his military service, he couldn't change his official bachelor story so, he returned to China and remarried Ping. She had to pretend to be a new bride and leave her eight-year-old son with relatives to move to the United States. Like most other Chinese war brides, she was not a young bride.

This is the last couple to be married in Tokyo under a law that made more than 1,300 American GI–Japanese marriages possible (1951).

Reunited with her husband of many years, Ping's future was filled with challenges.

Immigration was particularly difficult for Chinese immigrants like Ping. Following a harrowing interrogation process at immigration stations, they had to adapt to an entirely new culture. Most Chinese war brides were uneducated women from rural parts of China. In this urban American setting, conflicts arose when husbands considered their wives to be socially inadequate and culturally backward. Americanized husbands put tremendous pressure on their traditional wives to modernize. Wives, meanwhile, missed family and friends in China and often felt isolated and displaced. One Chinese newspaper observed that Chinese women lacked a place to "let off their emotions and frustrations. . . . In America, they have no companions but the refrigerator and the stove. They have no relatives, friends, or social life." In addition, most Chinese immigrant women faced the double burden of working in family businesses and caring for homes and children.

*"It was difficult to work in a laundry and to have a family at the same time. My husband never helped me out by watching the kids while **I was busy working and cooking at the same time**. Often the food would be burned because I had to do so many things at once. Feeding the children and changing their diapers consumed most of my time, so I almost never had any time to spare for myself."*

—**Yuen Ock Chu,**
immigrant to Los Angeles in 1947

CHANGING TRENDS
WHEN "NORMAL" WAS NOT NORMAL

Following two world wars and the Depression, Americans were anxious for things to return to "normal." For the multitudes of women who had grown up during difficult times, a chance to be primarily a wife and a homemaker felt like a dream come true. In fact, this move to "normal life" was enacted on such a massive scale that the 1950s were actually not normal at all.

As Americans raced to claim the promises of middle-class life, they reversed and accelerated many social trends. What we often view as the "traditional" 1950s represents a disruption in otherwise steady patterns of marriage, fertility, education, and prosperity in the twentieth century.

MARRIAGE During the first half of the century, the female age at marriage had risen. After the war, however, young Americans rushed headlong into matrimony. Millions of girls were engaged by the age of seventeen and married by the time they were twenty. The average marriage age dropped to 20 for women and 22 for men. In 1940, only 42 percent of women were married by the age of 24; by the late 1950s, the percentage had shot up to 70 percent. In the fifties, not getting married seemed a calamity. An unmarried woman was considered an "old maid" by her midtwenties. **Alice Bell**, raised in Utah, was one of many who watched her high school friends tie the knot and worried that it would never be her turn. While those friends were having babies, she worked and went to college. When she finally wed at the age of twenty-five, she felt she had escaped a fate worse than death.

FERTILITY Not only did women marry earlier, they had more babies in quicker succession than their mothers or grandmothers. One-third of all women had babies before they turned twenty. In what came to be known as the "Baby Boom," a vast number of families desired and had third and fourth children. With the availability of contraceptives, this increase was largely based on deliberate choices. The Baby Boom crossed all racial and class lines—

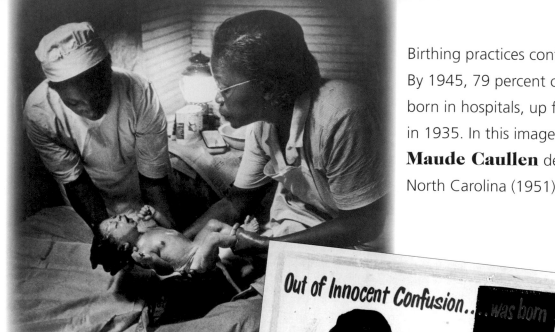

Birthing practices continued to change. By 1945, 79 percent of babies were born in hospitals, up from 37 percent in 1935. In this image, nurse–midwife **Maude Caullen** delivers a baby in North Carolina (1951).

The Riesan family of Milwaukee was not alone in being surrounded by children. Following a two-hundred-year decline in the birth rate, fertility increased by 50 percent between 1940 and 1957.

Out of Innocent Confusion... ...was born Heartbreak!

IDA LUPINO presents "Not Wanted"

An Emerald Production with
SALLY FORREST
KEEFE BRASSELLE · LEO PENN
Produced by
IDA LUPINO and ANSON BOND · Directed by ELMER CLIFTON
Original story by Paul Jarrico and Malvin Wald
Screenplay by Paul Jarrico and Ida Lupino
FILM CLASSICS, INC.

The most talked about picture of the year. This story of "Sally" is one which could happen to anyone's daughter in the same circumstances... It happens to 100,000 daughters every year in the U. S... The 100,000 beaten, bewildered girls who become mothers... unloved... unwanted... unwed!

Like the girl in this film, unwed teenagers who got pregnant faced exclusion and embarrassment. **Martha Corson** recalled, "Two or three girls got pregnant in high school. In those days, either there was a quick marriage or they went and stayed with relatives or at unwed mothers' homes. They gave their babies up for adoption and then came back."

Postwar parents were more permissive than in the past. Dr. Benjamin Spock, a pediatrician-turned-writer, became the parenting guru for the 1950s. Dr. Spock emphasized children's need to express themselves. Babies, he said, should not be forced into routines. A child having a tantrum should be distracted rather than punished. Moms were advised to be firm, but also patient, understanding, and willing to let their kids go at their own pace.

Have you ever heard of . . . Marion Donovon?

Tired of bulky cloth diapers, she devised her own disposable version out of a shower curtain and padding in 1951. She called her new invention "the boater." Although America was experiencing baby mania, Donovon could not convince anyone to manufacture her product. She paid to produce the first disposable diapers out of her own pocket. By the time she sold her business, it was worth one million dollars.

people from every group in America wanted and had bigger families. One Jewish woman who had four children recalled, "After the Holocaust, we felt obligated to have lots of babies. But it was easy because everyone was doing it." Indeed, there were one million more babies born every year during the 1950s than during the 1930s. After the 1950s, smaller families were again the norm. The baby boomer generation was unique in its size and influence for many years to come.

EDUCATION The government's GI Bill, which sent thousands of returning soldiers to college, did not include military women. Policy makers assumed that female veterans would become wives rather than students. A 1952 department store ad asked, *"What's college? That's where girls who are above cooking and sewing go to meet a man so they can spend their lives cooking and sewing."* One woman later remembered that her father frequently said, "Send 'em to college for a couple of years to get a little polish and meet the kind of boys you want 'em to marry." A *Ladies' Home Journal* writer advised college men to get young women "out of their dreams and into their kitchens." Indeed, the percentage of women in college was not very promising. In 1920 they made up 47 percent of college students. By 1958 they accounted for only 35 percent, with only 37 percent of those finishing degrees. Believing that a woman's fundamental role was that of wife and mother, most dropped out to marry. One cookbook author insisted, *"A man is in general better pleased when he has a good dinner upon his table, than when his wife talks Greek."*

In 1920 women earned one in six doctorates; in 1959 the number was one in ten. Graduates had few options for a professional life; those who sought jobs outside of secretarial, teaching, and nursing occupations had little success. Consequently, one Radcliffe College graduate explained,

"We married what we wanted to be. If we wanted to be a lawyer or a doctor we married one."

The great exception to this trend was among black women, who assumed they would have to work. Though far fewer black women entered college,

This woman and her neighbors enjoy life in Chicago's south suburb of Park Forest, honored as an "All-America City" in 1954.

more than 90 percent of those who began completed degrees. Chinese American women also graduated from college in increasing numbers, although advanced education frequently did not result in higher-paying jobs for women.

PROSPERITY AND THE SUBURBS The economic boom and high employment rates of World War II carried over into the postwar years, bringing new prosperity to many Americans. Money made but not spent during the war (when there was little to buy) went for down payments on houses, cars, and appliances. By 1960 the number of those who considered themselves middle class had doubled. Many working-class families were able to buy homes for the first time. Daughters of immigrant and working-class parents were grateful for their sudden inclusion in the American dream. White Americans took their newfound dollars and fled cities in a mass exodus to the newest suburbs. Lured by ads promising that *"A vacation that lasts a lifetime begins here,"* they moved into newly constructed, mass-produced, inexpensive single-family homes. Levittown was the first and most famous suburb built after the war. Beginning in 1949, entrepreneur William J. Levitt built homes in a Long Island, New York, potato field at an unprecedented rate. Millions of new homes went up around the country and by the end of the 1950s, more than one-fourth of Americans lived in the suburbs.

Bessie Delaney's family built a house in an all-white Virginia neighborhood in 1957, because no one would sell them one. She later wrote: "The first time I answered the door at our house in Mount Vernon, it was some white lady from Welcome Wagon and she went on and on about this and that and then she said to me, 'And be sure you tell the owner'... And I said, 'Lady, I have news for you. I am the owner.' Well, she about dropped dead. It was clear that she thought I was the maid."

The 1950s didn't mean Tupperware parties and suburbs for everyone. This woman weaves in a hogan on a New Mexico Navaho reservation.

This lifestyle continued to elude many minorities. Excluded by discriminatory housing practices, African Americans, Hispanics, and Asian Americans were heirs to crowded housing in aging cities. More than 50 percent of U.S. minorities lived below the poverty line. Of the 82,000 residents of Levittown in 1960, not a single person was black. William Levitt officially refused to sell to blacks. He said, "We can solve a housing problem, or we can try to solve a racial problem. But we cannot combine the two." In 1957, *Life* magazine pointed out that "10,000 Negroes work at the Ford plant in nearby Dearborn, [but] not one Negro can live in Dearborn itself." Living in the suburbs, white people rarely interacted with nonwhites. As late as 1970 the suburbs were 95 percent white.

ARTS IN THE SPOTLIGHT

"PEOPLE WHO ARE THE VERY ESSENCE OF DIGNITY"

Occasionally a literary work comes along at a pivotal moment and charts a new path for those that follow. Such was the case with **Lorraine Hansberry**'s *Raisin in the Sun,* which portrayed the conflict in a black family over whether to move to a white neighborhood. In the 1950s almost no one imagined that a play about an average black family could draw racially mixed audiences, but after Hansberry's play opened on Broadway in March of 1959, critics raved. One wrote that the actors drew him "unresisting into a world of their making, their suffering, their thinking, and their rejoicing." For the first time, audiences were a mix of black and white. Writer James Baldwin later wrote, "I had never in my life seen so many black people in the theater. And the reason was that never before, in the entire history of the American theater, had so much of the truth of black people's lives been on the stage." Fans were also amazed that the playwright was only twenty-eight years old.

The intelligent and charming Lorraine Hansberry was from a middle-class black family and had studied drama and art in college. She was working as a waitress, however, when she struck up a friendship with a Jewish musician named Philip Rose. They talked long hours about politics and social justice. After seeing a theater production at an African American church, Hansberry told her friend, "I can write a better play than that." Rose responded, "Well, why don't you then?"

The result was a story with autobiographical roots. As a child, Hansberry's family had moved into a white neighborhood where neighbors threw bricks through their windows. Her experiences with social exclusion found their way into the fictional lives of the Younger family. The plot of *Raisin in the Sun* revolves around what to do with the insurance money that is coming after the death of the father. Each family member has a dream of how the money should be used. Without telling anyone, the mother puts a down payment on a house. The family is shocked and dismayed to discover the house is in a white neighborhood.

In act 3 of *Raisin in the Sun,* son Walter Lee lashes out at his family:

What's the matter with you all! I didn't make this world! It was give to me this way! Hell, yes, I want me some yachts someday! Yes, I want to hang some real pearls 'round my wife's neck. Ain't she supposed to wear no pearls? Somebody tell me—tell me, who decides which women is suppose to wear pearls in this world? I tell you I am a *man*— and I think my wife should wear some pearls in this world!

Despite tough competition, *Raisin in the Sun* won the New York Drama Critics Circle Award in 1959. The play was made into a successful movie in 1961. It also opened the door for other big theater productions by and about African Americans, and many followed. Hansberry continued to write until her death from cancer only six years later. She died just before the opening of her next play.

> *"I think* [Raisin in the Sun] *will help a lot of people understand how we are just as complicated as they are— and just as mixed up—but above all, that we have among our miserable and downtrodden ranks—people who are the very essence of human dignity."*
>
> —Lorraine Hansberry
> in a letter to her mother

Ruby Dee, an actor, recalled meeting Lorraine Hansberry: "Lorraine was so young, I thought. She looked like a teenager, but there was a definite air of maturity about her. Hearing her speak, I quickly forgot her youth. She spoke with an authority, tinged with wit. I felt I was in the presence of a superior intellect."

Lorraine Hansberry

AMUSEMENTS

FAMILY-FRIENDLY ENTERTAINMENT

Postwar Americans had more money than ever, and more to spend it on. Even poorer families found ways of participating in the new prosperity. With marriage and babies preoccupying the youthful population, family-friendly entertainment was very popular.

BOWLING During the 1950s, women of all ages and classes donned bowling shoes and headed for the alleys. Although the Women's National Bowling Association was founded in 1916, pre–World War II bowling was mostly a male activity. Bowling alleys tended to be smoky places where men drank and gambled. During the war, numerous female workers joined leagues sponsored by their employers. Alleys worked to become more respectable. When the war ended and women lost their jobs, proprietors convinced retailers to sponsor women's leagues. They also promoted family activities and children's leagues. Consequently, by 1946, bowling was more popular than any other amateur sport.

TELEVISION People still tuned in to the radio, and thanks to car and transistor radios, they could now take their music with them. But the latest entertainment drew Americans into living rooms to sit transfixed in front of a box of flickering images. The number of televisions in U.S. homes grew almost overnight, from over 3 million in 1950 to 52 million in 1960. Newly invented TV dinners meant that people didn't even have to leave the screen to eat a meal. Shows like *Leave It to Beaver* and *Father Knows Best* were about white, middle-class families living in the suburbs. In these model families, moms vacuumed in high heels, kept spotless houses, and were always available to help their children solve problems.

The most popular sitcom of the decade was, however, one that

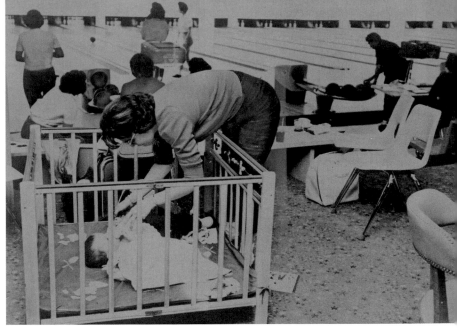

In 1963, even babies sometimes got in on the bowling action. This bowler has figured out how to mix responsibility and recreation. For many mothers of the era, the portable "playpen" was the answer to mobile toddlers.

challenged a number of cultural barriers. Real-life husband and wife Desi Arnaz, a Cuban bandleader, and **Lucille Ball**, an actress, played screen couple Ricky and Lucy Ricardo in *I Love Lucy*. The marriage gave audiences a window into Cuban American culture. Redheaded Lucy, a housewife, had dreams of stardom and wealth. Her antics allowed audiences to laugh at the tensions of marriage. When Lucille Ball became pregnant, CBS, the network that produced *I Love Lucy*, insisted that she not use the word on television and wanted to photograph her standing behind chairs. Instead of hiding her state, Lucy highlighted it, pushing Ricky into the hospital in a wheelchair for the delivery. Sixty-seven percent of television sets were tuned in the night Ricky Jr. was born. Twice as many people watched Lucy's baby's birth as watched Dwight D. Eisenhower's presidential inauguration the next day.

TEENAGE FUN Although youth culture had its roots in the 1920s, it wasn't until after World War II that teenagers became such a tremendous force in American life. Like their parents, postwar teens had more money and more free time than ever before. More of them went to school, hung out with people their age, and worried about fitting in. Advertisers recognized the moneymaking possibilities of this growing population and set out to make them enthusiastic consumers.

The experiences of **Hannah Mason** were similar to those of other teenage girls in the 1950s.

Did you know?

Cheerleading was originally an all-male college activity. By the 1950s cheerleading had filtered down into high schools and junior highs. Girls cheered. Boys played sports.

Mason recalled that when she was thirteen, "we used to have parties with boys—this was like pre-dating—and we would play spin the bottle. You got an empty coke bottle and put it on the ground. Everybody would be sitting in a circle, and *the person who was up would spin the bottle and had to kiss the person of the opposite sex closest to where the bottle landed."* Girls also invited their friends for "slumber parties" where they put each other's hair in curlers, painted fingernails, talked on the phone to boys, and practiced dancing to the newest records.

Vinyl records became more affordable after the war and Americans bought ten times as many as they had a decade earlier. The fifties were a time of music fusion when many different styles came together and growing numbers of black singers signed record contracts. After 1954 teens

Archery at a teen party in 1956.

Did you know?

Until the first issue of *Seventeen* magazine came out in 1944, few people paid attention to the money that could be made by selling products to teenage girls. The magazine positioned itself as the expert on how to be a successful teenager. It was a huge hit with adolescent girls. Within ten years, *Seventeen* completely changed the marketing landscape. Manufacturers developed teen-friendly products, clothes stores opened teen departments, and both looked for ways to sell to increasingly younger consumers.

increasingly chose rock and roll. Five out of nine top singles in 1956 were by the heartthrob Elvis Presley.

DATING Dating was the central and defining teen activity of the decade, with girls and boys going on dates as young as eleven or twelve. Boys were expected to ask girls out and pay for the date. Dating expectations created complicated situations because many Americans thought that sexual activity was acceptable for boys, but not for girls. People assumed that boys could not help themselves and told girls it was their responsibility to put on the brakes. The pinnacle of dating was "going steady." According to Hannah Mason, going steady meant dating one person exclusively. Wearing a boy's fraternity pin or his class ring was serious. "It was engaged to be engaged." For girls, high school dating was the first step in the serious business of finding a husband.

Schools held regular dances called "sock hops." At Mason's high school the dances were held in the gym. "It would be decorated and sometimes there'd be a live band, and we usually came in our fathers' cars." Teens did the fox trot, the waltz, the rumba, the samba, and the jitterbug. Elsewhere around the country they strolled, bunny hopped,

Nancy Douglas remembered, "I would never have called a boy. I waited for the proper phone call."

and shagged. Black teens added the dirty boogie, and Latino teens danced the cha-cha and merengue. Mason recalled, "If it was a prom you'd dress in a gown.... You didn't usually go in a shirt and sweater and bobby socks even if they called them sock hops. You dressed more elegantly. You'd wear a cocktail dress."

Some minority teens transformed mainstream cultural trends into their own personal style. Mexican American "pachequitas" and "pachucos" created their own hairdos, clothing styles, and ways of speaking. According to one pachequita, *"Mexican girls are full of fun, they laugh and joke with boys, but there is nothing bad between them.... we ride around and sing and laugh... and have a lot of fun talking and singing and stuff. Americans do that too."*

Teenagers cruised around in souped-up cars and skated at roller rinks. They also drank milk shakes and ate hamburgers at drive-in restaurants. Hannah Mason described pulling up next to "what looked like a country mailbox," checking off her order, watching the box make its way to the kitchen, then waiting for the carhop to deliver the food. "There were drive-ins where the carhops were on roller skates." To parents' dismay, teens also slipped off to drive-in movies where kissing was the featured activity. Between 1948 and 1958 the number of drive-ins grew from 480 to 4,000.

Although movie theater attendance declined after the invention of the television, movies were still popular, and they increasingly catered to teenage audiences. One Arkansas girl remembered one "way to keep cool was to go to the movies because that was the only place that was air conditioned. . . . I liked the Rialto. . . . It had . . . two carved staircases, plush red velvet, thick, thick carpet, and it was cool. So we went to the movies two and three times a week—the girls together. It was thirty-nine cents and I could make that babysitting."

It's hard to imagine a time when phone conversations with friends were limited to a public phone in the family's kitchen, but in the 1950s, there were no cell phones, instant messaging, or Facebook. This teen takes advantage of the family phone (and the kitchen counter).

Anna Davis, who was fourteen in 1955, recalled:

When I was a young teenager, if you went bowling, you didn't want to bowl better than the guy because you didn't want to hurt his ego. Today if I can bowl better than the guy, I'm going to bowl better than the guy, but when I was a young teenager, **you didn't excel because you didn't want to damage his ego.** They didn't care about ours but you had to worry about theirs.

Top ten girl's names of the 1950s: *Mary, Linda, Patricia, Susan, Deborah, Barbara, Debra, Karen, Nancy, and Donna.*

What did audiences see in the cool dark? Black actresses such as **Lena Horne** and **Dorothy Dandridge** appeared in a wider range of parts, and **Katy Jurado** and other Latinas made their mark in westerns. Actresses like **Katharine Hepburn** and **Bette Davis**, who had played strong, able characters in the thirties and early forties, gave way to sex symbols like **Elizabeth Taylor** and perky, sunny blondes like **Doris Day**. But fewer films were about

The school dance was the site of both romance and racial tension in the musical *West Side Story.* A take-off of Shakespeare's *Romeo and Juliet,* the play was set in 1950s New York, where the population of Puerto Ricans was rapidly increasing. Actress **Rita Moreno** had spent ten years playing exotic, demeaning roles when she landed the part of Anita in the 1961 film. She later recalled, "The more I played those dusky innocents, the worse I felt inside." This role was different. Having moved to New York from Puerto Rico when she was five, Moreno could relate to teenage immigrant Anita. Not only did the film win best picture, but Moreno took home an Academy Award for best supporting actress.

Did you know?

Marilyn Monroe, born Norma Jean Mortenson, was raised in foster homes and orphanages after her mother was institutionalized. Mortenson married at sixteen. Her life was changed when an army photographer took her picture at the factory where she was working during the war. Becoming a wartime pinup led to Marilyn Monroe's acting career.

women, and those that were dealt increasingly with questions of domesticity—marriage, family, and courtship.

Even female movie stars were under pressure to demonstrate that in their private lives, they washed dishes. Movie stars appeared in magazines dressed in aprons cooking and cleaning. Previously independent, glamorous female stars like **Joan Crawford** were featured as happy homemakers hanging laundry and mopping floors. A magazine photo of **Joan Fontaine** was accompanied by text that read, ***"We like our stars to be glamorous on the screen but at home girls at heart."***

A new type of film was on the rise: the teenage drama. *Rebel Without a Cause* and other movies explored teenage alienation. But not all were about angry boys driving around in fast cars. *Susan Slade, The Summer Place, Where the Boys Are, Splendor in the Grass,* and others were about girls. Central to many of their plots was the dilemma of the adolescent girl who wanted a boy's love but feared the consequences of "going all the way." Sometimes called "pregnancy melodramas," the stories often ended with the heroine marrying the father and having the baby.

Three contestants in a 1954 nationwide triple-crown beauty contest: **Marilyn Abromowitz**, **Maryann Karasik**, and **Jean Simon**.

BEAUTY

WAIST CINCHERS AND POINTY BRAS

The fashionable female of the 1950s molded her body to accentuate her maternal, feminine qualities. She was expected to be trim and appealing, relying on all sorts of undergarments and beauty aides. These included a pointy bra (padded if necessary) to make her breasts her most prominent feature, and a girdle to create a tiny waist. One woman described *"this instrument of torture called a waist cincher. It would pull in your waist fully two inches.... It was thought that if you had any flesh jiggling, this was just not ladylike."* For fancy occasions, cocktail dresses topped off layers of crinoline petticoats and white gloves. Hats got smaller and smaller and then disappeared altogether. Pink was the hot

color and showed up in clothing, appliances, and bathroom tile. Hair dye and hair sprays came into vogue, as did big hoop and button earrings.

As makeup became an absolute must, the cosmetics industry shifted into high gear. Avon ladies traveling door-to-door sold $87 million worth of cosmetics in 1956. Women began using eye shadow, mascara, and eyebrow pencils. By 1948, nearly 90 percent of women wore lipstick—quite a change from fifty years earlier when women who wore makeup were considered loose and immoral.

AT HOME

"MRS. MIDDLE MAJORITY"

After the war, the amount spent on household purchases increased 240 percent. As factories switched quickly from producing war goods to consumer goods, families used their wartime savings to buy homes, appliances, and automobiles. Almost immediately, items that had been luxuries were

This photo portrays the domestic ideal—a young mom with well-dressed, happy children in her clean, well-equipped kitchen.

A rising standard of cleanliness kept wives scrubbing and dusting. Homemakers were led to believe that floors should be mopped weekly, if not daily. According to one woman, "Decent women in South Arkansas did not have dust." Though people owned and dirtied more clothes than in the past, laundry had to be "whiter than white." One mother, who changed her sheets twice a week, recalled a time when her dryer broke and the family couldn't have clean sheets for 10 days: "Everyone complained. We all felt dirty. I felt guilty."

Many upwardly mobile Americans felt anxious when facing new social situations. As Americans looked to others for social cues, a culture of conformity emerged that was unparalleled in American history. Newly middle-class families wanted to fit in. Advertisers manipulated their insecurities and set out to make consumers believe that buying products would make them socially acceptable. Ads offered to help "Mrs. Middle Majority" to *"make herself and her family as happy, healthy, popular, and charming as the people in the advertisements."* A woman was

now considered essential: dishwashers, can openers, washing machines, and televisions. Specialized cleaning supplies replaced simple soap for household chores. After fifteen years of hardship and sacrifice, women were again showered with promises that gadgets and cleaning supplies would relieve the drudgery of housework.

For many, the opportunity to retreat into domestic life felt like a dream come true. In suburban neighborhoods women could enjoy the middle-class life that had eluded their mothers, spending their days caring for their families. They played with their children, drove carpools, and volunteered in PTA, scouting, and women's clubs. When a black woman was able to stay at home, her family viewed it as a triumph. An *Ebony* article entitled "Goodbye Mammy, Hello Mom" pointed out that World War II "took Negro mothers out of white kitchens, put them in factories and shipyards. When it was all over, they went back to kitchens—but this time their own. . . . *And so today in thousands of Negro homes, the Negro mother has come home, come home for the first time since 1619 when the first Negro families landed at Jamestown, Virginia."*

Whereas the beginning of the war had seen an upsurge in marriage, the end was marked by unprecedented numbers of divorces. **While one in six marriages ended in divorce in 1940, by 1946 it was one in four.**

reminded that even her husband's job promotions rested on her ability to properly perform her womanly tasks. One cookbook author advised, *"A failed company dinner can lose you a client or a friend. Bad dinners nightly can lose you a good deal more. Like your husband, for instance."*

Processed, packaged, frozen, and canned foods increasingly found their way onto America's tables. Velveeta cheese, canned soups, TV dinners, Jell-O salads, and casseroles saved time, but with a catch. Marketing research revealed that wives who used processed foods were afraid of being considered lazy homemakers. Soon industry dedicated itself to teaching cooks how to make packaged food appear homemade. Cake mixes that originally required only water now added "fresh eggs and milk" for that personal touch. Cookbooks featured elaborate cover-up schemes to alter the look and taste of prepackaged foods. A 1947 magazine revealed how to disguise canned peas in Jell-O with the heading, "Three of the Finest Ways to Win Friends and Influence Husbands."

FAMILY LIFE As in years past, all the family's home needs rested on the shoulders of Mom. Husbands were the providers, women the homemakers. Anna Davis recalled, "My mother took care of the inside of the house and my father took care of the outside." Davis, along with millions of other girls, made her brothers' beds and did the dishes. **Jenny Alvarado** remembered, "Mom was from that generation of women—she used to wait

on [my dad]. *He sat down to the dinner table and she was always bringing the food to him and if he needed anything she'd of course jump up and go get it for him."* In one study, researchers found that of eighteen major household jobs, men tended to do three—locking up at night, fixing broken things, and doing yard work. Women were responsible for the rest.

HEALTH

"ONE BIG CLOSET": ANOTHER SIDE OF THE STORY

The 1950s offered a woman few alternatives to motherhood and domesticity. If she failed to marry or didn't find happiness in her female roles, she might be labeled mentally unstable. Fear of this label kept many women quiet. In a rare voice of dissent, **Mrs. R. A. Koller** wrote to the editors of the *Ladies' Home Journal* in 1947, "The minute this dainty doll trips up the aisle and the honeymoon is over, she is handed a scrub bucket, ladder and strong soap." She continued that following a day of "endless boring tasks," washing dirty diapers, cleaning house, and ironing, *"you're so tired you can hardly drag yourself, but you must look like a dream, smell like a flower, have beautiful polished nails*—and above all, cheer up your husband when he comes home from a hard day at the office…pushing his pencil around….Get his slippers and give him his pipe and the newspaper—he's had a hard day and he's tired."

For women such as Mrs. Koller, therapists dished out advice on how to adapt to the situation, rather than how to change it. A number of prominent sociologists warned the public that females wishing to step away from their prescribed roles were a danger to themselves and their families. In the best-selling *The Modern Woman: The Lost Sex,* the "experts" declared that those who were unable to accept their dependent, nurturing, passive roles in life were "sick, unhappy, neurotic, and wholly or partially incapable of dealing with life." The only true woman was married with children. The authors suggested that all unmarried, "spinster" teachers be fired as they damaged their students

"I never had opinions; I was not allowed to. I had ulcers."

—Barbara Aoki

psychologically. Spinsters could not "be an adequate model of a complete woman for boys or girls." The American public agreed that marriage was a prerequisite for happiness. A 1957 poll showed that 80 percent of those surveyed believed that those who chose not to marry were sick and immoral.

For those who didn't fit the mold, there was nowhere to turn for support or understanding. Some found escape through alcohol—women's alcohol consumption soared. Others turned to newly invented tranquilizers—virtually nonexistent in 1955, more than one million pounds were consumed in 1959. One wife described her life in the fifties as "booze, bowling, bridge, and boredom." Problems in families were exacerbated by a tendency to deny that there were problems and keep issues hush-hush. **Benita Eisler** criticized this tendency when she said, *"If I had to choose one image of the decade, I would say that the fifties were one big closet."* Wife battering was not taken seriously; often it was assumed that a victim had provoked her husband. America in general continued to turn a blind eye to abuse, rape, and incest. Those who suffered from these abuses mostly suffered in silence.

THE WOMEN'S MOVEMENT

"SOMETHING HAD GONE WRONG"

Early women's rights proponents may not have lived to see suffrage in 1920, but neither did they watch the mass retreat from the fight for equality. That was left to a small group of dedicated but aging feminists who were members of the National Women's Party (NWP). The NWP, headed by **Alice Paul**, continued to push for the passage of an Equal Rights Amendment (ERA) that would outlaw discrimination based on sex. Alice Paul, who had so proudly hung the banner announcing women's new right to vote in 1920, watched as America became increasingly inhospitable to feminism and women's aspirations for equality. One NWP staff member hoped to pass the ERA "before the dreadful antifeminist reaction we are facing closes all doors to us."

Some in the NWP declared that members of the younger generation were "hopeless" and

By the 1950s, most women did not breast-feed their babies. In this photo, **Hilda Kassell** of New York City bottle feeds her baby behind a partition where her husband can't see.

"not interested in anything but cosmetics, TV and modern amusements." And indeed, the movement had difficulty attracting the younger generation. The exceptions were often women brought in by older relatives. One woman said, ***"Mother had fought so***

> **"Unlike the strident suffragettes who were once eager to prove their equality with men, the typical working wife of 1953 works for the double pay check that makes it possible to buy a TV set, a car—or in many cases simply to make ends meet."**
>
> —*Life* magazine

many battles for women, from suffrage on, that it was time I took up the sword." A few women were related to or descended from the pioneers of the original woman's movement. **Anna Lord Strauss**, great-granddaughter of Lucretia Mott, and **Nora Stanton Blatch**, granddaughter of Elizabeth Cady Stanton, were involved in women's causes. **Susan Anthony II**, grandniece of Susan B. Anthony, found life as a feminist "very lonely."

NWP members were not entirely alone in their concerns. Others also noted differences in the new generation of women. An English professor at the University of Illinois wrote that during the late forties and fifties,

> *"I felt increasingly that something had gone wrong with our young women of college age.... I noted it with growing alarm and anger.... I thought when I started teaching that since the battle to open doors to women had been won, all that was needed was for us to buckle down and show what stuff we were made of. I think I was confident the will was there—I knew the capacity was. But I was mistaken about the will."*

When professors urged their students to marry later, they could never "get it across" and were "characterized as bitter, unromantic old witches."

Older women continued to be a strong force during this period. **Eleanor Roosevelt** wrote a newspaper column, served as the U.S. ambassador to the United Nations, and helped author the Universal Declaration of Human Rights. Other women, such as anthropologist **Margaret Mead**, photographer **Dorothea Lange**, and artist **Georgia O'Keefe**, were still hard at work in their respective fields.

Have you ever heard of . . . Dolores Huerta?

While raising eleven children, Huerta worked to educate and empower migrant farm workers and protect their basic rights. Together with Cesar Chavez she founded the United Farm Workers Union in 1962 and became one of its primary lobbyists and spokespersons. Frequently jailed and beaten by police for union activities, Huerta was nicknamed "the Dragon Lady" by landowners she opposed.

Have you ever heard of . . . Maria Tallchief?

Born on the Osage Indian Reservation in Oklahoma to a Native American father and white mother, Tallchief sang at rodeos as a small child. Her talent led her family to move to Los Angeles, where she studied both concert piano and ballet. Tallchief danced with a number of famous companies and was the prima ballerina for the New York City Ballet between 1947 and 1960. She went on to found the Chicago City Ballet.

Have you ever heard of . . . Jackie Cochran?

A trained beautician who spent her childhood working in a sawmill, Cochran got her pilot's license when she was twenty-two, and was put in charge of women pilots during World War II. Cochran set over 200 flying records, but her best-known feat was being the first woman to break the sound barrier in 1953.

PAID WORK

TO WORK OR NOT TO WORK

With the end of World War II, government propagandists went from churning out posters, movies, and advertisements persuading women to don overalls and pick up welders, to notifying them that the crisis was about over and that it was time to go home. Clearly, paying women to build airplanes and tanks had not changed basic assumptions about "proper" roles.

While some women voluntarily quit their jobs, others were fired or demoted. Three-quarters of those working in war industries continued to work after the war—most in lower-skilled jobs for less pay. Government services for working women all but disappeared. The public judged the validity of a white woman wage earner by her reasons for going to work. People understood that widows, singles, minorities, and women with disabled husbands might need to earn money. Black working women tended to be respected in their communities because their work was so necessary for family survival.

On the other hand, women who admitted working because they liked it or because they wanted to buy things were frequently portrayed as unnatural. The urge to purchase the many newly available products conflicted with the ideal of keeping females at home because many families could not afford cars, televisions, and houses without a second income.

Although employers stopped the practice of firing women when they got married, they limited female ambition by offering only dead-end, low-paying jobs. Even so, one-third of women worked in 1950, mostly in "pink collar" service and clerical jobs. Working part-time was a new option that enabled women to earn some money without embarking on a career. Minorities continued to leave jobs as domestics, working instead as janitors, beauticians, waitresses, and hospital help. Minority women were employed in clerical jobs, but they earned less than half the wages of white women. Interestingly, however, minority women were much more likely than their husbands and sons to find white-collar work.

SCIENCE

In 1956, a *New York Times* article entitled **"Even a Ph.D. Can't Escape the Kitchen"** lamented that women with advanced degrees faced almost insurmountable obstacles to professional success. Even so, numerous brave individuals pushed their way into professions that had traditionally been male strongholds. One of these fields was science. Female scientists were often dismissed by male colleagues and unable to find jobs, but some found creative ways to pursue their careers and made significant contributions to their fields.

Virginia Apgar developed a uniform system for determining an infant's health in the first critical moments of life. Rating reflexes, muscle tone, skin color, breathing, and heart rate enables medical staff to act quickly if a newborn is in distress. Every baby born in U.S. hospitals today is given the Apgar test within sixty seconds of birth.

Grace Hopper helped program the first computer, a machine that was 50-feet long and 8-feet high. She invented an information compiler that made the computer more efficient and also helped to create a common computer language that could be shared by scientists.

In 1952, **Lora Bryning (Redford)** was one of only a handful of women in the U.S. Foreign Service. She thrived on the work that had taken her to Mexico, Belgium, Japan, and Burma. When she fell in love with a fellow officer, Ralph Redford, she faced a "stark choice." Married women could not be diplomats. The policy stated that an officer's wife was expected to "contribute to the realization of our foreign objectives: by creating a home environment which enables her husband to do his work most effectively." She chose to marry. "She was making policy one week and being a wife the next," recalled her son. When the policy was changed in 1972, she applied to rejoin the Foreign Service, but was informed that she was too old.

Gertrude Elion shared the Nobel Prize with a colleague for developing a drug to cure childhood leukemia and a drug that made organ transplants possible. Elion's scientific methods were later used to create AZT, a drug used today to treat AIDS.

Stephanie Kwolek, a chemist, discovered the synthetic fabric Kevlar, which is used in radial tires, bullet-proof vests, fireproof clothing, airplanes, and space ships.

Barbara McClintock, a Nobel Prize winner, found that genes could jump from one place on a chromosome to another. It wasn't until thirty years later that scientists realized that this knowledge was critical to explaining certain mutations and diseases.

Rosalyn Yalow invented radioimmunoassay, a way to measure minute substances in the body. This technology is used today in diagnosing certain diseases. It also helps criminologists find lethal substances in dead bodies.

Rachel Carson examines a specimen (1961).

NEW TECHNOLOGY During World War II the U.S. government poured money into the development of science and technology. Many of these discoveries improved life during peacetime. Demand for new technologies was so great that they were sometimes adopted before they could be proven reliably safe. The world was especially enthusiastic about a new pesticide called DDT that appeared to be the answer to all sorts of bug-related problems. Dusted on soldiers, it killed body lice and decreased the incidence of the disease typhus. Mixed with oil and sprayed on lush vegetation, it killed mosquitoes, the carriers of malaria.

In the United States, the government sent out airplanes to spray both neighborhoods and wilderness areas with this poison-laced oil. Nature lovers noted with alarm that DDT seemed to kill birds and helpful insects. Not only that, mosquitoes lingered on. But the government and chemical companies—who made millions of dollars producing DDT—did not want to hear complaints. They insisted that the pesticide was perfectly harmless. Scientists were only beginning to understand that ecosystems are interconnected and fragile. People were largely unaware of how poisons in the environment could affect human health.

What One Woman Did

"There Would Be No Future Peace for Me if I Kept Silent"

Rachel Carson, a successful oceanographer and writer, was busy writing her fourth book when she became aware of the controversy over DDT. As she conducted research and corresponded with other scientists, the evidence against the pesticide grew. But she had much to lose and little to gain by exposing what she knew.

Carson had succeeded in the scientific world thanks to her mother's sacrifices and her own hard work. Her mother sold the family china and silverware to send Carson to college. While attending graduate school during the Great Depression, Carson became the breadwinner for her family. She helped her mother raise two orphaned nieces while also working as a scientist for the U.S. Bureau of Fisheries. She also wrote magazine articles and books on the side, describing ocean life in a way that appealed to average Americans.

At the time Carson began researching the effects of DDT on the environment in 1957, she was caring for her aging mother and had just adopted an orphaned nephew. What began as an article turned into the book *Silent Spring*. In this book Carson demonstrated how pesticides become part of the food chain, resulting in declining bird populations, and causing cancer and birth defects in humans. She argued that humans do not have the right to pollute. Carson knew that her conclusions would make some people angry, but she wrote to a friend, "You do know . . . how deeply I believe in the importance of what I am doing. *Knowing what I do, there would be no future peace for me if I keep silent.*"

When *Silent Spring* was published in 1962, powerful people in the U.S. government and chemical industries accused Rachel Carson of not knowing what she was talking about. They tried to convince the public that she was overreacting. Carson stood her ground while fighting her own personal battle with cancer. She did not live to see the fruits of her courage, but many consider her the mother of the modern environmental movement. DDT was banned for use in the United States in 1972.

COLD WAR CONCERNS

THE SEARCH FOR SAFETY AND SECURITY

After the war, some Americans began saving their pennies to build bomb shelters in their yards and homes. The shelters of the 1950s were special reinforced concrete shells stocked with supplies for surviving a nuclear attack. In schools, students practiced crouching under desks in nuclear war drills. Why did these precautions suddenly appear necessary? After America dropped two atomic bombs in 1945, the Soviets began to explore nuclear technologies. They also went quickly from being our allies to being our enemies. Americans believed

that the Soviet Union and other Communists planned to take over the world and that it was the responsibility of the United States to stop them. The ensuing competition to build the deadliest weapons and gain the most political influence has been called the Cold War. The fear and distrust that it created lasted for more than forty years.

COLD WAR MOTHERS During the Cold War, the home became the symbol of safety and security from a menacing world. Portrayed as the heart of the home, women were reminded in numerous ways that the threat of Communism was on their very doorsteps. It was their duty to teach their children to love democracy. Housewives could reinforce their message about the evils of Communism when they purchased Kix cereal for their children. Hidden in each box was an atomic bomb ring with

Under the brand of **Communism** practiced in Soviet Russia, citizens worked for the government, which owned almost everything. The government had extensive power over individuals' lives. The capitalism of the United States, which upholds the rights of individual wealth and ownership, is in direct opposition to Soviet-style Communism.

"gleaming aluminum warheads." They could also take their kids to movies like *I Was a Communist for the FBI* and *The Red Menace*. According to the media, the safety of the country resided in the very living rooms and kitchens of America. And lest the message was missed, there was the infamous case of **Ethel Rosenberg** to remind women of their priorities. Rosenberg and her husband, Julius, were executed in 1953 for allegedly selling the secrets of the atomic bomb to the Soviets. They left behind two young sons.

MORE WAR After World War II, writer **Pearl S. Buck** pointed out that "Peace is shaped by war." Buck wrote that although the allies had won the war, leaders had not planned for peace. ***"The war ends, then, with mankind holding the atomic bomb in one hand and in the other . . . prejudice and distrust. We cannot believe in a long peace ahead."*** In this, she was right. In 1950 American troops were sent to help South Korea repel attacks by communist North Korea. Although the U.S. government purposely limited the number of women in the military, about 120,000 female recruits participated in the Korean War, mostly as clerical support staff and nurses. Thirteen platoons of female U.S. Marine reserves were also mobilized. During the next five years, 600 nurses served behind the lines in mobile surgical units like the one portrayed on the television show *M.A.S.H.*

MCCARTHYISM Meanwhile, Joseph McCarthy, a brassy senator from Wisconsin, stirred the government into a communist-hunting frenzy. While soldiers fought Communists abroad, McCarthy made it his job to expose them at home. The climate of fear was so great that many people supported him. Between 1950 and 1954 artists, movie stars, writers, politicians, and many others had their reputations ruined as they were called before the House Committee on Un-American Activities, charged

To many war-weary Koreans, America seemed like a place where everyone was rich and no one went hungry. For Korean women working on military bases or in the nearby brothels, marriage to a soldier appeared to be the ticket out of misery. **Cho Soonyi** was one of the first **Korean military brides** who entered the United States in 1951. She recalled, "I was lucky to meet nice young man. . . . I got very fortunate, lucky." In the years that followed, the numbers of Korean wives swelled to the hundreds and then the thousands. Though they had escaped one set of problems, many found equally challenging ones in their new homes: unfamiliar language, food, and customs, not to mention social exclusion from the Korean American community, which was convinced that Korean women who married American soldiers must be immoral.

with disloyalty or subversive activities. Summoned to testify against friends, playwright **Lillian Hellman** wrote, *"I cannot and will not cut my conscience to fit this year's fashions."* Anyone advocating peace, human rights, or justice was in peril of being labeled a communist, losing their job, or even being imprisoned.

What One Woman Did

"A Declaration of Conscience"

McCarthy's opponent came in unlikely form. **Margaret Chase Smith** was a fellow Republican, an ardent believer in the need for military strength, and the only woman in the Senate. At first this senator from Maine wondered if the Communist allegations were true, but as she watched McCarthy bully people she knew to be upright, she recognized him to be power hungry and dishonest. Other politicians agreed but were afraid to confront McCarthy for fear that he would also accuse them. But Smith had heard enough.

Four months after McCarthy began his smear campaign, Margaret Chase Smith surprised the

Wives of jailed communists picket in front of the New York Federal Courthouse in 1949.

Senate with a document entitled "A Declaration of Conscience," which had also been signed by six other Republican senators. She distributed it and gave an impassioned speech. Although she never once mentioned McCarthy by name, everyone knew to whom she was referring when she denounced "those of us who shout the loudest about Americanism" but "ignore some of the basic principals of Americanism—the right to hold unpopular beliefs; the right to protest, the right of independent thought." Exercising these rights, she said, should not cost a person's reputation or livelihood.

When Smith finished her speech, she waited for a rebuttal from McCarthy. Instead, the normally opinionated man sat silent and white-faced. The next day he dismissed the declaration as a "spanking," called Smith and her signers "Snow White and her six dwarves," and sneered that he never fought with women senators. Republicans who believed she was hurting her own party agreed with him. Others were impressed with her nerve.

Margaret Chase Smith campaigning in 1948 to become the first woman in the U.S. Senate.

Smith's speech received glowing reports in many newspapers and her office was flooded with letters thanking her for her courage.

Historians debate how much influence Smith's declaration had on McCarthyism. McCarthy's reign of terror continued for another four years. However, it is significant that when even the most powerful individuals in American society were too afraid or blinded to stand up for basic constitutional rights, Smith confronted them head on. McCarthy was discredited in 1954 and died from complications of alcoholism in 1957. Smith remained in public office another twenty-two years.

THE TECHNOLOGY RACE The race against Communism took other forms as well. In 1957 the Soviet Union beat the United States into space by launching Sputnik, a rocket-powered satellite with a dog on board. Americans scrutinized the school systems that were to produce the next generation of rocket scientists and began pouring money into education at all levels. Girls as well as boys benefited. **Susan Douglas**, in elementary school at the time, recalled:

> *Nothing less than the survival of the free world rested on our puny, puff-sleeved shoulders.* As we earnestly studied our *Weekly Readers* and heard how if we didn't shape up fast we'd all be living on borscht, sharing an apartment the size of a refrigerator carton with all our relatives, and genuflecting to Nikita Khrushchev, one thing was clear: No one said, "Just boys—just you boys study hard." *This was on everyone's heads, girls too,* and we were not let off the hook. . . . we had to get A's as well, to fend off the red peril and save our country and ourselves.

Americans and Soviets competed to produce the best televisions, refrigerators, and washing machines. The two-day-long televised "kitchen debates" in 1959 between Vice President Richard Nixon and Soviet Premier Nikita Khrushchev did not focus on who had better military technology, but instead on who had better lives, Americans or Soviets. The vice president insisted that the many handy appliances in America helped women to be better wives and mothers. Nikita Khrushchev

When the National Aeronautics and Space Administration (NASA) began training men to beat the Soviets to the moon in 1959, they became immediate celebrities. What the public and NASA did not know was that thirteen talented female pilots were also secretly (and successfully) undergoing the same rigorous testing as the men. Having proved their physical capabilities, the women and their male allies lobbied government officials to be included in the space program. **Jane Hart**, one of the pilots, told a Congressional subcommittee, **"I am not arguing that women be admitted to space merely so they won't feel discriminated against. I'm arguing that they be admitted because they have a very real contribution to make."** Vice President Lyndon Johnson scrawled across their proposal, "Let's stop this now." Though the pilots were only steps away from becoming astronauts, it would be more than twenty years before the first American woman was allowed to go into space.

responded that the truly beautiful and happy woman was the one working productively in a Soviet factory.

While Americans worried about the lack of freedom and capitalism in Communist countries, too many continued to turn a blind eye to injustices

Thousands of Americans constructed bomb shelters in an effort to protect their families from the effects of a nuclear attack.

at home. And there were many injustices at home. Some found courage to fight discrimination and seek equality.

THE CIVIL RIGHTS MOVEMENT

"TIRED OF GIVING IN"

In the early 1950s, the Rutland family moved to California. Although the Rutlands were black, their first-grader, Elsie, attended the neighborhood school. She made friends with a white classmate, Janey, who said she would come over and play. **Eva Rutland** knew that Janey would not show up because Janey's mother did not want her daughter playing with a black child. Rutland later wrote, "That day that Elsie pressed her little face against the window eagerly, expectantly, my heart turned over. *How could I explain, what could I do?* It's something you always think you're prepared for but you know you'll never really be prepared. You just hope you can soften the blow." Racism was alive and well in the United States.

SOME PROGRESS In the wake of World War II, the government grudgingly integrated the armed forces. Gestures such as this, and an executive order outlawing discrimination in federal employment,

gave African Americans hope that things might be changing. Many continued to migrate in search of opportunity, so that by 1950 one-third of the black population lived ouside of the South. Black celebrities found a place in the public eye. In 1948 **Alice Coachman** high jumped her way to fame as the first African American woman to win an Olympic gold medal, followed twelve years later by runner **Wilma Rudolph**. **Althea Gibson**, a talented tennis player, competed at the prestigious Wimbledon tournament in England in 1951. Record stores were full of albums made by women singing jazz, blues, spiritual, and classical music. Popular musicians included **Leontyne Price**, **Marian Anderson**, **Shirley Verrett**, **Mahalia Jackson**, **Billie Holiday**, and **Pearl Bailey**. The best-known black singer of the time was **Ella Fitzgerald**. **Gwendolyn Brooks** published poetry for which she won the Pulitzer Prize in 1950.

THE REALITIES In day-to-day life, blacks and whites were segregated—in schools, neighborhoods, and public places. No matter how educated, African Americans had difficulty finding adequate employment and housing. Black mothers sent their children to poor, overcrowded schools and tried to explain why they could not play at the parks or cool off at the swimming pools with white children. If they went to the movies at all, it was to sit in the least desirable seats. One woman wrote that her heart "skipped a beat" when her tiny child drank from a public fountain in Georgia labeled "whites only." Nowhere were race restrictions more rigorously enforced than in parts of the South where the majority of blacks still lived in poverty and worked for whites. The most basic American rights, such as voting and fair trial, were denied blacks, and the choice to buck the system could be more than frightening; it could be fatal.

THE MONTGOMERY BUS BOYCOTT Discontent came to a head in 1955 when a dignified seamstress (and civil rights worker) on her way home from work refused to give up her bus seat to a white man. **Rosa Parks** later commented, "People always say that I didn't give up my seat because I was tired, but that isn't true." She continued, "I was not

Members of the 1960 U.S. women's 400-meter relay team, the "Tennessee Tigerbelles," standing together in Rome after setting a world record.
Left to right: **Wilma Rudolph**, **Lucinda Williams**, **Barbara Jones**, and **Martha Hudson**.

tired physically, or no more than I usually was.... I was not old.... I was forty-two. *No, the only tired I was, was tired of giving in."*

Black leaders recognized Parks's case as an opportunity to challenge unfair bus policies in Montgomery, Alabama. **Jo Ann Robinson**, a leader of the Women's Political Council, pushed for a boycott. Leaders met to discuss the matter in the church of a young minister named Martin Luther King Jr. When some ministers were afraid to list their names as boycott leaders, NAACP leader E. D. Nixon shamed them: *"You guys have went around here and lived off these poor washerwomen all your lives and ain't never done nothing for 'em.* Now you got a chance to do something for 'em, you talking about you don't want the White folks to know about it." The ministers signed on.

For more than a year, the majority of Montgomery's black population refused to ride buses. Maids, cooks, and nannies walked the

long miles to their jobs in all kinds of weather. When offered a ride, one woman replied, *"I'm not walking for myself, I'm walking for my children and grandchildren."* Another said, "My feet is tired, but my soul is rested." Though men assumed the public face of the boycott, it was the hard work and community connections of women that sustained it. People with cars gave rides to those without, taxi drivers charged bus fare, and the Montgomery Improvement Association used donations to purchase station wagons. Some people chose to walk anyway, just to make a point.

Scattered whites supported the efforts of the black community. In a letter to a Montgomery

Church ladies of Woodville, Georgia, in 1941, above, and church ladies of Montgomery, Alabama, in 1956 giving a standing ovation to bus boycott leaders, left.

Coretta Scott King, the wife of Martin Luther King Jr., gave birth to her first child, a girl, only two weeks before the boycott began. She later wrote:

Being in Montgomery was like a drama that was unfolding. Martin and I and the other people of that small southern city were like actors in a play, the end of which we had not yet read. **Yet we felt a sense of destiny, of being propelled in a certain positive direction**.

Ella Baker, a college graduate and the granddaughter of slaves, had long worked for social justice when the bus boycott took place. She offered strategic advice to its leaders. Baker believed that everyone, not just leaders, should be strong and play a part. She wanted "people to understand that *in the long run they themselves are the only protection they have against violence or injustice.*"

Baker and other female leaders often felt pushed aside by male civil rights activists who had traditional views of women. The organization she founded, the Student Nonviolent Coordinating Committee (SNCC), helped college students to be a positive force for change. Baker was determined that SNCC would be more democratic than the other civil rights organizations, and that it would nurture young female leadership. After a number of black students staged sit-ins to integrate public spaces in 1960, members of SNCC, both black and white, began to do so on a larger scale.

newspaper, librarian **Juliette Morgan** wrote: *"Their cause and their conduct have filled me with great sympathy, pride, humility, and envy.* I envy their unity, their good humor, their fortitude, and their willingness to suffer for great…principles, or just plain decent treatment." **Virginia Foster Durr**, a white civil rights activist, described the ways the boycott influenced relationships between white and black women: "A vast deceit went on. Everybody knew that everybody else was lying, but to save face, they had to lie. The black women had to say that they weren't taking part in the boycott. The white women had to say that their maids didn't take part in any boycott." Montgomery's mayor begged white women to stop giving black women rides to or from work, but some just kept doing it.

The boycott ended, not because the bus company or city backed down, but because the Supreme Court decided that segregated seating violated the Fourteenth Amendment (which says the government should not limit the rights of citizens or deny them equal protection under the law). More important, the boycott set the ball rolling for the civil rights movement.

"NOT EASY TO BE A PIONEER"

In 1954 the Supreme Court declared segregated schools unconstitutional in a case called *Brown v. Board of Education*. Still, many white Americans were entrenched in destructive habits and ways of thinking about race relations. Around the country, young African Americans endured isolation and disrespect as they became the first blacks to attend white schools. Arkansas governor Orval Faubus used National Guardsmen to bar nine black students from attending an all-white high school in Little Rock. President Dwight Eisenhower responded by

"Until the killing of a black mother's son becomes as important as the killing of a white mother's son, we who believe in freedom cannot rest."—ELLA BAKER

ENTIRE PROCEEDS TO N.A.A.C.P. NATIONAL OFFICE
and SOUTHERN LEADERSHIP CONFERENCE

RALLY

'The Right to Vote" "The Fight to Vote"

THE FEDERATION OF NEGRO CIVIL SERVICE ORGANIZATIONS, INC.

PRESENTS

Jackie Robinson   Daisy Bates   Dr. Martin Luther King   Roy Wilkins

MANHATTAN CENTER

34th St. & 8th Ave., N. Y. C.

8pm Thursday, October 29

TICKETS $1.00   NO SEATS RESERVED

MEMBER ORGANIZATIONS OF FEDERATION

CERBEREAN SOCIETY   AEGIS SOCIETY
CORRECTIONAIRES   COUNSELIERS
PRAETORIAN SOCIETY   RUTLEDGE SOCIETY
VULCAN SOCIETY, INC.   SENTINEL SOCIETY, INC.
GUARDIANS ASSOCIATION
NEGRO ASS'N OF WELFARE WORKERS
N. Y. STATE CAREERISTS, INC.
NEGRO BENEVOLENT OF SANITATION
COMMUNITY TEACHERS ASSOCIATION
ASSOCIATED TRANSIT GUILD

TICKETS
may be obtained
by contacting

WILLIAM R. BRACEY
176-20 SUNBURY ROAD
JAMAICA 34, NEW YORK
LA 5-1629
and

Daisy Bates worked with other leaders on many civil rights issues. This flyer was posted for a 1959 Right to Vote Rally in New York.

black girl to attend Nolfolk High School in Virginia. Looking back, **Ricki Eleanor Gilbert**, a white senior at Norfolk High School that same year, regretted that she didn't befriend Reed. She watched her from afar and made sure that her picture appeared in the yearbook, but she never talked to her. "I was scared of losing my exalted position in school leadership," she said. *"I was scared of my friends turning their backs on me.* My reasons were pretty shallow."

Black parents faced risks for urging integration. In some towns they could lose their jobs for simply signing a petition. Even worse, they feared putting their children in harm's way. "I just had to let her go," stated one mother. "There is a principle involved. If our boys and girls enter the white school now it will be easier for others to get in later. *It's not easy to be a pioneer though."*

In 1952, United Women Methodists, one of the largest white women's organizations in the United States, made integrated schools and housing their mission. They knew that the biggest hurdle to desegregation was white attitudes, so they set

sending 1,200 U.S. Army paratroopers to enforce the students' rights. On September 23, 1957, **Carlotta Walls**, **Gloria Ray**, **Elizabeth Eckford**, **Thelma Mothershed**, **Melba Pattillo**, **Minniejean Brown**, Terrence Roberts, Ernest Green, and Jefferson Thomas officially started school at Central High School. Every day they endured cruel taunts and pranks.

Daisy Bates, the president of the local NAACP, attended school with the students all year to make sure they were safe. She helped them talk about their anger and about ways to survive. Bates and her family were threatened for her efforts, and her newspaper closed down. Even when the first of the group graduated, the battle was far from over. In Little Rock, as well as many other towns, officials closed schools rather than integrate.

While the integration of Central High School received massive media coverage, other less-publicized acts of courage were taking place around the country. In 1959, **Betty Jean Reed** was the only

Central High suspended Minniejean Brown after she poured chili on the heads of her tormenters. She had borne their harassment all year; she had been burned with hot soup, threatened with a knife, and called names. The lunch room was completely silent for a few moments after Minniejean's action; then the black lunch ladies applauded.

In 1961, Freedom Riders, testing a Supreme Court ruling that banned racial discrimination in interstate travel, rode in desegregated buses from New York to Washington, DC.

In Anniston, Alabama, a mob slashed the tires of the Freedom Riders' bus, set it on fire, and attempted to block the riders from exiting. Once they escaped the bus, riders were severely beaten.

out to systematically change those attitudes. Members challenged biblical excuses for racial prejudice and lobbied for fair housing policies. They also worked to inform their communities about the toll of segregation by bringing parents of both races together to talk about their children and their schools. Their work helped to prepare at least some white communities for change.

Pressuring schools to be inclusive was only the beginning. In 1962, **Fannie Lou Hamer**, a sharecropper in Mississippi, registered to vote. When she arrived home, her employer of eighteen years fired her and drove her whole family off the farm. The experiences of Hamer and many others like her set the stage for a widened arena of civil rights struggle that would continue into the following decades.

THE SEEDS OF CHANGE

SPEAKING OUT

As the 1950s turned into the 1960s, other changes were also afoot. Voices that had long been silent began to speak out and be heard. When the editors of *Redbook* magazine invited readers to submit essays on "Why Young Mothers Feel Trapped," more than a thousand manuscripts poured in each month for the next several years. When **Peg Bracken** published the *I Hate to Cook Book* in 1960, it became one of the best-selling cookbooks ever. Merely admitting that mothers sometimes felt trapped and that women didn't always like to cook was a huge step and an indication of things to come.

WOMEN STRIKE FOR PEACE Another surprising challenge to the status quo came on November 1, 1960, when fifty-thousand U.S. housewives seemed to emerge out of the blue to stage a massive protest against nuclear testing and military buildup. Pushing strollers and carrying picket signs, women around the country took to the streets, lobbied local officials, and sent telegrams to the White House. The group staging the protest called themselves "Women Strike for Peace." When the leaders were subsequently called in to the House Un-American Activities Committee, the absurdity of the situation became clear. The same American mothers whom society had held up as the mighty protectors against Communism were now being called Communists.

The hearing room was filled with women from eleven states with children in tow. They turned the courtroom upside down with their antics. When the first witness stood, so did the audience. The chairman outlawed standing, so the next woman was greeted with applause. The chairman outlawed clapping. With each new prohibition, the audience found creative ways to show support. Women ran up to embrace the witnesses, or give them flowers. The committee did not know how to respond. **Blanche Posner**, a retired schoolteacher, told them, "You don't quite

> "I was catapulted into the peace movement with the dropping of the bomb. . . . I was pretty apolitical up to that point. I used to get up in the morning and start polishing the furniture until I was polishing the polish. I thought, 'There must be more to life than this.' I had a daughter who was a small child. . . . When I read that the blast was so hot in some circumstances it incinerated people and left just a shadow against a stone wall. . . . I was numbed. I realized there were wars and there were wars, but this kind of war must never happen again."
>
> **—Ethel Barol Taylor**

understand the nature of this movement. This movement was inspired and motivated by mothers' love for their children. *When they were putting their breakfast on the table, they saw not only Wheaties and milk, but they also saw strontium 90 and iodine 131.*"

The proceedings demonstrated the irony of insisting that a buildup of deadly weapons was the only way to protect the innocent. A cartoonist portrayed the scene with a congressman asking the man next to him, "I came in late; which was it that was un-American—women or peace?"

"Mrs. Donald Davidson" and her baby **Denise** protest atomic-bomb testing in 1962.

The World Turned Upside-Down

1963–1990

In the spring of 1963 **Anne Moody** and two other black college students sat down at a "whites only" lunch counter at the Jackson, Mississippi, Woolworth store. When they attempted to order, waitresses fled to the kitchen, and patrons began to leave. As reporters gathered around, the high school lunch crowd arrived and quickly became violent. Moody later wrote that when she and her friends bowed their heads to pray, *"all hell broke loose."* People slapped, punched, and kicked them. Some high school boys made a noose out of a restaurant rope and tried to put it around their necks.

As police arrested her friend and carried him away bleeding, other protesters replaced him at the counter. "There were now four of us, two whites and two Negroes, all women," recalled Moody. "The mob started smearing us with ketchup, mustard, sugar, pies, and everything on the

John Salter, **Joan Trumpauer**, and Anne Moody endure mob actions during a 1963 sit-in.

counter." Other activists joined the women. The mob spray painted insults on their backs and poured salt in one man's wounds while ninety policemen stood outside and watched. The sit-in lasted for three hours. Like the sit-ins that preceded it, this protest did not gain immediate results. It was, however, a link in a chain of actions that began to change racial inequities in American society.

With U.S. troops gathering in Asia, protest marches, and a presidential assassination, 1963 was a year that divided the seemingly innocent fifties from the chaotic sixties. The mood in America was one of growing unrest and protest. Those denied equal rights battled to obtain them. As the emerging civil rights movement continued to dominate the news, other groups such as Hispanics and Native Americans were also pursuing change and challenging the status quo. When the best-selling book titled *The Feminine Mystique* questioned women's very roles as wives and mothers, it seemed to many as if the world were turning upside-down. The ensuing years brought a rapid pace of change. A new women's movement emerged. Women went to work and to college in increasing numbers. Activists worked to change laws that declared them unequal. Over the next twenty years, many women worked to more fully claim their rights as American citizens. Their efforts created a world of expanded opportunities and responsibilities for future generations.

CIVIL RIGHTS

"I'VE BEEN STANDING EVER SINCE"

Nearly ten years after the civil rights movement had begun, the majority of blacks still faced profound prejudice and inequality, especially in the South. In Southern states, county registrars employed a system of taxes and literacy tests to prevent blacks from voting. Whites were still the bosses, as well as land and bank owners. African American children still attended segregated and substandard schools. These and other factors reduced many Southern blacks to lives of grinding poverty without access to such basic services as running water, electricity, or paved roads. Violent reprisals for "stepping out of line" reminded blacks that justice was also reserved for whites. Yet, amid the danger, there were those like Anne Moody who continued to rise up and demand racial equality.

Unita Blackwell, a sharecropper in the Mississippi Delta, vividly recalled the day that civil rights workers came to town. Workers stood up

In Alexandria, Louisiana, black women picketed the local grocery store in 1964. Although the store was in a predominantly black neighborhood, its white owners refused to hire African Americans. Protesters gathered with posters that read, "Don't shop where you can't work." For six weeks they slowed business until the owners finally hired one of the protesters, **Miss Hobdy**. Black members of the community were so delighted that they purposely waited in her checkout line, however long.

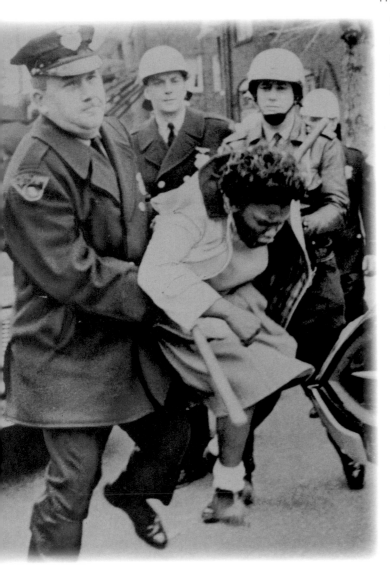

Though protesters used nonviolent methods, their efforts were often met with violence. In this photograph, a Cleveland, Ohio, civil rights protester is physically restrained as she reacts to the death of a fellow demonstrator who was struck and killed by a bulldozer (1964).

from having this important right. Some participated in acts of civil disobedience, peacefully integrating public places. Some attended marches. Others opened citizenship schools to teach people their rights and help them pass voting literacy tests. Still others canvassed neighborhoods and urged people to vote.

Women played a unique role in the struggle. Their networks of family, friends, and church helped them draw people into the civil rights movement. These connections also helped to sustain communities through the harsh and frightening backlash. For example, women created business cooperatives that gave jobs to those who had been fired for participating in civil rights activities. They also comforted and aided the families of victims of white violence.

A majority of Southern blacks worked on plantations and as sharecroppers in remote areas.

at church and talked about voting as the right of every individual. When they asked for volunteers to venture to the town hall and register to vote, Blackwell stood up. She recalled, *"My husband caught me by the dress tail and pulled me back down, because he was supposed to stand up first, you see, because he's the man. So he stood, then I stood up, and I've been standing ever since."* Blackwell and others charted a course that would alter the following decades.

VOTING RIGHTS Without access to the vote, African Americans were denied a powerful tool to change the system that oppressed them. Women like Unita Blackwell played a key role in community organizing, challenging the prejudice that kept them

Teenager **Euvester Simpson** *was jailed with civil rights worker* **Fannie Lou Hamer,** *who lay fevered and ill after being beat up by police. Simpson cared for Hamer all night. They made it through, she remembered, by singing:* **"We sang all night.** *I mean songs got us through so many things, and without that music I think many of us would have just lost our minds or lost our way completely."*

A number of women were widowed when their husbands were killed for their civil rights work. Civil rights activist Medgar Evers was shot to death in front of the house he shared with his wife and three children in 1963. His wife, **Myrlie Evers**, later wrote, "I flew to the door praying to be wrong. I switched on the light. Medgar lay face down in the doorway drenched with blood. I screamed, went to him, calling his name. . . . The children were around me now, pleading with him. 'Please, Daddy, please get up.'" In 1995, Myrlie Evers-Williams would become the first woman to head the civil rights organization the NAACP.

Courageous women ventured to these areas to promote civil rights. Those who listened also put themselves and their families in danger. Women were not immune from violent attacks. As Anne Moody became more involved in the movement, she was unable to return home because of threats made to her family by their local sheriff. Civil rights workers and their families were frequently bombed, beaten, arrested, threatened, and killed while law enforcement participated or looked the other way.

What One Woman Did

"I'm Sick and Tired of Being Sick and Tired"

In spite of limited education and savage beatings by police, sharecropper Fannie Lou Hamer became a powerful mouthpiece for the movement. Her famous phrase, *"All my life I've been sick and tired. Now I'm tired of being sick and tired"* spoke for many African Americans. In 1964, when the Southern Democrats continued to ban blacks from political participation, Hamer and other civil rights workers created the Mississippi Freedom Democratic Party (MFDP). When they sent delegates to the Democratic convention, they were refused seating. Nonetheless, Hamer addressed the convention, highlighting murders of civil rights leaders and her own suffering. She shared her experiences and sang freedom songs. In spite of presidential candidate Lyndon Johnson's attempts to direct attention back to himself, much of Hamer's speech was televised.

The efforts of the MFDP and other civil rights groups led to the Voting Rights Act a year later. The act banned polling places from discriminatory voting practices and gave the federal government power to enforce the law. The effects of the Voting Rights Act were profound. Federal Marshals were sent south to protect blacks registering to vote. In Mississippi, black voter registration rose from 6.7 percent in 1964, to 67.5 percent in 1970.

In 1964, Congress passed a landmark **Civil Rights Act** that prohibited (and continues to prohibit) job discrimination on the basis of race, color, religion, sex, or national origin. Many historians believe the word *sex* was added at the last minute in order to kill the bill. Imagine everyone's surprise when instead it became law. Those charged with enforcing the new law worked mainly to end racial discrimination and tended to ignore complaints of sexual discrimination.

A few white Mississippians braved the wrath of their neighbors to support civil rights. In 1962, **Winifred Green** and **Patricia Darian**, along with thirty others, founded Mississippians for Public Education. They worked to keep schools and public parks open for all races and monitored housing issues. Another organization run by **Connie Curry** helped black parents who lost their jobs after enrolling their kids in white schools.

FREEDOM SUMMER In 1964, leaders of the Student Nonviolent Coordinating Committee (SNCC), who had staged many sit-ins, tried a new tactic. They solicited the help of summer volunteers to fan out across Mississippi and promote voter registration, start freedom schools, and create community centers. They called the project "Freedom Summer." Over the course of three months, a thousand volunteers journeyed to Mississippi. Many of the volunteers were young, white Northerners. **Mary King**, a white SNCC staff member, wrote, "There was no line where the movement began and our personal lives left off." She felt that the movement "was about personhood, no matter what your race. It was about human promise and democracy."

Descending into the thick of the fray was a frightening, eye-opening experience for those

Protesters form a conga line as they prepare to spend a second night bedded down on a Selma, Alabama, street (1965).

involved—made more so by the brutal murders of three SNCC workers at the beginning of the summer. The Civil Rights Act, passed in July, had not made even a ripple in Mississippi. Volunteers were appalled at the poverty, illiteracy, and fear they encountered. One young woman recalled, *"For the first time in my life I am seeing what it is like to be poor, oppressed and hated."* Volunteers were equally amazed at the warm reception they received from people who took the huge risk of befriending, housing, and feeding them. They were especially impressed with the strength of African American women they encountered. "Our hostesses are brave women," wrote one volunteer to her family. Her hostess slept with a hatchet under her pillow, and rightly so—the violence against civil rights advocates accelerated. At the end of the summer, volunteers were afraid for those they left behind.

BENEFITS These individual and collective acts of bravery broadened public knowledge of the ugly realities of segregation and led to change. Just as important, numerous women were empowered by their experiences. By participating in the struggle, they discovered and honed their leadership abilities and gained confidence. Looking back, **Bernice Johnson Reagon**, founder of the a cappella music group Sweet Honey in the Rock, recognized that resisting oppression made her strong. *"There was a sense of power, in a place where you didn't feel you had any power. There was a sense of confronting things that terrified you, like jail, police. . . . so you were saying in some basic way 'I will never again stay inside these boundaries.'"*

"RED POWER"

African Americans were not the only minority group to protest their treatment by mainstream America. In the spring of 1964, a gun-toting Nisqually Indian woman informed police that she would shoot anyone who tried to stop her son from fishing in the river where the family had always fished. She, like many other Native Americans in Washington State, relied on fish for her livelihood. And yet, federal fishing regulations made fishing at certain times and places illegal. The resulting conflict over fishing rights

Have you ever heard of . . . Iolani Luahine?

As a child she dedicated her life to Laka, the ancient goddess of hula. Known foremost as a dancer, Luahine helped begin the Hawaiian renaissance. In the early 1970s, when many of the old Hawaiian ways were being lost, she called a meeting of prominent hula dancers and teachers to discuss how best to preserve Hawaiian culture. This meeting resulted in a number of new organizations dedicated to the preservation of traditional art, dance, music, and chant.

Many Native American communities were polarized by the explosive, and sometimes violent, American Indian Movement. **Delphine Red Shirt**, a Lakota teenager in the 1960s, recalled, "When I look back now, I realize that what it meant for the people in my community was a loss of innocence. . . . before the movement came, we were insulated from the world. . . . The time after the occupation, chaos came and settled in our midst. Guns and drugs became available."

highlighted many of the challenges that continued to plague Indian populations: a lack of political control, conflict between factions, loss of culture, unemployment, and racism. That same year, an estimated 74 percent of reservation families lived at or below poverty level.

Although Native Americans were a diverse group, many Native Americans began to argue that Indian survival required unification across tribal lines for mutual support. This "pan-Indianism" highlighted a person's dual identity as a member of a specific nation as well as a Native American in general. Many women joined the militant American Indian Movement (AIM) after it was founded in 1968, and participated in its activities to draw attention to Indian rights. The most dramatic was the group's 1973 seventy-two-day armed occupation of the village of Wounded Knee, the site of an 1897 massacre. In 1969, a group of Native Americans including women and children sought to call attention to their plight by peacefully occupying Alcatraz Island in San Francisco Bay for nineteen months. These, along with other forms of protest, eventually resulted in legislation granting more autonomy to Native Americans.

Did you know?

In 1985, **Wilma Mankiller** became the first female chief of the 150,000-member Cherokee Nation.

"IT WAS WRONG TO SIT BY AND LET IT HAPPEN"

Participation in civil rights movements lit the fire of activism in many youth. The 1960s were a confusing, yet interesting, time to be young. As the media carried news stories of political assassinations, the Vietnam War, political

Did you know?

More than 11,500 women served in Vietnam as nurses and military support staff. **Lynda Van Daventer**, an army nurse, wrote home, "I'm tired of going to sleep listening to outgoing and incoming rockets, mortars, and artillery. I'm sick of facing, every day, a new bunch of children ripped to pieces. They're just kids—eighteen, nineteen years old! It stinks! Whole lives ahead of them— cut off. I'm sick to death of it."

corruption, civil unrest, and economic downturns, youth cast about for answers to society's enormous problems. **Cathy Wilkerson**, a college student at the time, remembered, *"Every night we would gather and watch Vietnam on the TV, and watch black people being attacked and murdered....it just never stopped....I felt like we really needed to be disruptive to stop what was going on, that it was wrong to sit by and let it happen."* The largest segment of the U.S. population, people between ages fourteen and twenty-four (postwar baby boomers), came to view themselves as taking up the torch and forging a new, better way.

STUDENT GROUPS Colleges became a hot spot for political activity. And yet, as American youth looked critically at the issues, many came away with significantly different opinions. Some joined Young Americans for Freedom (YAF), a right-leaning college group that worked against Communism, unions, and welfare, and supported the Vietnam War. Others joined Students for a Democratic Society (SDS), a left-leaning college organization

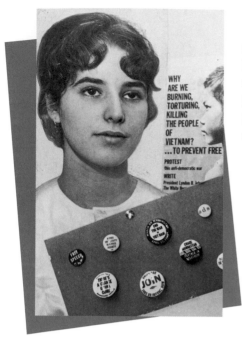

Students for a Democratic Society worker **Judy Pardun** displays buttons for the movement.

ideas struck such a chord that the paper found its way into a number of female circles where women were starting to find words for their concerns. Without knowing it, King and Hayden contributed in a profound way to the beginnings of a new women's movement, often called the second wave of feminism or the women's liberation movement.

THE SECOND WAVE OF FEMINISM

"A FULL EQUALITY OF THE SEXES": WOMEN'S GROUPS EMERGE

Imagine a time when the word *sexism* doesn't exist. Within this world, being a woman limits your every choice. Career aspirations beyond becoming a teacher, secretary, or nurse are frowned upon. This is a world where you make far less money than your male counterparts who do the same work. If you become pregnant, you can be fired from your job. There are no women on the Supreme Court and in some states, as a woman, you are not allowed to serve on a jury. You don't know of a single woman who runs a corporation or anchors the evening news. When you attempt to apply for a credit card or a loan, you are informed that you cannot do so without the consent of your husband or your father. Ivy League colleges refuse you admittance because you are female and medical and law schools across the country use female quotas to keep from accepting you. Welcome to the 1960s.

that worked for civil rights, welfare reform, and an end to the war.

As women in SDS and SNCC fought for racial equality, they realized that although they were taking risks and working every bit as hard as the men, their contributions were often dismissed as less important. Women rarely held leadership positions. Most often they found themselves cleaning up and doing secretarial work. They began to see the hypocrisy of a movement that was about gaining basic rights when they themselves were treated as second-class citizens. At a retreat after Freedom Summer, staff members Mary King and **Casey Hayden** submitted a paper about the status of women in the organization. They felt unsure how to explain their concerns because at that point no one was talking about women's rights. Afraid their ideas would be mocked, they submitted their paper anonymously.

They were right to worry. Most male peers criticized and ridiculed them. A male staff member joked that "the only position for women in SNCC is prone." These reactions led King and Hayden to write a second paper, "A Kind of Memo," which they sent to forty other female activists in 1965. Their

COMMISSION ON THE STATUS OF WOMEN As women in student groups began to protest their unequal status, other women pursued changes

"We women are doing pretty well. We're almost back to where we were in the twenties."

—**Margaret Mead**, anthropologist, 1976

Next time you look at nutrition information and "sell before" dates on your food, or compare food prices by ounce on grocery store shelves, you can thank Esther Peterson. In addition to advocating for women, she developed these consumer protections and fought for workers' rights.

through government channels. In 1961, it was legal to discriminate against women in many ways. **Esther Peterson**, head of the Women's Bureau, worked for change by convincing the new president, John F. Kennedy, that he should show his support for women voters by forming a commission to study the status of women in America. Consequently, Kennedy formed the Commission on the Status of Women headed by **Eleanor Roosevelt** to examine government and private sector hiring practices. It was the last project run by Roosevelt, who died in 1962.

The commission handed their report to President Kennedy in 1963, eleven days before his assassination. It confirmed what most women already knew: the workplace was profoundly and intentionally unequal.

The same year, Peterson worked with various groups to get Congress to pass the Equal Pay Act. This act required equal pay for equal work; however, the law did not create great change because women and men worked mostly at different jobs. The law was also difficult to enforce.

THE FEMININE MYSTIQUE A few months before the findings of the Commission on the Status

of Women were made public, **Betty Friedan**, a successful labor journalist and mother of three, touched a nerve when she published *The Feminine Mystique*. Friedan, who had herself given up graduate training for marriage and motherhood,

"[Women in America] were taught to pity the neurotic, unfeminine, unhappy women who wanted to be poets or physicists or presidents. They learned that truly feminine women do not want careers, higher education, political rights—the independence and the opportunities that the old-fashioned feminists fought for. Some women, in their forties and fifties, still remembered painfully giving up those dreams, but most of the younger women no longer even thought about them."

—BETTY FRIEDAN,
The Feminine Mystique

"A thorough-going, smirking disrespect for women permeated every aspect of society. I despair of conveying to young women...the chilling and depressing effect of this."

—**Dana Densmore**, radical feminist

pointed out a widespread discontentment among white, middle-class women. Some women reported feeling empty and incomplete, like they didn't exist. Some thought their problems must stem from husbands or children. Individual women coped with individual disappointment without seeing their struggles in a larger context.

After conducting questionnaires and interviews, Friedan offered her conclusions about "The problem with no name." The problem, Friedan believed, was that in spite of being told that they should gain complete fulfillment in domesticity, women were finding that they needed more. The feminine mystique, in limiting women's aspirations, had "succeeded in burying millions of women alive." The book became an instant best-seller. Some readers were outraged by Friedan's claims, and many women who were not white or middle-class could not relate to the book's themes. However, multitudes of others wrote letters expressing their gratitude to Friedan for clarifying their struggles. One woman wrote, *"It struck at the center of my being. I feel like I am on the threshold of a new life."*

THE BIRTH OF NOW On June 30, 1966, a group of professional women attended a government conference on the status of women. During the meetings, it became clear that the government did not take sexual discrimination seriously.

Frustrated, they decided that women needed a forum outside government agencies. Sitting at two tables at the back of the room, they "carried on whispered conversations" and created their own organization to work for women's equality. Betty Friedan scribbled the name of the new group on a napkin: NOW, the National Organization for Women.

The purpose of NOW, they decided, was "to take the actions needed to bring women into mainstream society *now*." Lawyer **Pauli Murray** recalled, *"The birth of NOW had happened so quickly and smoothly that most of the delegates left the conference unaware that a historic development in the women's movement had begun."* By the time they

Betty Friedan, president of NOW, explains to reporters the group's intention to insert the word *sex* into section I of the New York Constitution.

held their first conference that fall, their numbers had grown to three hundred. By 1974, NOW boasted 48,000 members in the United States and nine other countries.

NOW demanded *"a fully equal partnership of the sexes"* in pay, job opportunities, and education. They lobbied Congress, sued for reform through the courts, and put pressure on the executive branch of government. They attempted to create policy out of emerging feminist ideas and sought political and economic power for women. They promoted a national system of child care and encouraged a revised "concept of marriage" wherein partners would share household responsibilities. On the heels of NOW's creation, other women began to join together to create change.

"NEW EYES TO SEE": THE RADICAL FEMINISTS

Those who were frustrated by society's treatment of women began to share their experiences with one another. These were often younger women who had been involved in the civil rights or antiwar movements. In 1967, small radical feminist groups formed in New York, Boston, and Chicago. Each gathering had its own personality, and its own definition of women's problems and solutions. What the groups had in common was a burning desire to question everything in society. Of her experience with the New York Radical Women, **Anselma Dell'Olio** remembered "an outpouring of ideas, brains, wit, and talent, the likes of which I have never experienced again. . . . We all read and wrote frenetically, pressing books and essays on one another, talking, arguing, discussing until all hours of the night. *It was one huge, moveable, impromptu women's university."*

At meetings, women delved deep into their lives and asked difficult questions.

They discussed sex and pleasure, the politics of housework (Who does the dishes and laundry? Who vacuums and why?), husbands, abortion, and other issues that affected their lives. Were men the enemy? Was capitalism the enemy? They shared personal experiences. For example, **Shulamith Firestone** told of the pain of going to an Orthodox Jewish school where the boys said in morning prayers, "Thank you, lord, for not making me a woman." Other women told of their secret, illegal, back-alley abortions. **Rosalyn Fraad Baxandall** remembered a feeling of finally coming home when she attended early women's groups:

"Suddenly I had new eyes to see with and a new way to look at the past and the future. . . . Women were catching the fire and coming together to change the world. Changes started with everyday life and the relations between women and men. . . . His refusal to share housework; his arrogant assumption, reinforced by the society at large, that his work was most important—all those hidden injuries. . . . Discussion was intense because we were speaking about subjects formerly whispered or entirely suppressed. . . . finally letting out years of rage and learning where this rage came from."

Once they had identified problems, women's groups had to decide what to do about them. One reporter noted that where NOW members sought a "more equal share of the patriarchal pie," the women's liberation radicals "wanted a different pie altogether." The radicals weren't seeking powerful positions within society. They wanted to change society completely.

Beginning in 1970, the Chicago Women's Graphics Collective helped to increase the visibility of the women's liberation movement. Groups of two to four women created posters like this one. The Graphics Collective dissolved in 1983.

As women tried to understand the discrimination they faced, they came up with varying solutions. A group called the Boston Women promoted celibacy as an answer to the woman problem. In Chicago, women felt that capitalism, rather than men, was the enemy. **Naomi Weisstein** remembered, "We were ready to turn the world upside down." By 1969, the government was concerned enough about feminists that the FBI began to infiltrate their groups.

Some feminists worked to educate the public that rape was about violence and power, not sex. **Heather Booth** *remembered that when she took action to change her university's health policy toward rape victims, she was "petrified." "Would someone yell at me? Would I get thrown out of school? . . . My heart was always pounding. I almost never felt I knew enough, or was smart enough, to be confident. But* **we acted in spite of not knowing enough, being smart enough, or being confident enough**. *And the policy changed. We learned that if you act, you can change the world."*

TACTICS Armed with determination and a sense of drama, radical feminists demanded America's attention. One feminist theatre group calling themselves WITCH dressed in rags and put a hex on Wall Street. Shortly thereafter, they protested marriage by invading a Madison Square Garden bridal fair. Protesters arrived draped in gowns, black veils, and chains, singing, "Here come the slaves, off to their graves," and performing an "un-wedding ceremony" where they swore "not to obey." Hoping to reach working-class women, they performed skits in beauty parlors and laundromats.

On September 7, 1968, several busloads of women descended on Atlantic City to disrupt the annual Miss America Pageant. Beachgoers watched in surprise as protesters, led by actress **Robin Morgan**, fanned out with picket signs. To Morgan and some other feminists, the pageant was a *"degrading mindless-boobie-girlie symbol"* that turned female beauty into something like a cattle auction.

The protesters shocked the public with their capers. They crowned a live sheep Miss America and refused to talk to male reporters. **Carol Hanisch** recalled *"chaining ourselves to a large red, white, and blue Miss America dummy to highlight how women were enslaved by beauty standards."* They threw "'instruments of torture' (including high heels, nylons, girdles, hair curlers, false eyelashes, and *Playboy* and *Good Housekeeping* magazines) into a Freedom Trash Can." According to Hanisch, many women looked on "with skepticism or thoughtful silence." Several men grew "quite hostile." Donning dresses and high heels, a few protesters entered the hall and at a crucial moment dropped a banner reading "Women's Liberation" and chanted "Freedom for Women."

The Redstockings of New York disrupted a state hearing on abortion-law reform. At the hearing, one judge suggested that abortion might be made legal for women who had "done their social duty" by bearing four children. One woman shouted at the all-male legislators, "Men don't get pregnant, men don't bear children. Men just make the laws." Six weeks later, they held an "Abortion: Tell It Like It Is" speak out. While many mainstream Americans were appalled by these tactics, one journalist pointed out that *"without just this sort of excess, no one would have paid much attention to demands for women's equality."*

Only an estimated 15,000 women belonged to these radical groups. However, because of the media attention they received, their influence was far greater than their numbers suggest. This small group of women virtually defined women's liberation for most Americans. In the end, their outrageous tactics made the demands of other less radical feminist groups such as NOW seem far more acceptable to the larger public.

"FROM THE GUTS AND THE HEART": THE SHIFT TO FEMINISM

CLICKING MOMENTS Word of a women's movement began to spread. **Linda Nochlin**, a professor at Vassar College, remembered the "sheer exhilaration" of her introduction to feminism. It was 1969, and Nochlin had never heard of women's liberation. One day, she was visited by a friend with

> ## Did you know?
>
> The stereotype of feminists as bra burners was born at the Miss America Pageant protest in 1968, though not one bra went up in smoke. Fires on the boardwalk were against beach regulations.

> "We believed that it was the men who had to change and that we could force them to do it. We actually had truth squads where we confronted one another's mates. **Judy Thideau**'s husband, John Gabree, worked at *Penthouse* magazine. About six of us stormed into his office and demanded he resign from the sexist rag [magazine]. To our surprise, he did."
>
> —ROSALYN FRAAD BAXANDALL

a briefcase bulging with women's liberation essays. Once she started reading, Nochlin said, "I couldn't stop: this had nothing to do with old-fashioned ideas about getting the vote for women and getting men out of the saloons. *This was brilliant, furious, [quarrelsome] stuff written from the guts and the heart, questioning . . . the position of women within society in general."* She read until two AM, "making discovery after discovery, cartoonish light bulbs going off in my head at a frantic pace. . . . It was as though I kept opening doors onto an endless series of bright rooms . . . each moving me forward from a known space to a larger, lighter, unknown one." With that, Nochlin became a feminist and added her voice to the newly emerging women's movement.

Nochlin put her conversion into action by teaching the first class on women and art at Vassar. Art textbooks at the time contained no mention of women artists and their work. Because of this "everything had to be constructed from the beginning." Nochlin and her students began to ask new questions: *"Why are there so few male nudes by women artists and so many female ones by males? What does that say about power relations between the sexes, and about who is permitted to look at whom?"*

Teacher and students alike found the process energizing and empowering as they realized "that women mattered as creators of art and that their efforts, whether frustrated, failed, or successful, were worthy topics of study." Believe it or not, this was a revolutionary idea at the time.

The story of women's liberation is littered with life-altering experiences much like Nochlin's—"clicking moments" when the lights suddenly came on and shed rays on all aspects of a woman's life. One feminist likened the experience to the waking of Sleeping Beauty—"no kiss, no prince—just the click of consciousness that precedes self-possession."

Did you know?

Until 1976 married women were never listed in phone books under their own names.

The first consciousness-raising group in the New York City Women's Center in 1970. What might women discuss in a consciousness-raising group today? Would the issues be the same or different?

CONSCIOUSNESS-RAISING

One of the New York groups gave a name to women's sharing sessions. They called it "consciousness raising." Soon middle-class women around the country were congregating to reevaluate their lives and relationships. These discussions generated ideas that helped them take power over their lives.

During meetings, women found that they frequently lacked the words to explain the ways that society belittled them (now referred to as *sexism*). There was no name for the assumption that things male were superior to things female. Women also realized that the English language was male-centered. "Why," they asked, was the "word 'man' used to describe the whole human race?" No one would ever consider using the word *woman* to represent everyone. And why did the form of address *Mr.* apply to all males while *Mrs.* and *Miss* indicated a woman's marital status?

In a consciousness-raising group in California, women in the Asian American movement wondered why they were relegated to taking minutes for meetings, making coffee and food, and cleaning the toilets. They explored what it meant to be an Asian American woman. One woman remembered the experience: "So we each had a day where we spoke about our lives. We'd all start crying. I remember it being really scary for people. In fact, some people dropped out of the group when they found out we were going to do this. It was so vulnerable to say some of the things we said to each other."

Once **Jane McCall** attended a consciousness-raising group, she gained strength to confront her husband with the fact that he did only fifteen hours of housework for her eighty hours. She stated that this was no longer acceptable and that things needed to change. People began using the phrase *"the personal is political,"* coined by Carol Hanisch to explain that many women's problems were not individual at all. They were a part of a larger system of inequalities that oppressed women. Women's problems could not be solved without changing those inequalities through some sort of group action.

ONE MOVEMENT, MANY VOICES

WOMEN'S STRIKE FOR EQUALITY By 1970, the women's movement was in full force. Though different feminist groups had varying takes on the issues and solutions, many came together in a mass movement—the Women's Strike for Equality held on August 26, 1970. Organizers called for a nationwide strike to end discrimination against women. Strikers' demands focused on equal opportunities in employment and education, the creation of child-care centers, and legalized abortion. Some draped the Statue of Liberty with 40-foot banners that read, "Women of the World Unite" and "March on August 26 For Equality." In cities across the country, women marched with pots and pans and typewriters, learned self-defense, "liberated" male-only restaurants, and smashed teacups and dishware. With participants in forty-three states, the strike garnered much attention.

Not surprisingly, much of the media coverage was negative or dismissive of the women's concerns. ABC News began its report on the strike with a quote by Vice President Spiro Agnew: *"Three things have been difficult to tame. The ocean, fools, and women. We may soon be able to tame the ocean, but fools and women will take a little longer."* Agnew's smug response was only the beginning, as the news media went out of its way to portray feminists as humorless, hairy-legged, man-hating shrews.

Nevertheless, 1970 was a watershed year for women's liberation. Americans could not pick up a magazine or newspaper or watch TV without encountering the women's movement in some form. The wheels of change began to turn. Women united to organize child-care centers, women's

Women's Strike for Peace and Equality in New York City (1970).

Those marketing their products to women seemed decidedly oblivious to the women's liberation movement and continued to portray females in stereotypical roles. Feminists protested by giving "Plastic Pig" awards to offending companies and slapping "This Ad Insults Women" stickers on sexist ads.

The Moynihan Report, a government study made public in 1965, blamed the problems of urban poverty not on discrimination or lack of opportunity, but on **black, female-headed families**. It concluded that a mother-dominated culture created by slavery had led to families where women earned most of the money and favored their daughters over their sons. The report judged the black family to be "a tangle of pathology," which was the main obstacle keeping its members from getting ahead in the world. Though many scholars have since disputed the report's conclusions, it nonetheless shaped public opinion for years to come.

health collectives, rape crisis centers, and battered women's shelters.

MANY POINTS OF VIEW A major challenge facing the movement stemmed from the fact that feminists came from many different backgrounds. Consequently, they did not always agree on either the nature of the problems or the solutions. As one early feminist pointed out, *"There are almost as many points of view as there are women in the movement."* As in earlier generations, this made the movement tremendously complex and chaotic.

Black women were divided about whether race or sex was the larger issue. The Black Nationalist movement, which advocated violence and separatism, was in full swing by the late 1960s. It welcomed neither sympathetic whites nor women. Groups like the Black Panthers criticized women for taking on leadership roles. Their macho message, according to activist **Angela Davis**, was that a woman's job was to "inspire her man and educate his children." Female separatists felt sidelined in spite of the fact that **Elaine Brown** became the leader of the Black Panthers in the early seventies. Black Nationalists also accused black women of being so strong and domineering that they raised weak sons and undermined black men. This put black women in a tricky position, since by 1974, single moms stood at the head of one-third of black families. Writer **Maya Angelou** pointed out that black women tried to live in "the crossfire of masculine prejudice, white illogical hatred and black lack of power." **Michele Wallace**, a teenager at the time, remembered her shock at being dismissed because she was a girl: *"It took me three years to fully understand . . . that the countless speeches that all began 'the Black man' . . . did not include me."*

While some black women joined the feminist movement, others felt that racism was a far greater obstacle. **Ida Lewis**, the editor of *Essence* magazine, described women's liberation as "basically a family quarrel between white women and white men. And on general principles, it's not good to get involved in family disputes. The role of black women is to continue the struggle in concert with black men for the liberation and self-determination of blacks." Other black women, however, felt the need to organize, and formed the National Black Feminist Organization in 1973.

Latinas, an increasingly diverse group made up of individuals from numerous Latin American countries, had similar issues. They asked themselves, were they women first, or Chicanas? In 1972, when **Jennie Chavez** called for them to "rely on each other to fight the injustices of the society which is oppressing our entire ethnic group," she was accused of selling out to white ideas and of dividing the existing Chicano group. She responded that although "Chicanas, traditionally, have been tortilla makers, baby-producers, to be touched but not heard," she felt that they were now "ready to activate themselves" and begin "a new revolution within a revolution." In reality, loyalty to Hispanic men and feminist demands for abortion rights kept many Hispanic women from joining the movement.

On Mother's Day in 1973, **Yvonne Wanrow** was convicted by an all-white jury in the shooting death of a man who had attempted to molest her son. Her trial highlighted the unequal treatment of Native Americans in the criminal justice system. Native Americans and feminists rallied behind her. In the end, Wanrow was given probation and community service in lieu of jail time.

There were still other women who worried little about feminist concerns because they were too busy attempting to adjust to life in America. These included Vietnam War brides and thousands of Indochinese refugee women, many of whom had escaped Vietnam, Cambodia, and Laos crammed in dilapidated boats. Between 1965 and 1985 the number of Asian Americans increased from one to five million.

Native American women also charted their own course. Having discovered their voice during the activism of the sixties, a group of women from forty-three tribes and twenty-three states organized the North American Women's Association in 1970. Another group founded Women of All Red Nations (WARN) in 1974. With the women's movement raging around them, they did not seek liberation from their men, but rather worked to improve conditions for all Native Americans. **Madonna Gilbert**, one of WARN's founders, later explained that, *"Indian women have had to be strong because of what this…system has done to our men…alcohol, suicides, car wrecks, the whole thing. And after Wounded Knee, while all that persecution of the men was going on, the women had to keep things going."*

Even so, many of the causes that WARN members championed involved women's issues. They publicized the abuses of Bureau of Indian Affairs clinics that routinely sterilized Native American women without their consent. After discovering in 1974 that more than half of all Native

*"We are **American Indian** women, in that order. We are oppressed, first and foremost, as American Indians, as peoples colonized by the United States of America, **not** as women."*

—**Lorelei DeCora Means**, Winnebago activist

American children were living in non-Indian homes, institutions, or boarding schools, Indian women lobbied for an Indian Child Welfare Act, which was passed by Congress in 1978. The act granted Indian nations the right to control adoptions involving their tribal members. Activists also exposed the health hazards of uranium mining and toxic waste disposal on reservations.

Lesbians were another group who found themselves within and sometimes at odds with the women's movement. While individual women had chosen to live with female partners for hundreds of years without much notice, women's liberation provided a space for these women to more openly explore their relationships with other women. Daughters of Bilitis, a lesbian group formed in 1956, moved from a general policy of trying to quietly fit in, to that of going public. Younger lesbians split off to form their own more confrontational groups, including the Radicalesbians in 1970 and the Furies in 1971. Though focused on gaining acceptance within society, their members also participated in virtually every other aspect of the feminist movement.

Some radical feminists felt that having relationships with other women was the highest expression of women's liberation. While some

"Young women, especially, must take in these lessons so that instead of being intimidated by the activism of the 1960s, they will realize that they are basically like us and that, like us, they, too, can make change. If youth learns to build on the knowledge that lies in our history, they can go even further than we have. Who knows; together we may even be able to throw open the gate."

—feminist Carol Hanisch

In 1963, **Helen Andelin** published the best-selling book *Fascinating Womanhood.* In it she taught women how to become "domestic goddesses"—a role that brought "a different kind of glory than men enjoy." She told women that when a "red-blooded man comes in contact with an obviously able, intellectual and competent woman . . . he simply doesn't feel like a man any longer." Her recipe for true happiness included some dos and don'ts: Do be dependent, child-like, self-sacrificing, trustful, tender, and submissive. **"Don't be efficient in men's affairs such as leadership, making major decisions, providing a living, etc.**" She pointed out that by merely teaching a wife to admire her husband's manliness and muscles, one couple had averted divorce and the husband had bought the wife furniture rather than taking a trip to Japan.

heterosexual feminists accepted this, others feared that association with gay issues would turn mainstream Americans against feminism altogether. For this reason NOW initially rejected association with lesbians. Betty Friedan called them the "lavender menace." Lesbians within the movement decided to claim the name and "staged an invasion of the Second Conference to Unite Women wearing lavender T-shirts with 'lavender menace' emblazoned. During the welcoming address, they hit the lights and took over the stage." According to one onlooker, "It was great theater and good fun, and defused a potentially divisive issue." In the end, many feminists chose to accept their lesbian sisters; however, general acceptance of lesbians has been elusive.

AT HOME

"AREN'T YOU WORKING YET?"

HOMEMAKERS AND WOMEN'S LIBERATION In theory, many Americans believed that it was only fair to give women equal pay and access to work and education. To question the underlying beliefs that governed people's personal lives was another matter. Many stay-at-home moms felt attacked and undermined by feminists. One frustrated homemaker told a reporter,

"My wife doesn't work."

"I work all day at my job. I take pride in keeping my house not only clean but beautiful....I cook 'real' meals rich in nutrition and flavor. I do the research necessary so that my family can know and enjoy Strufoli at Christmas, Assata di Grano at Easter. I pass along to them their rich Italian heritage—songs I remember from my own childhood, stories I was told. I plan our vacations carefully. Yet liberated women keep asking me, 'Aren't you working yet?' What do they think I've been doing these past 18 years?"

The authors with their stay-at-home mother, **Alice Bell Hemming,** in 1967.

Another woman quipped, "Mothers of children from the ages of two to ten are too busy to be liberated." Some reasoned that they were already being pulled in so many directions, that the women's movement would only complicate their lives further. In 1965, one Pittsburgh housewife complained, *"I feel like a pie cut up in six pieces being served to a dinner party of ten."*

Some stay-at-home moms felt that they were dubbed as "either victims or fools." They felt scorned and defensive as some feminists gave little value to women's traditional contributions to society. In fact, in 1982, Betty Friedan admitted that the women's movement's "blind spot" was the family. "It was our own reaction against the wife-mother role that alienated women in middle class America."

Working-class women had never quite faced the sting of "the feminine mystique" in the same way as middle-class women. For one, most of them

As a result of the women's movement, many men took a more active role in parenting. However, in 1988, researchers at the University of Florida reported that married mothers who were employed full-time were still doing 70 percent of the housework.

were already working outside the home, and hadn't had the chance to experience the problem with no name. One woman pointed out, *"If your husband is a factory worker or a tugboat operator, you don't want his job."* Consequently, many working-class women placed high value on being able to stay at home. They retorted that their jobs did not leave them fulfilled, just tired. Their perception was often that the women's movement was only for white, middle-class, bored women who had nothing better to do with their time than stage protests.

Still others agreed with the move toward equality for women, but feared the consequences of voicing their agreement. **Louise Woodward** recalled that she quietly absorbed feminist beliefs and felt an inward "Yeah!" However, she said, *"I didn't say anything out loud because I didn't know what man would slap me down."* Reflecting this reluctance to be associated with the women's movement, a 1975

Until the 1960s, most Americans considered themselves plain meat and potatoes types. **Julia Child** revolutionized American cooking with the debut of her TV program *The French Chef* in 1962. A middle-aged woman who had learned to cook in Europe, Child demonstrated that gourmet food was within the grasp of the average cook. Cheery and humorous, she nonetheless was very serious about food and set the stage for a whole new generation of American chefs. Child's favorite motto? "Above all, have a good time."

Top ten girl's names of the 1970s: **Jennifer, Lisa, Michelle, Kimberly, Amy, Angela, Melissa, Heather, Maria, and Amanda.**

poll indicated that while 63 percent of the women interviewed favored most changes to improve the status of women, they did not want to be labeled as "women's libbers." A barrage of negative media took advantage of these differences of opinion and attempted to undermine the movement by pitting women against one another.

Whether or not a person agreed with women's liberation, the questions feminists asked affected people's personal lives. Change occurred in small, but important ways. Husbands began to take a larger role in child care. Many women sought more education. Marriage ages rose. Attitudes changed. **Anna Davis**, who had grown up doing housework and making her brothers' beds, remembered making changes within her own family. "I was very careful with my kids growing up. I made them both do everything. *I remember my son saying to me, 'doing the dishes that's a girl's job,' and I said, 'No, that's your job this week.'*"

> *When Dartmouth College went coed in 1973, students at the 200-year-old university hung sheets out their windows with the message, "No girls." Alumni threatened to withdraw their donations, and people lamented, "***There goes the football team***." Quotas remained in place; two boys were admitted for every girl. In 1983, Columbia College became the last Ivy League school to become coeducational.*

EDUCATION

"THERE GOES THE FOOTBALL TEAM": COLLEGE

Beginning in the 1960s, many all-male colleges began to worry about declining enrollments. In order to enlarge their applicant pools, more and more schools opened their doors to female students. Harvard granted its first degree to a woman in 1963 (though it took another ten years for it to open its libraries to women and become fully coed). Yale

> After MIT excused their low female enrollment by saying they lacked housing, philanthropist **Katherine Dexler McCormick** paid for construction of two women's dorms in 1962 and 1968.

began to admit women to undergraduate programs (as 15 percent of the class) in 1969. In order to accelerate the pace, the Women's Equality Action League (WEAL) filed lawsuits against more than one hundred colleges and universities. American medical schools responded by eliminating admission quotas for women. In 1959, only 504 women were admitted to medical school; by 1975 there were 3,647. With more options available, enrollment of young women in college shot up from 1.2 million to 3.5 million between 1960 and 1972. By 1979, there were more women than men going to college.

Many Hispanic American girls were the first in their families to attend college. Inspired by the movements for equality and civil rights, Latinas helped create campus organizations that emphasized unity and pride in their heritage. Among other activities, they protested the Vietnam War, donated their time to United Farm Worker efforts, pressured schools to institute Chicano studies programs, and volunteered in clinics and schools.

Christine Leonard, one of the February Sisters, during the occupation of the University of Kansas's East Asian studies building.

Gerda Lerner, one of women's history's founding mothers, wrote, "When I started working on women's history [in the early 1960s] the field did not exist. **People didn't think that women had a history worth knowing.**"

PAID WORK

WHAT SHALL I BE?

One dramatic example of college women working for change took place on a snowy night in Kansas. On February 4, 1972, a group of twenty students and four children sneaked into the East Asian studies building of the University of Kansas. These women, who came to be known as the February sisters, chained the doors and barricaded the windows. Several dozen women distributed leaflets, notifying the administration that they would occupy the building until the school agreed to improve health care, child care, pay, and employment opportunities for women. They also called for the formation of a women's studies department. The administration met their demands, creating long-term benefits for women and men at the University of Kansas.

Only four years after the first women's studies classes at San Diego State College in 1970, they were offered at more than one thousand colleges and universities. A growing number of academics questioned the prevailing assumption that only men "made" history. Historians began retrieving women's lives from historical obscurity. Academics also took a closer look at literature written by women.

In 1966 a girl could become the proud owner of the board game What Shall I Be? The Exciting Game of Career Girls. The object of the game was to "become a career girl," meaning that the player could be a ballet dancer, teacher, nurse, airline stewardess, or actress. As players moved their pieces around a board graced with smiling, uniformed women, they gathered heart-shaped cards highlighting personal qualities needed for each career.

At the time What Shall I Be? was created, few questioned the game's assumptions that women were naturally equipped for certain activities and not others, a belief that followed them from the home to the workplace. The presumption that men were smarter and more capable than women was so much a part of everyday life that even those dedicated to social causes didn't always see through it. According to writer Caroline Bird, racial discrimination made people angry, but discrimination against women "struck most people as funny." Even so, the core notion that a woman's only role was homemaker was beginning to collide with the reality of many women's lives.

"The other day my six-year-old daughter said she wanted to be a nurse when she grew up. 'Why not a doctor?' I asked. She looked at me scornfully. 'Only boys can be doctors.' Her words tore me to shreds. I will not allow her to believe them. I am a feminist."

—**Sophy Burnham**, reporter, 1970

PROFESSIONS, NOT JUST JOBS

More than ever before, women of all ages, marital status, and class earned wages. By the end of the 1960s, about half of all U.S. women were employed. Yet most worked in stereotypically female jobs, with low pay, low prestige, and limited advancement. The newest generation of young women emerged from college with higher expectations. Having watched their own mothers toil at dead-end jobs, they rejected the idea that they should do the same. Many took advantage of education, changing attitudes, and new laws to pursue better opportunities. Doors began to open.

Describing the problem young women faced when they tried to plan for their futures, writer Caroline Bird wrote in 1968, "Most girls find it hard to plan what they are going to do when they have reared children whose fathers they have not yet met."

Game pieces from What Shall I Be? The Exciting Game of Career Girls.

April Lou, a teacher in Manhattan, poses with her Chinese immigrant students.

In March of 1970 dozens of women marched into the offices of the Ladies' Home Journal and declared, "**We are the Women's Liberation Movement**. We shall now read our demands." They occupied the office of an editor who had once referred to his readers as "**mental defectives with curlers in their hair**." Protesters milled around the office, picnicked on the floor, and passed around the editor's cigars. After eleven hours, the head editor agreed to negotiate. In the end, the women won eight pages of space in the August issue and an agreement that the Journal would look into an on-site day-care center.

Women began training for and working in fields that had always been reserved for men. Between 1960 and 1970, the number of female dentists, lawyers, and doctors doubled. Those who paved the way felt they had to overachieve to win the respect of male colleagues. **Margaret Taylor**, one of the few women lawyers in the United States, remembered, "This was a man's profession and the harder you worked and the less you acted like a woman . . . the better off you were going to be. That's how you survived. The idea wasn't to change things around . . . it was to make yourself fit in." By 1988, there were more than 100,000 female physicians, making up 20 percent of all doctors. Their numbers had more than doubled in a decade.

In the 1970s some church congregations began ordaining women to their ministries. The first female disc jockeys hit the airwaves. For the first time, women were hired as conductors of symphony orchestras. Women also ventured into jobs as mechanics, construction workers, electricians, and carpenters. In spite of harassment from coworkers, **Kathleen Ryan** and her roommate paid their way through college by driving cabs in New York City.

Infiltrating the male work world was not easy; the women who did often felt like pioneers. **Susan Eisenberg** compared becoming an electrician in the 1970s to falling in love with someone forbidden. Her new knowledge of tools and her growing muscles gave her great pride. She also remembers that women who drove by where she worked would honk and wave in support.

At the same time, being the only woman on the job could be lonely. Some male coworkers resented

Have you ever heard of . . . Iris Rivera?

Thanks to Rivera, women no longer have to get coffee for their bosses. In 1977, Rivera, a legal secretary, was fired for refusing to make coffee. Women organized to get her job back. Rivera's action challenged a deeply ingrained notion that women should be responsible for domestic responsibilities even at work.

her presence and made her life miserable. Others became her friends and mentors. When Eisenberg realized she was expecting her first child, she was embarrassed to tell anyone. Like others in her position, it became her job to educate coworkers and figure out how to combine career and home life. Later, she loved to show her children the jobs they "worked together" while she was pregnant. "It gave me a powerful appreciation for the changes we have brought about. 'We built that, Susie?' my daughter asks as we drive by a big hotel. 'You bet!' I tell her."

The shift from working jobs to pursuing professions meant that more women viewed wage work as a long-term investment. Jobs opened up in a number of nontraditional fields such as aerospace, electronics, banking, insurance, and restaurant and

These Virginia coal miners were among the first women to work underground after winning that right by taking their fight all the way to the U.S. Supreme Court (1978).

Some women who chose to stay in traditionally female jobs felt disrespected by feminists. An African American nurse told *Ms.* magazine in 1973: "You will never know how hostile I become every time I hear a feminist berate a woman because she is a nurse. What can possibly be more liberating than an opportunity to earn money? Or does liberation mean we have to be doctors? I thought it meant being able to make choices." According to a veteran airline stewardess, "I don't think of myself as a sex symbol or a servant. **I think of myself as somebody who knows how to open the door of a 747 in the dark, upside-down and under water.**"

Have you ever heard of . . . Katherine Graham?

When her husband committed suicide in 1963, she was propelled into a world where men were in charge and women were invisible—she inherited the *Washington Post.* Graham quickly learned the ropes of newspaper production. Under her leadership, the *Post* became a first-rate newspaper that provided cutting-edge news, including uncovering the Watergate scandal. By the time Graham handed the *Post* over to her son almost thirty years later, she also owned *Newsweek* and a number of cable, TV, and radio stations—worth more than $2 billion.

After all their efforts, women still made significantly less money than men. In 1955, women working full time made 63.9 cents to a man's dollar. By 1968, that had fallen to 58 cents per dollar. Despite various efforts to create equality, in 1987, women still only earned 70 cents for every dollar earned by men. The difference in earning power could be catastrophic for single women with dependents. This became especially evident in the case of divorce or the death of a husband. Between 1965 and 1978 divorce rates doubled. Sociologists noted with concern that poverty was becoming an overwhelmingly female problem, with 40 percent of poor families headed by women.

FARMWORKER'S UNION Not all working women were able to pursue careers. Many continued to toil at difficult and low-paying jobs like housekeeping and farm work. These jobs were not even guaranteed minimum wage under the law. Although migrant farmworkers were the

hotel management. By 1975 women made up 40 percent of the workforce.

But the freedom to have a profession did not necessarily improve the quality of life for women. Family relationships, social programs, and salaries did not keep pace with changes in the workplace. Many women ended up working a double shift—going to work, then returning home to carry out traditional responsibilities. Decent and affordable day care was difficult to find. Opponents insisted that making day care more affordable would only encourage more women to work. In 1972, President Richard Nixon vetoed the Comprehensive Child Development Act, which would have provided day care for everyone who needed it, regardless of income level.

> "I'm a woman. I'm a black woman. I'm a poor woman. I'm a fat woman. And I'm on welfare. In this country, if you're any one of those things—poor, black, fat, female, middle aged, on welfare—you count less as a human being. If you're all those things, you don't count at all. Except as a statistic. . . . **Welfare is like a traffic accident**. It can happen to anybody, but especially it happens to women. That is why welfare is a women's issue."
>
> **—Johnnie Tillman**, chair of the National Welfare Rights Organization

backbone of U.S. agriculture, their living conditions were abysmal. Disease, malnutrition, and exposure to pesticides reduced life expectancy to about forty-seven years for these workers. The infant mortality rate for children of farmworkers was, and still is, double that of the rest of U.S. workers.

What One Woman Did

"It's Way Past Time"

When **Jessie Lopez de la Cruz** was thirteen years old she could carry a sack of cotton that weighed more than she did the length of a city block, weigh it, and haul it up an eight-foot ladder to dump it. Like other migrant farmworker children, she moved with her family from job to job and attended school when she could. De la Cruz remembered one camp where her family nailed together grape crates to live in. Employers were not small family farms, but large conglomerates that frequently used violence and underhanded means to quell worker discontent.

In the early 1960s, De la Cruz was married and had raised seven children when union organizer Cesar Chavez knocked on her door. All her life she had wondered what she could do about the injustices she and other migrant farmworkers experienced, and here was someone at her kitchen table insisting that women should be involved with the union of United Farm Workers. She knew immediately that she wanted to play a part and that she needed to get the word out to other women. De la Cruz talked as she worked. "I'd be chopping cotton," she recalled, "and I'd talk about the union to people in rows right next to me." She told them that it should no longer be taken for granted that women would stay home and do the cooking and cleaning. *"It's way past time when our husbands could say 'You stay home! . . . You have to do as I say!'"*

Nearly half of farmworker union organizers were women. They helped stage strikes and successful boycotts to demand fair working conditions. But they also focused on issues that directly influenced their quality of life, such as housing and sanitation, health, family and immigrant support services, care for the elderly, and bilingual education. As a result, the state of California passed laws protecting farmworkers in 1974.

HEALTH

WOMEN'S BODIES

By the 1960s, women were healthier than they had ever been. By 1990, life expectancy had risen even higher, with white women living to an average age of seventy-nine and black women living to almost seventy-four years of age (outliving men by seven to nine years). Advances in public health had radically checked the host of ills that had commonly taken

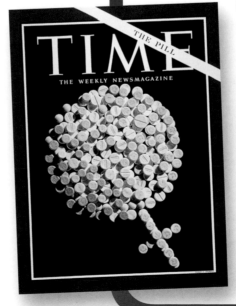

Did you know?

The first oral contraceptive, known as "the pill," went on the market in 1960. As the easiest and most effective means of preventing pregnancy, the pill revolutionized the bedroom, making it possible for women to separate sex from having babies. Journalists, social scientists, and church leaders looked on with interest to see how this would affect U.S. women. By the end of the decade it was the contraceptive of choice for 60 percent of married couples.

Roe v. Wade Perhaps no issue has created more controversy or divided more Americans than the question of who should control female fertility and sexuality. Until the mid-1800s, abortion was legal, if socially frowned upon. After it was outlawed in the United States, thousands of women lost their lives in secretive, botched attempts to end pregnancies. Some were young unmarried girls or victims of rape or incest. Most, however, were married women who for various reasons felt they could not care for another child. As the women's movement gathered steam in the 1960s, advocates for legal abortion argued that the question was not whether women should get abortions, because women were already risking their lives to get abortions. The question, they said, was who should decide when a woman's situation was such that she could not follow through with a pregnancy. In 1969, two young female lawyers agreed to take on the case of a pregnant twenty-one-year-old Texas woman who was divorced, jobless, and couldn't care for her five-year-old daughter. **Linda Coffee** and **Sarah Weddington** eventually argued her cause before the U.S. Supreme Court in a case known as *Roe v. Wade*. In a 1973 decision that generated fierce dissent and changed numerous lives, the court ruled that abortion was legal during the first three months of pregnancy. This shifted the responsibility of decision making from the government to individual women. This was not the end of the story, however. Battles over abortion rights raged throughout the eighties and have continued to the present.

lives earlier in the century. Even so, women had little specific knowledge about their own bodies and frequently felt misunderstood and dismissed by their doctors. This was particularly a problem among minority and poor women, who were more likely to receive substandard care. Some were even used as test populations for new medications and medical techniques.

By 1975, 98 percent of women delivered their babies in hospitals. While technology and scientific knowledge had decreased the risk of death and injury from childbirth, physicians had instituted a number of unnecessary medical procedures that made having a baby uncomfortable and embarrassing. These interventions made giving birth seem unnatural.

Newborn babies were immediately whisked away from their mothers to nurseries where they were often given baby formula rather than breast milk. Husbands were not allowed in delivery rooms.

The idea that a doctor always knew best was so prevalent that few women thought to challenge their treatment. However, in 1969, participants at a women's conference began chatting about their medical experiences. They found they shared much in common, including feeling "less valuable than men" and having been taught to have shame and embarrassment about their bodies. They decided that if women had more knowledge about their own health, they could make informed choices and advocate for themselves.

At the end of the conference, eleven women aged twenty-five to forty-one agreed to research women's health topics and write papers about them. They called themselves the Boston Women's Health Book Collective. Within a year, they transformed their papers into locally taught courses, and then into the first book on women's health written for women, by women: *Our Bodies, Ourselves.* The Collective explained why the book was exclusively about women:

"Our answer is that we are women and, as women, do not consider ourselves experts on men (although men through the centuries have presumed to be experts on us). We are not implying that we think...men are much less alienated from their bodies than women are. But we know that it is up to men to explore that for themselves."

International versions of *Our Bodies, Ourselves.*

Our Bodies, Ourselves addressed topics that were still often discussed in hushed tones: birth control, mental health, sexuality, abortion, rape, and sexually transmitted diseases. It also contained chapters about basic anatomy, health, nutrition, pregnancy, childbirth, and aging. In addition to creating an informational handbook, the Collective analyzed the health care system and proposed

Did you know?

The term *AIDS* (acquired immune deficiency syndrome) was used for the first time on July 27, 1982. The effects of this disease have grown to epidemic proportions, with an estimated 33 million people in 2007 infected with the virus worldwide.

concrete ways to better meet women's needs.

By 1976 the book had been reprinted three times in the United States, along with an edition in Braille. By the late 1970s, the book had been published in Spanish in the United States, as well as Japanese, French, and Italian for sale throughout Europe and Japan. With recent editions in Albanian (2006) and Russian (2007), *Our Bodies, Ourselves* has been culturally adapted into twenty-three languages worldwide and used for community outreach and advocacy on women's health issues.

Perhaps more important, *Our Bodies, Ourselves* became a starting point for those wishing to make health care more responsive to the specific needs of females. Gradually, more women attended medical school, women's clinics opened, and the public became better informed about female health. Some mothers reclaimed the experience of giving birth without medical interventions and attended childbirth classes. Breast-feeding came back in vogue. By 1979, the *New York Times* reported that the number of trained midwives was on the rise.

BEAUTY

"IS IT MATCHING YOUR SOUL?"

In 1962 nearly 56 million viewers gazed in awe as **Jacqueline Kennedy**, the new first lady, conducted

Have you ever heard of . . . Mary Kay Ash?

Following in the footsteps of earlier female entrepreneurs, she began Mary Kay Cosmetics in 1963 with $5,000, a shelf of skincare products, and the help of friends and her three children. She chose the bumblebee as her company symbol, saying, "It isn't supposed to fly but goes right on trying—just like women who didn't know they could fly but they did." Ash gave jewelry and pink Cadillacs as incentives to her beauty consultants. Her company was worth $22 million by the late seventies.

the first televised tour of the White House. Jackie Kennedy modeled grace and good taste. The youthful first lady was intelligent and fluent in French. She was also a fashion icon with coifed hair, pearls, crisp matching suit and gloves, and elegant pumps.

In the early 1960s, it was important to be a "lady," and ladies in schools and offices around the country followed dress codes. For example, the University of Kentucky instructed female coeds to wear wool dresses, hats, and gloves to church and tea, dresses to football games, and sweaters and skirts to class. According to one woman, *"When I was in college in the early sixties, women were required to wear skirts to classes—except when the weather was below zero!"* More adventurous women copied actress **Audrey Hepburn**'s boyish look—slim,

with short hair, fitted shirt, and pegged pants—but only out of the classroom or office.

"EVERYTHING WENT YOUNG IN '64" People had little warning of the huge fashion upheaval of the 1960s. Artist Andy Warhol later said, "Everything went young in '64. The kids were throwing out all the preppy outfits and dress-up clothes that made them look like their mothers and fathers, and suddenly everything was reversed—mothers and fathers were trying to look like their kids." Fashion was full of wild extremes. Women sported long dresses and "maxi" coats or miniskirts with knee socks or go-go boots that zipped to the knee. Animal prints and large, colorful, floral and striped patterns graced outfits, and fake fur was everywhere. Women strutted about in platform shoes. Fringe adorned shirts and jackets. Colorful crocheted ponchos masqueraded as coats.

Twiggy, a teenage fashion model from London, demanded attention in 1967 with her big-eyed, baby-doll look. At 5'6" and only 90 pounds, she had a "waif like body with thin shoulders and hollow chest, a pale face with huge, elaborately made-up eyes." Twiggy's unhealthy thinness set a damaging new ideal for girls to follow. Diet books and programs gained popularity. While the term

QUITE A CATCH!

Illustrator **Betty Brader**'s department store advertisement highlights the dramatically different fashions of the late 1960s.

anorexic was unknown until the 1980s, girls and women were already experiencing eating disorders.

Identifying with their African heritage, and the slogan Black Is Beautiful, some blacks wore African-print fabrics. Sixteen-year-old Michele Wallace gave up "makeup, high heels,

Have you ever heard of . . . Mary Quant?

In 1965, this Englishwoman introduced the miniskirt. For the first time in American history, girls wore skirts far above the knee. She explained, "You'll see the world differently from inside a mod minidress than in a shirtwaist and girdle." Quant also introduced makeup styles that featured pale pink or nude lip gloss and heavy black eyeliner around the eyes.

stockings, garter belts, girdles," and wore "T-shirts, dungarees, or loose African print dresses" with sandals.

"I wore black velvet hot pants [short shorts] and black boots to prom," laughed **Jane Lipscolm**, who was a high school senior in 1970. "My sister wore a belly outfit with puffed sleeves. I think she put a gem in her naval." The two girls from a small Midwestern town carried a needle and thread to hike up the skirts on their Catholic school uniforms once they left the building. Their mother, however, still tried to look more formal. "Oh, the ruined vacations because my mother's hairdo got messed up in the pool," recalled Lipscolm. "We spent all this time looking for the right bathing cap."

COUNTERCULTURE Some young people openly rejected mainstream American culture in a movement dubbed "counterculture." Hippies, as they were called, donned gauzy Indian print dresses or shirts and ratty bell-bottom jeans. They accessorized with headbands, sandals, strings of

beads called "love beads," peace signs on belts and jewelry, and tiny wire-rimmed "granny" glasses. Their point was antifashion—to prove that the way a person dressed didn't matter. But instead, hippie attire became the fashion and soon mainstream Americans wore tie-dyed shirts, sensible shoes, and ever-widening bell-bottoms. **Miyako Moriki**, raised by traditional Japanese parents, remembered, "When I was going to college my mother thought the way I dressed was outrageous. Like the hippie kids, [I wore] bright clothes, grew my hair long."

Like many, **Barbara Haber** temporarily "opted out of the system" and became a hippie. "I wore my hair in braids," she remembered. *"I smoked dope, I wore long dresses and sandals. Lived in collectives, made my own bread, ate granola, ate yogurt…was a vegetarian for awhile."* Hippies called themselves "flower children" and rebelled against what they viewed as the conformity and materialism of their parent's generation, often experimenting with hallucinogenic drugs. A popular slogan among hippies was "don't trust anyone over 30."

When the rock-musical *Hair* opened on Broadway in 1968, its title confirmed what people already knew: that **hair could be used to make a political statement**. Native Americans reclaimed the long braids of their past. Black youth scandalized their parents by growing long, nappy hair or brushing it out from their heads in big hairdos called Afros. Their message was that black was beautiful. Individual genders became less obvious as women clipped their locks and men grew theirs . . . or the other way around.

Elements of the **counterculture** *began to make their way into homes in the forms of patterns and colors, lava lamps, beads hung in doorways, and tie-dyed textiles. Many women began to reject the processed foods of their mothers' generation and took up baking their own bread, making their own yogurt, and drying their own fruit. Health food and making food from scratch became popular. Décor and diet often reflected where a person fit into the culture at large.*

Rocker **Janis Joplin** said of her hippie attire, "Anything that interferes with my thing, baby, forget it. The secret is freedom, and that means no bras or girdles. You got to do what you want to do and wear what you want to wear. Everybody is so hung up on the matching game—the shoes have to match the bag which matches the coat and dress. **But the big question is, is it matching your soul?"**

For women, the new, relaxed sexuality removed old restraints and stigmas. At the same time, it allowed men to exploit women by being sexually involved with them without any commitment. Many women felt pressured to have sex in order to prove that they were liberated, not "uptight."

By the late 1960s, many schools and workplaces began to relax their dress codes. The *New York Times* cheerfully reported in October 1970 that *"without any confrontation, demonstration or even artful campaigning, women are securing for themselves another human right: the right to wear pants to work.* The privilege is being granted by men in industry, government, and financial institutions who have long since given up the struggle to keep women from wearing pants at home." **Leslie Hampton**, a secretary who had sweltered in layers

Los Angeles, 1967: hippies gather for a "love-in," a celebration of peace and love.

of nylons, girdles, and clothing said, ***"What a moment of freedom that was when we decided not to do that anymore—no more girdles!"***

AMUSEMENTS

Raised in a time of relative prosperity and ease, 1960s middle-class adolescents joined their parents in considering entertainment a right. Creating fun for Americans was big business.

FIVE HOURS A DAY: TELEVISION

As more Americans sat glued to their TV sets for longer—an average of five hours a day by 1965—they participated in a national debate about women's changing roles and what they meant. Television sometimes celebrated women's aspirations, but just as often, it ridiculed and dismissed them. Sitcoms and variety shows frequently poked fun at feminism—depicting it as a silly notion being imposed upon women.

Television producers tried to attract the most viewers by shooting for the middle of the road. They didn't want to take on controversial subjects such as civil rights and the women's movement. But if you look closely at the shows that appeared in the sixties and seventies, you can glimpse the underlying tensions of American life. Just as women were underrepresented in powerful jobs, they were underrepresented in television. Only 30 percent of TV characters were female, and most of these were dependent, in one way or another, on the men in their lives.

The pioneering *Mary Tyler Moore Show* aired on television from 1970 to 1977. The first episode began with Mary, a single woman, moving to Minneapolis to take a job in a TV newsroom. She chose a traditionally male career over marriage. Critics complained that the show's writers did not make Moore independent enough. She still walked a fine line between femininity and assertiveness (few people believed a woman could be both feminine and assertive) and took on a nurturing role with office mates. Even so, *Mary Tyler Moore* was the first

For the first time, a number of black characters and sitcoms aired on TV. *Julia* was a show about the young widow of a Vietnam veteran. It broke ground in 1968 as the first television series featuring an African American woman as the main character. Other minorities continued to remain conspicuously absent from television.

In 1968, feminists were concerned when the new educational children's show *Sesame Street* featured "a world virtually without female people." Though a woman—**Joan Ganz Cooney**—created and produced the show, nearly all the original humans and puppets were male. **Jane Bergman** protested in the *New York Times,* writing, "For a little girl engaged in her own passionate struggle for self-definition, watching 'Sesame Street' last year . . . was like taking lessons in invisibility."

their next tough, independent, outspoken women leads until 1988–89, with the premiere of sitcoms *Rosanne* and *Murphy Brown.* Both shows took on a range of subjects untouched by other popular shows at the time. Behind the scenes, however, women made little progress in television production. They still earned substantially less than their male counterparts, and produced, directed, and wrote fewer than 21 percent of that season's top programs. The **Oprah Winfrey** *Show*'s first national broadcast in 1986 set into motion a long stream of successes that would result in Winfrey's current status as one of the world's most powerful women.

FROM "JELL-O DELIGHTS" TO *MS.* MAGAZINE

Since their inception, magazines aimed at women were almost completely owned, run, and edited by men. Activist **Susan Brownmiller** described them as "a make-believe world of perfect casseroles and Jell-O delights [where] marriages failed because wives didn't try hard enough [and] single parent households did not exist." For years men had written many of the articles offering women advice about how to live their lives.

show to suggest that a woman could find satisfaction in her job and that working was not just something to fill the time until she married. The show explored equality issues that popped up in homes and workplaces across the country.

The *Mary Tyler Moore Show* marked a larger trend in American society. No longer was a single woman automatically viewed as loveless, ugly, and deserving of pity. In fact, being single was fashionable and "cool." More women and men were waiting to get married, or not getting married at all. And in the meantime, they had fun. Nightclubs and discotheques catered to the new "swinging singles." The image of the single woman became one of independence and confidence.

In the early 1980s, television was not a hospitable place for most female characters. Shows such as *Dallas*, *Knots Landing*, and *Dynasty* captured audiences with catfighting, backbiting, money-grabbing shrews. Viewers wouldn't get

A 1972 children's album entitled *Free to Be . . . You and Me* promoted radically different ideas about what it meant to be female and male. This brainchild of actress **Marlo Thomas** used stories and songs to tell children that they could be anything they wanted, regardless of their gender. Girls could run fast and drive trucks; boys could cry and play with dolls; and both should help with the housework.

Gloria Steinem.

What One Woman Did

A New Kind of Magazine

Enter **Gloria Steinem**, a hardworking, glamorous freelance journalist who became the new feminist superstar. Steinem bucked media stereotypes that portrayed feminists as unattractive, lonesome, bitter women, by being simultaneously bright, beautiful, and successful.

Steinem was a relative newcomer to the women's movement, but she quickly found her place as one of its main voices by instigating a magazine run and written by women. Though for years feminists had produced hundreds of underground publications, none of them were designed for a widespread audience. *Ms.* magazine set out to provide a national forum for feminist ideas.

Founding a new kind of women's magazine proved to be complicated. Steinem and others had difficulty convincing prospective investors that a feminist magazine would sell. Even so, in December of 1971, a sample issue of *Ms.* magazine hit the shelves.

At the outset, newscaster Harry Reasoner predicted that *Ms.* would run out of material in six months. Instead, the magazine sold out in eight days and continued a long, successful run. It appealed to a broad readership from housewives to professional women.

Ms. magazine was experimental in a number of ways. First, because opinions about feminism varied, it was a place where numerous and sometimes opposing points of view could be discussed. The magazine also challenged trends and rejected standard beauty and food advertising. As a publishing enterprise, its offices doubled as a center of activism and a place to try out ideas about equity in the workplace. Some staff members brought their small children to work with them.

Spring 1972 issue of *Ms.*

"I AM WOMAN, HEAR ME ROAR": MUSIC

As much as any other medium, music marked the tides of social change through the 1960s and 1970s. From the girl groups of the early sixties to the disco and hard rock of the late seventies, young women had a wide range of musical role models.

Decked out in snappy, matching outfits and singing songs about teenage longing and relationships, girl groups topped the pop charts starting in 1960. Most successful girl groups, like the Shirelles, the Supremes, the Ronettes, and the Shangri-las, were African American. They set a black standard of beauty and were idolized by teenaged girls, regardless of race. They sang openly about conflicting teenage desires. For example, did "good girls" go all the way, and if they did, would the boy still love them? ("Will You Love Me Tomorrow," the Shirelles).

As social issues such as civil rights, the Vietnam War, and the environmental and women's movements captured the attention of America's youth, folk music joined rock and roll and jazz on college campuses. Folk music became a voice for many causes as young people tried to separate themselves from what they saw as mind-numbing conformity, materialism, and warmongering of the older generation. Musician Frank Zappa aptly noted in 1967 that many young people were no longer loyal to "flag, country or doctrine, but only to music."

The new folk singers were purposefully different from female performers of the past. They wore their hair long, shunned makeup, and opted for more comfortable garb. They also believed they could help change the world through music. Singers like **Joan Baez**, **Judy Collins**, and **Mary Travers** of Peter, Paul, and Mary demonstrated to girls that it was possible to be both political and female. Baez and black folk singer **Odetta** took up the cause of Hispanic farmworkers. Sioux Indian **Buffy Sainte-Marie** wrote songs about pacifism and the mistreatment of American Indians. **Malvina Reynolds** protested suburban conformity. America's young women sat up and listened.

Other singer/songwriters appealed specifically to the growing number of young, single, professional women. They also dressed for themselves, not for men, and sang about the complexities of their

Janis Joplin in 1970, the year of her premature death.

relationships. They celebrated friendship and sang about things that mattered to other women. **Carole King** won four Grammies in 1971 for her album *Tapestry*. **Helen Reddy**'s anthem "I Am Woman" rose to the top of the charts in 1972 and also won her a Grammy.

At the same time, rock music became more male-dominated, white, overtly sexual, and often antiwoman. Amid this "Under My Thumb" world of rock and roll of the late sixties and early seventies, women were camp followers and little else. Only a handful of women managed to rise through the ranks—among these were **Grace Slick** of Jefferson Airplane and **Janis Joplin** of Big Brother and the Holding Company. Joplin made her big debut in 1967 and worked to keep pace with male rock stars. She appeared intent on outdrinking and outswearing them, slept with members of her band, and became addicted to heroin. In 1968, *Life* magazine featured her in an article about "The New Rock." Describing her voice as "raw and tortured," the article continued, "Janis stomps. The band plays harder and faster. Faces twist. Janis screams.

In the 1960s dancing partners broke away from each other. **Dancing** was no longer a contact recreation where boys led and girls followed. Instead, dancers jerked and gyrated independently. Parents were baffled as young people did the twist, locomotion, pony, monkey, slop, and mashed potatoes. Kids also danced the go-go, hitchhiker, frug, watusi, and the woodpecker.

'Come on, come on, come on and take it. Take another little piece of my heart now baby. Oh yeah, now take it.'...Her hair thrashes, and she picks up a bottle she keeps with her and belts down more Southern Comfort." It seemed that only her mother asked, *"Janis, why do you scream like that when you've got such a pretty voice?"* Joplin's lifestyle was unsustainable and in October 1970, she died of a heroin overdose.

In the midseventies, disco made its debut. Unlike sixties protest music, disco was not particularly concerned with lyrics. Disco was about rhythm and dancing—dancing seductively in slinky synthetic dresses, shiny lip gloss, and tall shoes. Disco divas like **Donna Summer** celebrated a gyrating, sparkling sexuality that encouraged girls and women to be free. At the same time, disco lyrics said nothing about the consequences of such freedom. This was an easier kind of liberation that suggested girls did not need to attend law school—

they simply needed to become seductive dancing queens.

In the early 1980s, a new celebrity with sultry good looks and confidence to spare upped the ante. With her first hit single, "Holiday," in 1983, twenty-six-year-old **Madonna Louise Ciccone** was on the road to becoming a household name. Madonna paired openly sexual lyrics with catchy tunes. She also pushed at religious boundaries, juxtaposing sexuality with religious themes in songs such as "Papa Don't Preach" and "Like a Prayer." Even her name, a centuries-old term for the mother of Jesus, seemed to mock convention. While some were offended, others viewed Madonna as powerful and free of society's conventions. She also had a new medium—one that would carry her messages to a much wider audience. The invention of MTV and music videos added a new dimension to listening to music. Madonna's talent at reinventing herself ensured that she would continue churning out hits. However, when she appeared on stage sporting an iron cone bra, some wondered if this was progress for women.

GYM FLOORS AND PBJ SANDWICHES: SPORTS

In 1971, only one in twenty-seven girls played a sport of any kind. In spite of the numerous female athletes who had paved the way in the preceding decades, there were only a few poorly funded women's athletic programs. While male college athletes enjoyed great perks and huge budgets, female athletes shared uniforms, provided their own transportation, brought their own food, slept on gym floors, and often helped to set up and take down chairs for spectators. When the men's swim team at Michigan State decided they needed their pool for a practice, the women had to hold their meet in a pool that was too shallow. **Laura Siebald** remembered, *"Some of the divers came away from that meet with chipped teeth, bruised heads and scratches from colliding with the bottom of the pool."* Help was on the way in the form of government legislation.

TITLE IX Title IX stands out as some of the most important legislation passed for women since they

> "I think it's ridiculous the way we are treated. . . . They just wouldn't take us seriously. We practiced at 6 in the morning so we wouldn't get in the way of the men's team. . . . To compete in meets we had to borrow boats from other schools. We fund-raised with bake sales, raffles and car washes. . . . Crew is demanding and difficult under the best conditions, but practicing at six in the morning with flashlights when ice is forming on the oarlocks and you can't see two feet in front of you, well, it's almost unbearable."
>
> —**Betsy Hochberg**, member of Boston University's women's crew team, 1974

On September 20, 1973, thousands watched "the battle of the sexes" between top-ranked tennis star **Billie Jean King**, and former Wimbledon champion Bobby Riggs. Riggs had insisted for years that female athletes were inferior, and declared that even an "old man" could beat King. Billie Jean King trounced Bobby Riggs in three straight matches. Sports commentator Howard Cosell observed, "I suppose we all expected this match to have some high humor in it. Instead it seems to have become a very, very serious thing because the comedy has gone out of Bobby Riggs." King commented, "When I die, at my funeral, nobody's going to talk about me. They're all going to stand up and tell each other where they were the night I beat Bobby Riggs."

Have you ever heard of . . . Nancy Lopez?

Lopez won her first golf tournament at age nine and was the top amateur in the world at sixteen. As a twenty-one-year-old golfer in 1978, she made more money than any rookie, man or woman, ever had. California-born Lopez was a role model for other Latina athletes, and helped to move women's professional golf into the mainstream.

received the vote. Passed by Congress in 1972, Title IX stated that schools receiving federal funds could no longer discriminate on the basis of sex. In other words, high schools and colleges getting money from the government could not exclude women from programs like law and medicine. They risked losing money if they didn't provide equal athletic opportunities for women. Congress gave schools six years to comply.

Many schools dragged their feet and looked for ways to be exempt. Athletic directors across the country saw women's athletics funding as a threat to already established men's athletic programs. Many declared that Title IX would be the ruin of male college athletics. The athletic director at the University of Kansas, voicing the feelings of many other directors, announced that he would give women's athletics all the help he could "as long as it wasn't financial." The next year, women athletes at Ohio State received $40,000 out of a $6 million athletic budget. In 1974, the University of Maryland gave women's sports $30,000 out of its $2.2 million budget; Texas A & M gave $200 to ten women's sports.

But the threat of losing their federal funding proved a forceful incentive to change. The Women's Sports Foundation, founded by female athletes in

Have you ever heard of . . . Chris Ernst?

Ernst and her Yale Women's Crew teammates demanded equal treatment. They entered the athletic director's office and took off their shirts to reveal "Title IX" scrawled across their backs and chests. Ernst then read their demand for a women's locker room. Photos were published the next day in the *New York Times*. The women got their showers.

1975, pressured the government to follow through on its threat if schools did not comply.

Title IX promised equal access to such things as equipment, facilities, training, housing, travel allowances, scholarships, and publicity. The masses of girls and women who dove into sports proved that many had been standing on the sidelines just waiting for the opportunity to play. The number of women's high school cross-country teams increased from 77 in 1972 to 7,475 in 1982. During the same time span, the number of women participating in intercollegiate sports rose from 16,000 to 160,000. Physical fitness came to be seen as important for everyone, not just men. Finally it was acceptable for girls to have muscles, too.

"The sooner little boys begin to realize that little girls are equal and that there will be many opportunities for a boy to be bested by a girl, the closer they will be to mental health."—**Sylvia Presser**, *hearing examiner, ruling that girls be allowed to play little league baseball in New Jersey, 1973. Her ruling was upheld in superior court.*

In 1985, **Lynette Woodard**, a University of Kansas basketball star, was the first woman to sign with the Harlem Globetrotters. She was soon followed by **Jackie White**.

THE EQUAL RIGHTS AMENDMENT

"WHO'D BE AGAINST EQUAL RIGHTS FOR WOMEN?"

Feminists seeking equality for women in all facets of life resurrected an Equal Rights Amendment (ERA) suffragists had first put before Congress in 1923. The amendment stated: *"Equality of rights under law shall not be denied by the United States or any State on account of sex."* Between 1923 and 1970, the ERA had been introduced in every session of Congress, but had never even reached the House of Representatives or Senate. The time had finally come when there was enough popular support for this amendment to pass through Congress and make its way to the states for ratification.

The idea of equal rights for women had certainly gained popularity. In fact, by the early 1970s, both the Democratic and Republican parties had endorsed the ERA in their conventions. When the amendment came before Congress in 1972, it passed by large margins (354 to 23 in the House, 84 to 8 in the Senate) and was sent to the states for ratification. Twenty-two states ratified the amendment in the first year and eleven in the next two years. The ERA had to be ratified by 38 states by 1982 or die.

Congress buzzed with activity, and passed an abundance of equity laws. During this time, Representative **Bella Abzug** recalled, *"We put sex discrimination provisions into everything. There was no opposition. Who'd be against equal rights for women? So we just kept passing women's rights legislation."* In 1973, Congress passed the Equal Employment Opportunity Act. No longer could an employer turn a woman away saying that the job she was applying for was for men only. Other legislation included everything from improving training and counseling programs for women to tax deductions for child care. At the same time, the courts were busy striking down laws that gave preference to men

ERA supporters show their solidarity at the Alice Paul Memorial March in August 1977, a month after the suffragist and ERA author's death.

In 1968, **Shirley Chisholm** was the first black woman elected to the U.S. House of Representatives. This achievement was tempered by another decline. From 1962 to 1969, the number of women in the House of Representatives dropped from a record high of twenty down to eleven. One female member of the House complained, "There are three times as many whooping cranes as congresswomen. While many things are being done to protect the rare, long-legged bird, nobody seems concerned about our becoming an endangered species." In response, Chisholm and others founded the National Women's Political Caucus to help elect women at all levels of government. She went on to present herself as **the first black woman candidate for president** in 1972. Chisholm's campaign slogan was "Unbought and Unbossed."

in myriad ways. Schools began to look at curricula and textbooks to eliminate sexist attitudes. It seemed that nothing could slow the progress of the women's movement.

But somehow, by 1975, things had changed. Alselma Dell'Olio remembered her sense that *"feminism has lost forward movement."* In 1975, only one state ratified the ERA. Another state ratified in 1977. With so much initial support, how could things have turned around so completely within such a short period of time?

THE ANTI-ERA MOVEMENT The answer can be summed up in one name: **Phyllis Schlafly**. Schlafly founded a group called STOP ERA just after the ERA passed Congress. She and her followers denounced the ERA as antifamily and antireligion—an attack on the roles of women as wives and mothers. In her opinion, feminists were home wreckers who were "eroding the fabric of our families." On one ABC special, Schlafly stated that feminists "just

By 1981, 101 men had served on the U.S. Supreme Court. In that year, **Sandra Day O'Connor** became the first woman appointed to the Court. Though in childhood she dreamed of growing up to be a rancher, she attended law school instead. She graduated third in her class, but at her first job interview she was told, "I might be able to get you a position here as a legal secretary. But we've never hired a woman here as a lawyer and I don't see the time when we will do it." As a Supreme Court justice, she gained a reputation for evenhanded judgments.

Anti-ERA demonstrators protest at the White House in 1977.

don't want to be nice. They want to be ugly." She succeeded in convincing many Americans that if the ERA passed, their daughters would be drafted into the army, women and men would find themselves sharing public bathrooms, and women would no longer be able depend on a "traditional" system where men provided for their families. If the ERA passed, she told Americans, life as they knew it would completely disintegrate.

Change for women was and still is a contested topic, one that arouses a great deal of fear in some people. Catering to that uncertainty, Schlafly engaged women who had never before been involved in political action. She organized grassroots campaigns by using women's informal networks to spread the word about rallies and letter-writing campaigns. Anti-ERA activists created "telephone trees": each woman they called would call five more

women, and so on. In this way, thousands of women were rallied to action cheaply and efficiently.

Schlafly borrowed some of the theatrical tactics used by feminists to stage her own media-attention-grabbing events. As the Illinois legislature debated ERA ratification, her supporters converged on the capital wearing flowing white dresses, trailing flowers, and passing out homemade bread and apple pie to legislators. Holding rallies just before the evening news, Schlafly sometimes featured children carrying signs that read, "Please don't send my mommy to war." She made it appear that the fight over the ERA was between typical moms and fringe "women's libbers," often demonizing the women who spoke out against an unjust system that limited their choices.

Feminists could not combat the fear created by the well-organized anti-ERA movement. After

> *"The media image of feminists as unattractive women who are bitter because they can't get a man has frightened off women for decades and still does. Even many who were prepared to call themselves feminists have wanted to dissociate themselves from the unattractive, presumably bitter ones."*
>
> —*feminist* Dana Densmore

counterparts and continud to perform a majority of the housework and child care. Women chipped away at the barriers that kept them from reaching the upper levels in their jobs.

The media blamed the women's movement for "creating a generation of unhappy single and childless women." After all, hadn't they got what they wanted—equality and opportunity? **Susan Faludi**, in her best-selling 1991 book *Backlash: The Undeclared War Against American Women*, responded that American women's struggles stemmed not from too much equality, but from not enough. Many of the changes, as it turned out, were cosmetic, masking a lingering sense of female inferiority. Faludi wrote, *"Feminism asks the world to recognize at long last that women are . . . half (in fact, now more than half) of the national population, and just as deserving of rights and opportunities, just as capable of participating in the world's events, as the other half."* One group of artists in New York couldn't have agreed more.

1977, no more states ratified the ERA, and five attempted to rescind their ratifications. In the end, the amendment was three states shy of ratification. On June 30, 1982, feminists across the country mourned its death. Two thousand women stood across from the White House to support **Eleanor Smeal** of NOW when she announced that though the ERA was dead, "We are not going to be reduced again to the ladies' auxiliary." Meanwhile, Phyllis Schlafly and her supporters basked in a celebration where the band played "I Enjoy Being a Girl" and "Ding, Dong, the Witch Is Dead."

BACKLASH Though the women's movement had initiated noticeable changes in the lives and interactions of American families, many social inequalities continued to exist (and continue to this day). In the following decade, women made up two-thirds of America's poor adults. Most working women still earned considerably less than their male

ARTS IN THE SPOTLIGHT

"FIGHTING DISCRIMINATION WITH FACTS, HUMOR, AND FAKE FUR"

Imagine it is 1985, and the Museum of Modern Art in New York City is putting on a show that features the brightest stars in contemporary art. This show is so important that the curator insists that any artist not in the show "should rethink his career." Of course it will feature a wide range of artists, right? Wrong. Of the 169 artists exhibited, only 13 are women, and none are people of color. What is most surprising is that the art world hardly recognizes

> *"Sometimes, battling sexism in the normal way just won't do. Sometimes, you must don a gorilla mask, adopt the name of a dead female artist and send estrogen pills to the White House."*
>
> —**Heather Svokos,** Lexington (KY) *Herald-Leader*

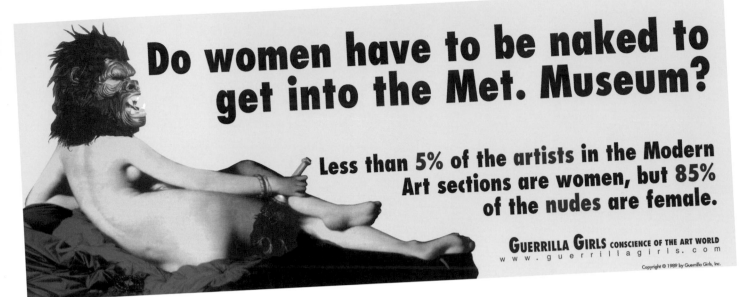

this omission as an oversight. You would like to do something to call attention to the ironies of the situation. A little humor perhaps? How about putting on a gorilla mask and plastering posters like the one above all around the city?

This is how a group called the Guerrilla Girls began. Since 1985, the Guerrilla Girls have dubbed themselves the "conscience of culture" and produced numerous posters, stickers, books, and billboards; staged protests; and given lectures combating sexism and racism in the arts. While performing missions, each Girl wears her mask and assumes the name of a dead female artist in order to remain anonymous.

> "Our situation as women and artists of color in the art world was so pathetic, all we could do was make fun of it. It felt so good to ridicule and belittle a system that excluded us."
>
> —Guerrilla Girl
> Paula Modersohn-Becker

When asked how they could stand wearing those masks all day, **Emily Carr*** responded, "It's hot." To which **Paula Modersohn-Becker** added, "Not as hot as we make it out there." **Alma Thomas** concluded, "But we look so beautiful, it's hard to complain."

Initially, the Guerrilla Girls' actions were met with "skepticism, shock, rage, and lots of talk," remembers **Anais Nin**. Another Girl, **Romaine Brooks**, recalls,

We just wanted to have a little fun with our adversaries and to vent a little rage. But we also wanted to make feminism (that "f" word) fashionable again, with new tactics and strategies. It was really a surprise when so many people identified with us and felt we spoke for their collective anger. We didn't have the wildest notion that women in Japan, Brazil, Europe and even Bali, would be interested in what we were doing.

In more recent years, Guerilla Girls have been invited to speak at some of the very institutions they have attacked. By jumping into the fray, they have joined the myriads of women past and present who have worked to give women an equitable and respected place at the American table.

*All Guerrilla Girl names are pseudonyms.

Your Time
1990–Present

This is your time. The story that begins this chapter is yours. You, your friends, and your family are participating in history as it unfolds. In 2006 the U.S. Census Bureau reported 151.9 million females and 147.5 males in the United States. Where do you fit in? How is your life experience typical or atypical when compared to other Americans? Is there even such a thing as typical? Writing history is the process of looking back at events and trying to make sense of what happened. If you were asked to write this chapter, what would you say? How would you characterize the last twenty years?

As with women in any previous generation, those living today have to adapt to the challenges of the times. Some of these challenges might be familiar to those living in earlier eras; others are particular to this moment in time. What struggles do you and your peers have that your parents or grandparents didn't have to face? What great strides have women made in your lifetime? What problems have continued to be frustratingly persistent? How has the world changed in the last two decades? Which of these changes do you view as positive ones? Which seem to you to be negative? Where do the women in your life fit into the historical narrative?

Looking back, it is easy to feel that historical outcomes were simply meant to be, and that the

Gabrielle Wyatt worked to improve her community by serving as a student member of the Baltimore County Public School Board in 2006.

future is always a move toward something better. For example, it might seem obvious that women would eventually get the right to vote or that U.S. courts would outlaw wife abuse. In reality, nothing in history was inevitable. While the world you live in is often the result of decisions made long before you were born, you have the opportunity, through the choices you make, to affect the world you will leave to your children and their children. Your legacy is up to you.

AT HOME

Look closely at the ways your family and the families around you operate. How would you describe your home life? How do you view marriage? Who does most of the work around your house? How much are you required to contribute? How is your family similar and different from others you've observed? Do you know any stay-at-home dads? How does our society respond to the women who choose to stay home with their children? Compare your household inventory (number of TVs, bathrooms, toys, computers, telephones, etc.) to what your parents had when they were growing up. How has technology changed household work?

On September 3, 2000, **Gloria Steinem**, famous second-wave feminist and founder of *Ms.* magazine, again made headlines when she chose to marry for the first time at the age of sixty-six. In responding to those who felt that this was a rejection of her former radical feminism, she said, *"Feminism is about the ability to choose what's right at each time in our lives."*

Did you know?

- In 2004, women bore an average of 1.9 children, down from 3.1 children in 1976.
- Following divorce, moms retain custody of their children nearly 70 percent of the time. With divorce ending one in two marriages, and with more than one-third of children born outside of marriage, single women head more households than ever before. Single women often struggle to keep their families housed, fed, and clothed. Researchers have expressed concern about this "feminization of poverty."
- Reported incidents of domestic violence dropped 21 percent from 1993–98.

In what ways have things stayed the same? What household technologies do you take for granted? What if you needed to live without these?

Not everyone has a home to return to. The National Law Center on Homelessness and Poverty estimates that, in the United States, 700,000 to 2 million people are homeless at any given time. Close to 36 percent of those are families with children. This out-of-work lumber worker and her children lived under an interstate highway bridge in Oregon (1992).

PAID WORK

What jobs do you see women doing? While women have made great progress in the workplace, there are still areas of inequality. In what areas do you see the need for improvement? How do the women around you balance the often-competing demands of work and home? Are there factors women need to consider when choosing a career that men do not? Which jobs are still carried out primarily by one gender or the other? Why do you think this is? Are there sufficient supports in place to help working parents with child care and other quality of life issues?

Nancy Pelosi, the first woman Speaker of the House of Representatives, brought her worlds of work and family together at her 2007 swearing-in ceremony in a way that few men would consider. Pictured here with her grandchildren and other children, she said, "*Having five children in six years is the best training in the world for Speaker of the House*.... It made me the ultimate multitasker and master of focus, routine, and scheduling."

The work of poorer women, often immigrants, makes it possible for other women to have careers. **Yessie Hernandez**, a high school student in Dallas, Texas, joins in a 2006 protest against an immigration reform bill that would put undocumented immigrants in jail.

Did you know?

- In a remarkable change from the previous generation, two-thirds of women with children under the age of three work for pay. This compares with 18 percent in 1900, 30 percent in 1950, and 48 percent in 2000.

- In September 2004, women made up 15 percent of the armed forces. Of 212,000 women on active duty, 35,100 women were officers and 177,000 were enlisted.

- In 2004, women aged 15 and older who worked full time, year-round, earned a median of $31,223. These workers made 77 cents for every dollar earned by males.

- In October 2001, only six of the 500 largest U.S. corporations where headed by a female CEO.

- In 1983, **Sally Ride** became the first American woman in space aboard the space shuttle Challenger. She was followed in 1984 by **Kathy Sullivan**, who was the first woman to walk in space. In 1992, **Mae Jemison** was the first African American woman in space. In 1999, NASA's 95th shuttle mission had a woman as commander—Colonel **Eileen Collins**.

- In 1992, Dr. **Antonia Novello**, a native Puerto Rican, became the first female surgeon general.

- The top ten occupations for women in 2001: manager, secretary, cashier, sales supervisor, registered nurse, elementary school teacher, nursing aide, bookkeeper, and waitress.

A migrant husband and wife team from Mexico harvest apples in Bridgeville, Delaware (2003).

EDUCATION

What is the main objective of education today? In other words, what do people hope to gain by going to school? How has your education differed from that of your parents? What levels of education have the women around you obtained? Have you observed any subtle or not-so-subtle biases in your own educational background? Are there differences in the ways girls and boys are taught? Do textbooks portray a world inhabited by women as well as men? Do they promote any gender stereotypes? What are the big educational debates at the moment?

> In 2001, when **Ruth Simmons** assumed the presidency at Brown University, she became the first African American woman to head an Ivy League university.

Did you know?

- In one recent study of teacher education textbooks, researchers **Karen Zittleman** and David Sadker found that only 7 percent of the material included women's contributions to history.

- In 2004, 88 percent of women graduated from high school. Thirty-one percent of women had attained a bachelor's degree or higher by the age of twenty-nine. The rates for men were slightly lower, with 85 percent finishing high school and 26 percent receiving bachelor's degrees.

- In 2006, women earned 59 percent of the bachelor's degrees and 60 percent of the master's degrees awarded in the United States.

AMUSEMENTS

What do you and your friends and family do for fun? If you watch sports on TV, do women's and men's teams or sports receive the same coverage? Do you see a difference in the ways that the women and men in your life use their free time? Do they have the same amount of free time? When you

Did you know?

- During the 2003–04 school year, 2.9 million girls participated in high school athletic programs. That same year, 162,752 college women participated in an NCAA sport. Compare this to 1972–73, when only 817,073 girls were involved in high school athletics.

- The popularity of Team USA soccer in 1999 helped to launch the first ever women's professional soccer league, the WUSA (Women's United Soccer Association). Though the league only lasted for three seasons, women's soccer lovers can look forward to newly forming professional soccer teams in WPS (Women's Professional Soccer), with games slated to begin in 2009.

- "[A] study published in December [2007] by the Pew Internet & American Life Project found that among Web users ages 12 to 17, significantly more girls than boys blog (35 percent of girls compared with 20 percent of boys) and create or work on their own Web pages (32 percent of girls compared with 22 percent of boys)."—*New York Times,* February 21, 2008, online edition

Players on Team USA wait for **Brandi Chastain** to take the final penalty shot in the FIFA Women's World Cup in July 1999. They beat Team China 5 to 4 after two overtimes.

read the newspaper or watch television or movies, how are women depicted? Have you looked at any teen magazines recently? What messages are they sending to young people?

In 1999, **Toni Murden** became the first woman to row alone across the 3,000 mile Atlantic Ocean. She docked her vessel, American Pearl, in Guadeloupe following her 81-day, 7-hour, 31-minute journey. She negotiated her way through the 20-foot seas of Hurricane Lenny. Quite an adventurer, Murden also cross-country skied to the South Pole in 1989.

Did you know?

- Cosmetic surgical and nonsurgical procedures have increased 456 percent in the last ten years. Women underwent 91 percent of those procedures, with breast enlargement and liposuction being the most common.
- The annual estimated revenue for the diet industry is $40 billion each year (up from $8 billion in 1990).

HEALTH

How knowledgeable do you think today's women are about health issues particular to women?

How do the problems of obesity and America's obsession with thinness affect women today? How has the process of pregnancy and childbirth

BEAUTY

What part does fashion play in America today? Who decides what is "in"? How would you describe today's fashions? Clothing? Hairstyles? Accessories? Are there any women's fashions that seem to defy common sense or that might seem silly to the next generation? Are there any trends that could actually be destructive to a woman's health? Who or what is considered beautiful? What messages do advertisements send about beauty and women's bodies?

Beth Russett, a Maine Migrant Health nurse–practitioner, told the photographer in 2007, "For me, practicing health care out of the back of a van in the middle of a migrant camp, handing out free medicines and talking to people about their story and how they got there and work they do, feels like a privilege."

changed for women of your generation? How has the wide availability of birth control changed the lives of the women around you? Does the fact that you could live to be eighty years old or older affect the decisions you make about exercise and eating?

Did you know?

- In 2005, life expectancy for black women was 76.5 years; for white women it was 80.8.

- The average age of an American woman having her first baby is 26.7. In 1970, it was 21.4.

- Many women changed their behavior when they learned that smoking could harm their infants' health. Cigarette smoking among pregnant women declined from 19.5 percent in 1989 to 11 percent in 2003.

- The American Anorexia and Bulimia Association estimates that 1 million women develop eating disorders each year.

- In 2002, the Centers for Disease Control and Prevention (CDC) reported that over 50 percent of American females are overweight and 25.8 percent are obese.

ARTS IN THE SPOTLIGHT

Do you think that women have achieved the same level of visibility as men in the arts?

What barriers might new female artists and musicians still face today? Of the movies you see, and the books that you read, how many of them are directed or written by women? How are women portrayed in current films, music, literature, and art?

"Why is it men are permitted to be obsessed about their work, but women are only permitted to be obsessed about men?"
—Barbra Streisand, performer and director

Professor, book editor, and novelist **Toni Morrison** is known for her intense stories set within black communities. Her best-selling novel *Beloved* earned her the Pulitzer Prize in 1988. In 1993 she became the first African American woman to win the Nobel Prize for Literature.

Top ten girls' names in 2007: ***Emily, Isabella, Emma, Ava, Madison, Sophia, Olivia, Abigail, Hannah, and Elizabeth.***

Did you know?

- Conductor **Marin Alsop**'s 2005 appointment as music director of the Baltimore Symphony Orchestra made her the first woman to lead a major American orchestra.

- In the spring of 2007 the Guerrilla Girls (see the end of chapter 9) completed a project for the *Washington Post* where they looked at the number of women and artists of color on display at the National Gallery of Art. When they revealed that the museum had only one (hastily installed) sculpture by an African American artist, a group of concerned employees at the museum formed an advocacy group called the Gallery Girls to address inequalities.

- When the 2007 Cannes International Film Festival commissioned thirty-four filmmakers to make special three-minute movies to be shown during the festival, they chose only one female director.

WHERE DO WE GO FROM HERE?

On June 7, 2008, **Hillary Rodham Clinton**, a U.S. senator from New York and former First Lady, concluded her run for the presidency of the United States. She came closer to victory than any woman in U.S. history. In conceding the Democratic primary presidential election to Senator Barack Obama of Illinois, she spoke of being unable "to shatter that highest, hardest glass ceiling this time." But, she said, "thanks to you, it's got about 18 million cracks in it. And the light is shining

In 1984, when **Geraldine Ferraro** became the first woman nominated by the Democrats for vice president of the United States, she said, "Tonight the daughter of an immigrant from Italy has been chosen to run for vice president in the new land my father came to love." The ticket lost, and it would be another 24 years before the next woman, **Sarah Palin**, of Alaska, would receive the Republican vice presidential nomination in 2008.

through like never before, filling us all with the hope and the sure knowledge that the path will be a little easier next time." She called to mind the struggles of suffragists, abolitionists, and civil rights workers to make a better world, and declared,

> *"Because of them, and because of you, children today will grow up taking for granted that an African American or a woman can yes, become President of the United States. When that day arrives and a woman takes the oath of office as our President, we will all stand taller, proud of the values of our nation, proud that every little girl can dream and that her dreams can come true in America. And all of you will know that because of your passion and hard work you helped pave the way for that day."*

How will your passion and hard work pave the way for those still to come? Will you help shatter remaining glass ceilings? Will you stand on the shoulders of the women who have gone before you to create a better world? The next chapter of American history belongs to you and your children and grandchildren. What will that story be?

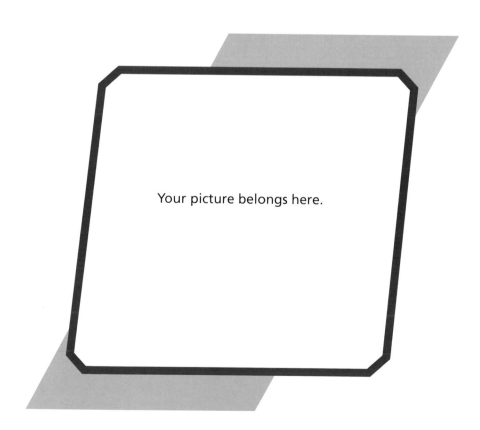

Your picture belongs here.

Bibliography

GENERAL HISTORIES

Ashelford, Jane. *The Art of Dress: Clothes and Society, 1500–1914.* London: National Trust, 1996.

Banner, Lois W. *Women in Modern America: A Brief History.* New York: Harcourt Brace College Publishers, 1984.

Berkin, Carol Ruth, and Mary Beth Norton. *Women of America: A History.* Boston: Houghton Mifflin Company, 1979.

Bolden, Tonya. *33 Things Every Girl Should Know About Women's History.* New York: Crown Publishers, 2002.

Collins, Gail. *America's Women: 400 Years of Dolls, Drudges, Helpmates, and Heroines.* New York: Perennial, 2003.

Colman, Penny. *Girls: A History of Growing up Female in America.* New York: Scholastic, 2000.

Cott, Nancy F., ed. *No Small Courage: A History of Women in the United States.* Oxford, UK: Oxford University Press, 2000.

DuBois, Ellen Carol, and Lynn Dumenil. *Through Women's Eyes: An American History.* Boston: Bedford/St. Martin's, 2005.

Eakins, Pamela, ed. *The American Way of Birth.* Philadelphia: Temple University Press, 1986.

Evans, Sarah M. *Born for Liberty: A History of Women in America.* New York: Free Press, 1989.

Faragher, John Mack, Mari Jo Buhle, Daniel Czitrom, and Susan H. Armitage, eds. *Out of Many: A History of the American People.* Upper Saddle River, NJ: Prentice Hall, 1997.

Harvey, Sheridan, Janice E. Ruth, Barbara Orbach Natanson, Sara Day, and Evelyn Sinclair, eds. *American Women: A Library of Congress Guide for the Study of Women's History and Culture in the United States.* Washington DC: Library of Congress, 2001.

Hymowitz, Carol, and Michael Weissman. *A History of Women in America.* New York: Bantam Books, 1978.

Jones, Jacqueline. *Labor of Love, Labor of Sorrow: Black Women, Work and the Family From Slavery to the Present.* New York: Vintage Books, 1985.

Keenan, Sheila. *Scholastic Encyclopedia of Women in the United States.* New York: Scholastic Reference, 2002.

Kessler-Harris, Alice. *Out to Work: A History of Wage-Earning Women in the United States.* New York: Oxford University Press, 1982.

McClellan, Elisabeth. *History of American Costume, 1607–1870.* New York: Tudor Publishing Company, 1969.

Mintz, Steven, and Susan Kellogg. *Domestic Revolutions: A Social History of American Family Life.* New York: Free Press, 1988.

Rappaport, Doreen. *American Women: Their Lives in Their Words.* New York: Harper Trophy, 1990.

Rosenberg, Rosalind. *Divided Lives: American Women in the Twentieth Century.* New York: Hill and Wang, 1992.

Skinner, Ellen. *Primary Sources in American History: Women and the National Experience.* 2nd ed. New York: Longman, 2003.

Steele, Valerie. *The Corset: A Cultural History.* New Haven, CT: Yale University Press, 2001.

Strasser, Susan. *Never Done: A History of American Housework.* New York: Henry Holt and Company, 1982.

Ware, Susan, ed. *Modern American Women.* New York: McGraw-Hill, 1997.

Weatherford, Doris. *American Women's History: An A-Z of People, Organizations, Issues, and Events.* New York: Prentice Hall General Reference, 1994.

————. *Milestones: A Chronology of American Women's History.* New York: Facts on File, 1997.

Woloch, Nancy. *Women and the American Experience.* New York: McGraw-Hill, Inc, 1984.

INTRODUCTION **WOMEN MAKING AMERICA**

Dobson, Shireen. *The Mother-Daughter Book Club: How Ten Busy Mothers and Daughters Came Together to Talk, Laugh and Learn Through Their Love of Reading.* New York: HarperCollins, 1997.

Lane, Ann J., ed. *Making Women's History: The Essential Mary Ritter Beard.* New York: Feminist Press at the City University of New York, 2000.

————, ed. *Mary Ritter Beard: A Sourcebook.* Boston: First Northeastern University Press, 1988.

National Women's History Project. "Our History." http://www.nwhp.org.

Pipher, Mary. *Reviving Ophelia: Saving the Selves of Adolescent Girls.* New York: Ballantine Books, 1994.

CHAPTER 1 **A REVOLUTIONARY GENERATION** *1770–1800*

Bartlett, Virginia K. *Keeping House: Women's Lives in Western Pennsylvania, 1790–1850.* Pittsburgh: University of Pittsburgh Press, 1994.

Berkin, Carol. *Revolutionary Mothers: Women in the Struggle for America's Independence.* New York: Alfred A. Knopf, 2005.

Berlin, Ira. *Many Thousands Gone: The First Two Centuries of Slavery in North America.* Cambridge, MA: Belknap Press of Harvard University Press, 1998.

Blakeley, Phyllis, and John N. Grant, eds. *Eleven Exiles: Accounts of Loyalists of the American Revolution.* Toronto, Canada: Dundurn Press Limited, 1982.

Blumenthal, Walter Hart. *Women Camp Followers of the American Revolution.* New York: Arno Press, 1974.

Bushman, Richard L., and Claudia L. Bushman. "The Early History of Cleanliness in America." *The Journal of American History* 74 (March 1988): 1213–38.

Cleary, Patricia. *Elizabeth Murray: A Woman's Pursuit of Independence in Eighteenth-Century America.* Amherst: University of Massachusetts Press, 2000.

Clinton, Catherine. *The Plantation Mistress: Woman's World in the Old South.* New York: Pantheon Books, 1982.

Cott, Nancy. *The Bonds of Womanhood: "Woman's Sphere" in New England, 1780–1835.* New Haven: Yale University Press, 1977.

————, ed. *History of Women in the United States: Historical Articles on Women's Lives and Activities,* Vol. 15, Women and War. Munich: K. G. Saur, 1992.

————, et. al., eds. *Root of Bitterness: Documents of the Social History of American Women.* Boston: Northeastern University Press, 1986.

Crane, Elaine Forman, ed. *The Diary of Elizabeth Drinker: The Life Cycle of an Eighteenth-Century Woman.* Boston: Northeastern University Press, 1994.

Dann, John C., ed., *The Revolution Remembered: Eyewitness Accounts of the War for Independence.* Chicago: University of Chicago Press, 1980.

D'Emilio, John, and Estelle B. Freedman. *Intimate Matters: A History of Sexuality in America.* New York: Harper and Row, 1988.

Dinkin, Robert J. *Before Equal Suffrage: Women in Partisan Politics from Colonial Times to 1920.* Westport, CT: Greenwood Press, 1995.

Ellet, Elizabeth F. *The Women of the Revolution.* Vols. 1–3. 1850. Reprint, New York: Hakell House Publishers, 1969.

Evans, Elizabeth. *Weathering the Storm: Women of the American Revolution.* New York: Charles Scribner's Sons, 1975.

Gelles, Edith B. *First Thoughts: Life and Letters of Abigail Adams.* New York: Twayne Publishers, 1998.

Gunderson, Joan. *To Be Useful to the World: Women in Revolutionary America, 1740–1790.* New York: Twayne Publishers, 1996.

Hoffman, Ronald, and Peter J. Albert, eds. *Women in the Age of Revolution.* Charlottesville, VA: University Press of Virginia, 1989.

Hoxie, Frederick E., Ronald Hoffman, and Peter J. Albert. *Native Americans and the Early Republic.* Charlottesville: University Press of Virginia, 1999.

Humphreys, Mary Gay. *Women of Colonial and Revolutionary Times: Catherine Schuyler.* Vol. 4, *New York Heritage Series.* Spartanburg, SC: Reprint Company, 1968.

James, Janet Wilson. *Changing Ideas About Women in the United States, 1776–1825.* New York: Garland Publishing, Inc., 1981.

Johansen, Bruce E. *Forgotten Founders: Benjamin Franklin, the Iroquois and the Rationale for the American Revolution.* Ipswich, MA: Gambit, Inc., 1982.

Kierner, Cynthia A. *Beyond the Household: Women's Place in the Early South, 1700–1835.* Ithaca: Cornell University Press, 1998.

———. *Southern Women in Revolution, 1776–1800: Personal and Political Narratives.* Columbia, SC: University of South Carolina Press, 1998.

Klinghoffer, Judith Apter, and Lois Elkis. "The Petticoat Electors: Women's Suffrage in New Jersey, 1776–1807." *Journal of the Early Republic* 12 (Summer 1992): 159–93.

Mann, Barbara Alice. *Iroquoian Women: The Gantowisas.* New York: Peter Lang, 2000.

Norton, Mary Beth. *Liberty's Daughters: The Revolutionary Experience of American Women, 1750–1800.* Ithaca: Cornell University Press, 1980.

Schafer, Daniel L. *Anna Madgigine Jai Kingsley: African Princess, Florida Slave Plantation Owner.* Gainesville, FL: University Press of Florida, 2003.

Thomas, Isaiah. *A Narrative of the Excursion and Ravages of the King's Troops under the Command of General Gage.* New York: *New York Times* & Arno Press, 1968.

Raphael, Ray. *A People's History of the American Revolution.* New York: New Press, 2001.

Reed, William B. *The Life of Esther De Berdt: Afterwards Esther Reed of Pennsylvania.* Philadelphia: C. Sherman, 1853.

Rappaport, Doreen. *American Women: Their Lives in Their Words.* New York: Harper Trophy, 1990.

Roberts, Cokie. *Founding Mothers.* New York: William Morrow, 2004.

Scholten, Catherine M. *Childbearing in American Society: 1650–1850.* New York: New York University Press, 1985.

Seaver, James E. *A Narrative of the Life of Mrs. Mary Jemison.* Norman, OK: University of Oklahoma Press, 1992.

Sedgwick, Catherine Maria. "Slavery in New England." *Bentley's Miscellany* 34 (1853): 417–24.

Stansell, Christine. *City of Women: Sex and Class in New York: 1789–1860.* Urbana: University of Illinois Press, 1987.

Tardiff, Olive. *They Paved the Way: A History of New Hampshire Women.* Bowie, MD: Heritage Books, 1980.

Thomas, Earle. *The Three Faces of Molly Brant.* Ontario, Canada: Quarry Press, 1996.

Tise, Larry, ed. *Benjamin Franklin and Women.* University Park: Pennsylvania State University Press, 2000.

Ulrich, Laurel Thatcher. *The Age of Homespun: Objects and Stories in the Creation of an American Myth.* New York: Vintage, 2001.

———. *A Midwife's Tale: The Life of Martha Ballard, Based on Her Diary, 1785–1812.* New York: Alfred A. Knopf, 1990.

Vare, Ethlie Ann, and Greg Ptacek. *Mothers of Invention: From the Bra to the Bomb, Forgotten Women and Their Unforgettable Ideas.* New York: William Morrow, 1987.

Dorothy Kelly tees off on a block of ice. She is joined by **Virginia Hunter, Elaine Griggs, Hazel Brown,** and **Mary Kaminsky,** all of Washington DC (sometime between 1920 and 1932).

Volo, James M., and Dorothy Deneen Volo. *Daily Life during the American Revolution.* Westport, CT: Greenwood Press, 2003.

Warwick, Edward, Henry Pitz, and Alexander Wyckoff. *Early American Dress: The Colonial.* New York: Random House Value Publishing, 1988.

Zagarri, Rosemarie. *A Woman's Dilemma: Mercy Otis Warren and the American Revolution.* Wheeling, IL: Harlan Davidson, Inc. 1995.

CHAPTER 2 **CIRCLES OF INFLUENCE** *1800–1840*

Bartlett, Virginia K. *Keeping House: Women's Lives in Western Pennsylvania, 1790–1850.* Pittsburgh: University of Pittsburgh Press, 1994.

Barton, Clara. *The Story of My Childhood.* New York: Arno Press, 1980.

Bergman, Jill, and Debra Bernardi, eds. *Our Sisters' Keepers: Nineteenth-Century Benevolence Literature by American Women.* Tuscaloosa: University of Alabama Press, 2005.

Berlin, Ira. *Many Thousands Gone: The First Two Centuries of Slavery in North America.* Cambridge, MA: Harvard University Press, 1998.

Bleser, Carol. *Tokens of Affection: The Letters of a Planter's Daughter in the Old South.* Athens, GA: University of Georgia Press, 1996.

Bolton, Ethel Stanwood, and Eva Johnston Coe. *American Samplers.* Princeton: Pyne Press, 1973.

Boylan, Anne M. *The Origins of Women's Activism: New York and Boston, 1797–1840.* Chapel Hill: University of North Carolina Press, 2002.

Brewer, Priscilla J. *From Fireplace to Cookstove: Technology and the Domestic Ideal in America.* Syracuse: Syracuse University Press, 2000.

Cott, Nancy. *The Bonds of Womanhood: "Woman's Sphere" in New England, 1780–1835.* New Haven: Yale University Press, 1977.

———, ed. *History of Women in the United States: Historical Articles on Women's Lives and Activities.* Vol. 11, *Women's Bodies: Health and Childbirth.* Munich: K. G. Saur, 1992.

———, ed. *History of Women in the United States: Historical Articles on Women's Lives and Activities.* Vol. 12, *Education.* Munich: K. G. Saur, 1993.

———. *Root of Bitterness: Documents of the Social History of American Women.* Boston: Northeastern University Press, 1986.

Delfino, Susanna, and Michele Gillespie. *Neither Lady nor Slave: Working Women of the Old South.* Chapel Hill: University of North Carolina Press, 2002.

Dewhurst, C. Kurt, Betty MacDowell, and Marsha MacDowell. *Artists in Aprons: Folk Art by American Women.* New York: E. P. Dutton/Museum of American Folk Art, 1979.

Dublin, Thomas. *Women at Work: The Formation of Work and Community in Lowell, Massachusetts, 1826–1860.* New York: Columbia University Press, 1993.

Fenelon, Francois. *The Education of a Daughter.* Baltimore: John Murphy & Co., 1847.

Fox-Genovese, Elizabeth. *Within the Plantation Household: Black and White Women of the Old South.* Chapel Hill: University of North Carolina Press, 1988.

Gates Jr., Henry Louis, ed. *Six Women's Slave Narratives.* New York: Oxford University Press, 1988.

Genovese, Eugene D. *Roll Jordan, Roll: The World the Slaves Made.* New York: Vintage Books, 1976.

Godey's Lady's Book. September 1832: 244.

Grimshaw, Patricia. *Paths of Duty: American Missionary Wives in Nineteenth-Century Hawaii.* Honolulu: University of Hawaii Press, 1989.

Groneman, Carol, and Mary Beth Norton, eds. *"To Toil the Livelong Day:" America's Working Women at Work, 1780–1980.* Ithaca: Cornell University Press, 1987.

Gutman, Herbert G. *The Black Family in Slavery and Freedom, 1750–1925.* New York: Pantheon Books, 1976.

Hall, Margaret. *The Aristocratic Journey: Being the Outspoken Letters of Mrs. Basil Hall Written during a Fourteen Months' Sojourn in America, 1827–1828.* New York: Putnam, 1931.

Hansen, Debra Gold. *Strained Sisterhood: Gender and Class in the Boston Female Anti-Slavery Society.* Amherst: University of Massachusetts Press, 1993.

Jacobs, Harriet A. *Incidents in the Life of a Slave Girl: Written by Herself.* Cambridge: Harvard University Press, 1987.

Jeffrey, Julie Roy. *The Great Silent Army of Abolitionism: Ordinary Women in the Antislavery Movement.* Chapel Hill: University of North Carolina Press, 1998.

Lerner, Gerda. *The Grimké Sisters from South Carolina: Pioneers for Women's Rights and Abolition.* New York: Schocken Books, 1971.

Lindley, Susan Hill. *You Have Stept Out of Your Place: A History of Women and Religion in America.* Louisville, KY: Westminster John Knox Press, 1996.

Martin, Scott C. *Killing Time: Leisure and Culture in Southwestern Pennsylvania, 1800–1850.* Pittsburgh: University of Pittsburgh Press, 1995.

Miller, Lillian B. *The Peale Family: Creation of a Legacy, 1770–1870.* Washington, DC: Abbeville Press, 1996.

Norton, Mary Beth, and Ruth M. Alexander, eds. *Major Problems in American Women's History,* 2nd ed. Lexington, MA: Heath and Company, 1996.

Painter, Nell Irvin. *Sojourner Truth: A Life, A Symbol.* New York: W. W. Norton & Company, 1996.

Perdue, Theda. *Cherokee Women: Gender and Culture Change, 1700–1835.* Lincoln: University of Nebraska Press, 1998.

Rawick, George P., ed. *The American Slave: A Composite Autobiography.* Vols. 1, 7, 9, 12. Westport, CT: Greenwood Press, 1977–79.

———. *From Sundown to Sunup: The Making of the Black Community.* Westport, CT: Greenwood Publishing Company, 1972.

Ryan, Mary P. *Cradle of the Middle Class: The Family in Oneida County, New York, 1790–1965.* Cambridge, MA: Cambridge University Press, 1981.

Samuels, Shirley, ed. *The Culture of Sentiment: Race, Gender, and Sentimentality in Nineteenth-Century America.* New York: Oxford University Press, 1992.

Shoemaker, Nancy. *A Strange Likeness: Becoming Red and White in Eighteenth-Century North America.* New York: Oxford University Press, 2004.

Smith-Rosenberg, Carroll. *Disorderly Conduct: Visions of Gender in Victorian America.* New York: Oxford University Press, 1985.

Sterling, Dorothy, ed. *We Are Your Sisters: Black Women in the Nineteenth Century.* New York: W. W. Norton & Company, 1984.

Theriot, Nancy M. *Mothers and Daughters in Nineteenth-Century America: The Biosocial Construction of Femininity.* Lexington: University Press of Kentucky, 1996.

Wertheimer, Barbara Mayer. *We Were There: The Story of Working Women in America.* New York: Pantheon Books, 1977.

White, Deborah Gray. *Ar'n't I A Woman? Female Slaves in the Plantation South.* New York: W. W. Norton & Company, 1985.

Wilcox, R. Turner. *Five Centuries of American Costume.* New York: Charles Scribner's Sons, 1963.

Yarbrough, Fay. "Legislating Women's Sexuality: Cherokee Marriage Laws in the Nineteenth Century." *Journal of Social History* 38 (2004): 385–406.

Yellin, Jean Fagan. *Women and Sisters: The Anti-Slavery Feminists in American Culture.* New Haven: Yale University Press, 1989.

CHAPTER 3 **GROWING DIVISIONS** *1840–1865*

Acosta, Teresa Palomo, and Ruth Winegarten. *Las Tejanas: 300 Years of History.* Austin: University of Texas Press, 2003.

Attie, Jeanie. *Patriotic Toil: Northern Women and the American Civil War.* Ithaca, NY: Cornell University Press, 1998.

Baker, Nina Brown. *Cyclone in Calico: The Story of Mary Ann Bickerdyke.* Boston: Little, Brown and Company, 1952.

Bank, Mirra. *Anonymous Was a Woman.* New York: St. Martin's Press, 1979.

Blight, David W., ed. *Passages to Freedom: The Underground Railroad in History and Memory.* Washington, DC: Smithsonian Books, 2004.

Bureau of Refugees, Freedmen, and Abandoned Lands. Freedmen and Southern Society Project, University of Maryland, College Park, MD. Original documents at National Archives, Washington, DC.

Bynum, Victoria E. *Unruly Women: The Politics of Social and Sexual Control in the South.* Chapel Hill: University of North Carolina Press, 1992.

Cayleff, Susan E. *Wash and Be Healed: The Water-Cure Movement and Women's Health.* Philadelphia: Temple University Press, 1987.

Clifford, Louise, and Candace Clifford. *Women Who Kept the Lights: An Illustrated History of Female Lighthouse Keepers.* Alexandria, VA: Cypress Communications, 2001.

Clinton, Catherine. *The Other Civil War: American Women in the Nineteenth Century.* New York: Hill and Wang, 1984.

Cowan, Ruth Schwartz. *More Work for Mother: The Ironies of Household Technology from the Open Hearth to the Microwave.* New York: Basic Books, 1983.

Craft, William. *Running a Thousand Miles for Freedom; Or the Escape of William and Ellen Craft from Slavery.* London: William Tweedie, 1860.

Cumming, Kate. *Kate: The Journal of a Confederate Nurse.* Baton Rouge: Louisiana State University Press, 1959.

Diner, Hasia R. *Erin's Daughters in America: Irish Immigrant Women in the Nineteenth Century.* Baltimore: Johns Hopkins University Press, 1983.

Drago, Harry Sinclair. *Outlaws on Horseback: The History of the Organized Bands of Bank and Train Robbers Who Terrorized the Prairie Towns of Missouri, Kansas, Indian Territory, and Oklahoma for Half a Century.* Lincoln: University of Nebraska Press, 1998.

Fales, Martha Gandy. *Jewelry in America, 1600–1900.* Woodbridge, UK: Antique Collector's Club, 1995.

Faragher, John Mack. *Men and Women on the Overland Trail.* New Haven, CT: Yale University Press, 1979.

Fields, Annie. *Life and Letters of Harriet Beecher Stowe.* Boston and New York: Houghton, Mifflin and Company, 1897.

Finley, Ruth E. *The Lady of Godey's: Sarah Josepha Hale.* New York: J. B. Lippincott, 1931.

Fischer, Christiane. *Let Them Speak: Women in the American West 1849–1900.* Hamden, CT: Archon Books, 1977.

Fleischner, Jennifer. *Mrs. Lincoln and Mrs. Keckly: The Remarkable Story of the Friendship between a First Lady and a Former Slave.* New York: Broadway Books, 2004.

Frye, L. Thomas, ed. *American Quilts: A Handmade Legacy.* Oakland, CA: Oakland Museum History Department, 1981.

Green, Rayna. *Women in American Indian Society.* New York: Chelsea House Publishers, 1992.

Hersh, Blanche Glassman. *The Slavery of Sex: Feminist-Abolitionists in America.* Urbana: University of Illinois Press, 1978.

Humez, Jean M. *Harriet Tubman: The Life and the Life Stories.* Madison: University of Wisconsin Press, 2003.

Jacobs, Harriet. *Incidents in the Life of a Slave Girl, Written by Herself.* Cambridge, MA: Harvard University Press, 1987.

Jameson, Elizabeth, and Susan Armitage, eds. *Writing the Range: Race, Class and Culture in the Women's West.* Norman: University of Oklahoma Press, 1997.

A mother and child in about 1911.

Jeffrey, Julie Roy. *The Great Silent Army of Abolitionism: Ordinary Women in the Antislavery Movement.* Chapel Hill: University of North Carolina Press, 1998.

Johnson, Susan Lee. *Roaring Camp: The Social World of the California Gold Rush.* New York: W. W. Norton & Company, 2000.

Kerr, Andrea Moore. *Lucy Stone: Speaking out for Equality.* Piscataway, NJ: Rutgers University Press, 1992.

Larson, Kate Clifford. *Bound for the Promised Land: Harriet Tubman, Portrait of an American Hero.* New York: Ballantine Books, 2004.

Leavitt, Judith Walzer. *Brought to Bed: Childbearing in America, 1750–1950.* New York: Oxford University Press, 1986.

Leonard, Elizabeth D. *Yankee Women: Gender Battles in the Civil War.* New York: W. W. Norton & Co., 1994.

Lerner, Gerda. *The Female Experience: An American Documentary.* Indianapolis: Bobbs-Merrill Educational Publishing, 1977.

Madsen, Susan Arrington. *I Walked to Zion: True Stories of Young Pioneers on the Mormon Trail.* Salt Lake City, UT: Deseret Book Company, 1994.

Maher, Sister Mary Denis. *To Bind Up the Wounds: Catholic Sister Nurses in the U.S. Civil War.* New York: Greenwood Press, 1989.

Million, Joelle. *Woman's Voice, Woman's Place: Lucy Stone and the Birth of the Woman's Rights Movement.* Westport, CT: Praeger, 2003.

Orlofsky, Patsy, and Myron Orlofsky. *Quilts in America.* New York: McGraw-Hill Book Company, 1974.

Pryor, Elizabeth Brown. *Clara Barton: Professional Angel.* Philadelphia: University of Pennsylvania Press, 1987.

Riley, Glenda. *The Female Frontier: A Comparative View of Women on the Prairie and Plains.* Lawrence: University Press of Kansas, 1988.

Roberts, Giselle. *The Confederate Belle.* Columbia: University of Missouri Press, 2003.

Ruiz, Vicki L., and Virginia Sanchez Korrol, eds. *Latina Legacies: Identity, Biography, and Community.* Oxford, UK: Oxford University Press, 2005.

Schlissel, Lillian. *Women's Diaries of the Westward Journey.* New York: Schocken Books, 1982.

Scott, Anne Firor. *The Southern Lady: From Pedestal to Politics, 1830–1930.* Chicago: University of Chicago Press, 1970.

Smith, Adelaide W. *Reminiscences of an Army Nurse during the Civil War.* New York: Greaves Publishing Company, 1911.

Stanton, Elizabeth Cady. *Eighty Years and More: Reminiscences, 1913-1897.* New York: Schocken, 1988.

Sterling, Dorothy, ed. *We Are Your Sisters: Black Women in the Nineteenth Century.* New York: W. W. Norton & Company, 1984.

Still, William. *The Underground Railroad: A Record of Facts, Authentic Narratives, Letters, etc. Narrating the Hardships, Hair-breadth Escapes and Death Struggles of Slaves in Their Efforts for Freedom.* Philadelphia: Porter and Coates, 1872.

Taylor, Susie King. *A Black Woman's Civil War Memoirs: Reminiscences of My Life in Camp with the 33rd U.S. Colored Troops, Late 1st South Carolina Volunteers.* New York: Markus Wiener Publishing, 1988.

Tobin, Jacqueline L., and Raymond G. Dobard. *Hidden in Plain View: A Secret Story of Quilts and the Underground Railroad.* New York: First Anchor Books, 2000.

Tortora, Phyllis, and Keith Eubank. *Survey of Historic Costume: A History of Western Dress.* New York: Fairchild Publications, 1994.

Vincent, Margaret. *The Ladies' Work Table: Domestic Needlework in Nineteenth-Century America.* London, PA: University Press of New England, 1988.

Von Mehren, Joan. *Minerva and the Muse: A Life of Margaret Fuller.* Boston: University of Massachusetts Press, 1994.

Wagner, Sally Roesch. *Sisters in Spirit: Haudenosaunee (Iroquois) Influence on Early American Feminists.* Summertown, TN: Native Voices, 2001.

Ward, Geoffrey C., and Ken Burns. *Not For Ourselves Alone: The Story of Elizabeth Cady Stanton and Susan B. Anthony.* New York: Alfred A. Knopf, 1999.

Waterford Foundation, Inc. *The Waterford News.* Winchester, VA: Winchester Printers, 1999.

Weatherford, Doris. *Foreign and Female: Immigrant Women in America, 1840–1930.* New York: Facts on File, 1995.

Wellman, Judith. *The Road to Seneca Falls: Elizabeth Cady Stanton and the First Women's Rights Convention.* Urbana: University of Illinois Press, 2004.

Wertheimer, Barbara Mayer. *We Were There: The Story of Working Women in America.* New York: Pantheon Books, 1977.

Williams, Nancy Clement. *After One Hundred Years.* Independence, MO: Zion's Printing and Publishing Co., 1951.

Wright, Helen. *Sweeper in the Sky: The Life of Maria Mitchell, First Woman Astronomer of America.* New York: Macmillan Co., 1949.

CHAPTER 4 **NEW WAYS OF LIVING** *1865–1890*

Abelson, Elaine S. *When Ladies Go A-Thieving: Middle-Class Shoplifters in the Victorian Department Store.* New York: Oxford University Press, 1989.

Ashelford, Jane. *The Art of Dress: Clothes and Society 1500–1914*. London: Harry N. Abrams, 1996.

Benson, Susan Porter. *Counter Cultures: Saleswomen, Managers, and Customers in American Department Stores 1890–1940*. Urbana: University of Illinois Press, 1986.

Boston Women's Heritage Trail: Four Centuries of Boston Women. Gloucester, MA: Curious Traveler Press, 1999.

Bothume, Elizabeth Hyde. *First Days Amongst the Contrabands*. Boston: Lee and Shepherd Publishers, 1893. Reprint, New York: Arno Press/*New York Times*, 1968.

Brown, Dee. *Bury My Heart at Wounded Knee: An Indian History of the American West*. New York: Bantam Books, 1972.

Bureau of Refugees, Freedmen, and Abandoned Lands. Freedmen and Southern Society Project, University of Maryland, College Park, MD. Original documents at National Archives, Washington, DC.

Burke, John. *Duet in Diamonds: The Flamboyant Saga of Lillian Russell and Diamond Jim Brady in America's Gilded Age*. New York: G. P. Putnam's Sons, 1972.

Censer, Jane Turner. *The Reconstruction of White Womanhood 1865–1895*. Baton Rouge: Louisiana State University Press, 2003.

Clark, Beverly Lyon, ed. *Louisa May Alcott: The Contemporary Reviews*. Cambridge, UK: Cambridge University Press, 2004.

Dirlik, Arif, ed. *Chinese on the American Frontier*. New York: Rowman & Littlefield Publishers, 2001.

Foner, Eric. *Reconstruction: America's Unfinished Revolution*. New York: Harper & Row, 1988.

Forbes, Malcolm. *Women Who Made a Difference*. New York: Simon and Schuster, 1990.

Green, Harvey. *The Light of the Home: An Intimate View of the Lives of Women in the Victorian America*. New York: Pantheon Books, 1983.

Gutman, Herbert G. *The Black Family in Slavery and Freedom, 1750–1925*. New York: Pantheon Books, 1976.

Harris, Katherine. *Long Vistas: Women and Families on Colorado Homesteads*. Niwot: University Press of Colorado, 1993.

Herndl, Diane Price. *Invalid Women: Figuring Feminine Illness in American Fiction and Culture, 1840–1940*. Chapel Hill: University of North Carolina Press, 1993.

Hook, Jason, and Martin Pegler. *To Live and Die in the West: The American Indian Wars*. Chicago: Fitzroy Dearborn Publishers, 2001.

Hunter, Tera W. *To 'Joy My Freedom: Southern Black Women's Lives and Labors after the Civil War*. Cambridge, MA: Harvard University Press, 1997.

This portrait of the Sisters of the Holy Family in New Orleans, Louisiana, was displayed at the 1900 Paris Expo.

Leach, William. *Land of Desire: Merchants, Power, and the Rise of a New American Culture*. New York: Pantheon Books, 1993.

Leavitt, Judith Walzer. *Brought to Bed: Childbearing in America, 1750–1950*. New York: Oxford University Press, 1986.

Lehman, David. "Colossal Ode." *Smithsonian Magazine* (April 2004): 120–22.

Moynihan, Ruth B., Susan Armitage, and Christine Fischer Dichamp. *So Much to Be Done: Women Settlers on the Mining and Ranching Frontier*. Lincoln: University of Nebraska Press, 1990.

Moynihan, Ruth B., Cynthia Russett, and Laurie Crumpacker. *Second to None: A Documentary History of American Women.* Vol.1. Lincoln: University of Nebraska Press, 1993.

Myers, Sandra L. *Westering Women and the Frontier Experience 1800–1915.* Albuquerque: University of New Mexico Press, 1982.

Ohio Historical Society, "The African-American Experience in Ohio 1850–1920." *Afro-American* 4, no. 2: 4.

Oppedisano, Jeannette M. *Historical Encyclopedia of American Women Entrepreneurs: 1776 to the Present.* Westport, CT: Greenwood Press, 2000.

Peiss, Kathy. *Hope in a Jar: The Making of America's Beauty Culture.* New York: Metropolitan Books, 1998.

Poll, Richard D. et al. *Utah's History.* Provo, UT: Brigham Young University Press, 1978.

Pryor, Mrs. Roger A. *My Day: Reminiscences of a Long Life.* New York: Macmillan Co., 1909.

Rawick, George P., ed. *The American Slave: A Composite Autobiography, Oklahoma Narratives.* Supplement, series 1, vol. 12. Westport, CT: Greenwood Press: 1977.

Riley, Glenda. *The Female Frontier: A Comparative View of Women on the Prairie and the Plains.* Lawrence: University Press of Kansas, 1988.

Robinson, Sherry. *Apache Voices: Their Stories of Survival as Told to Eve Ball.* Albuquerque: University of New Mexico Press, 2000.

Rosenblum, Robert, Maryanne Stevens, and Ann Dumas. *1900: Art at the Crossroads.* New York: Harry N. Abrams, 2000.

Sapiro, Virginia. *Women in American Society: An Introduction to Women's Studies.* Mountain View, CA: Mayfield Publishing Company, 1999.

Schlissel, Lillian, and Catherine Lavender, eds. *The Western Woman's Reader: The Remarkable Writings of Women Who Shaped the American West, Spanning 300 Years.* New York: HarperCollins, 2000.

Schwalm, Leslie A. *A Hard Fight for We: Women's Transition from Slavery to Freedom in South Carolina.* Urbana: University of Illinois Press, 1997.

Sivulka, Juliann. *Soap, Sex, and Cigarettes: A Cultural History of American Advertising.* Belmont, CA: Wadsworth Publishing Company, 1997.

Smith, Adelaide W. *Reminiscences of an Army Nurse during the Civil War.* New York: Greaves Publishing Company, 1911.

Smith, Betsy Covington. *Women Win the Vote.* Englewood Cliffs, NJ: Silver Burdett Press, 1989.

Smith-Rosenberg, Carroll. *Disorderly Conduct: Visions of Gender in Victorian America.* New York: Oxford University Press, 1985.

Sterling, Dorothy, ed. *We Are Your Sisters: Black Women in the Nineteenth Century.* New York: W. W. Norton & Company, 1984.

Stockel, H. Henrietta. *Women of the Apache Nation: Voices of Truth.* Reno: University of Nevada Press, 1991.

Stratton, Joanna L. *Pioneer Women: Voices from the Kansas Frontier.* New York: Simon and Schuster, 1981.

VanWagenen, Lola. "Sister-Wives and Suffragists: Polygamy and the Politics of Woman Suffrage, 1870–1896." PhD diss., New York University, 1992.

Wagner, Sally Roesch. *Matilda Joslyn Gage: She Who Holds the Sky.* Aberdeen, SD: Sky Carrier Press, 2002.

Ward, Geoffrey C. Ward. *Not For Ourselves Alone: The Story of Elizabeth Cady Stanton and Susan B. Anthony.* New York: Alfred A. Knopf, 1999.

Ward, Jean M., and Elaine A. Maveety. *Yours for Liberty: Selections from Abigail Scott Duniway's Suffrage Newspaper.* Corvallis: Oregon State University Press, 2000.

Yung, Judy. *Unbound Feet: A Social History of Chinese Women in San Francisco.* Berkeley: University of California Press, 1995.

Zipf, Karin L. "Reconstructing 'Free Woman:' African-American Women, Apprenticeship, and Custody Rights during Reconstruction." *Journal of Women's History* 12, no. 1 (2000): 8–31.

CHAPTER 5 **WIDER PATHS** *1890–1920*

Addams, Jane. *Twenty Years at Hull House.* Macmillan Publishing Co., 1910. Reprint, Franklin Center, PA: Franklin Library, 1981.

Baxandall, Rosalyn, and Linda Gordon, eds. *America's Working Women: A Documentary History 1600 to the Present.* New York: W.W. Norton & Co., 1995.

Bederman, Gail. *Manliness and Civilization: A Cultural History of Gender and Race in the United States 1880–1917.* Chicago: University of Chicago Press, 1995.

Bogardus, R.F. "The Reorientation of Paradise: Modern Mass Media and the Narratives of Desire in the Making of American Culture." *American Literary History* 10, no. 3 (1998): 508–23.

Bohlke, Brent L., ed. *Willa Cather in Person: Interviews, Speeches, and Letters.* Lincoln: University of Nebraska Press, 1986.

Bowen, Louise de Koven. *The Public Dance Halls of Chicago.* Chicago: The Juvenile Protective Association of Chicago, 1917.

Brown, Dee. *Bury My Heart at Wounded Knee: An Indian History of the American West.* New York: Bantam Books, 1970.

Bundles, A'Lelia. *On Her Own Ground: The Life and Times of Madam C. J. Walker.* New York: Simon & Schuster, 2001.

Cohn, David L. *The Good Old Days: A History of American Morals and Manners as Seen through the Sears, Roebuck Catalogs 1905 to the Present.* New York: Simon & Schuster, 1940.

Crichton, Judy. *America 1900: The Turning Point.* New York: Henry Holt and Company, 1998.

Deutsch, Sarah. *No Separate Refuge: Culture, Class, and Gender on an Anglo-Hispanic Frontier in the American Southwest 1880–1940.* Oxford, UK: Oxford University Press, 1987.

DuBois, Ellen Carol, and Vicki L. Ruiz, eds. *Unequal Sisters: A Multicultural Reader in U.S. History.* New York: Routledge, 1990.

Edelman, Bernard. *Centenarians: The Story of the 20th Century by the Americans Who Lived It.* New York: Farrar, Straus and Giroux, 1999.

Edgerly, Lois Stiles. *Give Her This Day: A Daybook of Women's Words.* Gardiner, ME: Tilbury House Publishers, 1990.

Enstad, Nan. *Ladies of Labor, Girls of Adventure: Working Women, Popular Culture, and Labor Politics at the Turn of the Twentieth Century.* New York: Columbia University Press, 1999.

Ewing, Elizabeth. *History of 20th Century Fashion.* New York: Costume & Fashion Press, 1992.

Faulkner, T. A. *The Lure of the Dance.* Los Angeles: T. A. Faulkner, 1916.

Fine, Lisa M. *The Souls of the Skyscraper: Female Clerical Workers in Chicago, 1870–1930.* Philadelphia: Temple University Press, 1990.

Forbes, Malcom. *Women Who Made a Difference.* New York: Simon & Schuster, 1990.

Franklin, Penelope, ed. *Private Pages: Diaries of American Women, 1930s–1970s.* New York: Ballantine Books, 1986.

Goldman, Emma. *Living My Life: An Autobiography of Emma Goldman.* New York: Knopf, 1931. Reprint, Salt Lake City, UT: Gibbs M. Smith, 1982.

Gordon, Lois, and Alan Gordon. *The Columbia Chronicles of American Life, 1910–1992.* New York: Columbia University Press, 1995.

Greenwald, Maurine Weiner. *Women, War, and Work: The Impact of World War I on Women Workers in the United States.* Westport, CT: Greenwood Press, 1980.

Grunwald, Lisa, and Stephen J. Adler. *Letters of the Century: America 1900–1999.* New York: Dial Press, 1999.

Henry, Alice. *The Trade Union Woman.* New York: D. Appleton & Co., 1915.

Hill, Patricia R. *The World Their Household: The American Woman's Foreign Mission Movement and Cultural Transformation 1870–1920.* Ann Arbor: University of Michigan Press, 1985.

Historical Statistics of the United States. Washington DC: U.S. Government Printing Office, 1976.

Hunter, Tera W. *To 'Joy My Freedom: Southern Black Women's Lives and Labors after the Civil War.* Cambridge, MA: Harvard University Press, 1997.

Jacobs, Margaret D. *Engendered Encounters: Feminism and Pueblo Cultures, 1879–1934.* Lincoln: University of Nebraska Press, 1999.

Jellison, Katherine. *Entitled to Power: Farm Women and Technology, 1913–1963.* Chapel Hill: University of North Carolina Press, 1993.

Katzman, David M. *Seven Days a Week: Women and Domestic Service in Industrializing America.* New York: Oxford University Press, 1978.

Klein, Laura F., and Lillian A. Ackerman, eds. *Women and Power in Native North America.* Norman: University of Oklahoma Press, 1995.

Kornbluh, Joyce L., and Brigid O'Farrell. *Rocking the Boat: Union Women's Voices, 1915–1975.* New Brunswick, NJ: Rutgers University Press, 1996.

Kurian, George. *Datapedia of the United States 1790–2000: America Year by Year.* Lanham, MD: Bernan Press, 1994.

Lovett, Robert Morss. *Edith Wharton.* New York: Robert M. McBride & Company, 1925.

Marton, Kati. *Hidden Power: The Presidential Marriages That Shaped Our Recent History.* New York: Pantheon Books, 2001.

Morris, Lloyd. *Not So Long Ago.* New York: Random House, 1949.

Nakano, Mei. *Japanese American Women: Three Generations 1890–1990.* Berkeley, CA: Mina Press Publishing, 1990.

Niederman, Sharon. *A Quilt of Words: Women's Diaries, Letters & Original Accounts of Life in the Southwest, 1860–1960.* Boulder, CO: Johnson Books, 1988.

Nies, Judith. *Nine Women: Portraits from the American Radical Tradition.* Berkeley: University of Berkeley Press, 2002.

Oppendisano, Jeanette M. *Historical Encyclopedia of American Women Entrepreneurs: 1776 to the Present.* Westport, CT: Greenwood Press, 2000.

Overlock, M. G. *A Nurse in Every Home.* Worcester, MA: Overlock Associates for the Protection of Health, 1913.

Payne, Karen, ed. *Between Ourselves: Letters between Mothers and Daughters 1750–1982.* Boston: Houghton Mifflin Company, 1983.

Peiss, Kathy. *Cheap Amusements: Working Women and Leisure in Turn-of-the-Century New York.* Philadelphia: Temple University Press, 1986.

———. *Hope in a Jar: The Making of America's Beauty Culture.* New York: Henry Holt and Company, 1998.

Peterson, Barbara Bennett, ed. *Notable Women of Hawaii.* Honolulu: University of Hawaii Press, 1984.

Report by the Juvenile Protective Association of Chicago, 1917.

Sanger, Margaret. *Margaret Sanger: An Autobiography.* New York: W. W. Norton and Co., 1938.

Sanger, Margaret, and Havelock Ellis. *Women and the New Race.* New York: Truth Publishing Company, 1920.

Scott, Emmett J. *Negro Migration during the War.* New York: Arno Press, 1969.

Shapiro, Laura. *Perfection Salad: Women and Cooking at the Turn of the Century.* New York: Henry Holt and Company, 1986.

Shapiro, Virginia. *Women in American Society: An Introduction to Women's Studies.* Mountain View, CA: Mayfield Publishing Company, 1999.

Smith, Robert A. *A Social History of the Bicycle: Its Early Life and Times in America.* New York: American Heritage Press, 1972.

Sterling, Dorothy, ed. *We Are Your Sisters: Black Women in the Nineteenth Century.* New York: W. W. Norton & Company, 1984.

Tinling, Marion. *Women Remembered: A Guide to Landmarks of Women's History in the United States.* New York: Greenwood Press, 1986.

Toth, Emily. *Unveiling Kate Chopin.* Jackson: University Press of Mississippi, 1999.

Voget, Fred W. *They Call Me Agnes: A Crow Narrative Based on the Life of Agnes Yellowtail Deernose.* Norman: University of Oklahoma Press, 1995.

Waal, Carla, and Barbara Oliver Korner. *Hardship and Hope: Missouri Women Writing about Their Lives, 1820–1920.* Columbia: University of Missouri Press, 1997.

Ward, Geoffrey C. *Not For Ourselves Alone: The Story of Elizabeth Cady Stanton and Susan B. Anthony.* New York: Alfred A. Knopf, 1999.

Weinberg, Sydney Stahl. *The World of Our Mothers: The Lives of Jewish Immigrant Women.* Chapel Hill: University of North Carolina Press, 1988.

White, Burton L. *The First Three Years of Life.* New York: Prentice Hall Press, 1990.

White, Deborah G. *Too Heavy a Load: Black Women in Defense of Themselves.* New York: W. W. Norton & Company, 1999.

Wilson Jr., Vincent. *The Book of Distinguished American Women.* Brookeville, MD: American History Research Associates, 1983.

Woolum, Janet. *Outstanding Women Athletes: Who They Are and How They Influenced Sports in America.* Phoenix, AZ: Oryx Press, 1992.

CHAPTER 6 **PUSHING THE LIMITS** *1920–1930*

"Aeronautics: Freak." *Time,* October 5, 1925: 30.

Bailey, Beth L. *From Front Porch to Back Seat: Courtship in Twentieth-Century America.* Baltimore: Johns Hopkins University Press, 1988.

Blee, Kathleen M. *Women of the Klan: Racism and Gender in the 1920s.* Berkeley: University of California Press, 1991.

Boole, Ella A. *Give Prohibition Its Chance.* Evanston, IL: National Women's Christian Temperance Union Publishing House, 1929.

Condon, Robert. *Great Women Athletes of the 20th Century.* Jefferson, NC: McFarland & Company, Inc. 1991.

Congoleum Gold Seal Art-rugs Ad. *Saturday Evening Post,* July 23, 1927: 35.

Conway, Jill Ker, ed. *Written by Herself, Autobiographies of American Women: An Anthology.* Vintage Books: New York, 1992.

Cowan, Ruth Schwartz. *More Work for Mother: The Ironies of Household Technology from the Open Hearth to the Microwave.* New York: Basic Books, 1983.

Dunkel, Bob. "Gertrude Ederle." National Public Radio. December 1, 2003.

Engelmann, Larry. *The Goddess and the American Girl: The Story of Suzanne Lenglen and Helen Wills.* New York: Oxford University Press, 1988.

Evaporated Milk Ad. *Saturday Evening Post,* July 9, 1927: 164.

Fairbanks, Carol, and Bergine Haakenson, eds. *Writings of Farm Women: An Anthology.* New York: Garland Publishing, 1990.

Fass, Paula. *The Damned and the Beautiful: American Youth in the 1920s.* New York: Oxford University Press, 1977.

Forbes, Malcom. *Women Who Made a Difference.* Simon & Schuster: New York, 1990.

Franklin, Penelope, ed. *Private Pages: Diaries of American Women, 1930s–1970s.* New York: Ballantine Books: 1986.

Friends gather for the Pie Town, New Mexico Fair in 1940.

"Golf: Shenecossett Invitation." *Time,* August 10, 1925: 31.

Huggins, Nathan Irvin. *Voices from the Harlem Renaissance.* New York: Oxford University Press, 1994.

"Ice Cream for Health." *Saturday Evening Post,* July 16, 1927: 106.

Hune, Shirley, and Gail M. Nomura, eds. *Asian and Pacific Islander American Women: A Historical Anthology.* New York: New York University Press, 2003.

Kurian, George Thomas. *Datapedia of the United States 1790–2000: America Year by Year.* Lanham, MD: Bernan Press, 1994.

Kyvig, David E. *Daily Life in the United States, 192–1939: Decades of Promise and Pain.* Westport, CT: Greenwood Press, 2002.

Langley, Winston E., and Vivian C. Fox, eds. *Women's Rights in the United States: A Documentary History.* Westport, CT: Praeger, 1998.

Latham, Angela J. *Posing a Threat: Flappers, Chorus Girls, and other Brazen Performers of the American 1920s.* Hanover, NH: Wesleyan University Press, 2000.

Lynd, Robert, and Helen Lynd. *Middletown.* 1929. New York: Harcourt, Brace, 1959.

Marks, Carol, and Diana Edkins. *The Power of Pride: Stylemakers and Rulebreakers of the Harlem Renaissance.* New York: Crown Publishers, 1999.

May, Elaine Tyler. *Great Expectations: Marriage and Divorce in Post-Victorian America.* Chicago: University of Chicago Press, 1980.

May, Larry. *Screening Out the Past: The Birth of Mass Culture and the Motion Picture Industry.* New York: Oxford University Press, 1980.

McClatchy, J. D., ed. *Selected Poems: Edna St. Vincent Millay.* New York: Library of America, 2003.

Milbank, Caroline Rennolds. *New York Fashion: The Evolution of American Style.* New York: Harry N. Abrams, 1989.

Modell, John L. *Into One's Own: From Youth to Adulthood in the United States, 1920–1975.* Berkeley: University of California Press, 1989.

Monroy, Douglas. "Making Mexico in Los Angeles." In *Metropolis in the Making: Los Angeles in the 1920s,* edited by Tom Sitton and William Deverell, 161-78. Los Angeles: University of California Press, 2001.

Putnam, Nina Wilcox. "Ventures and Adventures in Dress Reform." *Saturday Evening Post,* October 7, 1922: 15, 93–4.

Raub, Patricia. *Yesterday's Stories: Popular Women's Novels of the Twenties and Thirties.* Westport, CT: Greenwood Press, 1994.

"Religion: Wickedness." *Time,* September 7, 1925: 26.

Rogers, Agnes. *Women Are Here to Stay: The Durable Sex in Its Infinite Variety through Half a Century of American Life.* New York: Harper & Brothers Publishers, 1947.

Rose, Kenneth D. *American Women and the Repeal of Prohibition.* New York: New York University Press, 1996.

Roses, Lorraine Elena, and Ruth Elizabeth Randolph. eds. *Harlem Renaissance and Beyond: Literary Biographies of 100 Black Women Writers 1900–1945.* Boston: G. K. Hall & Co., 1990.

———, eds. *Harlem's Glory: Black Women Writing 1900–1950.* Cambridge, MA: Harvard University Press, 1996.

Ruiz, Vicki. *From Out of the Shadows: Mexican Women in Twentieth-Century America.* New York: Oxford University Press, 1999.

Sitton, Tom, and William Deverell. *Metropolis in the Making: Los Angeles in the 1920s.* Los Angeles: University of California Press, 2001.

Sivulka, Juliann. *Soap, Sex, and Cigarettes: A Cultural History of American Advertising.* Belmont, CA: Wadsworth Publishing Company, 1998.

Stockings Ad. *Saturday Evening Post,* July 9, 1927: 135.

Strausser, Susan. *Never Done: A History of American Housework.* New York: Henry Holt and Company, 1982.

CHAPTER 7 **MAKING IT THROUGH** *1930–1945*

Anderson, Karen. *Wartime Women: Sex Roles, Family Relations, and the Status of Women during World War II.* Westport, CT: Greenwood Press, 1981.

Armor, John, and Peter Wright. *Manzanar.* New York: Times Books, 1988.

Arnold, Eleanor, ed. *Voices of American Homemakers.* Bloomington: Indiana University Press, 1985.

Bain, Robert, and Joseph M. Flora, eds. *Fifty Southern Writers after 1900: A Bio-Bibliographical Sourcebook.* New York: Greenwood Press, 1987.

Balderrama, Francisco E., and Raymond Rodriguez. *Decade of Betrayal: Mexican Repatriation in the 1930s.* Albuquerque: University of New Mexico Press, 1995.

Berg, Gordon. "Labor Hall of Fame: Frances Perkins and the Flowering of Economic and Social Policies." *Monthly Labor Review* 112, no. 6 (1989): 28.

Bernstein, Alison R. *American Indians and World War II: Toward a New Era in Indian Affairs.* Norman: University of Oklahoma Press, 1991.

Best, Gary Dean. *The Nickel and Dime Decade: American Popular Culture during the 1930s.* Westport, CT: Praeger, 1993.

Bird, Caroline. *The Invisible Scar.* New York: David McKay Company, 1966.

Blackwelder, Julia Kirk. *Women of the Depression: Caste and Culture in San Antonio, 1929–1939.* College Station: Texas A&M University Press, 1984.

Blake Allmendinger. "Little House on the Rice Paddy." *American Literary History* 10, no. 2 (1998): 369.

Borhan, Pierre, ed. *Dorothea Lange: The Heart and Mind of the Photographer.* Boston: Little, Brown and Company, 2002.

Campbell, D'Ann. *Women at War with America: Private Lives in a Patriotic Era.* Cambridge: Harvard University Press, 1984.

Campbell, Karlyn Kohrs, ed. *Women Public Speakers in the United States, 1925–1993: A Bio-Critical Sourcebook.* Westport, CT: Greenwood Press, 1994.

Chadakoff, Rochelle, ed. *Eleanor Roosevelt's My Day: Her Acclaimed Columns 1936–1945.* New York: Pharos Books, 1989.

Colman, Penny. *A Woman Unafraid: The Achievements of Frances Perkins.* New York: Atheneum, 1993.

Condon, Robert J. *Great Women Athletes of the 20th Century.* Jefferson, NC: McFarland & Co., 1991.

Conn, Peter, Elizabeth J. Lipscolm, and Frances E. Webb, eds. *The Several Worlds of Pearl S. Buck: Essays Presented at a Centennial Symposium.* New York: Greenwood Press, 1994.

Conway, Jill Ker. *Written by Herself, Autobiographies of American Women: An Anthology.* New York: Vintage Books, 1992.

Cook, Blanche Wiesen. *Eleanor Roosevelt.* Vol. 1. New York: Penguin Books, 1992.

————. *Eleanor Roosevelt.* Vol. 2. New York: Viking, 1999.

Doherty, Thomas. *Pre-Code Hollywood: Sex, Immorality, and Insurrection in American Cinema, 1930–1934.* New York: Columbia University Press, 1999.

Gordon, Lois, and Alan Gordon. *The Columbia Chronicles of American Life, 1910–1992.* New York: Columbia University Press, 1995.

Grunwald, Lisa, and Stephen J. Adler. *Letters of the Century: America 1900–1999.* New York: Dial Press, 1999.

Hasday, Judy L. *Extraordinary Women Athletes.* New York: Children's Press, 2000.

Hemming, Cora Pearson. *Personal History of Cora Pearson Hemming.* (manuscript in authors' possession).

Hershan, Stella K. *The Candles She Lit: The Legacy of Eleanor Roosevelt.* London: Praeger, 1993.

Honey, Maureen. "Remembering Rosie: Advertising Images of Women in World War II." In *The Home-front War: World War II and American Society,* edited by Kenneth Paul O'Brian and Lynn Hudson Parsons, 83-106. Westport, CT: Greenwood Press, 1995.

Inada, Lawson Fusao, ed. *Only What We Could Carry: The Japanese Internment.* Berkeley, CA: Heyday Books, 2000.

Jacobs, Christopher P., and Donald W. McCaffrey. *Guide to the Silent Years of American Cinema.* Westport, CT: Greenwood Press, 1999.

Kennedy, David M. *Freedom from Fear: The American People in Depression and War: 1929–1945.* New York: Oxford University Press, 1999.

Kurth, Peter. *American Cassandra: The Life of Dorothy Thompson.* Boston: Little, Brown, 1990.

Low, Ann Marie. *Dust Bowl Diary.* Lincoln: University of Nebraska Press, 1984.

Orleck, Annelise. *Common Sense and a Little Fire: Women and Working-Class Politics in the United States, 1900–1965.* Chapel Hill: University of North Carolina Press, 1995.

Martin, Patricia Preciado, ed. *Songs My Mother Sang to Me: An Oral History of Mexican-American Women.* Tucson: University of Arizona Press, 1992.

McElvaine, Robert S. *The Great Depression: America, 1929–1941.* New York: Times Books, 1984.

————. *The Depression and the New Deal: A History in Documents.* New York: Oxford University Press, 2000.

Melosh, Barbara. *Manhood and Womanhood in New Deal Public Art and Theater.* Washington, DC: Smithsonian Institution Press, 1991.

Milkman, Ruth. *Gender at Work: The Dynamics of Job Segregation by Sex during World War II.* Urbana: University of Illinois Press, 1987.

Miller, Ernestine Gichner. *Making Her Mark: Firsts and Milestones in Women's Sports.* New York: Contemporary Books, 2002.

Miner, Madonne M. *Insatiable Appetites: Twentieth-Century Women's Bestsellers.* Westport, CT: Greenwood Press, 1984.

Nakano, Mei. *Japanese American Women: Three Generations 1890–1990.* Berkeley, CA: Mina Press Publishing, 1990.

Noun, Louise Rosenfield. *Iowa Women in the WPA.* Ames: Iowa State University Press, 1999.

Payne, Karen, ed. *Between Ourselves: Letters Between Mothers and Daughters 1750–1982.* Boston: Houghton Mifflin Company, 1983.

Phillips, Cabell. *From the Crash to the Blitz: 1929–1939.* New York: Fordham University Press, 2000.

Read, Phyllis J., and Bernard L. Witlieb. *The Book of Women's Firsts.* New York: Random House, 1992.

Reynolds, Bernice Weaver. Conversation with Heidi Hemming, March 2004.

Roosevelt, Eleanor. *On My Own.* New York: Harper, 1958.

Ruiz, Vicki L. *Cannery Women, Cannery Lives: Mexican Women, Unionization, and the California Food Processing Industry, 1930–1950.* Albuquerque: University of New Mexico Press, 1987.

Sanders, Marion K. *Dorothy Thompson: A Legend in Her Time.* Boston: Houghton Mifflin Company, 1973.

Scharf, Lois. *Eleanor Roosevelt: First Lady of American Liberalism.* Boston: Twayne Publishers, 1987.

Shannon, David A., ed. *The Great Depression.* Englewood Cliffs, N.J.: Prentice-Hall, Inc., 1960.

Sherrow, Victoria. *Hardship and Hope: America and the Great Depression.* New York: Twenty-First Century Books, 1997.

Shindo, Charles J. "The Dust Bowl Myth." *The Wilson Quarterly* 24, no. 4 (2000): 25.

Soderbergh, Peter A. *Women Marines: The World War II Era.* Westport, CT: Greenwood Press, 1992.

Spangenburg, Ray, and Diane K. Moser. *Eleanor Roosevelt: A Passion to Improve.* New York: Facts on File, 1997.

Stock, Catherine McNicol. *Main Street in Crisis: The Great Depression and the Old Middle Class on the Northern Plains.* Chapel Hill: University of North Carolina Press, 1997.

Stoddard, Hope. *Famous American Women.* New York: Thomas Y. Crowell Company, 1970.

Stuart, Ray, ed. *Immortals of the Screen.* Los Angeles, Sherbourne Press, 1965.

Terkel, Studs. *The Good War: An Oral History of World War Two.* New York: Pantheon Books, 1984.

————. *Hard Times: An Oral History of the Great Depression.* New York: Pantheon Books, 1970.

Tong, Benson. *The Chinese Americans.* Westport, CT: Greenwood Press, 2000.

U.S. Holocaust Memorial Museum. "Voyage of the 'St.Louis.'" http://www.ushmm.org (accessed May 15, 2004).

Vare, Ethlie Ann, and Greg Ptacek. *Mothers of Invention: From the Bra to the Bomb: Forgotten Women and Their Unforgettable Ideas.* New York: William Morrow, 1987.

Watkins, T. H. *The Hungry Years: A Narrative History of the Great Depression in America.* New York: Henry Holt and Company, 1999.

Weatherford, Doris. *Milestones: A Chronology of American Women's History.* New York: Facts on File, 1997.

Zhao, Xiaojian. *Remaking Chinese America: Immigration, Family, and Community, 1940–1965.* New Brunswick, NJ: Rutgers University Press, 2002.

CHAPTER 8 **SECURITY AT LAST?** *1945–1963*

Ackmann, Martha. *The Mercury 13: The True Story of Thirteen Women and the Dream of Space Flight.* New York: Random House, 2004.

Adamson, Lynda G. *Notable Women in American History: A Guide to Recommended Biographies and Autobiographies.* Westport, CT: Greenwood Press, 1999.

Auster, Albert. *American Film and Society since 1945.* New York: Praeger, 1991.

Bernikow, Louise. *The American Women's Almanac: An Inspiring and Irreverent Women's History.* New York: Berkley Books, 1997.

Boyd, Herb. *Autobiography of a People: Three Centuries of African American History Told by Those Who Lived It.* New York: Doubleday, 2000.

Coontz, Stephanie. *The Way We Never Were: American Families and the Nostalgia Trap.* New York: Basic Books, 1992.

Delany, Sarah L., and A. Elizabeth Delaney. *Having Our Say: The Delany Sisters' First 100 Years.* New York: Kodansha International, 1993.

Douglas, Susan J. *Where the Girls Are: Growing Up Female with the Mass Media.* New York: Three Rivers Press, 1994.

Grunwald, Lisa, and Stephen J. Adler. *Letters of the Century: America 1900–1999.* New York: Dial Press, 1999.

Hansberry, Lorraine. *A Raisin in the Sun.* New York: Random House, 1959.

Hasday, Judy L. *Extraordinary Women Athletes.* New York: Children's Press, 2000.

Haygood, Wil. "45 Years Ago, a 'Raisin' to Cheer." *Washington Post,* March 28, 2004.

Hine, Darlene Clark, ed. *Women in the Civil Rights Movement.* New York: Carleson Publishing, 1990.

Igus, Toyomi, ed. *Book of Black Heroes: Great Women in the Struggle.* Orange, NJ: Just Us Books, 1991.

Jackson, Kenneth T. *Crabgrass Frontier: The Suburbanization of the United States.* New York: Oxford University Press, 1985.

Kaledin, Eugenia. *Mothers and More: American Women in the 1950s.* Boston: Twayne Publishers, 1984.

Keene, Ann T. *Earthkeepers: Observers and Protectors of Nature.* New York: Oxford University Press, 1994.

Kerber, Linda, and Jane DeHart-Mathews, eds. *Women's America: Refocusing the Past.* New York: Oxford University Press, 1982.

King, Coretta Scott. *My Life with Martin Luther King, Jr.* New York: Henry Holt and Company, 1993.

Lear, Linda. *Rachel Carson: Witness for Nature.* New York: Henry Holt and Company, 1997.

Lee, Steven Hugh. *The Korean War.* New York: Longman, 2001.

May, Elaine Tyler. *Homeward Bound: American Families in the Cold War Era.* New York: Basic Books, 1988.

Miedzian, Myriam, and Alisa Malinovich, eds. *Generations: A Century of Women Speak About Their Lives.* New York: Atlantic Monthly Press, 1997.

Miller, Ernestine. *Making Her Mark: Firsts and Milestones in Women's Sports.* Chicago: Contemporary Books, 2002.

Mulvey, Kate, and Melissa Richards. *Decades of Beauty: The Changing Image of Women.* New York: Reed Consumer Books, 1998.

Nowell-Smith, Geoffrey, ed. *The Oxford History of World Cinema.* Oxford, UK: Oxford University Press, 1997.

Patrick, Diane. *Amazing African American History: A Book of Answers for Kids.* New York: John Wiley & Sons, 1998.

Pressley, Sue Anne, and Bobbye Pratt. "Va. High School Classmates Face Their Own Legacy." *Washington Post,* May 2, 2004: C1, C8.

Puerto Rico Herald. "Puerto Rico Profile: Rita Moreno." www.puertorico-herald.org/issues/vol4n32/ProfileMoreno-en.html (accessed March 12, 2005).

Rodriguez, Clara E. ed. *Latin Looks: Images of Latinas in the U.S. Media.* Boulder, CO: Westview Press, 1997.

Rogers, Agnes. *Women are Here to Stay: The Durable Sex in Its Infinite Variety Through Half a Century of American Life.* New York: Harper Brothers Publishing, 1949.

Rollin, Lucy. *Twentieth-Century Teen Culture by the Decades: A Reference Guide.* Westport, CT: Greenwood Press, 1999.

Rupp, Leila J., and Verta Taylor. *Survival in the Doldrums: The American Women's Rights Movement, 1945 to the 1960s.* New York: Oxford University Press, 1987.

Rutland, Eva. *The Trouble with Being a Mama.* New York: Abingdon Press, 1964.

Shaffer, Robert. "Women and International Relations: Pearl S. Buck's Critique of the Cold War." *Journal of Women's History* 11 (1999): 151–75.

Sherman, Janann. *No Place for a Woman: A Life of Senator Margaret Chase Smith.* New Brunswick, NJ: Rutgers University Press, 2000.

Sibley, Katherine A. S. *The Cold War.* Westport, CT: Greenwood Press, 1998.

Sivulka, Juliann. *Soap, Sex, and Cigarettes: A Cultural History of American Advertising.* Belmont, CA: Wadsworth Publishing Co., 1998.

Sklar, Kathryn Kish, and Thomas Dublin, eds. *Women and Power in American History Volume Two—From 1870.* Upper Saddle River, NJ: Prentice Hall, 2002.

Skolnick, Arlene. *Embattled Paradise: The American Family in an Age of Uncertainty.* New York: Basic Books, 1991.

Stein, Robert, ed. *Why Young Mothers Feel Trapped.* New York: Trident Press, 1965.

Still, Darlene R. *Extraordinary Women Scientists.* Chicago: Children's Press, 1995.

Vare, Ethlie Ann, and Greg Ptacek. *Women Inventors & Their Discoveries.* Minneapolis: Oliver Press, 1993.

Yuh, Ji-yeon. *Beyond the Shadow of Camptown: Korean Military Brides in America.* New York: New York University Press, 2002.

Zhao, Xiaojian. *Remaking Chinese America: Immigration, Family, and Community 1940–1965.* New Brunswick, NJ: Rutgers University Press, 2002.

CHAPTER 9 **THE WORLD TURNED UPSIDE-DOWN** *1963–1990*

"Balancing the Scales of Justice: Sandra Day O'Connor, the First Woman on the Supreme Court, Has the Last Word." *Washington Post,* March 24, 2005: C 14.

Baxandall, Rosalyn, and Linda Gordon, eds. *Dear Sisters: Dispatches from the Women's Liberation Movement.* New York: Basic Books, 2000.

Bernikow, Louise. *The American Women's Almanac: An Inspiring and Irreverent Women's History.* New York: Berkley Books, 1997.

Blewen, John. "Oh Freedom Over Me." *American RadioWorks,* Minnesota Public Radio, February 2001.

Boston Women's Health Book Collective. *Our Bodies, Ourselves: A Book by and for Women.* New York: Simon & Schuster, 1971.

Braunstein, Peter, and Michael William Doyle, eds. *Imagine Nation: The American Counterculture of the 1960s and '70s.* New York: Routledge, 2002.

Broude, Norma, and Mary D. Garrard, eds. *The Power of Feminist Art: The American Movement of the 1970s, History and Impact.* New York: Harry N. Abrams, 1994.

Brownmiller, Susan. *In Our Time: Memoir of a Revolution.* New York: Random House, 1999.

Cantarow, Ellen. *Moving the Mountain: Women Working for Social Change.* New York: McGraw-Hill Book Company, 1980.

Carabillo, Toni, Judith Meuli, and June Bundy Csida. *Feminist Chronicles: 1953-1993.* Los Angeles: Women's Graphics, 1993.

Chamberlin, Hope. *A Minority of Members: Women in the U.S. Congress.* New York: Praeger Publishers, 1973.

Condon, Robert J. *Great Women Athletes of the 20th Century.* Jefferson, NC: McFarland and Company, 1991.

Daniel, Robert L. *American Women in the 20th Century: The Festival of Life.* San Diego: Harcourt Brace Jovanovich, 1987.

Douglas, Susan J. *Where the Girls Are: Growing up Female with the Mass Media.* New York: Three Rivers Press, 1995.

DuPlessis, Rachel Blau, and Ann Snitow. *The Feminist Memoir Project: Voices from Women's Liberation.* New York: Three Rivers Press, 1998.

Echols, Alice. *Daring to Be Bad: Radical Feminism in America, 1967–1975.* Minneapolis: University of Minnesota Press, 1989.

Everett, Richard. Conversation with Heidi Hemming, September 2004.

Evers, Mrs. Medgar [Myrlie]. *For Us, the Living.* Garden City, NY: Doubleday & Company, 1967.

Freeman, Jo. *The Politics of Women's Liberation: A Case Study of an Emerging Social Movement and Its Relation to the Policy Process.* New York: David McKay Company, 1975.

Friedan, Betty. *The Feminine Mystique.* New York: W. W. Norton & Company, 1963.

Gatlin, Rochelle. *American Women Since 1945.* Jackson: University Press of Mississippi, 1987.

Geracimos, Ann. "TV's Great Chef Feted on 90th; Julia Child Kitchen Exhibit Opens." *Washington Times,* August 21, 2002.

Goldin, Claudia. *Understanding the Gender Gap: An Economic History of American Women.* New York: Oxford University Press, 1990.

Greenburg, Doreen L., Karen L. Hill, Frances Johnson, Carole A. Oglesby, and Sheila Easterby Ridley. *Encyclopedia of Women and Sport in America.* Phoenix, AZ: Oryx Press, 1998.

Guerrilla Girls. "Guerrilla Girls Bare All: An Interview." www.guerrillagirls.com.

Hartman, Susan. *From the Margin to Mainstream: American Women and Politics Since 1960.* Philadelphia: Temple University Press, 1989.

Hatch, Rebecca. *A Generation Divided: The New Left, The New Right, and the 1960s.* Berkeley: University of California Press, 1999.

Women shown in various occupations available to them in about 1915.

Hine, Darlene Clark, ed. *Black Women in United States History: Trailblazers and Torchbearers, 1941–1965.* Brooklyn, NY: Carlson Publishing 1990.

Iggers, Jeremy. *The Garden of Eating: Food, Sex, and the Hunger for Meaning.* New York: Basic Books, 1996.

Inness, Sherrie A., ed. *Disco Divas: Women and Popular Culture in the 1970s.* Philadelphia: University of Pennsylvania Press, 2003.

Johnston, Carolyn R. *Sexual Power: Feminism and the Family in America.* Tuscaloosa: University of Alabama Press, 1992.

King, Billie Jean. *Billie Jean.* New York: Viking Press, 1982.

King, Mary. *Freedom Song: A Personal Story of the 1960s Civil Rights Movement.* New York: William Morrow and Company, 1987.

Lev, Peter. *American Films of the 70s: Conflicting Visions.* Austin: University of Texas Press, 2000.

Levine, Suzanne, and Harriet Lyons, eds. *The Decade of Women: A Ms. History of the Seventies in Words and Pictures.* Chicago: Putnam, 1980.

Lipscolm, Jane. Conversation with Heidi Hemming, May 2004.

Linden-Ward, Blanche, and Carol Hurd Green. *American Women in the 1960s: Changing the Future.* New York: Twayne Publishers, 1993.

Matthews, Glenna. *American Women's History: A Student Companion.* New York: Oxford University Press, 2000.

Miedzian, Myriam, and Alisa Malinovich, eds. *Generations: A Century of Women Speak About Their Lives.* New York: Atlantic Monthly Press, 1997.

Moody, Anne. *Coming of Age in Mississippi.* New York: Dial Press, 1968.

Murray, Pauli. *Song in a Weary Throat: An American Pilgrimage.* New York: Harper & Row, 1987.

Peterson, Barbara Bennett. *Notable Women of Hawaii.* Honolulu: University of Hawaii Press, 1984.

Powers, Stephen, David J. Rothman, and Stanley Rothman. *Hollywood's America: Social and Political Themes in Motion Pictures.* Boulder, CO: Westview Press, 1996.

Rix, Sara E. *The American Woman 1988-89: A Status Report.* New York: W.W. Norton & Co., 1988.
———. *The American Woman 1990-91: A Status Report.* New York: W.W. Norton & Co., 1991.

Rodnitzky, Jerome L. "The Sixties Between the Microgrooves: Using Folk and Protest Music To Understand American History, 1963–1973." *Popular Music and Society* 23, no. 4 (1999): 105–22.

Rollin, Lucy. *Twentieth Century Teen Culture by the Decades: A Reference Guide.* Westport, CT: Greenwood Press, 1999.

Rollins, Judith, ed. *All Is Never Said: The Narrative of Odette Harper Hines.* Philadelphia: Temple University Press, 1995.

Rosen, Ruth. *The World Split Open: How the Modern Women's Movement Changed America.* New York: Viking, 2000.

Rothenberg, Fred. "Women Athletes Pick up the Crumbs." *Kansas City Star,* November 13, 1974.

Schlafly, Phyllis. *The Power of the Positive Woman.* New Rochelle, NY: Arlington House Publishers, 1977.

Schlissel, Lillian, and Catherine Lavender, eds. *The Western Women's Reader: The Remarkable Writings of Women Who Shaped the American West, Spanning 300 Years.* New York: Harper Perennial, 2000.

Shulman, Bruce J. *The Seventies: The Great Shift in American Culture, Society, and Politics.* New York: Free Press, 2001.

Skolnick, Arlene. *Embattled Paradise: The American Family in an Age of Uncertainty.* New York: Basic Books, 1991.

Steinem, Gloria. *Outrageous Acts and Everyday Rebellions.* New York: Henry Holt and Company, 1995.

Stone, Ken. "Ante Goes Up, Gals Look to Happier Days." *University Daily Kansan,* 1974.
———. "Women's Sports Put on the Defensive" *University Daily Kansan,* 1974.

Sutherland, Elizabeth, ed. *Letters from Mississippi.* New York: McGraw-Hill Book Company, 1965.

Thom, Mary. *Inside Ms.: 25 Years of the Magazine and the Feminist Movement.* New York: Henry Holt and Company, 1997.

Tobias, Sheila. *Faces of Feminism: An Activist's Reflections on the Women's Movement.* Boulder, CO: Westview Press, 1997.

White, Deborah Gray. *Too Heavy a Load: Black Women in Defense of Themselves.* New York: W. W. Norton, 1999.

Woodward, Louise. Conversation with Julie Hemming Savage, October 2004.

Woolum, Janet. *Outstanding Women Athletes: Who They Are and How They Influenced Sports in America.* Phoenix, AZ: Oryx Press, 1998.

1st International Congress of Working Women called by the National Women's Trade Union League of America, Washington, DC, October 28, 1919.

Picture Credits

SOURCE ABBREVIATIONS

DPL   Denver Public Library, Western History Collection

DU   Duke University Hartman Center for Sales, Advertising & Marketing History

ED   Courtesy of Earl Dotter, photojournalist, Silver Spring, Maryland

GI   Getty Images

Granger The Granger Collection, New York

JF   Courtesy of Jo Freeman

LC   Library of Congress

NWP   Courtesy of the National Woman's Party Collection, the Sewall-Belmont House and Museum, Washington, DC

NYPL   Schomburg Center for Research in Black Culture, The New York Public Library, Astor, Lenox and Tilden
            Foundations

SI   Smithsonian Institution

SSC   Sophia Smith Collection, Smith College

WHS   Wisconsin Historical Society

Picture positions are noted with T (top), B (bottom), L (left), R (right), and M (middle).

FRONTMATTER

iv LC-USZ62-42067

INTRODUCTION **WOMEN MAKING AMERICA**

xii LC-USZ62-104928 **xiii** T: LC-USZC2-5511; B: ED **xiv** T: LC-DIG-ppmsca-02941; B: LC-U9-1033-16
xv T: LC-USZC4-644; B: LC-USZ62-120768 **xvi** T: LC-USZ62-10284; B: LC-USZC4-1841

CHAPTER 1 **A REVOLUTIONARY GENERATION** *1770–1800*

1 Granger **2** National Museum of American History, SI, DL*388164 **4** Courtesy of Historic New England
5 T: LC-USZ62-40500; B: LC-USZ62-97560 **7** LC ppmsca-02973 **9** LC-USZ62-52098 **10** T: Granger; B: LC-USZC4-4617
11 Collection of Penny Colman **12** LC-USZ62-54 **13** LC-USZ62-2727 **14** LC-USZ62-48859 **15** LC-USZCN4-165
16 Granger **18** T: LC-USZC4-1111; B: LC-USZ62-1410 **21** Granger **22** Granger **24** LC-USZ62-60923
27 LC-USZ62-100353 **28** LC-USZ62-56050 **30** Granger **31** Photograph ©2009 Museum of Fine Arts, Boston
33 LC-USZ62-31864 **34** Granger **35** LC-USZC4-5316 **37** The Connecticut Historical Society, Hartford, Connecticut
39 LC-DIG-pga-00010 **40** Granger

CHAPTER 2 **CIRCLES OF INFLUENCE** *1800–1840*

CHAPTER 3 **GROWING DIVISIONS** *1840–1865*

Michi Otani holds her daughter, **Marjorie Otani (Baird)** on her lap in New York City (1958).

CHAPTER 4 **NEW WAYS OF LIVING** *1865–1890*

CHAPTER 5 **WIDER PATHS** *1890–1920*

157 LC-DIG-ppmsca-13707 **158** LC-USZ62-67910 **160** LC-DIG-nclc-04305 **161** Granger **162** LC-DIG-ggbain-29988 **164** T: WHS 1919; B: LC-USZ62-47559 **166** LC-MS-34363-1 **167** LC-USZ62-111391 **168** T: LC-USZ62-121145; B: LC-USZ62-116310 **169** L: LC-USZC4-3029; R: LC-USZ62-70538 **172** LC-USZ62-126851 **173** T: Elias Goldensky/GI; B: LC-USZ62-86967 **176** Granger **177** General Research & Reference Division, NYPL 1216617 **178** DU Advertising Ephemera Collection, A 0620 **179** SSC Azalia Emma Peet Papers, 2223 **180** LC-USZ62-105893 **181** LC-USZ62-115744 **182** LC-USZ62-102002 **183** Photographs and Prints Division, NYPL 1168439 **185** LC-USZ62-56041 **186** LC-DIG-ppmsca-12512 **187** LC-USZC2-1206 **188** T: LC-USZ62-98405; B: LC-USZ62-7089 **190** L: LC-USZ62-48792; R: LC-USZ62-48718 **191** NWP SB001205 **192** WHS 25985 **193** LC-DIG-ppmsca-02944 **195** SSC Margaret Sanger Papers, 372 **195** LC-USZ62-137707 **199** National Afro-American Museum and Cultural Center, Columbus, OH 88-3 **200** LC-DIG-ggbain-18848 **201** Clockwise from left: LC-USZC4-12617; LC-USZC4-9551; LC-USZC4-1342; LC-USZC4-10671; LC-USZC4-10234

CHAPTER 6 **PUSHING THE LIMITS** *1920–1930*

203 LC-USZ62-99824 **204-05** LC-USZC4-8150 **206** R: NWP SB002041; L: WHS 37894 **208** LC-USZ62-38343 **209** T: Scurlock Studio Records, Archives Center, National Museum of American History, SI; B: WHS 35073 **210** LC-USZC4-12986 **211** LC-USZ62-26742 **213** T: LC-USZ62-113284; B: Granger **216** T: Douglas Fairbanks Museum; B: DU, Ad*Access Online Project Database, BH1184 **217** LC-USZC2-6150 **218** LC-USZ62-119368 **219** T: Granger; WHS 6701 **220** LC-USZ62-96020 **221** LC-USZ62-132291 **223** L: LC-USZ62-108549; R: Granger **224** LC-USZ62-111359 **225** LC-USZ62-111705

CHAPTER 7 **MAKING IT THROUGH** *1930–1945*

227 WHS 10936 **228** LC-USF351-585 **229** in authors' possession **230** LC-DIG-fsa-8b37356 **231** T: LC-DIG-fsa-8a16722; B: LC-DIG-fsa-8a16676 **233** LC-USZ62-29821 **235** LC-USZ62-111456 **236** LC-USZ62-36649 **237** LC-USZ62-58355 **238** LC-USF-34-9058 **239** LC-USZ62-137708 **240** LC-USZ62-66161 **242** LC-DIG-ppmsca-07216 **243** National Portrait Gallery, SI, NPG.72.75 **244** LC-USZC2-1500 **245** T: LC-USF33-006159-M1; B: LC-USF34-036636 **246** T: USF33-005147-M5; B LC-DIG-fsa-8c36090 **247** LC-USZ62-113279 **248** LC-DIG-ppmsca-02922 **249** LC-USZ62-112059 **250** LC-USZC2-1108 **252** LC-USZC4-3357 **253** T: LC-USZC2-5599; B: LC-USZ62-94040 **254** LC-DIG-fsa-8e09351 **255** LC-USZC4-5597 **256** T: WHS 35126; M: LC-USZ62-104148; B: LC-DIG-fsac-1a34808 **257** LC-USF33-013288-M5 **258** T: LC-USZ62-75794; M: LC-USZ62-17121; B: LC-USZ62-88122 **259** T: LC-USZ62-17124; M: LC-USF34-073882-D

CHAPTER 8 **SECURITY AT LAST?** *1945–1963*

261 Alfred Eisenstaedt/GI **262** LC-USZ62-85807 **264** T: LC-USZ62-121893; M: LC-DIG-ppmsca-02989; B: WHS, photo by Milwaukee Journal Sentinel, 10845 **266** T: LC-USZ62-132141; B: LC-USZ62-133880 **268** LC-USZ62-111432 **269** T: LC-USZ62-120830; B: DU Ad*Access Online Project Database, TV 0213 **270** Yale Joel/GI **271** WHS 8434 **273** T: LC-USZ62-120128; B: WHS 27019 **274** T: LC-USZ62-51415; B: Granger **276** LC-G613-T-57610 **277** NWP Equal Rights, 28, No 6 (June, 1942) **279** LC-USZ62-111439 **280** Alfred Eisenstaedt/GI **283** T: LC-USZ62-111605; B: Robert W. Kelley/GI **285** WHS, photo by Milwaukee Journal Sentinel, 1941 **286** T: LC-USZ62-113285; BL: LC-USZ62-135428; BR: LC-USF34-046153-D **288** WHS 3993 **289** L: LC-DIG-ppmsca-08129; R: LC-USZ62-118472 **290** LC-USZ62-126854

CHAPTER 9 **THE WORLD TURNED UPSIDE-DOWN** *1963–1990*

291 WHS 2381 **293** LC-USZ62-127369293 **294** LC-USZ62-119494 **295** LC-USZ62-127737 **298** L: LC-USZ62-122604; R: JF **299** Francis Miller/GI **300** L: JF; R: LC-USZ62-122632 **301** T: LC-USZC4-8103; B: JF **302** LC-USZC4-7235 **304-305** courtesy of Bettye Lane **307** LC yan 1a38634 **309** T: LC yan 1a38701; L: in authors' possession **310** WHS, photo by Milwaukee Journal Sentinel, 6769 **312** Spencer Research Library, University of Kansas **313** in authors' possession **314** LC-USZ62-112148 **315** ED **317** Time Life Pictures/GI **319** Erin Habecker/*Our Bodies Ourselves* **320** Joseph Magnin Poster Collection, Archives Center, National Museum of American History, SI **321** LC-USZ62-121469 **323** Michael Ochs

EPILOGUE: **YOUR TIME** *1990–PRESENT*

BACKMATTER

Poster for the exhibition of Works Progress Administration (WPA) women painters in Boston (between 1936 and 1938).

Index

In 1912, **Juliette Gordon Low** called a friend, declaring, "I've got something for the girls of Savannah, [Georgia] and all of America, and all the world, and we're going to start tonight." Low founded the Girl Scouts, and in the ensuing years, millions of girls have benefited from her vision. These Girl Scouts pose in 1920.

This 1902 photograph of a woman doing laundry in Newport, Rhode Island, was taken by noted portrait and art photographer, **Gertrude Käsebier**.

Child laborers in the artificial flower industry in New York City (1924).

A poster from the
U.S. Printing Office in 1944.

Heidi Hemming and Julie Hemming Savage wrote this book to draw readers into the wonders of American women's history. Not surprisingly, they have come to view the women they have written about as old friends, and hope their readers will too. Heidi has a master's degree in history; Julie's master's degree is in American studies. *Women Making America* has grown out of their love of women's history and years of practical experience as teachers working with students and educators. The sisters live with their families in Silver Spring, Maryland. Contact them at www.womenmakingamerica.com.

An attached caption to this 1924 photo reads, *"Five sisters who helped to run things on Capitol Hill. They were employed as secretaries by five members from as many states. L to R* **Goldie Dunn, Jeane, Marge, Belle, Vera.**"